A Note on the Type

This book was set in Fairfield, a typeface designed by the distinguished American artist and engraver Rudolph Ruzicka (1883–1978). Fairfield is an original typeface which displays the qualities of the master craftsman whose talent was dedicated to clarity. Rudolph Ruzicka was born in Bohemia and came to America in 1894. He designed and illustrated many books, and was the creator of a considerable list of individual prints—wood engravings, line engravings on copper, and aquatints.

Composed by North Market Street Graphics,
Lancaster, Pennsylvania
Printed and bound by R. R. Donnelley & Sons,
Harrisonburg, Virginia
Designed by Anthea Lingeman

A DAY IN THE LIFE

compiled & edited by
Tom Schultheiss

A DAY
IN THE
LIFE

The Beatles
Day-By-Day

1960-1970

pierian
press
1980

ISBN 0-87650-120-X
LC 79-91185

THE PIERIAN PRESS
Post Office Box 1808
Ann Arbor, MI 48106

contents

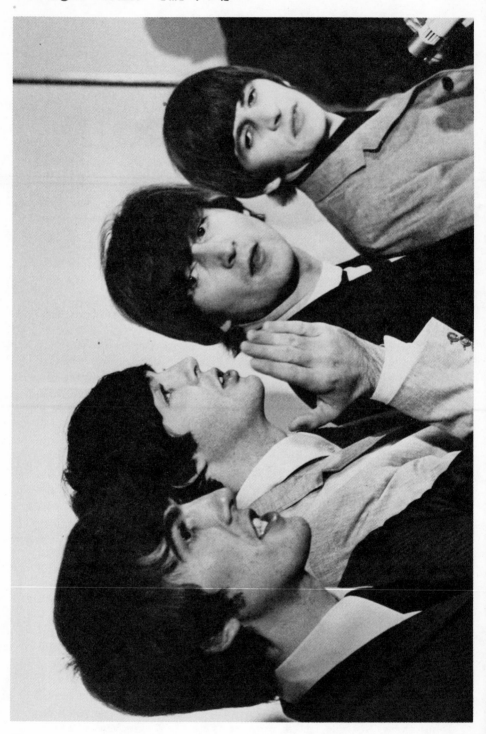

introduction

Hundreds of books and thousands of periodical issues devoted to The Beatles have been published over the years; not a single one of them can be totally trusted, including the one you hold in your hands.

THE DISAPPEARANCE OF THE BEATLES

A trustworthy history or biography of The Beatles does not yet exist, despite all claims to the contrary. It does not exist principally because a biographer or historian with the appropriate concerns, background, perceptiveness and motivation has yet to be attracted to the subject which, like the entire field of contemporary popular (and particularly rock) music, is apparently still too much in the news to be taken seriously. It is certainly not my purpose to presume such a role; rather, the chronology which follows is at best merely a groundwork or basis for someone's future undertaking, and repre-sents an attempt to make The Beatles accessible to historical method. A sorting out, a sifting through — bare bones history, if you will.

The most important and influential group of popular musicians of this century, after nearly twenty years, goes without an accurate and reliable telling of their story. The Beatles are disappearing into history. Even as tens of millions listen to them daily on the airwaves, even as millions play carefully preserved or newly acquired records and tapes, even as tens of thousands mingle at fan conventions to discuss, watch, listen, appreciate, and sense through absorption the enormous power and appeal which memory preserves nearly a decade after their disbandment, The Beatles — historically speaking — con-tinue to disappear.

It is, perhaps, precisely the perpetual activity, adoration and interest which continues to surround the group members, mirrored in a steady stream of books, fan magazines, articles and news reports, that keeps many from an awareness that, in fact, they "know" very little indeed about The Beatles. Everybody *does* something about The Beatles, to mangle Mark Twain, but nobody really *says* anything about them. Nothing, at any rate, consistently reliable and accurate.

The problem is that The Beatles are probably still so much with us that few would concede to an uncertainty or unfamiliarity with at least the basic facts of their lives and careers. Especially those who write books about them which rely, in turn, on earlier books!

This volume makes an attempt to report what many think they know about The Beatles, to codify the vast amalgam of facts, half–truths, lies, fiction, guesswork and mistakes contained in diverse published sources. It seeks to compare, contrast and organize every–one else's history or biography of the group into a chronological outline which both exposes areas of error, uncertainty and disagree–ment and, as a result, isolates and illuminates, if not the truth, at least a consensus of opinion.

THE MYSTERY OF ASTRID K

I first began to entertain some mild doubts about the accuracy of many of the accounts about The Beatles when I added up six versions of the name Astrid Kirschner Kircherr Kichener Kirchner Kirchherr Kitchener. I still don't know what her name is, do you? According to whom? I've decided to call her Astrid Kirschner, sparingly, because . . . well, because it's the first name on my list, and also to quickly resolve what could develop into an incredible identity crisis for her.

Poor Astrid K. Should she really suffer such abuse in the annals of history? The person credited with restyling the hair of our four lovable Mop Tops? (An event that, for many, ranks with the in–vention of gunpowder and, for many others, is right up there with the creation of plastic flowers that smell just like your favorite bath–room deodorizer.) The person who, thereby, influenced the appear–ance of millions of people? The person who helped send hundreds of barbers into unemployment lines throughout the civilized world?

Fortunately, Astrid K had married and so, hopefully, had been saved from the trauma of having to choose which version of her maiden name to use. "Hi, I'm Astrid Kirschner Kircherr Kichener Kirchner Kirchherr Kitchener." What a drag. Unfortunately, two versions of her married name turned up: Astrid Kemp Kempe. Sorry, Astrid. Picture the driver's license.

Astrid suffers not alone, however. There are also such notables as Rory Storm Storme. Take your pick. There's more: Allan Alan Allen Williams is as fortunate as Allen Alan Allan Klein that their last names aren't Allen, too. Or Allan. Alan?

WHICH DAY IN THE LIFE?

Moving on to even more knotty and profound problems, we find that the permutations above represent only the tip of the ice cube.

Remember the day John Lennon married Cynthia Powell? Well, Cynthia doesn't. In her recent book, *A Twist Of Lennon* (delightful reading, but about as reliable as a California used-car salesman), the first Mrs. Lennon well remembers her wedding date, August 23, 1963. Unfortunately, everybody else remembers it as August 23, 1962, including everyone in Britain who saw the photocopy of the marriage certificate published as part of a year-old newspaper report, "£100 for a scrap of Lennon."*

Who can forget the birth of John and Cynthia's son, Julian, on April 8, 1963? Wait for it. Anthony Fawcett, who, "after spending two years (1968-1970) working and traveling with the Lennons . . . " (John and Yoko), began to piece together his 1976 volume *One Day At A Time*, points our memories in the direction of April 18, 1964. Missed a piece. Julian, who has probably been happily celebrating two birthdays a year for the past 16 years now, must be grinding his teeth at me this very moment.

The day John Lennon met Paul McCartney? Get ready. It was either June 15, 1955, June 15, 1956, or June 15, 1957. Cover your eyes and throw a dart.

The day Brian Epstein first heard mention of a recording called *My Bonnie* from a young man named Raymond Jones? October 28, 1961. August 1961. November 1961. October 29, 1961. September 1961. None of the above.

The day Brian Epstein first saw The Beatles perform on stage at the Cavern? Hunter Davies, from whom we have the *authorized* biography (newly "revised"), would have you believe it was November 9, 1962 which, by all other accounts, would have Brian gasping in ecstasy over the discovery that he'd been managing this fabulous group of musicians for nearly a year, unbeknownst even to himself. November 9, 1961.

George Harrison's authorized birth, also according to the *authorized* biography, took place on two occasions: February 25, 1943 (page 35) and again in 1944 (page 37). Birth is, after all, a somewhat disquieting experience (the whole series of events perhaps explains why his first song was called *Don't Bother Me*?), but to do it *twice*?

Pattie Boyd Harrison, George's first wife, also had some pretty disturbing experiences of her own. Davies' biography, after unmistakably referring to an incident which occurred to Pattie "through being a Beatle wife" (page 316), quotes Pattie's own account of an attack upon her by a pack of "horrid little girls" at a Beatles' Christ-

---

*"Current owner, Keef R," the report reads, "lead guitarist/vocalist with [the] virtually unknown suburban band Scarab, from Addlestone, Surrey, who bought the certificate from a Cheshire greengrocer earlier this year, isn't willing to let it go for under £100. Keef is also selling individual photocopies at £1 a throw."

mas Show in Hammersmith, "the Christmas of 1965." The problem is, first, that Pattie did not become a "Beatle wife" until January 21, 1966 and, second, that there was no Beatles' "Christmas Show" in Hammersmith in 1965, although the group did perform at the Odeon in Hammersmith on December 10th as part of their final tour of the U.K. The probability is that the incident occurred during the 1964 "Christmas Show" at the Odeon in Hammersmith, when Pattie was far from being a "Beatle wife," the couple having met the previous March on the set of "A Hard Day's Night."

Before you are overcome with a total feeling of confusion and hopelessness, let me assure you of one thing: it gets worse.

THE BEATLES AND "THE BATHTUB HOAX"

Contrary to what Henry Ford may have believed, not all history is bunk; all bunk, however, does have the unfortunate potential and the too often curious distinction of fitting somewhere into the chronicles of history. The sad fact that a good deal of nonsense is actually believed is unsurprising. Literary familiars of H.L. Mencken, for example, are well aware of his view that the appetites of most for comfortable and convenient "truths" are as instinctive as eating, and the end results, in terms of historical accuracy, are as predictable as that of the digestive process.

Our story begins in 1917, when the American journalist Henry Louis Mencken concocted a whimsical historical spoof called "A Neglected Anniversary," a ridiculous "history" of the bathtub in America which has come to be called, of all things, "The Bathtub Hoax."

The bathtub, for the benefit of the unwashed among us, is thought to be conceptually as old as humankind; extant physical remains of tubs, basins and bathing chambers predate Christ by some two thousand years, and the embellishment of such facilities with hot and cold running water supplies and waste-water drainage systems was apparently commonplace even in the early stages of what we know as Greek Civilization, reaching still higher levels of development under the Romans.

Mencken's bogus history, first published in the December 28, 1917 issue of the New York *Evening Mail*, was a mock celebration of the seventy-fifth anniversary of what he identified as the first use of a bathtub in the United States. The historic date was December 20, 1842, when Adam Thompson, a Cincinnati merchant, took not one but two baths in a tub of his own design and manufacture. The tub, constructed of mahogany lined with sheet lead and weighing over 1,700 pounds, had been modelled by Thompson after one he had seen in England (where the bathtub was first introduced in 1828), and became the forerunner of the modern American bathtub. The Cincinnati tub site was later visited by then Vice President Millard Fillmore who, upon his succession to the presidency in 1850, wasted no time in ordering the construction of the first bathtub in the White House. The example of the President, presumably the first holder of the office to bathe regularly, was instrumental in the acceptance of bathing and bathtubs by the American people.

Mencken's fanciful piece, representative of his style but unre--markable in most other respects, gains its overriding notoriety from one central fact: it was accepted as the truth. Written in a tone of casual but serious credibility, supported by references to and quota--tions from equally fake medical journals, garnished with fraudulent dates and statistics, adorned with reassuring but totally contrived details, the article sports all the trappings of history and yet tells a story which Mencken assumed would be recognized as what he later called a "tissue of absurdities."

In 1926, Mencken's "melancholy reflections" on his previous article were published, an unbelieving lament on the gullibility of his fellows. "Pretty soon I began to encounter my preposterous 'facts' in the writings of other men," he wrote. "They got into learned journals. They were alluded to on the floor of congress. They crossed the ocean, and were discussed solemnly in England, and on the continent. Finally, I began to find them in standard works of refer--ence."*

All of this, Beatle fans, does have a point. There are references throughout *A Day In The Life* to dates and "events" mentioned in three recent parodies of The Beatles' lives and careers: *National Lampoon*'s Beatles issue of October 1977, Mark Shipper's *Paperback Writer* (1978), and the satirical contents of the album **The Rutles** (1978). All of these have been included to provide for something more than comic relief, although some will feel that a good deal of what is mentioned, especially out of context, is decidedly un-funny, and still others that the story of The Beatles is such that it needs no comic relief. They are included, nonetheless, *in order to prevent the "facts" they contain from turning into history* and, by identifying them as non-history, to diminish the likelihood of creating and per--petuating The Beatles' very own "bathtub hoax."

For the scoffers and unbelievers among us, let us here recount the story of the origin of the name Shea Stadium. The tale begins in Mark Shipper's *Paperback Writer* (1978), where a spoof of a Beatles' performance at Shea Stadium refers, parenthetically, to the "fact"

---

*From Mencken's "Melancholy Reflections" in *The Bathtub Hoax and Other Blasts & Bravos from the Chicago Tribune*, edited by Robert McHugh. (New York: Knopf, 1958.) For those interested in similar burlesques and hoaxes, see Richard Wormser's "Fabulous Fiction" in *The Papers of the Bibliographical Society of America*, Volume 47 (1953), pages 231--247.

that the stadium was named in memory of the great Cuban guerrilla leader, Che Stadium. The tale ends, hopefully, in the pages of a mid–1979 issue of *Beatles Unlimited*, a fine little fan magazine published in Holland, where the column of an American contributor, written in a tone of casual but serious credibility, carries mention of the little-known "fact" that the stadium where The Beatles performed on August 23, 1966 was named for the famed Cuban guerrilla leader, Che Stadium. All in good fun. *Obviously* silly. Doubtless tongue-in-cheek. Many, I'm sure, will by now have stopped laughing and said to themselves: "Who'd be so damned stupid that they'd believe *that*?!" The answer, patient readers, awaits you in your bathtub.

HAPPINESS IS A WARM TYPEWRITER

By now it will be abundantly clear to anyone who has bothered to come this far that, when reading about The Beatles, a little healthy scepticism directed toward the printed word is advisable. Until recently, the words "research," "scholarship," and "standard reference source" could not be applied to any piece of writing about the group. Happily, a few books grounded in reality have appeared; some of the information they contain is still faulty, but what they may lack in reality of facts they more than make up for in reality of attitude, in method of arriving at conclusions. When your local newspaper embroiders a story on solar energy with some lines from George Harrison's *Here Comes The Sun*, and then credits them to John Lennon and Paul McCartney (it happened here, yesterday), the point is made: journalism is not history, and common knowledge is only common, not knowledge.*

The preparation of this book has made it apparent that most writing about The Beatles can be easily recognized and assessed as to type: there are those few serious attempts by informed, interested writers who simply labored without a full, professional range of research skills or resources (yet produced remarkable, solid work); next, journalism (most of it bad) spawned of necessity to produce, greed, or both; a large body of literature reflective of caring and sincere efforts by devoted fans who, untrained and sometimes too accepting, at least can't be accused of not being involved in what they write; lastly, hack writing, which is all that need be said of it. In all cases except the first, carelessness, the tendency to make ill-founded assumptions, and a simple disinterest in detail take their toll. The fan can be excused. The uncritical writer or journalist who ignores contradictions, who is unquestioning, unobservant and given to unrestrained regurgitation of someone else's information, can't.

_____

* Mark Twain's earlier (mangled) quip on the weather is now supposedly more accurately attributed to a late 19th century editor of the *Hartford Courant*, Charles D. Warner. File under: knowledge, common.

It has been quite an easy thing to trace, in the compilation of this work, where a particular "fact" originated, and who believed and repeated it. *A Day In The Life*, apart from being a Beatles' chronology, is very much a chronicle of writing *about* The Beatles.

"THE GOOD IS OFT INTERRED WITH THEIR BONES"

This volume, as stated, draws its own existence from previous writing about The Beatles, contrasting and incorporating information from all the types of sources discussed. It makes no pretense to adding anything new, except organization, and is admittedly as right or wrong as the books and periodicals upon which it is based. These include biographies, autobiographies, reminiscences, discographies, periodical articles, fan magazines and newsletters — even a book of sheet music and a recording.

A Day In The Life proceeds from the assumption that The Beatles ought to be taken seriously. That doesn't mean "no fun." It simply means *caring* about the truth and reality of what is enjoyed. Being "serious" in history, in this case music history, involves the idea that at the root of historical knowing is verification, and at the root of verification is chronology, the positioning of events in time. This bare bones history, then, draws its form from the very backbone of history: chronology.

THE DAYS IN THE LIFE OF *A DAY IN THE LIFE*

It was from this standpoint, and with only a passing acquaintance with how muddled The Beatles' history had become, that work on this project began some two years ago. The idea was simple: to search through all The Beatles' literature of any real significance and look for dates (days, months, seasons, years, or a combination of these), record these dates on cards along with a reference to the event or fact connected with it, and also a reference to exactly where the date/event was discussed. Where approximate dates could be extracted from phrases like "the next day," "two weeks later" or "the month before," appropriate cards were made. Then again, not every single date found during the search was recorded. Such dates, however, were important to someone's understanding of The Beatles, figuring prominently in their thinking about or experience of the group. The policy, therefore, was to include 99.9% of the dates encountered, because the significance of what might appear trivial to some — a fan's recollections of freezing on a London street corner in anticipation of The Beatles' subsequent arrival at a recording studio — only becomes clear when it proves that the group was *not* somewhere else at the time. Where no date was mentioned, the subject was passed over, however interesting or important. The card file presently surpasses 10,000 cards, chronologically arranged. The result, in effect, is a "date index" to the materials covered in the search.

A Day In The Life represents only about a third of the information in the card file, which will be continued and form the basis of a larger and more detailed work. Coverage of the years 1971 into 1980 has been withheld, perhaps to form the basis of a second interim ten-year work, as have *most* of the references to the sources in which more information about a particular day's "event" can be found. The release of this edition was felt to be an appropriate step in the process of compiling the larger work based on the conclusion, as will be amply illustrated by the confusion of sources in the pages which follow, that it could fulfill a function and was needed right now.

DAY–BY–DAY PIECE--BY--PIECE

Certain peculiarities of the text of *A Day In The Life*, and some overall policies affecting its compilation, have yet to be touched upon.

Throughout the book, the reader will encounter occasional coded references to one or more of the sources which have treated a particular date/event. Such concluding notations represent examples of variant spellings, disparate dates, conflicting information, and uncertain details commonly found in the materials searched. They have been included merely as indicative of the large body of confused and imprecise "knowledge" circulating in the literature about The Beatles, and are placed following what has been determined to be the "correct" date, or at least the most *probable*, based on an overall familiarity with the *general* reliability of the conflicting sources. Determining the objective truth of any particular point in the chronology has been left to the more historically disciplined; the aim here has been simply to provide a starting point. Source codes are further explained in the section which follows.

The entire chronology has been organized as a progression from the general to the particular, from the larger time frame down to the particular day. Entries in the chronology begin with the year in general, and proceed to the early year, the month in general, early month, specific date(s) within month(s), mid-month, late month, seasons between months, mid-year, and continue in a similar fashion to late year, and spans of years. Certain "early-," "mid-," and "late-" references which could be placed with some certainty within the day-by-day chronology have been so positioned.

It may appear strange that some "events" have been fragmented into smaller parts: that which immediately precedes, the core event itself, that which immediately follows, all of which are or relate to really only one event. This practice grew out of a necessity to ac--commodate the interest range of the varying narratives, which them--selves may emphasize not a performance itself, but whether a per--formance was recorded, or which treat only the arrival of The Beatles at a city, not the course of events during their trip to that city. At--tribution of *only those details actually mentioned* in a particular book or periodical thus becomes more precise.

The tendency throughout has been to minimize the inclusion of extraneous details, to avoid analysis, subjective opinions and edito--rializing, and to simply report what occurred based on a synthesis of information from the many diverse observations and commen--taries examined. Hence, entries are usually brief and non-judge--mental; those that appear to add a value judgement usually reflect the point of view of the source of the date.

ACCORDING TO WHOM?

The books and periodicals listed below, arranged by the coded abbreviation assigned them for the indexing process, represent the complete body of sources so far surveyed for the overall "date index" project (encompassing the period from The Time B.B. into 1980), and form the basis of the present edition. They are noted here merely to allow readers to interpret the occasional coded references sprinkled throughout the text.

Two- or three-letter source codes have usually been derived from the initial letters of words within the titles of books or, for period--icals, from their titles coupled with actual or assigned issue numbers. Source codes are then followed by specific page number(s).

A complete list of all the periodical issues scanned is not included in the present volume — degree of coverage has varied according to availability — because references to sources of the dates in the chronology, as mentioned previously, are not really intended to be followed up at this point and have been withheld except to random--ly illustrate representative dates and events surrounded by error, confusion and uncertainty between sources.

Many other books and periodicals have yet to be searched for dates and corresponding facts or events, and references from them fitted into the chronology. Their absence is due more to their cur--rent unavailability, for various reasons, than to a lack of awareness about their existence.

AAB   *ALL ABOUT THE BEATLES*, by Edward De Blasio.
AR   *ATLANTIC RECORDS; A DISCOGRAPHY*, compiled by Michel Ruppli.
ATC   *APPLE TO THE CORE*, by Peter McCabe and Robert Schonfeld.
ATN   *ALL TOGETHER NOW*, by Harry Castleman and Wally Podrazik.

BAB   *THE BEATLES; THE AUTHORIZED BIOGRAPHY*, by Hunter Davies.

BB   *THE BEATLES MONTHLY BOOK* (Reprint ed.) Beat Publications.

BBS   *BEHIND THE BEATLES SONGS*, by Philip Cowan.

BC   *THE BEATLES COMPLETE*. Warner Brothers Publications.

BCE   *THE BEATLES: CONCERT--ED EFFORTS*, by Jan Van de Bunt, et.al.

BD   *BEATLES DISCOGRAPHY*, by Arno Guzek.

BEA   *BEATLEFAN*. The Goody Press.

BF   *THE BEATLES FOREVER*, by Nicholas Schaffner.

BFC   *OFFICIAL BEATLES FAN CLUB [BOOK] 1971*. Apple Music, Inc.

BIH   *THE BEATLES IN HELP!*, by Al Hine.

BIR   *THE BEATLES; AN ILLUSTRATED RECORD*, by Roy Carr and Tony Tyler.

BIT   *BEATLES IN THEIR OWN WORDS*, compiled by Barry Miles.

BM   *BEATLE MADNESS*, by Martin A. Grove.

BPB   *BEATLES PRESS BOOK*. Apple Press Office.

BU   *BEATLES UNLIMITED*. Editor: Erik Bakker.

BYT   *THE BEATLES – YESTERDAY & TODAY*, by John Swenson.

CON   *A CELLARFUL OF NOISE*, by Brian Epstein.

CS   *CLUB SANDWICH*. Wings Fun Club.

DI   *DIG IT; THE BEATLES BOOTLEG BOOK*, by Koos Janssen & Erik Bakker.

GBR   *THE GREAT BEATLE RIP OFF*, by Bob Sullivan.

GUB   *GROWING UP WITH THE BEATLES*, by Ron Schaumburg.

HH   *HARRISON HERALD*. Official George Harrison Fan Club.

HHG   *GEORGE GERNAL*. Published by Harrison Herald, Official George Harrison Fan Club.

IR   *THE BEATLES; AN ILLUSTRATED RECORD* (Revised ed.), by Roy Carr and Tony Tyler.

JLS   *THE JOHN LENNON STORY*, by George Tremlett.

LCP   *THE LONGEST COCKTAIL PARTY*, by Richard Di Lello.

LMD   *LOVE ME DO*, by Michael Braun.

MB   *MERSEY BEAT; THE BEGINNINGS OF THE BEATLES*, edited by Bill Harry.

MOB   *THE MUSIC OF THE BEATLES*, by Wilfrid Mellers.

MWG   *THE MAN WHO GAVE THE BEATLES AWAY*, by Allan Williams and William Marshall.

N   Refers to dated newsletters of the New York–based Beatles (U.S.A.) Limited, renamed Official Beatles Fan Club in 1969.

NL   *NATIONAL LAMPOON*. (October 1977)

OBF   *THE OFFICIAL BEATLES' FAN CLUB [BOOK, 1970]*. Apple Music, Inc.

ODT   *JOHN LENNON – ONE DAY AT A TIME*, by Anthony Fawcett.

OSP   *THE OFFICIAL SGT. PEPPER'S LONELY HEARTS CLUB BAND SCRAPBOOK*, by Robert Stigwood and Dee Anthony.

PMA   *PAUL MC CARTNEY AND WINGS*, by Tony Jasper.

PMB   *PAUL MC CARTNEY – BEATLE WITH WINGS*, by Martin A. Grove.

PMI   *PAUL MC CARTNEY IN HIS OWN WORDS*, by Paul Gambaccini.

PMS   *THE PAUL MC CARTNEY STORY*, by George Tremlett.

PMW   *PAUL MC CARTNEY & WINGS*, by Jeremy Pascall.

PW   *PAPERBACK WRITER*, by Mark Shipper.

RO   *RECORDINGS OF JOHN, PAUL, GEORGE & RINGO*, by Arno Guzek & C. Mattoon.

SFF   *STRAWBERRY FIELDS FOREVER*. Editor: Joe Pope.

SPL   *SGT. PEPPER'S LONELY HEARTS CLUB BAND*, by Henry Edwards.
SU1   *STARR UNLIMITED 1*, published by *Beatles Unlimited*.
TB   *THE BEATLES*, by Hunter Davies.
TBA   *THE BEATLES AGAIN*, by Harry Castleman and Wally Podrazik.
TBD   *THE BEATLES DISCOGRAPHY* (Revised ed.), by Mitchell McGeary.
TM   *THE MESS* (later *THE WRITE THING*) Editor: Barb Fenick.
TOL   *A TWIST OF LENNON*, by Cynthia Lennon.
TR   **THE RUTLES** (LP) Warner Brothers.
TSB   *THE TRUE STORY OF THE BEATLES*, by Billy Shepherd.
WL   *WITH A LITTLE HELP FROM MY FRIENDS*. Co-editors: Joy
            Kilbane & Pat Simmons.
WT   *THE WRITE THING*. Editor: Barb Fenick.

In conclusion, readers can only be urged to recognize that today there exist many Beatles' stories of varying degrees of accuracy and truth (there are few, certainly, who would dispute that The Beatles really did exist, however). A small arsenal for the deflation of your neighborhood Beatles "expert" now rests in your hands. When next you feel intimidated by an authoritative assertion made by some--one with an "I Love Paul" button on their lapel, simply remember the plight of Astrid K, the lady with eight last names, and ask the question: "Says who?"   **T.S.**

ACKNOWLEDGEMENTS

The efforts and cooperation of the following individuals during the creation of this book are gratefully acknowledged:

Harry Castleman and Wally Podrazik, without whom it would not have occurred to me to do this book, and who had the good sense not to let me talk them into doing it . . .

Barb Fenick, editor of *The Write Thing* (1792 Sunny Slope, St. Paul, MN 55116), for trusting me with all her rare and treasured back issues . . .

Pat Simmons, co-editor of *With A Little Help From My Friends* (9836 Pleasant Lake Blvd., U-24, Cleveland, OH 44130), for copies of her own publication (with Joy Kilbane), plus a priceless stack of all sorts of early fan magazines, and for other courtesies & encouragements . . .

Bill King, editor of *Beatlefan* (Box 33515, Decatur, GA 30033) and

Erik Bakker, editor of *Beatles Unlimited* (P.O. Box 259, Alphen aan de Rijn 2470, Holland) for supplying issues of their respective fanzines . . .

Hannah B. Bruce of the *Life* Picture Service, for her prompt, tho--rough and reasonable approach to business . . .

Tony Curbishley of ATV Music for his many kindnesses, which go far beyond the bounds of his permission to utilize the lyrics from

A Day In The Life . . .

Stan Yinger, for allowing me to peruse his collection of Beatles liter--
ature for "useables" . . .

Peggy Cabot, who made a tough typesetting job look easy, put up
with my handwriting, and now knows more about The Beatles
than she ever probably wanted to know.

Woke up, fell out of bed

A DAY IN THE **LIFE**

The Beatles
Day-By-Day

BEFORE
BEATLES

OVER THE YEARS (The Time B.B.) . . .

1807
Birth year of Blind Lemon Preston, original composer of songs like *Back in de U.S.S.R., Boys, Rocky Raccoon, Lucy in de Sky wit de Diamonds,* and *I Ain't Not Beleebin*, according to *National Lampoon*'s parody of Beatles' history.

1902
Jim McCartney, Paul McCartney's father, is born.

1904
Copyright year of the song *I Ain't Not Beleebin* (forerunner of John Lennon's *God*) by Blind Lemon Preston, according to *National Lampoon*'s parody of Beatles' history.

1915
WINTER
"Sgt. Pepper's Lonely Hearts Club Band," led by American Sergeant Phineas Patrick Paul Pepper, marches to the front lines of the Battle of Pomme de la Pomme, their music ending the battle, according to Henry Edwards' novel, *Sgt. Pepper's Lonely Hearts Club Band.*

1917
John Lennon's father, Alfred Lennon, is orphaned at age five after his father, Jack Lennon, dies.

1919
Jim McCartney, Paul McCartney's father, begins a small ragtime band in Liverpool at the age of 17.

1920
Dick James, Beatles' first music publisher, born Richard Leon Vapnick, is born in London's East End.

1926
George Martin is born in North London, son of a carpenter.

Harold Harrison, George Harrison's father, begins ten years at sea as a ship's steward with the White Star Line.

1927
Fred Lennon, John Lennon's orphaned father, leaves the orphan-- age after ten years there, aged 15.

1929
Harold Harrison, George Harrison's father, meets his future wife, Louise French.

1930s
James McCartney, Paul's father, has his own band -- Jim Mac's Jazz Band -- and plays at numerous Liverpool dance halls.

1930
Harry Epstein marries Brian Epstein's future mother, Queenie.

Harold and Louise Harrison, George Harrison's parents, place their name on a list for a council house in Speke, which they finally move into 18 years later.

MAY 20   Harold and Louise Harrison are married.

1931
Louise, the first child of Harold and Louise Harrison -- George Harrison's parents -- is born.

DEC 18   Allen Klein is born in Newark, New Jersey.

1933--34
Allen Klein's mother dies; his father subsequently places Klein and two older sisters in an orthodox Hebrew orphanage for ten years.

1934
Harold, the second child of Harold and Louise Harrison -- George Harrison's parents -- is born.

BEFORE BEATLES

FEB 18   Yoko Ono, later Mrs. John Lennon, is born.

SEP 19   Brian Epstein is born in Liverpool, England.

1935
Mal Evans, later Beatles' road manager, is born.

1936
Harold Harrison, George Harrison's father, leaves his position as a ship's steward with the White Star Line after ten years.
Richard Starkey and Elsie Gleave, co--workers at a Liverpool bakery, get married.

1937
Dick James, then Richard Leon Vapnick, and later The Beatles' first music publisher, is a professional singer with Al Berlin and his band.
Harold Harrison, George Harrison's father, gets a job as a bus conductor.

1938
Harold Harrison, George Harrison's father, becomes a bus driver.

DEC 3   Julia Stanley marries Alfred Lennon.

1939
FALL
Cynthia Powell's expectant (with Cynthia) mother and her two sons are evacuated from Liverpool to Blackpool--by--the--Sea at the outbreak of World War II.

SEP 10   Cynthia Powell's father arrives in Blackpool by train from Liverpool, unaware of Cynthia's impending birth.
Cynthia Powell is born in Blackpool, England.

OCT 20   Raymond Jones, later an original member of the group The Dakotas, is born.

1940
Brian Epstein, age six, moves with his family to Prestatyn, North Wales.

Elsie and Richard Starkey, Ringo Starr's parents, get a small house in Liverpool just prior to Ringo's birth.

Peter Harrison, third child of Harold and Louise Harrison – George Harrison's parents – is born.

JUN 23   Stu Sutcliffe is born in Edinburgh, Scotland.

SUMMER

Julia Lennon, John Lennon's mother, finds out she is pregnant with John.

JUL 7   Richard Starkey, Jr., (later, Ringo Starr) is born in Dingle, Liverpool.

OCT 9   John Winston Lennon is born at Oxford Street Maternity Hospital during a German Luftwaffe air raid on Liver-- pool. AAB--30 (Oct 10)

DEC 25   Phillip Spector is born in the Bronx, New York.

1941

Jim McCartney marries Paul McCartney's mother, Mary.
Pete Best is born.

1942

Dick James, later The Beatles' first music publisher, records with Primo Scala's Accordian Band.

Neil Aspinall's parents return to Liverpool from an evacuation settlement on the North Wales coast.

APRIL

Alfred Lennon, working as a ship's steward, jumps ship, leaving his wife and child without support funds; John is cared for by his mother's sister, John's Aunt Mimi Stanley.

JUN 18   James Paul McCartney is born at Walton Hospital, Liver-- pool, first son of Jim and Mary Patricia McCartney.

SEP 24   Linda Louise Eastman is born in Scarsdale, New York.
PMB--183 (1941) PMS--123 (1941)

1943

Richard Starkey and Elsie Gleave end their marriage.

Brian Epstein enters Liverpool College, after the family returns
to Liverpool.

FEB 25   George Harrison is born, fourth child of Louise and Harold
          Harrison, near Arnold Grove, Wavetree, Liverpool.
              BAB--35 (Wavertree; 1943), 37 (1944) BB1--7 (1942)
              BIR--25 (1942)

MAY 27   Priscilla Maria Veronica White, later Cilla Black, is born in
          Liverpool.
MAY 28   Tony Mansfield, later an original member of the group The
          Dakotas, is born.

JUL 18   Robin MacDonald, later an original member of the group
          The Dakotas, is born.

AUG 19   William Ashton, later "Billy J. Kramer," is born.

1943--44
Allen Klein and his two older sisters return to their father after
spending ten years in an orphanage.

1944
Brian Epstein is expelled from Liverpool College.

JAN 7   Michael McCartney (later Mike McGear) is born in Liver--
          pool.

FEB 23   Mike Mansfield, later an original group member of The
          Dakotas, is born.

JUL 22   Peter Asher, brother of Jane Asher and later part of the
          duo Peter and Gordon, and still later the staff producer
          at Apple Records who signed James Taylor, is born.

OCT 29   Denny Laine is born in Birmingham.

1945
Peter McCabe, later co--author of *Apple to the Core* (1972), is
born in Liverpool.
Richard Leon Vapnick, professional singer, changes his name to
Dick James.
Alfred Lennon returns to England and visits John, intending to

take him to New Zealand. At the last moment, John decides to remain with his mother, who returns him to be raised by his Aunt Mimi.

MAR 17   Pattie Boyd, later Mrs. George Harrison, is born.

APRIL
H.M.S. Mull of Kintyre, a Royal Navy repair ship built in Canada, is launched; Paul McCartney was unaware of this fact when he wrote and recorded his *Mull of Kintyre* in 1977.

JUN 4   Gordon Waller, later of the musical duo Peter and Gordon, is born.

1946
Ringo Starr develops appendicitis and must undergo operation after his appendix bursts; due to complications, he remains in the hospital for over a year.
John Lennon enters Dovedale Primary School in Liverpool.

APR 5   Jane Asher is born in London.

AUG 4   Maureen Cox, later Mrs. Richard Starkey, is born.

1947
George Martin leaves the British Fleet Air Arm after wartime service, enrolling in Guildhall School of Music.
Norman Smith, later to become The Beatles balance--and--control engineer for recordings, leaves the R.A.F. at age 23; John Lennon later refers to Smith as "Normal" Smith, and Paul McCartney calls him "Two D--B's Smith."
Ringo Starr is released after a year in a hospital, and returns to St. Silas's School.

1948
Harold and Louise Harrison, along with their four children (in--cluding George Harrison, age six), move into the council house in Speke which they had applied for 18 years earlier.

FALL
Brian Epstein, age 14, enters Wrekin College, a private school in Shropshire.

BEFORE BEATLES

1949

Phil Spector's father dies in the boy's ninth year.

FEB 7   Joe English, later a drummer for Wings, is born in
Rochester, New York.

SUMMER
John Lennon, age 8½, poses for photographs with his cousins
Michael, David, Leila and sister Julia.

1950s

Sir Lew Grade, creator of Associated Television Corporation (ATV)
which later purchases Northern Songs, manages singer Dick
James as his show business agent.

1950

SEPTEMBER
John Lennon is awarded a beginners (25 yards) swimming certificate by the Liverpool Association of Schoolmasters.

SEP 10   Brian Epstein first begins work at the family business in
Liverpool, a furniture store.

LATE 1950
George Martin takes a job as an assistant A&R man at EMI's
Parlophone label.

1951

Ringo Starr enters Dingle Vale Secondary Modern School.

1952

Dick James signs with Parlophone records.
John Lennon enters Quarry Bank High School in Liverpool.
Elsie (Gleave) Starkey begins to date Harry Graves, soon to be–
come Ringo Starr's stepfather.

JUNE
John Lennon, age 11, draws the pictures later used in 1974 on the
sleeve of his LP **Walls and Bridges**.

NOVEMBER
New Musical Express begins the first British pop record charts,
publishing its Top Fifteen.

DEC 9   Brian Epstein receives notice to report for a British armed forces medical examination.

Christ--
mas   Ringo Starr's half--yearly report card describes him as quiet, thoughtful, a slow worker but trying his best.

1953

Ringo Starr contracts pleurisy, beginning a stint of nearly two more years of hospitalization, from age 13 to 15.

Tony Barrow, later The Beatles' senior press officer, becomes record critic -- "Disker" -- for the Liverpool *Echo*.

Paul McCartney receives a school prize for an essay: a copy of a book called *Seven Queens of England*.

APR 17   Ringo Starr's mother, Elsie Starkey, remarries Harry Graves in Ringo's thirteenth year.

JUNE

John Lennon's Uncle George, with whom John had been staying along with his Aunt Mimi, dies of a hemmorhage.

JUN 4   Jimmy McCulloch, later a guitarist in Paul McCartney's Wings, is born in Glasgow, Scotland.

SEPTEMBER

Paul McCartney enters Liverpool Institute high school.

1954

FEB 25   George Harrison's eleventh birthday. Soon, he passes his "eleven--plus" exam.

APR 12   *Rock Around the Clock*, by Bill Haley and The Comets, is released.

1955

Richard Starkey leaves the hospital after two years. Too old to return to school, he becomes a messenger boy for British Railways.

Dick James records *Robin Hood*, theme song for the TV series, for George Martin of Parlophone.

George Harrison moves to Liverpool Institute high school.

JUNE

Bill Haley and The Comets' *Rock Around the Clock* hits number

BEFORE BEATLES

1 on the record charts in the U.S.

NOVEMBER
RCA buys Elvis Presley's contract from Sun Records.

1956
The earliest known picture of The Beatles -- then The Quarrymen --
is taken at a Liverpool church--hall dance, featuring John, Paul
and three others.

Klaus Voorman arrives in Hamburg, Germany, to study at the Art
School.

George Harrison, age 13, purchases a guitar from a schoolmate
for three pounds.

George Harrison and some friends form The Rebels, first playing
at the Speke British Legion Club, Liverpool.

EARLY 1956
John Lennon forms The Quarrymen, a skiffle group, while attending
Quarry Bank High School.

Paul McCartney's mother dies in Liverpool at age 47. BM--103
(1958) JLS--106 (Oct 31) PMB--184 (Oct 31)

Following the death of his mother, Paul McCartney's interest in
music is evidenced as never before; he buys his first inex--
pensive guitar.

JANUARY
Bill Haley's *Rock Around the Clock* is number 1 on the charts in
the U.K.

Rock Island Line, by Lonnie Donegan, is released.

FEBRUARY
Elvis Presley's *Heartbreak Hotel* is released.

MARCH
Carl Perkins is almost killed in a car crash.

MARCH--APRIL
Cynthia Powell's mother learns that Cynthia's father is terminally
ill with cancer.

APRIL
Elvis Presley's *Heartbreak Hotel* hits number 1 in the U.S.

Carl Perkins' *Blue Suede Shoes* tops both the pop music, rhythm &

blues, and country charts at the same time.

LATE APRIL
  Bill Haley's *See You Later, Alligator* and Lonnie Donegan's *Lost John* are popular in England.

MAY
  Elvis Presley's *Heartbreak Hotel* tops the charts in fourteen countries.

JUNE
  Cynthia Powell's father dies of cancer following a six--month illness.

early Jun Elvis Presley appears on the "Milton Berle Show" in the U.S.
JUN 15   One of John Lennon's friends, Ivan Vaughan, brings Paul McCartney to meet John at a Quarrymen concert at a church picnic in Woolton, a Liverpool suburb; McCartney is invited to join the group. BB2--9 (Jun 15, 1955) BBS--47 (Jun 15, 1955) BYT--26 (Jun 15, 1957)

AUG 16   Heartland U.S.A. erects a weathervane to honor Sgt. Phineas Patrick Paul Pepper, according to Henry Edwards' novel *Sgt. Pepper's Lonely Hearts Club Band.*

SEP 9   Elvis Presley appears on the "Ed Sullivan Show."

1957
  Ringo Starr, then working at Hunt's Sports' Equipment store in Speke, starts the Ed Clayton Skiffle Group with friend Roy Trafford.
  Cynthia Powell, age 18, begins attending Liverpool Junior Art School.
  Percy Phillips, who had built a small demo studio in his Liverpool home, records four teenagers calling themselves The Quarrymen; Phillips erases the tapes afterward in order to reuse them.
  John Lennon and Paul McCartney are part of a Liverpool skiffle group managed by Nigel Whalley.

JAN 16   The Cavern Club is opened as a jazz club in a former wine store cellar on Mathew Street in Liverpool by Alan Sytner; presenting only jazz and skiffle groups, Sytner

once fines Rory Storm and The Hurricanes for perform–
ing *Whole Lotta Shakin'*.

SUMMER
Brian Epstein leaves the Royal Academy of Dramatic Arts to go
   back to work for his father, managing the record department at
   one of the family stores in Liverpool.
Dick Clark's "American Bandstand" joins the national ABC
   network in the U.S.

FALL
Cynthia Powell moves her studies from the Liverpool Junior Art
   School to the Liverpool College of Art.
John Lennon begins attending Liverpool Art College.

NOVEMBER
Eddie Cochran reaches recognition for his *Twenty Flight Rock*, the
   song which earned Paul McCartney a place in John Lennon's
   group, The Quarrymen.

1958
Maharishi Mahesh Yogi arrives in Hawaii.
Paul McCartney introduces John Lennon to George Harrison.
George Harrison joins The Quarrymen.
John Lennon and Paul McCartney write *Love Me Do*.

EARLY 1958
Dick Clark's daily "American Bandstand" is so popular that a
   Saturday evening version begins.

MAR 24   Elvis Presley sails for Germany to begin two years in the
              U.S. Army.

MAY 3   Alan Freed's Boston rock 'n' roll show is the scene of a
              riot, complete with assaults and stabbings.

JUL 15   John Lennon's mother is killed in an auto accident.

SEP 28   The Phil Spector composition *To Know Him Is to Love
              Him* is released in the U.S.; the title is taken from an
              inscription on the tombstone of Phil's father. It is
              number 1 by the end of the year.

LATE DECEMBER
John Lennon meets Cynthia Powell in a class in lettering at the Liverpool College of Art. TOL–15 (1959)

LATE 1958
Cliff Richard, British rock 'n' roll star, is ignored when his movie -- "Move It" -- is released in the U.S.

John Lennon and Paul McCartney perform briefly together as The Nurk Twins.

The Quarrymen, including Lennon, McCartney and Harrison, perform using the name Johnny and The Moondogs.

1958--59
Paul McCartney writes *Hot as Sun*, later released on **McCartney** (LP).

1959
John Lennon, Paul McCartney and George Harrison all leave their respective schools; they invite Stu Sutcliffe (who couldn't play) to join as bass guitarist, with Thomas Moore on drums.

The Phil Spector recording group, The Teddy Bears, breaks up despite the success of *To Know His Is to Love Him*.

Liverpool boasts a dozen "beat" clubs and numerous suburban "dance halls" where groups like The Beatles regularly perform.

John Lennon and Paul McCartney have written around 100 songs since their meeting in 1956.

Promoter Harry Bostock, manager of the Plaza, St. Helens, begins to present local groups four nights a week, including The Beatles.

Brian Epstein's family business, NEMS (North End Music Stores), opens a new store in White Chapel, the center of Liverpool's shopping district.

The Maharishi comes to England to espouse his philosophy of transcendental meditation; he is not to meet The Beatles until August 1967.

Brian Epstein and Terry Doran meet in a Liverpool pub.

John Lennon originates a new group name -- The Beatles, a musically influenced variation of "beetles," growing out of the group's admiration of Buddy Holly and The Crickets; they settle first on using The Silver Beatles.

Little Richard stops his career as a rock singer to briefly espouse the ministry.

Dick James ends his singing career.

BEFORE BEATLES

JAN 21   Ron Nasty and Dirk McQuickly first meet at 43 Egg Lane,
Liverpool, after Dirk accidentally knocks Ron to the
floor, according to the album send--up of The Beatles,
The Rutles.

FEB 3   Buddy Holly, J.P. Richardson and Ritchie Valens are all
killed in the crash of a private plane; the cuff links worn
by Buddy Holly will be given to Paul McCartney twenty
years later.

MAY
Doug Martin's "Ivor Promotions" opens a venue called "The Jive
Hive" in St. Lukes Hall, Crosby, with Wednesday and Saturday
shows; The Beatles perform hundreds of times at this and other
"jive hives," homes for the developing "Mersey Beat."

JUNE
The Moondogs audition for the "Carroll Levis Discovery Show"
in Liverpool.

SUMMER
Johnny and The Moondogs (John, Paul & George) perform on the
British TV talent show "Discoveries," held in Manchester.
"Oh Boy," England's best rock 'n' roll TV show, bombs after a
brief run on ABC--TV in the U.S.
Pete Best and friends clear out the basement of Best's mother's
house, soon to become The Casbah Club.
George Harrison leaves school without a graduating certificate to
go to work.

JULY
Neil Aspinall leaves Liverpool Institute to study accounting.

AUGUST
Promoter Sam Leach begins to present local groups at places like
St. George's Hall and the Tower Ballroom, including The
Beatles.
Ray McFall assumes responsibility for The Cavern Club, a Liver--
pool jazz club, when founder Alan Sytner leaves as manager.

LATE AUGUST
The Casbah Club, run by Pete Best's mother, opens in West
Derby, Liverpool.

AUG 29   The Quarrymen become regulars at Mona Best's Casbah Club, Liverpool, when George Harrison and drummer Ken Wood (then members of the Les Stewart Quartet) call upon John Lennon and Paul McCartney to help form a quartet after Les Stewart decides not to play at the Casbah. Ken Wood is later replaced by Pete Best.
JLS–107 (Aug 29, 1958) BB30–iv (1958)

NOVEMBER
The Quarrymen disband; George Harrison gets a job as an appren–tice electrician at a Liverpool department store, Blackers.
Later, the group re–forms, changing its name to "The Silver Beatles," shortened from "Long John and The Silver Beatles."
BB3–7 (Nov 1958)

NOV 20   Alan Freed, America's premiere rock disc jockey, is fired from WABC radio after a payola scandal.

NOV 28   Alan Freed, America's premiere rock disc jockey, is fired from WNEW–TV after a payola scandal.

Christ–   Ringo Starr gets his first drum kit at age 18½; at the time
mas   he is working as an apprentice engineer for H. Hunt and Sons.

LATE 1950s–EARLY 1960s
The Beatles perform regularly at dances held at the Liverpool College of Art.
Denny Laine has his own group, Denny and The Diplomats.

EARLY 1960s
Drummer Denny Seiwell, ten years later the first Wings' drummer, plays in jazz clubs in Chicago, then New York.
Yoko Ono works as a short–order cook at the House of Pancakes in New York, according to Mark Shipper's humorous spoof of Beatle history, *Paperback Writer.*

MID–1960s
Denny Laine, born Brian Hines, is signed to Decca Records new label, Deram.

Nobody was really sure

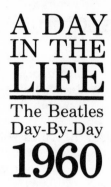

A DAY
IN THE
LIFE
The Beatles
Day-By-Day
1960

DURING THIS YEAR ...
   The Beatles refuse several chances to advance their careers when it
   is stipulated that they must get rid of Stuart Sutcliffe, not the
   best of musicians.

EARLY 1960
   John Lennon, Paul McCartney and George Harrison form The
   Moondogs out of the previously disbanded Quarrymen;
   their name soon changes again to become The Silver
   Beatles.

JANUARY
   Cliff Richard's **Expresso Bongo** (EP) sells 181,000 copies in the
   U.K.

MID--MARCH
   Elvis Presley is discharged from the U.S. Army.

APR 17   Eddie Cochran is killed in a car crash in England. Allan
         Williams, promoter of a concert scheduled to include
         Cochran, considers lesser acts to replace him -- among
         them The Silver Beatles, whom he rejects.
April   John, Paul, George, Pete Best, and Stu Sutcliffe, who
         has joined the group, audition for promoter Larry
         Parnes (after the intercession of Allan Williams);
         Parnes is arranging a tour of Scotland for performer
         Johnny Gentle.
Spring   The Silver Beatles tour Scotland performing as backing
         musicians for Johnny Gentle. (BU8--14 (1959)
              JLS--107 (Oct)   PMS--31,125 (Oct)

MAY
   Elvis Presley appears on the "Frank Sinatra" TV show.
   The Beatles back a stripper named Shirley in a number of

15

appearances in a club in the Upper Parliament Street area, Liverpool.

Wednesday nights become the regular "beat" night at the Liverpool jazz club, The Cavern.

MAY 20   Allan Williams secures the "Silver Beetles" their first con--tract with Paramount Enterprises; the group is to per--form at the Grosvenor Ballroom, Wallasey.

MAY 25   The Cavern Club in Liverpool, for three years a jazz club, begins to offer rock groups as entertainment.

JUNE

Tony Sheridan comes to Hamburg, after a year in London as a session musician, to play at the Kaiserkeller.

JUN 6   The Silver Beatles and Gerry and The Pacemakers perform at the Grosvenor Ballroom, Wallasey. MWG--p27 of photos (Silver Beetles)

SUMMER

Iain Hines' band, The Jets, rehearses at the Top Ten Club; The Beatles arrive and invite the group to a meal at the British Sailors Society.

Pete Best leaves school to work full--time at the Casbah Club and with his own group, The Blackjacks.

AUGUST

Paul McCartney invites Pete Best to travel to Hamburg as the steady drummer for The Silver Beatles.

The Silver Beatles – John, Paul, George, Pete and Stu -- travel to Hamburg, Germany, in place of Cass and The Casanovas, who fail to make the club date at the Indra Club; they remain in Hamburg for four--and--a--half months, moving from the Indra, to the Kaiserkeller, to the Top Ten Club. ATC--11 (early 1960) BCE--7 (Apr) JLS--107 (Apr) PMS--125 (Apr) ODT--184 (Apr)

En route to Hamburg, Germany, John Lennon photographs Paul McCartney, George Harrison, Stu Sutcliffe, Pete Best and "Lord Woodbine" -- a Liverpool strip--club owner -- at the Arnhem War Cemetery.

The Berlin Wall is erected.

AUG 13   Stu Sutcliffe is issued a British passport in Liverpool.

AUG 16   John Lennon is issued a British passport in Liverpool.
Aug 17-- The Beatles perform at the Indra Club, Hamburg,
  Oct 16   Germany.
AUG 18   A Beatles' contract of this date engages them for perfor-
              mances at one of Bruno Koschmeider's clubs, the Indra,
              in Hamburg until Oct 16, 1960.

SEP 21   Just prior to the renewal of their contracts, Allan
              Williams writes to The Beatles in Hamburg chiding
              them on their performances at Bruno Koschmeider's
              Indra Club.

FALL

In a recording session arranged by Allan Williams, John Lennon,
Paul McCartney, George Harrison, Stu Sutcliffe and Ringo
Starr (subbing for Pete Best) make their first recording at
Akustik studios, Hamburg, Germany, for Ł 10 – a 78 rpm
demonstration record of which four copies are made -- as they
back up bass guitarist and vocalist Lu Walters from the lineup
of Rory Storm and The Hurricanes; they record *Fever*, *Summer--
time* and *September Song*.
The Beatles meet Astrid Kirschner, creator of their later hairstyle,
and Klaus Voorman.
John, George and Paul again meet Ringo Starr, who was playing
with Rory Storm at the Kaiserkeller in Hamburg, Germany.

OCTOBER

The Indra Club, Hamburg, is closed by German authorities; The
Silver Beatles move to the Kaiserkeller, where they play seven
days a week, alternating with Rory Storm and The Hurricanes,
into December.

OCT 16   The Beatles contract of August 18, 1960 with Bruno
              Koschmeider expires, but is renewed until the end of the
              year.

NOVEMBER

Stu Sutcliffe and Astrid Kirschner get engaged, two months after
their first meeting.

NOV 11   Allan Williams, Beatles' manager, writes to Bruno Kosch--
              meider in Hamburg about the fact that no commissions
              from their various agreements have lately been deposited

in Williams' Hamburg bank account.

DECEMBER

The Beatles perform at the Top Ten Club in Hamburg on one
night only, prior to George Harrison's deportation and the
expiration of the rest of the group's work permits.

George Harrison is deported from Germany as underage and in--
eligible for a work permit.

Bob Wooller becomes disk jockey at The Cavern Club.

The Beatles debut at The Cavern Club. BM--109 (Jan 1961)

EARLY DECEMBER

The Beatles return to Liverpool from Hamburg, after an attempt
to find work in Paris, having been asked to leave Germany on
the basis of a complaint by Bruno Koschmeider that they had
started a fire in one of his clubs. JLS--39,107 (*went to*
Hamburg) PMS--125 (*went to* Hamburg)

DECEMBER 1960--FEBURARY 1962

Bob Wooller, the disk jockey at Liverpool's Cavern Club, recalls
introducing The Beatles 292 times on stage during this period.

DEC 17   Allan Williams secures a contract for The Beatles to per--
form at the Grosvenor Ballroom, Wallasey, on December
24.

DEC 24   The Beatles perform at the Grosvenor Ballroom, Wallasey.

DEC 27   The Beatles in concert at Liverpool's Litherland Town
Hall, an engagement booked by promoter Brian Kelly
after Bob Wooller brings the band to Kelly's attention.

I'd love to turn you on

A DAY
IN THE
LIFE

The Beatles
Day-By-Day

1961

DURING THIS YEAR . . .

Over 350 groups play at clubs and concert halls in Liverpool's Merseyside area.

Liverpool explodes with new "beat" venues in the heart of the city.

Derry and The Seniors become one of the first Liverpool groups to have a recording released; saxaphonist Howie Casey of the group later plays background for Wings, beginning with **Band on the Run** (LP).

Phil Spector and Leslie Sill form the Philles record label in New York.

Tony Sheridan records the unreleased song *Tell Me If You Can*, written by Sheridan and Paul McCartney in Hamburg, Germany.

The Silver Beatles change their name to The Beatles.

Ringo Starr goes very steadily with a girlfriend named Jerri.

John Lennon is photographed by Jurgen Vollmer in a Hamburg doorway, the photo to adorn the cover of John's **Rock 'N' Roll** (LP) in 1975.

John Lennon is photographed by Jurgen Vollmer while performing on stage in Hamburg, Germany.

Yoko Ono's first avant garde creation to cause a sensation -- "Milk Bottle in a Blanket of Snow (Aerial View)" -- hangs in New York's House of Pancakes on 34th Street, according to Mark Shipper's humorous spoof of Beatle history, *Paperback Writer.*

All I've Got to Do, by Lennon/McCartney, is first copyrighted in U.K., later to be re-copyrighted in 1964 by Northern Songs Ltd.

The Beatles are photographed playing at the New Brighton Tower.

The owner of New York's 34th Street House of Pancakes pins one of Yoko Ono's culinary masterpieces -- a cheese blintz -- to the wall, where it hangs proudly until early 1973, according to Mark Shipper's humorous spoof of Beatle history, *Paperback Writer.*

19

George Harrison, Pete Best, John Lennon and Paul McCartney pose
for a photograph outside Liverpool's Cavern Club.

The Beatles are photographed playing in the Ballroom at Aldershot,
in the south of England.

John Lennon heads up the little--known Beatles, including George
Harrison, Pete Best and Stuart Sutcliffe; Paul McCartney, already
involved in an established solo career with an album on the
LiverPool label (**Paul McCartney**), decides to join them, according
to Mark Shipper's humorous spoof of Beatle history, *Paperback
Writer.*

The Beatles play regularly at the Aintree Institute.

EARLY 1961

The Beatles become the top rock 'n' roll group in Liverpool's
\Merseyside, playing regularly at the Casbah Club.

George Harrison, Pete Best, Paul McCartney and John Lennon are
photographed backing American black singer Davy Jones at the
Cavern.

JAN 25   The Beatles perform in an evening concert at Hambleton
Hall, Liverpool, along with Derry and The Seniors, and
Faron and The Tempest Tornadoes.

FEBRUARY

Stu Sutcliffe applies for an entry visa to re--enter Germany.

FEB 17   Allan Williams secures a contract for The Beatles to perform
at the Grosvenor Ballroom, Wallasey, on February 24.

FEB 24   The Beatles perform at the Grosvenor Ballroom, Wallasey.

FEB 25   George Harrison turns 18.

FEB 28   John Lennon applies for an entry visa to re--enter Germany.

MAR 1   Allan Williams writes a letter to the German Consulate in
Liverpool imploring them to allow The Beatles to return
to Germany to perform.

MAR 15   On or about this date, The Beatles originally intended to
--16   return to Germany for three months to perform at the
Top Ten in Hamburg.

MAR 21   The Beatles debut at Liverpool's Cavern Club as "guests"

of the regular Tuesday night group, The Bluegenes
(later, The Swinging Blue Jeans).

SPRING
Tony Sheridan leads The Star Band at Hamburg's Star Club.

APRIL
The Beatles return to the Top Ten Club in Hamburg, Germany,
for three months.

APR 20   Allan Williams writes a letter to The Beatles after Stu
Sutcliffe informs him that the group has decided not to
pay Williams' 10% commission.

EARLY 1961
In Hamburg, The Beatles live together in a small flat above the Top
Ten Club; clothes--lines criss--cross the room, furnished mainly
with Army--style beds.

APRIL--JUNE
John Lennon, Paul McCartney and George Harrison pose for a
photograph on a rooftop in Hamburg.

MAY
Tony Sheridan and The Beat Brothers record versions of *Ain't
She Sweet, If You Love Me, My Bonnie, The Saints, Why,
Nobody's Child, Cry for a Shadow, Sweet Georgia Brown,
Kansas City, Hey Hey Hey Hey* and *What'd I Say* for Polydor
Records.   BD--2 (adds *Some Other Guy* and *Rock and Roll
Music*)   BU8--14 (Apr)   JLS--107 (Apr)   RO--1 (adds
Skinny Minny and *Tell Me If You Can*)

JUNE
Stu Sutcliffe and Astrid Kirschner marry; Sutcliffe leaves The
Beatles.
1961   Stu Sutcliffe enters the "Master Class" headed by Eduardo
Paolozzi at Hamburg's State High School for art instruction.
My Bonnie/The Saints (45) by Tony Sheridan and The Beat
Brothers, is released in Germany on the Polydor label.

LATE JUNE
The Beatles leave Hamburg for Liverpool.

JULY
The Beatles return to Liverpool after being signed to Polydor Records in Germany.

Neil Aspinall, a friend of Pete Best's working as an accountant, quits his job and becomes road manager for The Beatles.

The Beatmakers (The Beatles and Gerry and The Pacemakers together for one night) perform at the Litherland Town Hall, arranged by promoter Brian Kelly.

The Beatles appear regularly at The Cavern Club in Liverpool.

JUL 6   The first issue of Liverpool's *Mersey Beat* is published.
Bob Wooller, disk jockey at The Cavern Club, has his praise of the Beatles published in an article in the new Merseyside music newspaper, *Mersey Beat.*
"Being a Short Diversion on the Dubious Origins of Beatles," translated from the John Lennon, is published on the front page of vol. 1, no. 1 (July 6--20, 1961) of *Mersey Beat.*

JUL 8   Ringo Starr spends his 21st birthday in Liverpool, returning to Butlins to continue as drummer for The Hurricanes until September 3.

JUL 14   A "Welcome Home" night is held for The Beatles at Liverpool's Cavern Club.

JUL 20   *Mersey Beat* reports the signing of The Beatles -- Pete Best, George Harrison, John Lennon, Paul MacArthy, and Stuart Sutcliffe -- to Germany's top recording company, Polydor, by Bert Kaempfert.

JUL 21   The Beatles perform at the lunch--time session at Liver--pool's Cavern.

JUL 25   The Beatles perform at an evening session at The Cavern, Liverpool, along with The Bluegenes, Gerry and The Pacemakers and others.

JUL 26   The Beatles perform at an evening session at The Cavern, Liverpool, along with The Remo Four, The Four Jays, and others.

AUGUST
The Beatles perform regularly at Liverpool's Cavern Club.

AUG 2   The Beatles' first night as Cavern Club regulars at which they act as hosts to other groups, much as the Bluegenes had hosted them on March 21, 1961.

AUG 3   "Stop the World," record reviews by Brian Epstein, are printed in *Mersey Beat.*

AUG 5   The Beatles play at Liverpool's Cavern in a show beginning after midnight, along with The Remo Four, Kenny Ball's Jazzmen and Mike Cotton's Jazzmen.

AUG 17   "I Remember Arnold," a poem by John Lennon, appears in the Aug 17–31 issue of *Mersey Beat.*

The first Beatles fan letters are printed in *Mersey Beat.*

AUG 31   *Mersey Beat* carries an article on The Beatles' popularity by Bob Wooller, "Well Now – Dig This!"

Brian Epstein's two NEMS record shops in Liverpool are touted as containing "The finest record selections in the North" in an advertisement in *Mersey Beat.*

Mersey Beat magazine reports the formation of the first Beatles fan club, opening officially in September 1961.

SEPTEMBER

John Lennon receives a gift of money from his aunt in Edinburgh prior to his 21st birthday in October; he and Paul McCartney leave for a holiday in Paris.

My Bonnie (EP) released in Germany.

Brian Epstein first begins to hear about an unfamiliar group, The Beatles.

Dick James opens his own music publishing firm in Charing Cross Road, London.

SEP 1   The Beatles perform at lunchtime and during the evening at The Cavern.

The Beatles are the only "beat" group to remain on the bill at Liverpool's Cavern Club, a jazz club.

SEP 5   The Beatles perform at The Cavern, with The Bluegenes, The Remo Four, and The Pacemakers.

SEP 6   The Beatles perform at The Cavern's evening show, along with Ian and The Zodiacs, and Sandon and The Searchers.

SEP 7   The Beatles perform at The Cavern, alone on the bill.

SEP 13   The Beatles perform at The Cavern, along with The Remo Four, and The Pressmen.

SEP 14   The September 14–28 issue of *Mersey Beat* reports The Beatles in performance at the Litherland Town Hall "every Thursday."

"Around and About," by the Beat Comber, an installment of an occasional column by John Lennon, appears in *Mersey Beat* issue for September 14–28.

SEP 15 The Beatles perform at lunchtime at The Cavern Club.

SEP 19 The Beatles perform at the lunchtime show at The Cavern.

SEP 20 The Beatles perform at the evening show at The Cavern, along with Ian and The Zombies, Karl Terry and The Cruisers.

SEP 21 David Plowright, producer of the "People and Places" show on the Granada TV Network in Manchester, England, replies to a letter by Pete Best's mother, Mrs. M. Best, indicating that he will contact her "if it is possible" to invite The Beatles on the show.
The Beatles perform at the lunchtime show at Liverpool's Cavern.

FALL
Brian Epstein vacations for five weeks in Spain.

LATE FALL
Stu Sutcliffe collapses.

OCTOBER
Leggy Mountbatten, a retail chemist from Bolton, stumbles down the steps of a disco club, where he learns about The Rutles from a sailor, according to the album send--up of The Beatles, **The Rutles.**
John Lennon and Paul McCartney vacation in Paris.

OCT 5 Bob Wooller's column in the October 5–19 issue of *Mersey Beat* rates The Beatles as the number one most popular rock group – exluding The Bluegenes, who are "beyond comparison."

OCT 18 The Beatles perform at The Cavern's evening show along with The Four Jays, and Ian and The Zodiacs.

OCT 19 A group called "The Beatmakers," comprised of members of The Beatles and Gerry & The Pacemakers, perform at the Litherland Town Hall.

OCT 24 The Chamber of Commerce of Houston, Texas, replies to a letter from Richard Starkey, who had previously inquired about securing employment in Houston.

OCT 28 A youth named Raymond Jones attempts to purchase *My Bonnie* (45) at Brian Epstein's Liverpool record store.

AAB–55 (Aug 1961)   ATC–20 (Nov 1961)   BM–110
(Oct 29)   TSB–82 (Sep 1961)

OCT 30   Two more inquiries by young girls are made at Brian
Epstein's NEMS record store about the same Beatles'
record that Raymond Jones had asked about the previous
Saturday.
Brian Epstein is unable to find any record importer who has
heard of a record by The Beatles.

NOVEMBER
Brian Epstein, Liverpool plumber visiting The Cavern Club to fix
a clogged pipe in the ladies' room, offers to become The
Beatles' manager, according to Mark Shipper's humorous spoof
of Beatle history, *Paperback Writer.*

NOV 9   Brian Epstein first sees The Beatles perform at a lunchtime
session at The Cavern Club.   BAB–124 (Nov 9, 1962)
TB–124 (Nov 9, 1962)
NOV 10   The Beatles perform at the Tower Ballroom, New Brighton,
as part of a show called "Operation Big Beat."

DECEMBER
John Lennon and Paul McCartney fill in dozens of entry blanks --
under assumed names -- putting The Beatles first in the balloting
for the *Mersey Beat* popularity poll.

DEC 1   The Beatles perform at the Tower Ballroom, New Brighton,
one of six groups featured.
DEC 3   In Epstein's office, The Beatles agree to allow Brian Epstein
to act as their manager.
DEC 8   The Beatles perform at the Tower Ballroom, New Brighton,
one of five groups featured below Davy Jones in "The
Davy Jones Show."
DEC 13   The Beatles perform at the Casbah Club, Liverpool.
The Beatles and Brian Epstein sign a formal contract
covering their agreement.   ATC–40 (Jan 1962)   CON–
55 (Jan 24, 1962)   TSB–88 (Oct 1961)
DEC 14   Bob Wooller's "The Roving 'I'," a *Mersey Beat* column,
reports the upcoming January release of Polydor's
The Saints/My Bonnie (45) in England.
DEC 15   The Beatles perform at the Tower Ballroom, New Brighton,
one of four groups featured.
Dec   Mike Smith, A&R manager from Decca records, visits The

Cavern and sees The Beatles.

DEC 23   The Beatles perform at an all night session at The Cavern, one of four groups.

Christ–   The Beatles find themselves playing at venues farther and
mastime   farther from Liverpool, with less and less audience attention.

DEC 27   The Beatles perform at The Cavern, along with Gerry and The Pacemakers and Kingsize Taylor and The Dominoes.

DEC 29   The Beatles perform at The Cavern, along with The York–shire Jazz Band.

LATE 1961

Stu Sutcliffe collapses at the Art College in Hamburg.

A DAY IN THE LIFE

The Beatles
Day-By-Day

1962

DURING THIS YEAR . . .

George Martin, in an early conversation with Brian Epstein, utters
the words: "Liverpool? So what's from Liverpool?"

Pattie Boyd leaves home and moves to London, hoping to become
a model.

According to John Lennon, true co--composition efforts of
Lennon and McCartney end this year.

The Beatles record an unreleased version of *Hello Little Girl* for
their Parlophone audition tapes.

Please Please Me, words and music by Lennon/McCartney, is
copyrighted in the U.K. by Dick James Music, Ltd., while
Love Me Do and *P.S. I Love You*, words and music by
Lennon/McCartney, are copyrighted by Ardmore and Beech--
wood Ltd.

Mal Evans, age 27, leaves his job in the Post Office at lunchtime
and enters a club for the first time in his life -- The Cavern on
Mathew Street.

Ringo Starr and his estranged natural father, Ritchie Starkey, meet
by chance at the Starkey family's residence.

Michael McCartney changes his name to Michael McGear, after
joining the group Scaffold.

London musician Billy Shears first meets The Beatles; he later
becomes Paul McCartney's double after cosmetic surgery,
replacing McCartney following his bogus 1966 "demise,"
according to Lee Merrick in *Rat Subterranean News*.

Rock musician Billy Shears plays stints in London nightclubs,
according to an article by Lee Merrick in the *Rat Subterranean
News*.

Billy Shears plays at the same nightclub as Paul McCartney; their
resemblance is recognized, save for Billy's larger nose, according
to an article by Lee Merrick in the *Rat Subterranean News*.

EARLY 1962

Brian Epstein approaches Gerry Marsden of Gerry and The Pace--

makers about a management contract.

The Beatles, having cleaned up their act and donned modish suits at the behest of Brian Epstein, are photographed during an appearance at The Cavern.

EARLY--MID 1962

The Beatles record a demonstration tape for submission to Decca Records containing the songs *Catcall* (then called *Catswalk*), *I Lost My Little Girl, Looking Glass, Thinking Of Linking, The Years Roll Along, Winston's Walk* and *Keep Looking That Way*; the tunes are never officially released by the group.

1962--1966

The Beatles record 102 songs, appearing in the U.K. on eight albums, 12 extended play recordings, and 13 singles, and in the U.S. on 11 albums, four extended play recordings, and 20 singles.

JANUARY

The Star Club opens in Hamburg, Germany, with The Beatles as first--nighters; they stay for only a few weeks, returning in April. BAB--96 (opened in May) BCE--15 (Jan 1961)

JAN 1   The Beatles travel to London for their audition at Decca Records, driven there in a van by Neil Aspinall.

The Beatles perform 15 songs for their first audition before a major record company, Decca Records; Mike Smith, Decca A&R man, auditions them at Decca's Hampstead studios, London, along with another group, Brian Poole and the Tremoloes. (The other group is subsequently signed by Dick Rowe, Mike Smith's superior -- The Beatles are not.)

JAN 2/3 Music critic of the Liverpool *Echo*, Tony Barrow (known as "Disker"), mentions the possibility of The Beatles recording for Decca, the first printed notice about The Beatles.

JAN 4   The front page of *Mersey Beat* proclaims The Beatles -- John Lennon, George Harrison, Paul "McArtrey" and Pete Best -- Liverpool's top beat group in *MB*'s popular--ity poll.

JAN 5   *My Bonnie/The Saints* (45) is released in the U.K. on the Polydor label.

JAN 6   The Beatles perform at The Cavern with The Collegians in an evening show.

1962   Brian Epstein first writes to "Disker," music critic of the
          Liverpool *Echo* – Tony Barrow, later The Beatles'
          senior press official -- after Barrow's paragraph about the
          possibility of The Beatles recording for Decca appeared.

JAN 10   The Beatles perform at The Cavern, part of an evening show
          with The Strangers and Gerry and The Pacemakers.

JAN 12   The Beatles perform during an evening show at The
          Cavern, along with Mike Cotton's Jazzmen.

JAN 17   The Beatles perform as part of an evening show at The
          Cavern, along with The Remo Four and Ian and The
          Zodiacs.

LATE JANUARY--MARCH

Sometime during this period, before their turndown by
Decca, The Beatles play their first engagement as artists
contracted by Brian Epstein at the Thistle Cafe in West
Kirby, ten miles from Liverpool.

FEBRUARY

Stu Sutcliffe again collapses in Hamburg, returns to his room and
remains there writing, drawing and enduring headaches and
temper tantrums.

FEB 3   The Beatles perform in an evening session at The Cavern,
          along with Gerry and The Pacemakers and The Saints
          Jazzband.

FEB 24   The Beatles perform as part of an all--night session at The
          Cavern, along with four other groups.

FEB 28   The Beatles perform at an evening session at The Cavern,
          along with The Searchers, and Gerry and The Pace--
          makers.

LATE FEBRUARY--EARLY MARCH

The Beatles perform at the BBC's Playhouse Theatre, Manchester.

MARCH

Decca Records turns down Brian Epstein and The Beatles after
reviewing the audition tapes made January 1; executive Dick
Rowe tells Brian Epstein that groups of guitars are on the
"way out."

MARCH–MAY

Brian Epstein takes a copy of the Decca audition tapes to EMI's London record store, H.M.V. Records, to have the tapes recorded on discs for circulation to other record companies; the person cutting the discs is so impressed that he contacts Syd Coleman, manager of Beechwood Music and Ardmore Music, with offices directly over the record store. Epstein plays the tapes for Coleman, who in turn contacts George Martin of EMI's Parlophone label.

MAR 2   The Beatles perform at an evening session at The Cavern Club.

MAR 3   The Beatles perform at an evening session at The Cavern Club, along with Jim McHarg's Jazzmen.

early Mar   The Beatles give performances in Southport, Chester and Gloucester.

MAR 22   The March 22–April 5 issue of *Mersey Beat* carries a two–line advertisement offering The Beatles for hire as per--formers: "THE BEATLES -- 12/14 Whitechapel, Royal 7895."

In the March 22–April 5 issue, *Mersey Beat* magazine re--ports that former Beatle Stu Sutcliffe recently returned to Hamburg, Germany, after a visit to Liverpool.

In the March 22–April 5 issue, *Mersey Beat* reports that John Lennon and Paul McCartney have written over 70 songs together to date.

Mersey Beat columnist "Virginia," in the March 22–April 5 issue, speculates on whether Ringo Starr, drummer for The Hurricanes, will join with a group called The Seniors in a series of one--nighters.

MAR 23   The Beatles perform at The Cavern Club, along with Gerry and The Pacemakers. MB–30 (Friday, 23rd) MB–31 (Friday, 24th)

MAR 24   The Beatles perform at the Jazzclub in Hewall during the afternoon.

The Beatles perform at the Barnston Women's Institute during the evening.

MAR 28   The Beatles perform at The Cavern, together with Gerry and The Pacemakers and The Remo Four.

MAR 29   The Beatles perform at the Liverpool club, The Odd Spot, along with The Mersey Beats.

MAR 30   The Beatles perform at The Cavern, along with The Dallas Jazz Band.

APR 2   The Beatles, billed as "Merseyside's Joy," perform at the
            Pavilion Theatre in Liverpool, second act to The Royal
            Show Band.
APR 4   The Beatles perform at The Cavern Club, along with The
            Dominoes and The Four Jays.
APR 5   "An Evening with John, George, Paul & Pete," presented
            by The Beatles Fan Club, is held at The Cavern be-
            ginning at 7:30 p.m. as a send–off for their journey
            to Hamburg.
APR 7   The Beatles perform at The Cavern in an evening session,
            along with The Saints Jazz Band.
APR 10   Stu Sutcliffe dies of a brain hemorrhage in Hamburg,
            Germany, at the age of 21.
APR 11   The Beatles fly off to a seven–week engagement in Ham-
            burg, Germany, leaving from Ringway Airport, Man-
            chester.
early Apr   The Beatles arrive back in Hamburg, Germany, having thus
            taken their first plane ride.
APR 13   *Mersey Beat* reports that The Beatles will begin a seven–
            week stint at the Star Club in Hamburg, Germany, on
            this date.   BCE–19 (Apr 13)   ODT–184 (Apr–June)
                  TBA–73 (Apr 23), 126 (Apr 23)
APR 19   "News from Germany," a piece on The Beatles reception
            and activities in Hamburg, appears in *Mersey Beat.*
            The obituary of Stu Sutcliffe is printed in the April 19–
            May 3 issue of *Mersey Beat,* along with a story about
            The Beatles debut at Hamburg's Star Club on the same
            page.
            The Beatles Fan Club runs an ad for new members in the
            classified column of *Mersey Beat*'s April 19–May 3
            issue.
            Mersey Beat's April 19–May 3 issue reports that Ringo
            Starr is spending his third summer season as drummer for
            The Hurricanes at Butlin's Holiday Camp, Skegness.
APR 23   *My Bonnie/The Saints* (45) is issued in the U.S. on the
            Decca label.

MID–1962
    Brian Epstein approaches London recording studios with tapes
    by The Beatles.

MAY

John Lennon and Paul McCartney write *P.S. I Love You* in Hamburg, Germany.

Bobbie Brown begins The Beatles Fan Club in Liverpool, England.

Brian Epstein visits Kenneth Boast in London; Boast contacts Syd Coleman, a music publisher, who shows George Martin Epstein's demonstration tapes of The Beatles. George Martin finds The Beatles' Decca audition tapes interesting enough to grant an audition for Parlophone.

MAY 9   Brian Epstein wires news of EMI Records audition to The Beatles.

Brian Epstein wires *Mersey Beat* that he has secured an EMI contract for The Beatles to record on the Parlo–phone label.

MAY 31   *Mersey Beat* reports to its readers on the recording contract secured by Brian Epstein for The Beatles with EMI's Parlophone label.

JUNE

My Bonnie (LP) is released in Germany on the Polydor label.

Brian Epstein signs Gerry Marsden to a management contract.

JUNE–SEPTEMBER

George Martin is uninterested in signing The Beatles to a contract and takes no action until Brian Epstein, through an EMI sales--man who serviced Epstein's record outlets, threatens to cancel all his business with EMI unless a Beatles' single is released promptly.

JUNE 1962--DECEMBER 1968

Excluding income from song--writing, The Beatles earn 7.8 million pounds during this period.

EARLY JUNE

The Beatles return from Hamburg, Germany.

JUN 6   Beatles audition before George Martin of EMI/Parlophone, performing six songs at the Abbey Road studios, London.

JUN 9   The Beatles first scheduled appearance at The Cavern after their return from their stint at Hamburg's Star Club.

Beatles in concert at The Cavern Club in Liverpool.

JUN 11   The Beatles first radio broadcast on the BBC, "The
          Beatles In Concert."
JUN 15   The Beatles perform in an evening session at The Cavern,
          along with The Spidermen.
JUN 16   The Beatles perform in an evening session at The Cavern
          Club, along with Tony Smith's Jazzmen.
JUN 19   The Beatles perform in an evening session at The Cavern,
          together with The Bluegenes, and Ken Dallas and The
          Silhouettes.
JUN 20   The Beatles perform in an evening session at The Cavern,
          together with The Sorrals, and The Strangers.
JUN 21   The Beatles perform in the "Bruce Channel Show" at
          Liverpool's Tower Ballroom. TBA--229 (Tower Ball--
          room in New Brighton)
JUN 22   The Beatles, along with The Cyclones, perform at an even--
          ing session at Liverpool's Cavern.
JUN 26   NEMS Limited, the Epstein family business, forms NEMS
          Enterprises Ltd., to handle show--business activities.
JUN 27   The Beatles, along with The Big Three, perform at a Cavern
          Club evening session.
JUN 28   The Beatles perform at The Majestic in Birkenhead, near
          Liverpool.
JUN 29   The Beatles perform at the Tower Ballroom, New Brighton.

SUMMER
Cynthia Powell finds out she is pregnant.
Ringo Starr plays drums in Skegness at Butlin's holiday camp.
Songs performed on BBC Radio during this period later appear on
    bootleg albums **Yellow Matter Custard** and **As Sweet As You
    Are.**
The son of a friend brings Dick James the song *How Do You Do
    It* for publishing consideration. James offers it to George
    Martin, who tries to get The Beatles to record it.

JULY
Anticipated release time for The Beatles' first Parlophone single.

JUL 1   Dick James meets with The Beatles and Brian Epstein to
          discuss recording a song that James was publishing; The
          Beatles decide not to record it.
          The Beatles perform at Liverpool's Cavern Club, on the
          bill with Gene Vincent and others.
JUL 26   *Mersey Beat* reports an ever widening audience for The
          Beatles, with club bookings in Manchester, Rhyl,

Swindon, Crewe, Chester, Stroud, Doncaster, St. Helens and Warrington.

The Beatles, billed second to Joe Brown and His Bruvvers, perform at Cambridge Hall, Southport.

JUL 27   The Beatles, billed second to Joe Brown and His Bruvvers, perform at the Tower Ballroom, New Brighton.

JUL 28   The Beatles take top billing at the "Mersey Beat Ball," presented at The Majestic Ballroom, Birkenhead, 7:30–11:30 p.m.

The Beatles perform at The Cavern, in an evening session with Dee Fenton and The Silhouettes, and The Red River Jazzmen.

LATE JULY

Brian Epstein signs a recording contract for The Beatles on EMI's Parlophone label.

JULY--AUGUST

The Beatles perform at the Plaza Ballroom, St. Helens, in four Monday night engagements.

AUGUST

Frank Ifield's *I Remember You* tops the British charts for the entire month.

AUG 1   The Beatles perform during the evening at The Cavern, along with The Mersey Beats, and Gerry and The Pace--makers.

AUG 2   The Beatles perform at the River Park Ballroom, Chester.

AUG 5   The Beatles perform in an evening session with The Saints Jazzband at The Cavern.

AUG 6   The Beatles perform at a Bank Holiday special show at the Grafton Ballroom, along with Gerry and The Pace--makers and The Big Three.

AUG 8   The Beatles, billed second, perform at The Cavern along with Shane Fenton and The Fentones, and The Big Three.

AUG 15   The Beatles perform at the evening show at The Cavern. Brian Epstein calls Pete Best and asks to see him next morning at his office.

AUG 16   The Beatles begin an engagement at the Riverpark Ball–
              room, Chester, a series of four Thursday night sessions.
           Pete Best is told by Brian Epstein that Ringo Starr will
              replace him as The Beatles' drummer.   JLS–109 (Aug 1)
AUG 17   The Beatles perform at The Cavern; Pete Best's last session
              with the band.
early Aug After four years as their drummer, Richard Starkey leaves
              Rory Storm and The Hurricanes to join The Beatles.
AUG 18   The Beatles perform at The Cavern; Ringo Starr's first
              session as a group member.
           The Beatles are recorded at The Cavern Club, Liverpool,
              performing *Some Other Guy.*
AUG 23   "Small Sam," a short piece by John Lennon (aka Beat–
              comber) is published in *Mersey Beat.*
           Mersey Beat reveals the replacement of Pete Best by
              Ringo Starr to Beatles' fans.
           John Lennon marries Cynthia Powell at the Mount
              Pleasant register office, Liverpool. Paul McCartney is
              best man.   TOL–74 (Aug 23, 1963)
           Following the wedding of John Lennon and Cynthia
              Powell, a lunch–time "wedding reception" is held at
              Reeces Cafe; after waiting for a table in the crowded
              restaurant, the couple is toasted with glasses of water.
              Brian Epstein pays for the lunch.   TOL–78 (places this
              in 1963)
           The Beatles perform at the River Park Ballroom, Chester.
AUG 28   The Beatles perform at an evening session at The Cavern,
              along with The Bluegenes, and Gerry Levine and The
              Avengers.
AUG 30   The Beatles perform at the River Park Ballroom, Chester.

LATE AUGUST–EARLY SEPTEMBER
Earliest sound film of Beatles on stage is made by Granada TV.

FALL
Cynthia Lennon persuades John to visit his Aunt Mimi who,
   along with Lennon's other blood relatives, had boycotted his
   wedding; the reunion is a happy one.
The Beatles appear on BBC radio singing *I'll Be On My Way.*

SEPTEMBER
Mersey Beat carries a photo and front page headline: "Beatles
   to Record for Parlophone."

In one 16 hour session, The Beatles record their first album –
We're Gonna Change the Face of Pop Music Forever – at EMI's
London studios, according to Mark Shipper's humorous spoof
of Beatle history, *Paperback Writer.*

EARLY SEPTEMBER
The Beatles back sixteen--year--old vocalist Simone Jackson at
The Cavern.

SEP 3   The Beatles perform at Queen's Hall, Widnes, along with
Billy Kramer and The Coasters, and Rory Storm and
The Hurricanes.

SEP 4   The Beatles arrive in London from Liverpool to begin
their first week--long major recording session for EMI/
Parlophone.
The Beatles register at a Chelsea hotel and later arrive at
EMI's St. John's Wood No. 2 studio. Rehearsals and
final recording takes last until midnight.

SEP 6   "On Safairy with Whide Hunter," by Beatcomber (John
Lennon), is published in *Mersey Beat.*
Mersey Beat publishes reminiscences by Paul "McArtney"
about The Beatles earlier days, when they played
backup for a stripper named Janice.
The Beatles perform at the River Park Ballroom, Chester.

SEP 8   The Beatles perform at the Majestic Ballroom, Birkenhead.

SEP 9   The Beatles perform in an evening session at The Cavern,
along with Billy Kramer and The Coasters, and Clinton
Ford.

SEP 10   The Beatles perform at Queens Hall, Widnes, along with
Rory Storm and The Hurricanes, and Geoff Stacey and
The Wanderers.
Pete Best, former Beatles' drummer, makes his first
appearance as a member of Lee Curtis and The All Stars,
at the Majestic Ballroom, Birkenhead.

SEP 11   *Love Me Do* and *P.S. I Love You* are recorded for The Beatles'
first single at EMI studios in London; this day's re--
cording of *Please Please Me* is not released.

mid--Sep   Brian Epstein brings The Beatles to the offices of *Record
Mirror* in London for an interview with Peter Jones,
arranged by photographer Dezo Hoffman; Jones con--
cludes, after the group's first interview outside Liver--
pool, that they are "a nothing group" in terms of
national interest.

SEP 17   The Beatles, along with Billy Kramer and The Coasters,
           and The Vikings, perform at Queens Hall, Widnes.
SEP 20   *Mersey Beat* finally spells Paul McCartney's name
           correctly -- having previously printed it as McArthy,
           McArtrey and McArtney.
           Mersey Beat publishes more of Paul McCartney's remin--
           iscences of The Beatles' early days, this time a re--
           counting of their first four--and--one--half months in
           Hamburg.
SEP 22   The Beatles perform at the Majestic Ballroom, Birkenhead.
SEP 23   The Beatles perform in an evening session at The Cavern,
           along with The Saints Jazz Band, and The Dominoes.
SEP 26   The Beatles perform at The Cavern in a lunchtime session.
           The Beatles perform in an evening session at The Cavern,
           together with The Spidermen, and The Dominoes.
SEP 28   The Beatles perform at The Cavern Club in a lunchtime
           session.
SEP 30   The Beatles perform in an evening session at The Cavern,
           along with The Red River Jazz Men, and Clay Ellis
           and The Raiders.

OCTOBER
EMI decides to play *Love Me Do* only two times per week for
three weeks on its own Radio Luxembourg program.
Ya--Ya (EP), by Tony Sheridan and The Beat Brothers, is released
in Germany on the Polydor label.

OCT 1   The Beatles sign a new five--year contract with Brian
           Epstein's NEMS Enterprises.
OCT 3   The Beatles perform in an evening session at The Cavern,
           together with The Echoes, and Billy Kramer and The
           Coasters.
OCT 4   *Mersey Beat* reports that former Beatles' drummer Pete
           Best is playing regularly at the Majestic Ballroom,
           Birkenhead, as one of The All Stars.
OCT 5   The Beatles first single for EMI, *Love Me Do/P.S. I Love
           You* (45), is released in the U.K. on Parlophone, and
           is first aired on Radio Luxembourg. BM--114 (Oct 4)
               CON--20 (Nov) CON--60 (Sep 11, same day re--
               corded) TB--163 (Oct 4); 354 (Nov)
OCT 6   The Beatles make a personal appearance at Dawson's
           Music Shop, Widnes, to autograph copies of their first
           single, *Love Me Do/P.S. I Love You.*

OCT 7   The Beatles perform in an evening session at The Cavern, along with The Red River Jazzmen, The Bluegenes, and The Zodiacs.

OCT 8   The Beatles perform in a lunchtime session at The Cavern.

OCT 10   The Beatles perform in both a lunchtime and an evening session at The Cavern, along with The Four Jays, and Ken Dallas and The Silhouettes in the evening.

OCT 12   The Beatles perform at the Tower Ballroom in New Brighton, on the bill with Little Richard, Billy J. Kramer, The Undertakers and Rory Storm.

Brian Epstein's NEMS Enterprises stages a rock spectacular at the Tower Ballroom, New Brighton, with The Beatles on the bill with Little Richard.

The Beatles play at The Cavern Club with Little Richard.

OCT 13   The Beatles perform in an evening session at The Cavern, together with The Zenith Six, and Group One.

OCT 17   The Beatles perform in both a lunchtime and an evening session at The Cavern; along with The Big Three, and Group One in the evening.

OCT 18   *Love Me Do* hits number 1 in *Mersey Beat*'s top twenty listing "Merseyside Tops."

Mersey Beat indicates that The Beatles have an upcoming concert at the Royal Lido, in the Welsh seaside resort of Prestatyn.

mid–Oct   The Beatles perform at the Royal Lido, Prestatyn.

OCT 22   The Beatles perform at the Queens Hall, Widnes, along with The Mersey Beats, and Lee Curtis and The All--Stars.

OCT 25   The Beatles record for the BBC's "Teenagers' Turn" pro--gram in Manchester, singing *Love Me Do*.

OCT 26   BBC's "Teenagers' Turn" program, featuring The Beatles, is broadcast.

Love Me Do enters the *New Musical Express* charts.

OCT 27   *Love Me Do* becomes the first Beatles' record ever charted, entering the *Melody Maker* singles charts at 48 in the U.K.

OCT 28   The Beatles perform in concert at the Empire Theatre in Liverpool, their first major concert appearance, along with Little Richard and others.

OCT 31   The Beatles again travel to Hamburg.

NOVEMBER

Love Me Do appears in the U.K. on the *Record Mirror* charts in the 49th slot.

Beatles' performances on BBC radio are recorded, later to be illegally included on the following bootleg LPs: **As Sweet As You Are, Once Upon a . . . , Don't Pass Me By, Outakes Volume II, Have You Heard the Word, Yellow Matter Custard, Original Audition Tape Circa 1962 and Judy.**

Brian Epstein discusses the publication of *Please Please Me* with Dick James; Epstein brings along a Decca demonstration tape of the song, which every other major music publisher had re--jected for publication.

Dick James becomes Beatles' music publisher and booking agent.

Dick James arranges The Beatles' first London TV appearance.

NOV 1--   Beatles return to Hamburg, Germany for the fourth time,
14   again appearing at the Star Club. BB7--13 (mid--Nov--
          mid--Dec) BCE--23 (Nov 1--13)

NOV 3   *Love Me Do/P.S. I Love You* hits number 32 in the *New Record Mirror* charts.

NOV 7   Granada TV airs film of The Beatles performing *Love Me Do* on the "People and Places" show. ATN--248 ("earliest sound film of the Beatles performing") BCE--22 (Oct 26) BIR--15 ("first--ever television appearance")

NOV 10   *Love Me Do* enters the *Disc Weekly* charts at number 28, rises to 24, then drops from the charts.

NOV 15   Alan Smith's column, "London Beat," in *Mersey Beat* asks: "Can The Beatles become national stars . . . ?"

NOV 17   The Beatles record performances for Granada TV's "People and Places" show.

NOV 18   The Beatles perform in an evening session at The Cavern, along with The Mersey Beats.

NOV 19   The Beatles perform at a lunchtime session at The Cavern.

NOV 21   The Beatles perform in an evening session at The Cavern, together with The Zodiacs, and Johnny Templer and The Hi--Cats.

NOV 22   The Beatles perform at the Majestic Ballroom, Birkenhead.

NOV 23   The Beatles perform at a lunchtime session at The Cavern. In the evening, The Beatles perform at the 12th Annual Arts' Ball at the Tower Ballroom, New Brighton, along with two other bands.

NOV 25   The Beatles perform in an evening session at The Cavern, along with The Zenith Six, The Four Mosts, and The Dennisons.

NOV 26   The Beatles leave for London for more EMI recording sessions.

How Do You Do It, Please Please Me and *Ask Me Why*
recorded; *How Do You Do It* is never released.

late   The Beatles refuse George Martin's recommendation that
1962   they record and release *How Do You Do It*, by Mitch
              Murray, choosing *Please Please Me* instead (released in
              January 1963); Martin had almost refused to allow them
              to record this, The Beatles second single and their first
              really big hit.
NOV 28   The Beatles perform in an evening session at The Cavern,
              along with The Remo Four, and Dee Young and The
              Pontiacs.
NOV 29   The Beatles perform at the Majestic Ballroom, Birkenhead.

LATE 1962

The Beatles perform eleven songs on the British radio program
"Stramash."

The Beatles performance on the radio program "Stramash" is
illegally recorded by a Liverpool art teacher, later to be in--
cluded on the bootleg recording **Youngblood** (LP).

Two of The Beatles argue against returning to Hamburg to fulfill
the contracted club date at Star Club, in order to be in England
in case any television offers are made now that *Love Me Do* is
on the charts.

DECEMBER

Love Me Do climbs steadily on the *New Musical Express* charts
in the U.K.

DEC 1   *Love Me Do* enters *Billboard*'s British top twenty singles
              charts, remaining on the charts for six weeks during
              which time it reaches a high point of number 17.
DEC 4   The Beatles appear on the BBC's "Talent Spot" show.
DEC 10   The Beatles perform at the Embassy Theater, Peter--
              borough, England, on the bill with Frank Ifield, Ted
              Taylor and Julie Grant.   MB--46 (Dec 2)
DEC 12   George Martin comes to Liverpool to see Brian Epstein's
              new protege, Gerry Marsden.
              Brian Epstein and George Martin attend an evening concert
              by The Beatles at The Cavern; Martin first sees Priscilla
              White (later Cilla Black) working as the cloakroom
              attendant in The Cavern.
mid--Dec *Love Me Do/P.S. I Love You* enters the top twenty in

	England, remaining there only a week.
DEC 17	The Beatles again appear on Granada television show "People and Places."
Dec 18– Jan 1	The Beatles final trip to Hamburg, Germany, performing at the Star Club.
Christ– mastime	John Lennon appears on–stage at the Star Club during one performance with a toilet seat draped around his head in a dispute with the club's management.
late Dec	Ted "Kingsize" Taylor records The Beatles on stage at the Star Club in Hamburg, Germany.
DEC 30	Heather, Linda (Eastman) McCartney's daughter by her first marriage, is born.

LATE 1962

John Lennon and George Harrison purchase a pair of Gibson Jumbo guitars as spares.

Yoko Ono's avant garde creations begin to garner attention in London's artistic circles, according to Mark Shipper's humorous spoof of Beatle history, *Paperback Writer.*

The Beatles record *I Forgot to Remember to Forget, Lucille,* and *Dizzy Miss Lizzie*; never released.

WINTER 1962–1963

Through bad snow and freezing conditions, Cynthia Lennon visits her doctor and hospital twice a week during her pregnancy, constantly attempting to avoid being recognized by avid Beatle fans.

1962–1963

When I'm Sixty–Four is written during The Beatles Cavern Club days.

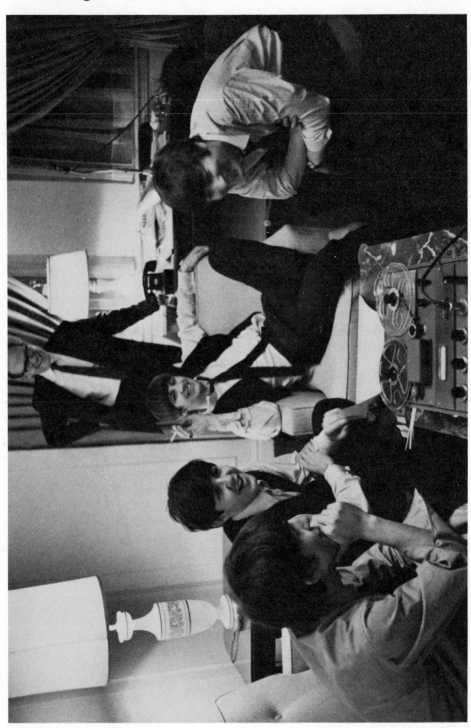

I read the news today
oh boy

A DAY
IN THE
LIFE

The Beatles
Day-By-Day

1963

DURING THIS YEAR . . .

The Beatles record the unreleased song *How Do You Do It?* at the
behest of George Martin; Gerry and The Pacemakers later
release their version.

Alistair Taylor, Brian Epstein's former assistant who had signed
the original Beatles contract with NEMS, rejoins NEMS after a
period with Pye records.

John Lennon and Mick Jagger's girlfriend, Yoko Ono, begin to see
each other secretly, according to Mark Shipper's humorous spoof
of Beatle history, *Paperback Writer*.

The following singles by The Beatles are released in Australia:
*Please Please Me/Ask Me Why, From Me to You/Thank You
Girl, She Loves You/I'll Get You, I Want to Hold Your Hand/
This Boy.*

She Loves You is written while travelling on a bus in Yorkshire
during the Helen Shapiro tour.

The Beatles record an unreleased version of their song *Love of the
Loved*.

The following EP by The Beatles is released in Australia: **Twist
and Shout**.

George Harrison writes *Don't Bother Me*, his first song.

The Beatles (LP) is released in Italy, with tracks identical to those
on the U.K. album **Please Please Me**.

The following singles by The Beatles are released in Italy: *Please
Please Me/Ask Me Why, She Loves You/I'll Get You, P.S. I
Love You/I Want to Hold Your Hand, Twist and Shout/Misery*.

I Wanna Be Your Man (45) by The Rolling Stones, written by
John Lennon after his overtures to Mick Jagger's girlfriend
(Yoko Ono) are rejected, is released in the U.K. on Decca,
according to Mark Shipper's humorous spoof of Beatle history,
Paperback Writer.

Rutlemania hits England, according to the album send-up of The

Beatles, **The Rutles**.

EARLY 1963
Brian Epstein tries to promote The Beatles in the U.S., approach–ing promoters and record companies, but comes away with no results.

Yoko Ono first meets and impresses Mick Jagger with her painting "Stairway to Abuse," at her one–woman exhibition in London, according to Mark Shipper's humorous spoof of Beatle history, *Paperback Writer*.

George Harrison comes to the U.S. to visit his sister Louise, married to an American and living in St. Louis.

Billy Shepherd begins work on his book, *The True Story of The Beatles*.

Singer Paul Simon first hears of The Rutles while in England, according to the album send-up of The Beatles, **The Rutles**.

Mal Evans works part–time as a bouncer at the Cavern; three months later The Beatles' hire him as road manager to work with Neil Aspinall.

Ringo Starr buys a new set of gray/blue perloid Ludwig drums, after which the words "The Beatles" are first painted on the bass drum in the now familiar stylistic characters.

Freda Kelly takes over management of The Beatles Fan Club from Bobbie Brown, who began it in Liverpool in May 1962.

Promoter Arthur Howes places The Beatles under contract as their manager for tour and live performance booking.

JANUARY
Plans for recording an album, their first, live at the Cavern are considered but dismissed by The Beatles.

Misery, written by John Lennon and Paul McCartney, is recorded at EMI's Abbey Road studios, London.

JANUARY–MARCH
The Beatles begin to notice an improvement in their financial situation, each receiving Ł 200 a week from Brian Epstein, who, at this point, is actually over–paying them with a view to a profitable future.

JAN 1   The Beatles begin a brief tour of Scotland, flying there straight from Germany.

JAN 3   *Mersey Beat* carries an article by Alan Smith about the
           recording of The Beatles' second single on November 26,
           1962.
           Mersey Beat announces that The Beatles have won its
           popularity poll for the second year in a row.
JAN 5   "Disker," the Liverpool *Echo*'s record critic, reviews
           The Beatles' forthcoming record – *Please Please Me* –
           at length; Tony Barrow didn't mention that he also
           worked for The Beatles at the time.
           The Beatles tour of Scotland ends.
           Love Me Do reaches its highest point on the *Melody Maker*
           singles charts, 21, dropping down after two weeks in this
           position.
JAN 7   Five hundred fans are turned away from a packed–house
           performance by The Beatles at the Majestic Ballroom,
           Birkenhead.
JAN 10   The Beatles perform at the Grafton Ballroom, Liverpool.
JAN 11   The Beatles appear on ABC's "Thank Your Lucky Stars"
           television show.   BCE–24 (Beatles *record* an appearance)
JAN 12   *Please Please Me/Ask Me Why* (45) is released in the U.K.
           ATN–15 (Jan 11)
JAN 16   A BBC recording of The Beatles is broadcast as a tie–in
           with the release of their second single.
JAN 17   *Mersey Beat* carries an ad announcing the release of *Please
           Please Me/Ask Me Why.*
JAN 18   A Beatles broadcast over Radio Luxembourg features John
           Lennon as lead vocalist on *Carol*, and Paul McCartney
           and George Harrison on *Lend Me Your Comb*; the songs
           later appear on the bootleg records **Peace of Mind** and
           Buried Treasures.
JAN 19   *Please Please Me* enters the *Melody Maker* singles charts in
           the U.K. at 47.
JAN 22   Recordings of Beatles' performances for BBC's "Talent
           Spot" and "Saturday Club" are made.
JAN 25   Vee Jay signs The Beatles for U.S. release.
           Cilla Black makes her singing debut at The Cavern Club,
           where she formerly worked checking hats and coats.
               JLS–108 (1962)
JAN 31   *Please Please Me* hits number 1 in *Mersey Beat*'s "Mersey–
           side Tops" listing, a Liverpool popularity poll.
           Mersey Beat reports the publicity agent Andrew Oldham
           has taken over publicity for The Beatles.
           The Beatles perform at the Majestic Ballroom, Birkenhead.

FEBRUARY

The Beatles appear on "Scene" at the Manchester Granada TV studios.

The Beatles receive national exposure for the first time in the U.K. in an article by Maureen Cleave in London's *Evening Standard.*

Billy J. Kramer, under the management of Brian Epstein, combines with a backing group to form Billy J. Kramer and The Dakotas.

While touring as a backing group on the Helen Shapiro tour, The Beatles are thrown out of a hotel restaurant as they attempt to dine in their leather jackets.

FEBRUARY--MARCH

The Beatles tour the U.K., backing such artists as Helen Shapiro, Chris Montez, and Tommy Roe.

FEB 1 *Please Please Me* enters *Billboard*'s British top twenty singles charts, remaining on the charts for a period of eleven weeks during which time it reaches a high point of number 2.

FEB 2 The Beatles perform at the Gaumont in Bradford, England, beginning the Helen Shapiro tour; the show is recorded by ABC--TV and rebroadcast in part on "Thank Your Lucky Stars."

   Please Please Me enters the British pop charts at number 16.

FEB 3 The Beatles top the bill at the Cavern Club's "Rhythm and Blues" festival.

FEB 4 *Love Me Do/P.S. I Love You* (45) is released in Canada.

FEB 5 The Beatles perform at the Gaumont in Doncaster, England, as part of the Helen Shapiro tour. BBS--26 (Feb 3)

FEB 6 The Beatles appear at the Granada in Bedford, England, as part of the Helen Shapiro tour. BBS--26 (Feb 4)

FEB 7 The Beatles perform at the Odeon in Wakefield, England, as part of the Helen Shapiro tour.

FEB 8 The Beatles perform at the ABC in Carlisle, England, as part of the Helen Shapiro tour.

early 1963 During the Helen Shapiro tour, Ringo Starr is ejected from a ball held in a Carlisle hotel for "extreme scruffiness."

FEB 9 The Beatles perform at the Odeon in Sunderland, England, as part of the Helen Shapiro tour.

FEB 10 The Beatles perform at the Embassy in Peterborough, England, as part of the Helen Shapiro tour.

FEB 11 At EMI's Abbey Road studios in London, The Beatles

record *I Saw Her Standing There, Misery, Anna, Chains, Boys, Baby It's You, Do You Want to Know a Secret, A Taste of Honey, There's a Place,* and *Twist and Shout* for **Please Please Me** (LP); also recorded are the unreleased songs *Bad to Me, I'm in Love, Hold Me Tight, Keep Your Hands Off My Baby* and *I'll Keep You Satisfied.*
BB29–25 (March)   BD–4 (Mar 3–9)   TSB–179 (March)

FEB 13   The Beatles appear on ABC's "Thank Your Lucky Stars" television show.

FEB 14   The Beatles perform at The Locarno Ballroom on St. Valentine's Night.

FEB 16   *Please Please Me* becomes the first Beatles number 1 single.

FEB 16   The Beatles leave the Helen Shapiro tour, rejoining on
–22   February 23.

FEB 21   George Harrison, columnist for the Liverpool *Echo*, plugs a forthcoming TV appearance by The Beatles on "Thank Your Lucky Stars."

FEB 23   The Beatles perform at the Granada in Mansfield, England, as part of the Helen Shapiro tour.

FEB 24   The Beatles appear at the Coventry Theater in Coventry, England, as part of the Helen Shapiro tour.

FEB 25   The Beatles finish recording *Can't Buy Me Love* on George Harrison's 21st birthday.
Please Please Me/Ask Me Why (45) is released in the U.S.; some issues of the record misprint the group's name as The Beattles.   TBD–3 (Mar)

FEB 26   The Beatles perform at the Odeon in Taunton, England, as part of the Helen Shapiro tour.
Northern Songs Ltd., The Beatles' music publishing company, is formed, with Brian Epstein and Dick James as directors.   ATC–142 (Jan)

late Feb   *Love Me Do* drops from the top fifty in the *Melody Maker* charts.

FEB 27   The Beatles perform at the Rialto in York, England, as part of the Helen Shapiro tour.

FEB 28   *From Me to You* is written in a bus travelling between York and Shrewsbury.
The Beatles perform at the Granada in Shrewsbury, England, as part of the Helen Shapiro tour.

MARCH

The Beatles record *The Tip of My Tongue* at EMI's Abbey Road studios, London.

The work of The Beatles and other Liverpool groups popularizes the phrase "Liverpool Sound" in music circles.

I'll Be On My Way, written by John Lennon and Paul McCartney, is recorded at EMI's Abbey Road studios, London, by Billy J. Kramer with The Dakotas.

Please Please Me stays in the top ten singles charts in the U.K.

MARCH--AUGUST

Beatles' songs broadcast over the BBC in London are later included on the following bootleg records: **Outakes/Studiosessions, Have You Heard the Word, Yellow Matter Custard, Stockholm 1964, Outakes Vol. 1** and **Outakes Vol. 2.**

MAR 1   The Beatles perform at the Odeon in Southport, England, as part of the Helen Shapiro tour.

MAR 2   *Please Please Me* hits number 1 on the *Melody Maker* singles charts, remaining there for two weeks.
The Beatles perform at City Hall in Sheffield, England as part of the Helen Shapiro tour.

MAR 3   The Beatles perform at the Gaumont in Hanley, England, ending the Helen Shapiro tour. BCE--24,25 (Henley)

MAR 4   *From Me to You* and *Thank You Girl* are recorded at EMI's Abbey Road studios, London.

MAR 9   The Beatles perform at the Granada in East Ham, England, first concert beginning the Chris Montez/Tommy Roe tour. BEA3--13 ("mid--March" tour was with Helen Shapiro) TOL--83 (Montez/Roe tour occurred "over the Christmas period")

MAR 10 The Beatles perform at the Hippodrome in Birmingham, England, as part of the Chris Montez/Tommy Roe tour.

MAR 12 The Beatles perform at the Granada in Bedford, England, as part of the Chris Montez/Tommy Roe tour; partially recorded by BBC Radio and broadcast on the show "Here We Go."
The Beatles appear on the BBC's "Here We Go" program.

MAR 13 The Beatles perform at the Rialto in York, England, as part of the Chris Montez/Tommy Roe tour.

MAR 14 The Beatles perform at the Gaumont in Wolverhampton, England, as part of the Chris Montez/Tommy Roe tour.

MAR 15 The Beatles perform at Colston Hall in Bristol, England, as part of the Chris Montez/Tommy Roe tour.

MAR 16 The Beatles perform at City Hall in Sheffield, England, as part of the Chris Montez/Tommy Roe tour.

MAR 17   The Beatles perform at the Embassy in Peterborough,
              England, as part of the Chris Montez/Tommy Roe tour.
MAR 18   The Beatles perform at the ABC in Gloucester, England, as
              part of the Chris Montez/Tommy Roe tour.
MAR 19   The Beatles perform at the ABC in Cambridge, England, as
              part of the Chris Montez/Tommy Roe tour.
MAR 20   The Beatles perform at the Ritz in Romford, England, as
              part of the Chris Montez/Tommy Roe tour.
MAR 21   The Beatles perform at the ABC in Croydon, England, as
              part of the Chris Montez/Tommy Roe tour.
MAR 22   **Please Please Me** (LP) is released in the U.K.   BBS–52
              (Mar 7)   BM–115 (Apr)   OBF–4 (Apr 11)
              Misery, written by Lennon/McCartney and recorded by
              Kenny Lynch, is released in U.K.
              The Beatles perform at the Gaumont in Doncaster, England,
              as part of the Chris Montez/Tommy Roe tour.
MAR 23   The Beatles perform at City Hall in Newcastle, England, as
              part of the Chris Montez/Tommy Roe tour.
MAR 24   The Beatles perform at the Empire in Liverpool, England,
              as part of the Chris Montez/Tommy Roe tour.
MAR 26   The Beatles perform at the Granada in Mansfield, England,
              as part of the Chris Montez/Tommy Roe tour.
MAR 27   The Beatles perform at the ABC in Northampton, England,
              as part of the Chris Montez/Tommy Roe tour.
MAR 28   The Beatles perform at the ABC in Exeter, England, as part
              of the Chris Montez/Tommy Roe tour; partially recorded
              by BBC Radio and broadcast on "On the Scene."
              The Beatles appear on the BBC's "On the Scene" program.
MAR 29   The Beatles perform at the Odeon in Lewisham, England,
              as part of the Chris Montez/Tommy Roe tour.
MAR 30   The Beatles perform at the Guildhall in Portsmouth,
              England, as part of the Chris Montez/Tommy Roe tour.
              BCE–27 (Guild Hall)
MAR 31   The Beatles perform at the De Montfort Hall in Leicester,
              England, as part of the Chris Montez/Tommy Roe tour.
              BCE–27 (De Montford Hall)

EARLY 1963
John and Cynthia Lennon occupy the flat offered them in the
lower portion of John's Aunt Mimi's house.

MID–SPRING
Brian Epstein opens an office in London.

APRIL

As The Beatles are about to appear on "Thank Your Lucky Stars," they learn that the Pete Best Combo has broken up due to lack of bookings.

The Beatles learn that they will tour the U.K. with top billing, together with Roy Orbison and Gerry and the Pacemakers.

The Beatles' money--making ability begins in earnest.

The Beatles become aware that they must become more disciplined and punctual, and more dress conscious, as their popularity grows.

Begins an extended period when the number 1 position on the British singles charts is held by one of several groups managed by Brian Epstein and produced by George Martin.

Beatles Monthly Book, official fan magazine, is founded.

EARLY APRIL

Please Please Me is in the number 11 slot in the U.K. singles charts as *From Me to You* is being pressed.

APR 6 **Please Please Me** (LP) enters the *Melody Maker* album charts in the U.K. at number 10.

early 1963 Cynthia Lennon and girlfriend Phyllis are driven to Sefton General Hospital in the middle of the night, both dressed in nightgowns, slippers and robes, after Cynthia's labor pains increase; the hospital refuses to transport Phyllis back home, and she walks for two miles before encountering an amazed taxi driver.

APR 8 John Charles Julian Lennon is born at Sefton General Hospital, Liverpool. ODT--184 (April 18, 1964)

APR 10 *From Me to You* enters *Billboard*'s British top twenty singles charts, remaining on the charts for 17 weeks during which time it reaches a high point of number 1.

early 1963 Two days after Julian's birth, Cynthia Lennon gets to hold her son for the first time.

APR 12 **Please Please Me** (LP) hits number 1 on the *New Musical Express* charts, remaining there for six months.
LCP--262 (Apr 11)   PMS--129 (mid--Apr)
From Me to You/Thank You Girl (45) is released in U.K.
BM--115 (Apr 11)   IR--16 (Apr 11)
The Beatles perform in an evening session at the Cavern, along with The Dennisons, Faron's Flamingos, and The Roadrunners.

mid--Apr *Please Please Me* drops to number 17 in the U.K. singles charts.

early   A week after the birth of his son, Julian, John Lennon
1963   finally returns from performing, although he has called
           his Aunt Mimi for progress reports.
           A week after the birth of his son Julian, John Lennon visits
           his wife in the hospital; before leaving he inquires if it
           would be alright if he vacationed in Spain with Brian
           Epstein, who had asked him to go on holiday after
           touring.
APR 16   The Beatles appear on the BBC's "6:25 Show" television
           program.
APR 20   *From Me to You* enters the *Melody Maker* singles charts in
           the U.K. at number 19.
APR 21   The Beatles perform at the Empire Pool in Wembley,
           England, at the *New Musical Express* Poll Winner's
           Concert. BCE–27 (Apr 28)   BEA3–13 (Mar)   LCP–
           262 (Apr 1)
APR 26   *I Saw Her Standing There*, recorded by Duffy Power, is
           released in U.K.
           Do You Want to Know a Secret/I'll Be On My Way (45),
           recorded by Billy J. Kramer with The Dakotas, is re--
           leased in U.K.

LATE APRIL
From Me to You hits number 3 on the singles charts in the U.K.

LATE APRIL–EARLY MAY
The Beatles vacation for 12 days in Teneriffe, The Canary Islands.

MAY
The Beatles, topping the bill for the first time, are signed to tour
   with Roy Orbison and Gerry and the Pacemakers.
The Beatles are pelted with jelly beans for the first time while on
   tour with Roy Orbison, after George Harrison's earlier remark
   that he liked "jelly babies."

MAY 1   Tony Barrow leaves Decca records to become press officer
           for Brian Epstein's NEMS Enterprises.
MAY 4   *Do You Want to Know a Secret* by Billy J. Kramer with
           The Dakotas, enters the *Melody Maker* singles charts in
           the U.K. at 47.
           From Me to You hits number 1 on the *Melody Maker*
           singles charts and remains there for 6 weeks.
           Please Please Me (LP) hits number 1 on the *Melody Maker*

album charts, remaining there for 30 weeks.

MAY 9   The Beatles perform at the Royal Albert Hall in London;
Paul McCartney meets Jane Asher after the concert.

MAY 11 The Beatles perform at the Imperial Ballroom in Nelson,
England.

early May After returning from his holiday break in Spain, John and
Cynthia Lennon go together to register their son's
birth just before The Beatles leave once again to tour
with Roy Orbison.

MAY 14 The Beatles perform at the Rank in Sunderland, England.

MAY 15 The Beatles perform at the Royalty in Chester, England.

MAY 17 The Beatles appear on the BBC's "Pops and Lennie"
television show.

MAY 18 The Beatles headline their own tour, beginning at the
Granada in Slough, England.

MAY 19 The Beatles perform at the Gaumont in Hanley, England,
headlining their own tour.

MAY 20 The Beatles perform at the Gaumont in Southampton,
England, headlining their own tour.

MAY 22 The Beatles perform at the Gaumont in Ipswich, England,
headlining their own tour.

MAY 23 The Beatles perform at the Odeon in Nottingham,
England, headlining their own tour.

MAY 24 *My Bonnie/The Saints* (45) is reissued in the U.K.
BIR–124 (June '63) GBR–1 (May 23)
The Beatles perform in Harrow, England.
The Beatles perform at the Granada in Walthamstowe,
England, headlining their own tour.

MAY 25 The Beatles perform at City Hall in Sheffield, England,
headlining their own tour; partially recorded for broad–
cast on BBC Radio's "Saturday Club."
The Beatles appear on the BBC's "Saturday Club" program,
singing *Happy Birthday, Johnny B. Goode, Memphis
Tennessee,* and *You Really Got a Hold on Me.*
Songs from The Beatles appearance on the "Saturday
Club" program are recorded, later to appear illegally on
the bootleg recordings: **Rare Beatles, Rare Sessions**
and **Happy Birthday.**

MAY 26 The Beatles perform at the Empire in Liverpool, England,
headlining their own tour. BEA3–13 (Apr)

MAY 27 *From Me to You/Thank You Girl* (45) is released in the
U.S. TBD–3 (June) BF–23,207 (Mar)
The Beatles perform at the Capitol in Cardiff, England,

headlining their own tour.

MAY 28   The Beatles perform at the Gaumont in Worcester,
        England, headlining their own tour.

MAY 29   The Beatles perform at the Rialto in York, England,
        headlining their own tour.

MAY 30   The Beatles perform at the Granada in Kingston, England.
        The Beatles perform at the Odeon in Manchester, England,
        headlining their own tour.

MAY 31   The Beatles perform at the Odeon in Southend, England,
        headlining their own tour.

EARLY 1963

Paul McCartney begins to live with Jane Asher and her parents
while in London, where he resides until the end of 1966 when
he buys his own house in St. John's Wood.

JUNE

The Official Beatles Fan Club begins to set up a network of Area
Secretaries to process new membership applications.

My Bonnie/The Saints, by Tony Sheridan and The Beatles, is re--
leased in Germany on the Polydor label.

The Tip of My Tongue, written by John Lennon and Paul
McCartney, is recorded by Tommy Quickly.

Polydor's reissue of their old Beatles' single tune, *My Bonnie*, is
attacked by The Beatles.

Bad to Me and *I Call Your Name*, both written by John Lennon
and Paul McCartney, are recorded at EMI's Abbey Road studios,
London, by Billy J. Kramer with The Dakotas.

The Beatles set up a company to receive profits from their music
careers called The Beatles Ltd.

JUN 1   The Beatles perform at the Granada in Tooting, England,
        headlining their own tour.

JUN 2   The Beatles perform at the Hippodrome in Brighton,
        England, headlining their own tour.

JUN 3   Del Shannon releases a single in the U.S. with his own version
        of Beatles' *From Me to You*, released in the U.S. by The
        Beatles just over a week before.
        The Beatles perform at the Granada in Walthamstow,
        England.
        The Beatles perform at the Granada in Woolwich, England,
        headlining their own tour.

JUN 4   The Beatles perform at Town Hall in Birmingham, England,
         headlining their own tour.
         The Beatles begin their own BBC radio series, "Pop Go
         The Beatles."
JUN 5   The Beatles perform at the Odeon in Leeds, England,
         headlining their own tour.
JUN 7   The Beatles perform at the Odeon in Glasgow, Scotland,
         headlining their own tour.
JUN 8   The Beatles perform at City Hall in Newcastle, England,
         headlining their own tour.
JUN 9   The Beatles perform at King George Hall, Blackburn,
         headlining the last stop on their own tour. PMS--130
             (St. George's Hall)   TBA--231 (King George's Hall)
JUN 10   *Do You Want to Know a Secret/I'll Be On My Way* (45),
         recorded by Billy J. Kramer with The Dakotas, is
         released in the U.S.
JUN 12   The Beatles perform at a charity concert at Grafton Ball--
         room in Liverpool, England, for the National Society
         for the Prevention of Cruelty to Children.
June 12 Versions of tracks are recorded for The Beatles' **With**
--July 20   **The Beatles** (LP).
JUN 14   The Beatles perform at New Brighton Tower in Liverpool,
         England.   BCE--30 (Tower Ballroom, New Brighton)
JUN 15   *Do You Want to Know a Secret*, by Billy J. Kramer with
         The Dakotas, hits number 1 on the *Melody Maker* charts,
         dropping to number 4 the next week.
         My Bonnie enters the *Melody Maker* charts in the U.K. at
         number 38, dropping to 46 the following week, and
         thereafter off the charts.
mid--Jun The Brian Epstein--managed group, Gerry and the Pace-
         makers, put their *I Like It* in number 1 chart position.
JUN 16   The Beatles perform at the Odeon in Romford, England,
         along with Gerry and the Pacemakers, and Billy J.
         Kramer.
JUN 17   The Beatles plan a private birthday party for Paul McCartney
         the following day.
JUN 18   At EMI studios, Paul McCartney is escorted out into the
         street where he receives a "bumping" on the pavement
         for his 21st birthday, to the amusement of crowds and
         reporters.

The Beatles perform at the Winter Gardens in Margate, staying at hotel on the sea--front.

Paul McCartney's 21st birthday party, which turns noisy and disorderly, is held at Paul's Aunt Jinny's home.

JUN 20   *Mersey Beat* carries a piece on Brian Kelly, Liverpool promoter responsible for The Beatles' early (1960) appearances at Litherland Town Hall.

Mersey Beat publishes an article by Howie Casey on The Beatles' early performances in Hamburg, Germany, as The Silver Beatles.

JUN 22   The Beatles perform at Town Hall in Abergavenny.

John Lennon records an appearance for the BBC's "Juke Box Jury" television show.

JUN 23   The Beatles appear on BBC's "Easy Beat" radio program.

JUN 28   The Beatles perform at Queen's Hall in Leeds, England.

JUN 29   John Lennon's "Juke Box Jury" appearance is televised.

"Thank Your Lucky Stars" TV program, covering The Beatles and other Liverpool acts, is televised; the show is rebroadcast October 9th and November 13th.

JUN 30   The Beatles perform at the Regal in Yarmouth, England.

MID--1963

Sid Bernstein, an American promoter, notes the continuing stories about The Beatles in the British press, and calls Brian Epstein to propose the Carnegie Hall concert.

The Beatles (John Lennon, lead vocalist) record *I Got a Woman* and *Soldiers of Love*; versions never released.

SUMMER

John Lennon, Paul McCartney, George Harrison, Billy J. Kramer, Tony Mansfield, Neil Aspinall and Mike Mansfield are photo--graphed together.

Brian Epstein moves NEMS Enterprises to larger offices in Liver--pool, hiring additional staff to handle his growing business.

Mal Evans, the bouncer from the Cavern Club, joins Neil Aspinall as The Beatles' equipment/road managers at the behest of Brian Epstein.

The Beatles express great enthusiasum for doing a film.

At a Sunday performance in Brighton, George Harrison begins his guitar introduction to *Oh My Soul*, only to have all the group's equipment go dead; the curtains are closed, the equipment checked and fixed; George begins again only to have the same thing occur. The trouble is traced to a heavy bass drum resting

on the main power supply backstage.
Paul McCartney and George Harrison are photographed with Billy
J. Kramer.

MID--SUMMER
Rumors begin to spread that John Lennon is a married man.

JULY
Love of the Loved, written by John Lennon and Paul McCartney,
is recorded at EMI's Abbey Road studios, London, by Cilla
Black.

JUL 1   Beatles record *She Loves You* and *I'll Get You.*
JUL 3   The Beatles appear on a radio show in Manchester.
    Hello Little Girl, written by John Lennon and Paul
    McCartney, is recorded at EMI's Abbey Road studios
    by The Fourmost.
JUL 5   The Beatles perform at the Plaza Ballroom in Oldhill,
    England.
JUL 7   Ringo Starr turns 23.
    The Beatles perform at the ABC in Blackpool, England.
JUL 8--   The Beatles perform at the Winter Gardens in Margate,
13   England, with Billy J. Kramer.
JUL 12   **My Bonnie** (EP), by Tony Sheridan and The Beatles, is re--
    released in the U.K. by Polydor.
    Twist and Shout (EP) is released in U.K. BBS--51 (Sep)
    LCP--274 (June 26th)
JUL 15   *All My Loving* is recorded.
JUL 16   BBC resumes "Pop Go The Beatles" radio series for
    another ten weeks. BBS--54 (Aug 16th)
JUL 18   A message from John Lennon is printed in *Mersey Beat*
    regarding rumors that he alone has been disparaging
    toward Ringo Starr, or that Ringo is being kept in the
    background by other group members.
JUL 21   The Beatles perform at Blackpool's Queen's Theatre to an
    overflow crowd.
JUL 22   *I'll Keep You Satisfied*, written by John Lennon and Paul
    McCartney, is recorded at EMI's Abbey Road studios,
    London, by Billy J. Kramer with The Dakotas.
    Introducing The Beatles (LP) is released in U.S.
JUL 22   The Beatles perform at the Super Mare Odeon in Weston,
--27   England, with Gerry and the Pacemakers, and Tommy

Quickly.
late Jul   EMI presses a quarter–million copies of *She Loves You/*
           I'll Get You in anticipation of heavy sales a month
           hence.
JUL 26   *Bad to Me/I Call Your Name* (45), written by Lennon/
           McCartney and recorded by Billy J. Kramer with The
           Dakotas, released in U.K.
JUL 27.   **Twist and Shout** (EP) enters the *Melody Maker* singles
           charts at number 14 in the U.K.
JUL 28   The Beatles perform at the ABC in Great Yarmouth,
           England.
JUL 29   The Beatles record new songs at EMI's London
--30   studios.
JUL 30   *Tip of My Tongue*, written by Lennon/McCartney, and
           recorded by Tommy Quickly, released on single in the
           U.K.
JUL 31   The Beatles perform at the Imperial Ballroom, Nelson,
           in the U.K.

AUGUST

The Beatles' performance of *Long Tall Sally* in London's Top Ten
Club is recorded, later to appear illegally on bootleg recordings
like **Have You Heard the Word**.
She Loves You is released in the U.K., according to Mark Shipper's
humorous spoof of Beatle history, *Paperback Writer.*
Billy Shepherd, author of *The True Story of The Beatles*, is
photographed talking to Ringo Starr and George Harrison in a
hotel in Bournemouth.
New Musical Express interview between Alan Smith and John
Lennon discusses the period in Lennon's life before formation
of The Quarrymen.
The Beatles give their final performance -- number 294 -- at The
Cavern Club, according to Mark Shipper's humorous spoof of
Beatle history, *Paperback Writer.*

AUG 1   The first issue of *The Beatles Book* is published. BB27--
           iii (Aug 1962)   TBA--138 (Jul)
           Allan Williams and others organize the largest open air
           Beat concert held to date; Brian Epstein earlier informs
           him that the Beatles won't attend due to their South-
           port concert.

The Beatles perform in Southport, England.

AUG 2   The Beatles perform at the Grafton Ballroom in Liverpool, England, with The Undertakers, The Dennisons, and The Cascades.   BB25--22 (Aug 1)   MB--52 (Grafton Rooms)

AUG 3   The Beatles perform in an evening show at Liverpool's Cavern Club -- their final performance at The Cavern -- along with The Mersey Beats, The Escourts, The Road Runners, The Sapphires, and Johnny Ringo and The Colts.   BAB--177 (Aug 23rd given as final per-- formance)

The first Beatles' single to register on the U.S. *Billboard* charts, *From Me to You*, enters at number 125.

Bad to Me by Billy J. Kramer with The Dakotas, written by Lennon/McCartney, enters the *Melody Maker* singles charts at number 31 in the U.K.

AUG 4   The Beatles perform at the Queens Theatre in Blackpool, England.

AUG 5   The Beatles appear at "A Twist & Shout Dance" in Abbotsfield Park, Urmston, Manchester, along with three other acts.

AUG 6   The Beatles perform at the St. Helier Springfield Ballroom
--9   in Jersey, England, during five days there.

AUG 8   Kyoko Cox, Yoko Ono's daughter by her first marriage, is born.

AUG 10 *From Me to You* reaches its highest 1963 position on the U.S. *Billboard* singles charts: number 116.

AUG 11 The Beatles perform at the ABC in Blackpool, England.

AUG 12 The Beatles perform at the Odeon in Llandudno, with
--17   Billy J. Kramer and Tommy Quickly.

AUG 15 An article by Pete Best describing his career with The Beatles is published in *Mersey Beat.*

AUG 16 The ten week radio series, "Pop Goes The Beatles," begins on the BBC in the U.K.

AUG 17 **Twist and Shout** (EP) reaches highest position -- number 2 -- on the *Melody Maker* singles charts.

AUG 18 The Beatles perform at the Princess Theatre in Torquay.

AUG 19 The Beatles appear on Granada TV's "Scene at 6:30" television program; *Twist and Shout, This Boy* and *I Want to Hold Your Hand* are recorded and later appear illegally on bootleg recordings.

AUG 19 The Beatles perform at the Gaumont in Bournemouth,
--24   England, with Billy J. Kramer and Tommy Quickly.

AUG 23 *She Loves You/I'll Get You* (45) is released in U.K.

AUG 24   The Beatles appear on ABC's "Thank Your Lucky Stars
         Summer Spin" television program.
         Bad to Me by Billy J. Kramer with The Dakotas, written
         by Lennon/McCartney, hits number 1 on the *Melody
         Maker* singles charts, remaining there for two weeks.
AUG 25   The Beatles perform at Queen's Theatre in Blackpool,
         England.
AUG 26   The Beatles perform at the Odeon in Southport, England,
--31   with Gerry and The Pacemakers and Tommy Quickly.
AUG 30   *Hello Little Girl,* written by Lennon/McCartney and
         recorded by The Fourmost, is released on a single
         in the U.K.
AUG 31   *She Loves You* enters the *Billboard* British top twenty
         singles charts, remaining on the charts for 24 weeks
         during which time it reaches a high point of number 1.
         She Loves You enters the *Melody Maker* singles charts at
         number 12 in the U.K.

SEPTEMBER
   Collarless "Beatles jackets" first go on sale across England.
   She Loves You sales reach 750,000 copies; total sales for Beatles'
   releases has reached two million.
   A Beatles' performance of *I Saw Her Standing There, From Me to
   You* and *Money* is recorded, later to appear illegally on bootleg
   recordings.
   Brian Epstein signs a management contract with Cilla Black
   (Priscilla White).

SEP 1   The Beatles perform at the Regal in Yarmouth; the show is
         filmed for ABC's "Big Night Out" television program.
SEP 3   The Beatles perform at the Queen's Theatre, Blackpool.
SEP 4   The Beatles perform at the Gaumont in Worcester, England,
         along with Mike Berry.
SEP 5   The Beatles perform at the Gaumont in Taunton, England,
         along with Mike Berry.
SEP 6   **The Beatles' Hits** (EP) is released in U.K.
         New Musical Express reports Cilla Black will record *Love
         of the Loved,* by Lennon/McCartney, for Brian Epstein.
         The Beatles perform at the Odeon in Luton, England,
         along with Mike Berry. TBA--232 (Sep 7)
SEP 7   *She Loves You* hits number 1 on the *Melody Maker* singles
         charts, remaining there for five weeks. PMS--131 (seven
         weeks)

"Big Night Out" performance, recorded on September 1, is televised on ABC.

The Beatles appear at the Fairfields in Croydon, England. BB26--21 (Fairfield Halls)

SEP 8   The Beatles perform at the ABC in Blackpool, England, along with Mike Berry.

SEP 10   Donald Zec of the *Daily Mirror* interviews The Beatles, one of their first long interviews.

SEP 13   The Beatles perform at the Public Hall in Preston, England.

SEP 14   The Beatles perform at the Memorial Hall in Nantwich, England.

SEP 15   The Beatles perform at the Royal Albert Hall in London.

mid--   John Lennon travels to Paris, Paul and Ringo to Athens
late Sep   and Greece, and George visits his sister in St. Louis, Missouri. JLS--113 (Sep 15)

SEP 16   *She Loves You/I'll Get You* (45) is released in U.S. BAB--346 (Aug)

SEP 17   The Beatles perform at the Queen's Theatre, Blackpool.

SEP 21   *Hello Little Girl* by The Fourmost, written by Lennon/McCartney, enters the *Melody Maker* singles charts at number 41 in the U.K.

SEP 23   *Bad to Me/I Call Your Name* (45) written by Lennon/McCartney and recorded by Billy J. Kramer with The Dakotas, is released in the U.S.

SEP 26   *Mersey Beat* magazine begins a regular special section devoted to news about The Beatles, "Mersey Beatle."

SEP 27   *Love of the Loved*, written by Lennon/McCartney and recorded by Cilla Black, is released on a single in U.K.

SEP 28   **The Beatles Hits** (EP) enters the *Melody Maker* singles charts at number 44 in the U.K.

FALL

Mike Hurst records Lennon/McCartney composition *Little Child* for a single, never released.

New York promoter Sid Bernstein calls Brian Epstein to propose the arrangement of the first American concerts for The Beatles.

Walter Shenson, film producer, first conceives of making a film built around The Beatles -- later to become "A Hard Day's Night."

"Beatlemania" begins in the U.K. following the group's return from Sweden; at this point fans begin to become hysterically excited.

LATE 1963
About six months after Julian Lennon's birth, Cynthia Lennon's
mother returns from a stay in Canada; Cynthia moves in with
her mother in Hoylake with plans to set up housekeeping with
John in London, much to the relief of John's Aunt Mimi, who
had grown tired of the split level arrangement in her own house.
John and Cynthia Lennon take a second honeymoon in Paris,
staying at the luxurious George Cinque Hotel.

OCTOBER
National coverage of The Beatles becomes widespread in the
British press.
Beatles fan clubs spring up in Germany and Canada.
WINS disc–jockey Murray Kaufman – Murray The K – first
becomes aware of The Beatles when someone provides a copy
of *She Loves You* for his weekly record contest. The single
places third in a field of five. He continues to play it for 2½
weeks with no special listener reactions.
The date for a "Northern Get Together" of members of The
Beatles fan club in announced.
The original date for the fan club Get Together this month at
Liverpool Stadium must be cancelled because The Beatles are
unable to attend on the date booked by the club.
Brian Epstein moves his office from Liverpool to London.
I Wanna Be Your Man, written by John Lennon and Paul McCartney,
is recorded at Kingsway studios, London, by The Rolling Stones.
I'm in Love, written by John Lennon and Paul McCartney, is
recorded at EMI's Abbey Road studios, London, by The Four–
most.
British press coins the term "Beatlemania," which "officially"
begins as of this month.

OCT 5   The Beatles perform at the Glasgow Concert Hall, Glasgow,
          Scotland.
OCT 6   The Beatles perform at the Regal in Kirkcaldy, Scotland.
OCT 7   The Beatles perform at the Dundee Caird Hall, Dundee,
          Scotland.
OCT 9   John Lennon turns 23.
          The Beatles appear on a rebroadcast of the BBC's "The
          Mersey Beat" television program, originally shown
          June 29. BBS–54 (Oct 19)
OCT 11   The Beatles appear at the Stoke Trentham Gardens.
          BCE–33 (Trentham Gardens, Stoke–On–Trent)

She Loves You becomes The Beatles first Gold Disc (sales over 1,000,000 units); sales of **Please Please Me** (LP) pass a quarter million.

OCT 13 Neil Aspinall's 22nd birthday.

"Beatlemania" is born as thousands jam the London streets outside the Palladium Theatre.

Beatles appear on BBC--TV show "Sunday Night at the London Palladium," seen by 15 million viewers.

Songs from The Beatles' London Palladium performance – broadcast on BBC radio -- are recorded, later to be illegally included on the following bootleg LPs: **Sunday Night at the London Palladium**, and **The Tour Album (Third Amendment)**.

OCT 14 London's *Daily Mirror* carries an editorial praising The Beatles following their performance at the Royal Variety Show the night before.

OCT 15 The Beatles perform at the Floral in Southport, England. MB--61 (Floral Pavilion)

Oct A few days after The Beatles' London Palladium concert, the London *Times* carries its first report on The Beatles: a report on the 40 policemen needed to control crowds of thousands of fans buying tickets in Newcastle for the group's November 23 concert.

OCT 17 Bond Street is mobbed when Paul McCartney arrives to eat lunch with the winner of a magazine contest, "Why I Like The Beatles."

OCT 18 The Beatles perform at the Music Hall in Shrewsbury, England.

OCT 19 *I Want to Hold Your Hand* and *This Boy* are recorded at EMI's Abbey Road studios, London.

OCT 20 Three thousand fans mob Birmingham studio where The Beatles are recording a performance for ABC's "Thank Your Lucky Stars" television show.

The Beatle Christmas Record is recorded at EMI's Abbey Road studios, London. BB4--4 (Oct 17) (BD--5 (Oct 19)

OCT 24 Over 600 teenagers wait all night long to buy tickets to The Beatles' concert scheduled for the ABC Cinema, Carlisle.

OCT 24 The Beatles perform five concerts in a tour of Sweden.
–29 BCE--33 (Oct 24--30) PMB--194 (Oct 14--29)

OCT 24 The Beatles perform at the Karlaplan in Stockholm, Sweden; recorded for Swedish radio.

Beatles' performance of *She Loves You, Twist and Shout, Long Tall Sally* and *I Saw Her Standing There* aired on Stockholm TV show "Drop In," are recorded, later to be illegally included on bootleg records like **Sweden 1963** and **Stockholm 1964**.

Mersey Beat reports on the 30--minute BBC TV documentary, "The Mersey Sound," featuring The Beatles and other Liverpool area groups.

OCT 25   **The Kramer Hits** (EP), featuring four songs penned by Lennon/McCartney, is released in U.K.

The Beatles perform two shows in Karlstadt, Sweden.

OCT 26   *Love of the Loved* by Cilla Black, written by Lennon/ McCartney, enters the *Melody Maker* singles charts at number 41 in U.K.

The Beatles perform two shows at the Kungliga Tennishallen, Stockholm, Sweden.

The Beatles "Thank Your Lucky Stars" appearance, recorded October 20, is televised.

A Brian Epstein appearance on "Juke Box Jury" is televised.

OCT 27   The Beatles perform two shows in Gothenburg, Sweden.

OCT 28   The Beatles perform in Boras, Sweden.

British press reports teenagers fighting to get tickets to The Beatles' forthcoming Newcastle concert, November 23.

Anthony Newley releases his own version of *I Saw Her Standing There*, barely four months after **Introducing The Beatles** (LP) is released in the U.S.

OCT 29   The Beatles perform in Eskilstuna, Sweden.

OCT 30   A Beatles' performance is filmed for Swedish TV show "Drop In," broadcast November 3.

OCT 31   The Beatles first realize their massive popularity -- the date which they themselves see as the start of "Beatlemania" -- when thousands of screaming fans greet them at London Airport on their return from Sweden.

NOVEMBER

The British press begins to report stories of schoolboys and shop apprentices being turned away from school and work because of their long "Beatle" haircuts.

Brian Epstein flies to New York, arranges the Ed Sullivan TV appearances and sets up The Beatles' recording association with Capitol Records.

John Lennon is not present at Trinity Road Parish Church,
Hoylake, when his son is christened John Charles Julian Lennon.

Songwriting credits on Beatle records change from "McCartney/
Lennon" to "Lennon/McCartney."

"Don't Bother Me, George Harrison's first song written for The
Beatles, appears on the album **With The Beatles.**

A Christmas Gift to You (LP), by Beatles' producer Phil Spector,
is first released, to be re-released in 1972 as **Phil Spector's
Christmas Album** on Apple Records. BU25-20 (late 1965)

EARLY NOVEMBER

Bernard Delfont announces the names selected for the Royal
Variety Performance at the Prince of Wales Theatre -- The
Beatles are on the list.

It is announced that The Beatles' next LP, **With The Beatles**, will
be released November 22, and their next single (*I Want to Hold
Your Hand*) on November 29; a quarter-million advance orders
for the LP are placed almost immediately.

NOVEMBER--DECEMBER

The Beatles tour with Peter Jay's Jaywalkers and The Brooks
Brothers.

NOV 1   *I Wanna Be Your Man*, written by Lennon/McCartney
and recorded by The Rolling Stones, is released on a
single in U.K.

British newspapers are filled with stories and pictures of
The Beatles' return to London Airport from a concert
tour of Sweden.

I'll Keep You Satisfied, written by Lennon/McCartney
and recorded by Billy J. Kramer with The Dakotas, is
released on a single in the U.K.

The Beatles No. 1 (EP) is released in U.K. JLS--112 (Jul
26) JLS--113 (Oct)

A short interview with Jane Asher is printed in a London
paper.

The Beatles perform at the Odeon at Cheltenham, England,
beginning their autumn tour. BB3-27 (Gaumont)
LCP--268 (Gaumont in Cheltenham)

NOV 2   The *Daily Telegraph* criticizes the hysteria over The
Beatles.

The London *Daily Worker* editorializes pridefully about

the success of four working lads named John, Paul,
George and Ringo.
The Beatles perform at City Hall in Sheffield, England, on
their autumn tour.

NOV 3   Swedish TV show "Drop In," with a performance by The
Beatles, is first broadcast.
The Beatles perform at the Odeon in Leeds, England, on
their autumn tour.

NOV 4   Royal Variety Performance at Prince of Wales Theatre,
featuring The Beatles, is attended by the Queen Mother,
Princess Margaret and Lord Snowdon.   AAB–72 (Oct)
BBC–TV films Beatles in Royal Variety Performance in
London.
Songs from The Beatles' Royal Variety show performance
are recorded, later to be illegally included on the
following bootleg LPs: **Cavern Club, Gone Are the Days,
The E.M.I. Outakes,** and **Cinelogue Six.**

NOV 5   The Beatles perform at the Granada in East Ham, England.
The Beatles perform at the Adlephi in Slough, England, on
their autumn tour.

NOV 6   The Beatles perform at the ABC in Northampton England,
on their autumn tour.

NOV 7   The Beatles perform at the Adelphi in Dublin, Ireland, on
their autumn tour. BBS–26 (Ritz) LCP–268 (Ritz in
Dublin)

NOV 8   *I Call Your Name*, written by Lennon/McCartney, is re–
leased on LP **Listen . . .** by Billy J. Kramer with The
Dakotas.
The Beatles perform at the Ritz in Belfast, Northern
Ireland, on their autumn tour. BBS–26 (Adelphi)
BCE–34 (Adelphi) LCP–268 (Adelphi in Belfast)

NOV 9   *Love of the Loved* by Cilla Black, written by Lennon/
McCartney, reaches its highest point on the *Melody
Maker* singles charts: number 31.
I'll Keep You Satisfied by Billy J. Kramer with The
Dakotas, written by Lennon/McCartney, enters the
Melody Maker singles charts at number 24 in the U.K.
The Beatles No. 1 (EP) enters the *Melody Maker* singles
charts at number 40 in the U.K.
The Beatles perform at the Adelphi in Slough, England.
The Beatles perform at the Granada in East Ham, England,
on their autumn tour.

NOV 10   TV broadcast of the November 4 filming of the Royal

Variety Performance, featuring The Beatles.

The Beatles perform at the Hippodrome in Birmingham, England, on their autumn tour.

NOV 11   The Beatles escape crowds of fans by disguising themselves as Birmingham policemen.

I'll Keep You Satisfied, written by Lennon/McCartney and recorded by Billy J. Kramer with The Dakotas, is released on a single in U.S.

NOV 12   Paul McCartney is stricken with gastric flu, forcing cancel--lation of concert at the Guildhall in Portsmouth, England. LCP--268 (lists the performance as uncan--celled)

NOV 13   BBC rebroadcasts the "Mersey Beat" television program, first shown June 29.

The London *Daily Mail* reports: "Teenagers Weep for The Beatle with a Temperature."

The Beatles perform at the ABC in Plymouth, England, on their autumn tour. LCP--263 (Dec)

NOV 14   In Plymouth, England, hoses are used to control screaming Beatle fans.

The Beatles perform at the ABC in Exeter, England, on their autumn tour.

NOV 15   *I'm in Love*, written by Lennon/McCartney and recorded by The Fourmost, is released on a single in the U.K.

Hello Little Girl, written by Lennon/McCartney and re--corded by The Fourmost, is released on a single in the U.S.

The Beatles perform at Colston Hall in Bristol, England, on their autumn tour.

NOV 16   *I Wanna Be Your Man*, by The Rolling Stones, written by Lennon/McCartney, enters the *Melody Maker* singles charts in U.K. at number 46.

American TV networks film The Beatles' Bournemouth concert at the Winter Gardens; it is shown in U.S. the following week.

NOV 17   The Beatles perform at the Coventry Theatre in Coventry, England, on their autumn tour.

NOV 18   British press reports that a Church of England vicar has proposed that The Beatles record a song called *Oh Come All Ye Faithful, Yeh, Yeh.*

The Beatles receive a silver LP from EMI Records for over 250,000 sales of **Please Please Me** (LP).

NOV 19   The winner of a pop magazine competition meets The

Beatles in their dressing room prior to their performance at the Gaumont, Wolverhampton.

The Beatles perform at the Gaumont in Wolverhampton, England, on their autumn tour.

NOV 20   Filming of The Beatles' Manchester, England, concert at the Ardwick Apollo, on their autumn tour.

The Beatles performance of *Twist and Shout* and *She Loves You* at their Manchester concert is recorded, the songs later appear illegally on the bootleg LPs **Rock 'N' Roll** and **ABC Manchester**.

NOV 21   The Beatles perform at the ABC in Carlisle, England, on their autumn tour.

NOV 22   In Parliament, Sir Charles Taylor asks the Home Secretary to withdraw police protection for The Beatles in the London area.

With The Beatles (LP) released in the U.K. with advance orders of 300,000, on the same day as the assassination of President John F. Kennedy in Dallas, Texas.

NOV 22   The Beatles perform at the Globe in Stockton, England, on their autumn tour.   PMS--133 (Stockton ABC)

NOV 23   *I'll Keep You Satisfied* by Billy J. Kramer with The Dakotas, written by Lennon/McCartney, reaches its highest point on the *Melody Maker* singles charts: number 4.

The Beatles perform at City Hall in Newcastle, England, on their autumn tour.

NOV 24   The Beatles perform at the ABC in Hull, England, on their autumn tour.

NOV 25   **Beatlemania with The Beatles** (LP) is released in Canada (Capitol of Canada).

NOV 26   The Beatles perform at the ABC in Cambridge, England, on their autumn tour.

NOV 27   The Beatles perform at the Rialto in York, England, on their autumn tour.

NOV 28   The Beatles perform at the ABC in Lincoln, England, on their autumn tour.

late Nov   Gossip spreads in Britain that Ringo Starr is about to marry someone named Elva Jamieson, 18--year--old sister of a friend of Ringo's, David Jamieson.

An advertisement in the local newspaper at Huyton, near Liverpool, proclaims: "Mr. and Mrs. Kenneth Jamieson wish to state that their daughter Elva is not marrying Ringo Starr."

NOV 29   *I Want to Hold Your Hand/This Boy* (45) is released in the U.K. with advance orders of 700,000.

The Beatles perform at the ABC in Huddersfield, England, on their autumn tour.

Elva Jamieson rushes by car from Kirkby, Liverpool, to see Ringo Starr at Huddersfield, Yorks, to explain the ad-- vertisement that her parents ran early in the month.

NOV 30   **With The Beatles** (LP) enters the *Melody Maker* album charts at number 1, remaining there for 22 weeks.

The Beatles perform at the Empire in Sunderland, England, on their autumn tour.

DECEMBER

Circulation of the *Beatles Monthly Book* fan magazine passes 300,000.

London Sunday papers at last begin to carry stories on The Beatles and Beatlemania.

Beatles Film Productions is founded.

John Lennon's Gibson Jumbo spare guitar is stolen during their two week Christmas show in Finsbury Park.

The Rutles have 19 hits in the top 20 in the U.K., according to the album send--up of The Beatles, **The Rutles.**

Beatles' songs broadcast over the BBC, London, later appear on the bootleg recording **Spicey Beatles.**

The decision to make a film around The Beatles -- "A Hard Day's Night" -- is announced, with Alan Owen to do the screenplay and Richard Lester to direct.

EARLY DECEMBER

Jacqueline Capstick, an EMI representative in France, brings two French reporters to England to meet The Beatles.

Seven Beatles' recordings are simultaneous Top Twenty hits in the U.K.

DEC 1   The Beatles perform at De Montfort Hall in Leicester, England, on their autumn tour.

DEC 2   The Beatles spend all day recording a TV show with Morecambe and Wise at ATV's Elstree studios.

The Beatles perform at an evening charity show at the Grosvenor Hotel in London while on their autumn tour. BB6--29 (at the Spastics Ball, Grosvenor House)

DEC 3   The Beatles perform at the Guild Hall in Portsmouth, England, on their autumn tour.

DEC 5   An advertisement for black leather, Cuban heel, pointed-- toe "Beatle Boots" appears in *Mersey Beat.*

DEC 6   *The Beatles Christmas Record* is released by Fan Club to its members, along with a copy of the Christmas Issue of the National Newsletter.

DEC 7   *I Want to Hold Your Hand* enters the *Melody Maker* singles charts at number 1 in the U.K., remaining there for four weeks.

Beatles Northern fan club convention is held at the Odeon in Liverpool.

BBC televises "It's The Beatles," film of the Northern Area Convention of the Official Beatles Fan Club.

The Beatles hold five positions in the British top twenty -- 1, 2, 11, 17, and 19 -- with Billy J. Kramer's Lennon/ McCartney composition, *I'll Keep You Satisfied*, in the number 6 slot; **With The Beatles** and **Please Please Me** simultaneously hold first and second positions on the album charts.

I Want to Hold Your Hand enters the *Billboard* British top twenty singles charts, remaining on the charts for 12 weeks during which time it reaches a high point of number 1.

The Beatles No. 1 (EP) reaches its highest point on the *Melody Maker* singles charts: number 19.

The Beatles perform at the Empire in Liverpool, on their autumn tour.

DEC 8   The Beatles perform at the Odeon in Lewisham, England, on their autumn tour.

DEC 9   *Roll Over Beethoven/Please Mr. Postman* (45) is released in Canada.

The Beatles perform at the Odeon in Southend, England, on their autumn tour.

DEC 10   The Beatles perform at the Gaumont in Doncaster, England, on their autumn tour.

DEC 11   The Beatles appear on the TV show "Juke Box Jury."

The Beatles perform at the Futurist in Scarborough, England, on their autumn tour.

DEC 12   The Beatles perform at the Odeon in Nottingham, England, on their autumn tour.

DEC 13   *New Musical Express* reports that The Beatles have signed with Capitol Records for U.S. release.

The Beatles perform at the Gaumont in Southampton, England, concluding their own autumn tour.

DEC 14   **The Beatles Hits** (EP) reaches its highest point on the *Melody Maker* singles charts: number 14.

The Beatles perform at the "Southern England Fan Club Convention" at the Wimbledon Palais to an audience of 3,000.

DEC 21   The Beatles' Christmas show is previewed with a perfor-- mance at the Gaumont in Bradford, England.

DEC 22   The Beatles' appearance on a special Christmas edition of "Thank Your Lucky Stars" television show is broadcast.

Film of The Beatles' Manchester concert of November 20 is released.

The Beatles' Christmas show is previewed at the Empire in Liverpool, England.

DEC 23   "It's The Beatles" weekly series begins broadcast on Radio Luxembourg.

Dec 24– Opening of The Beatles Christmas Show at the Astoria in
Jan 11   Finsbury Park, England. BB10–19 (Dec 26–Jan 11) TBA–233 (Dec 26–Jan 11)

DEC 25   The Beatles spend Christmas Day in Liverpool, flown from Astoria on a special charter arranged by Brian Epstein.

Christ- Cilla Black performs in The Beatles Christmas
mas   Show.

DEC 26   Capitol Records rush–releases their first Beatles' single in U.S., *I Saw Her Standing There/I Want to Hold Your Hand* (45). BEA2–17 (Jan 1964)

The Beatles appear on the two–hour BBC radio show "From Us To You."

DEC 27   Music critic of the London *Times* proclaims Lennon/ McCartney the outstanding composers of the year.

DEC 29   WMCA radio, New York, plays *I Want to Hold Your Hand* at 12:50 pm, claiming first "important" airplay of a Beatles record on American radio.

Richard Buckle of the *Sunday Times* calls Lennon and McCartney "the greatest composers since Beethoven."

DEC 31   Official Beatles Fan Club boasts 80,000 dues–paying members, with thousands of applications backed up and going unanswered for months at a time.

late Dec Dora Bryan's record, *All I Want for Christmas Is a Beatle,* gets into the hit parade in the U.K.

LATE 1963

The London *Times*' music critic first notes the "distinctly ingenious" character of the music by Lennon and McCartney.

About 150 licenses have already been granted by NEMS Enter-- prises for the manufacture and merchandising of Beatles souvenirs.

NEMS Enterprises grants a British company, Stramsact, the right to issue further licenses for the merchandising of Beatles souvenirs; NEMS receives 10% of monies received by Stramsact.

EMI raises the royalty rate for The Beatles from one penny per single sold to two pennies, owing to the large number of sales being made.

John Lennon and Paul McCartney are commissioned to write the music for a ballet called "Mods and Rockers."

Sid Bernstein, American promoter, books an appearance by The Beatles at Carnegie Hall for February 12, 1964.

LATE 1963--EARLY 1964

Newsmen finally learn of John Lennon's marriage and the birth of his son; his wife is phoned and pursued incessantly, until photographs appear on the front pages of daily newspapers.

A crowd of people stood and stared

A DAY IN THE LIFE

The Beatles
Day-By-Day

1964

DURING THIS YEAR ...

Fred Lennon, John Lennon's father, is a dishwasher at a hotel in Esher, England.

The Beatles dal film "Tutti per uno" (LP) is released in Italy by Parlophone.

Paul McCartney tells his father, Jim McCartney, to quit his job with the cotton firm he'd worked for for 48 years.

I Should Have Known Better/Tell Me Why (45) is released in Sweden by Parlophone.

En Flagrante Delire, a French translation of John Lennon's *In His Own Write*, is published by Simon and Schuster.

Stu Sutcliffe's paintings from the 1961–62 Hamburg period are exhibited at the Walker Art Gallery.

The following Beatles' singles are released in Holland: *Can't Buy Me Love/You Can't Do That, A Hard Day's Night/Things We Said Today, I Should Have Known Better/Tell Me Why, I'll Cry Instead/A Taste Of Honey, If I Fell/And I Love Her, I Saw Her Standing There/Matchbox, Eight Days A Week/Baby's In Black,* and *I Feel Fine/She's A Woman.*

A Hard Day's Night by John Burke is published.

Brian Epstein meets Nat Weiss, a New York divorce attorney, who becomes a close friend of Epstein's.

All About The Beatles by Edward De Blasio is published in the U.S. by McFadden–Bartell.

Bob Dylan exposes The Beatles to marijuana for the first time in their lives, although they were thoroughly versed on the use of pills from their Hamburg experience.

Dear Beatles, edited by Bill Adler, is published in the U.S. by Grossett & Dunlap.

Phil Spector produces The Righteous Brothers version of *You've Lost That Loving Feeling*, which hits number 1 and eclipses

Cilla Black's original version.

The True Story of The Beatles by Billy Shepherd is published in the U.S. by Bantam.

Denny Laine is a member of the Moody Blues, playing basically rhythym & blues.

At a press conference, John Lennon states that he feels The Beatles' success will last only five years.

The Beatles Beat (LP) is released in Germany by Odeon.

An interview with John Lennon traces the derivation of the name Beatles from his attempt to find something akin to Buddy Holly and The Crickets.

Several Beatles EPs are released in the U.S., but fail to catch favor with American record buyers favoring singles and albums.

Conozca Beatles (LP) is released in Mexico by Capitol.

The Beatles, Paul McCartney on lead, record the unreleased song *Woman.*

Love Letters to The Beatles, edited by Bill Adler, is published in the U.S. by Putnam.

The following singles by The Beatles are released in Italy: *From Me to You/Devil in Her Heart, You Can't Do That/Can't Buy Me Love, A Hard Day's Night/Things We Said Today, Thank You Girl/All My Loving, I Should Have Known Better/Tell Me Why.*

The following album by The Beatles is released in Australia: **With The Beatles.**

The Beatles Book, photographs by Dezo Hoffman, is published in the U.S. by Lancer.

The Beatles record versions of *One and One Is Two, Hello Little Girl, Home, Moonglow, Raunchy, You Are My Sunshine* and other songs, all unreleased.

The Beatles Up to Date is published in the U.S. by Lancer.

On their first trip to America, 10,000 screaming fans await The Rutles at Kennedy Airport; the Rutles, however, land at La Guardia, according to the album send--up of The Beatles, **The Rutles.**

Out of the Mouths of Beatles by Adam Blessing is published in the U.S. by Dell.

The Beatles record an unreleased version of *Shout* during a television special.

A Hard Day's Night (LP) is released in Italy.

The Beatles are recorded performing *Always and Only, You'll Know What to Do, From a Window, I Don't Want to See You Again, It's for You, Like Dreamers Do, Nobody I Know* and *One and One Is Two*, versions never released.

4 Garcons dans le Vent (LP) is released in France by Odeon.

The Beatles receive two Grammy Awards from the American National Academy of Recording Arts and Sciences: best new artist; and best vocal performance by a group (for *A Hard Day's Night*).

The Beatles Quiz Book by Jack House is published in the U.K. by William Collins.

I Favolosi Beatles (LP) is released in Italy, with the same songs as the U.K. **With The Beatles** (LP).

A Cellarful of Noise by Brian Epstein is published in the U.S. by Doubleday.

The following singles by The Beatles are released in Australia: *Love Me Do/I Saw Her Standing There, Roll Over Beethoven/ Hold Me Tight, Can't Buy Me Love/You Can't Do That, Komm gib mir deine Hand/Sie Liebt Dich, A Hard Day's Night/Things We Said Today, I Should Have Known Better/If I Fell, I Feel Fine/She's a Woman.*

The Beatles' Second Album (LP) is released in Japan by Odeon.

A Hard Day's Night by John Burke is published in the U.S. by Dell.

Pattie and George Harrison vacation in Tahiti.

John Lennon receives a solid–gold guitar pick when named *Melody Maker*'s choice as "Guitarist of the Year," according to Mark Shipper's humorous spoof of Beatle history, *Paperback Writer.*

The government of Israel rejects Brian Epstein's attempts to set up a performance there by The Beatles, claiming that the music would be harmful to Israeli youth and that security measures would be too expensive.

And Now: The Beatles (LP) is released in Germany by SR Inter--national (Odeon).

In a London club, Paul McCartney first hears *Those Were the Days*, sung by its composer George Raskin, a song McCartney would later produce on Apple for Mary Hopkin.

Please Please Me, by Lennon/McCartney, originally copyrighted in 1962, is recopyrighted in U.K. by Dick James Music Ltd.

Beatles (LP) is released in Japan by Odeon.

The following EPs by The Beatles are released in Australia: **The Beatles Hits, The Beatles No. 1, Twist and Shout, All My Loving, Requests, More Requests, Further Requests,** and **A Hard Day's Night.**
Meet The Beatles (LP) is released in Japan by Odeon.
The albums **The Beatles, Vol. 2,** . . . **Vol. 3,** and . . . **Vol. 4** are released in Mexico by Capitol.

EARLY 1964

The British based company, Stramsact, acting as licensee for NEMS Enterprises, grants a license to six young Englishmen who incorporate a U.S. company, Seltaeb, to act as their agent in America.
John Lennon compiles his first book, *In His Own Write,* during the filming of "A Hard Day's Night."
During the filming of "A Hard Day's Night" a good many paternity suits against Paul McCartney are filed in Liverpool, all deftly handled by Brian Epstein's attorney.
John and Cynthia Lennon move to London, finding a flat in Emperors Gate, Kensington.
Paul McCartney, then boyfriend of 19--year--old Jane Asher, offers Peter and Gordon (Peter Asher and Gordon Waller) the song *World Without Love* to record.
Phil Spector produces *I Love Ringo,* by Bonnie Joe Mason, soon to be known as "Cher."
Beatles' fan mail in the U.S. reaches one--quarter million letters, and must be stored in a New York City warehouse.
Cilla Black records *Anyone Who Had a Heart,* which tops the charts in the U.K. a few weeks later.
Copies of the first Beatles bootleg – **The Original Greatest Hits** – begin to appear in the U.S.

JANUARY

America is largely unaware of The Beatles, all of that to change in a matter of weeks.
From "Meet The Beatles" (EP), special juke box EP featuring six songs from **Meet The Beatles** (LP), is released on the Capitol label in the U.S.
Highlights From "Meet The Beatles," featuring an interview and three songs from **Meet The Beatles** (LP), issued to radio stations on a Capitol promotional disc.

In Britain, the Vernon Girls release *We Want The Beatles*, and American bluegrass singer Bill Clifton releases *Beatle Crazy*.

I Want to Hold Your Hand tops the singles charts in the U.K.; **Twist and Shout (EP)**, **The Beatles Hits (EP)**, and **The Beatles No. 1 (EP)** are the country's best selling EPs, and **With The Beatles** and **Please Please Me** hold first and second place in the album charts.

Anyone Who Had a Heart/Just for You (45), by Cilla Black, managed by Brian Epstein, is released in the U.K., eventually to hit number 1 on the charts.

The Beatles, during a three—week concert at the Paris Olympia, find two albums, **Bob Dylan** and **The Free--Wheelin' Bob Dylan** by Bob Dylan while visiting a radio station – having hitherto been familiar only with his U.K. hit *Blowin' in the Wind*; they play the albums over and over while in Paris.

Sweet Georgia Brown/Nobody's Child, by Tony Sheridan and The Beatles, is released in Germany on the Polydor label.

EARLY JANUARY
Brian Epstein, under great business strain, considers and eventually rejects offers to sell The Beatles' management contracts for large sums of money.

JANUARY 1964--JUNE 1965
Beatles' records remain in the Rhodesian top ten for a year--and--a--half, except for a two--week period.

JAN 2   *Mersey Beat* reports that Rory Storm and The Hurricanes, in the year and a half since Ringo Starr's departure to The Beatles, have been through at least five different drummers and still have no one suitable for the position.

JAN 3   *I Want to Hold Your Hand* hits number 1 in Australia.
NBC's "Jack Paar Show" includes a videotaped segment of The Beatles' Bournemouth concert of November 16, 1963, the first film of The Beatles shown to U.S. audiences.

JAN 4   *I'm in Love* by The Fourmost, written by Lennon/McCartney, enters the *Melody Maker* singles charts in the U.K. at number 50.
She Loves You enters Dutch radio's (VARA) "Time for Teenagers" top 10 charts at number 7.
I Wanna Be Your Man by The Rolling Stones, written by

77

Lennon/McCartney, reaches its highest point on the
Melody Maker singles charts: number 10.

I Want to Hold Your Hand enters Dutch radio's (VARA)
"Time for Teenagers" top 10 charts at number 10.

JAN 9   John Lennon comments that the slow rise of *I Want to
Hold Your Hand* on the American charts was merely a
"sympathy for Britain" phenomenon, and that he did
not expect it to be a hit in the U.S.

JAN 10   *I Want to Hold Your Hand* enters the charts in U.S., selling
a half–million copies in ten days.   TB–192 (Jan 1963)

JAN 11   The Beatles' Christmas show ends after two weeks at the
Astoria in Finsbury Park, England.

JAN 12   The Beatles second appearance on "Sunday Night at the
London Palladium" is televised; their performance is
recorded, later to be included on the bootleg re–
cording **Sunday Night at the London Palladium**.

JAN 13   Originally scheduled release date for *I Want to Hold Your
Hand/I Saw Her Standing There* (45) in the U.S.; the
single was rush–released on December 26, 1963.

Twist and Shout (LP) is released in Canada by Capitol of
Canada.   BF–23 (1963)

JAN 14   The Beatles, minus Ringo, along with Brian Epstein and
Mal Evans, fly out of London airport for Paris, several
thousand fans in attendance.   CON–94 (Jan 15)

Only forty newsmen – and virtually no fans – greet The
Beatles upon their arrival at Le Bourget airport, Paris.

John, Paul and George check into the George V Hotel,
near the Champs Elysees.

During the evening, George Harrison goes to the high–
priced cabaret, the Eve Club, while John and Paul are
visited in their hotel suite by Bruno Coquatrix of the
Olympia, and a representative of Odeon Records
handling Beatles' records in France.

JAN 15   John, Paul and George emerge from the George V in mid–
afternoon and walk along the Champs Elysees.

Ringo Starr, having been fog–bound in Liverpool the
previous day and unable to get to London airport,
finally makes the trip to Paris, arriving at Le Bourget
airport around 5 p.m.

At night the four Beatles perform at the Cyrano Theatre in
Versailles.

After the Cyrano Theatre concert, The Beatles return to
their hotel to learn that they have hit number 1 in the U.S.

Jan   The Beatles, George Martin, Brian Epstein and others hold a

celebration dinner at the George V Hotel after the news that
I Want To Hold Your Hand has hit number 1 in the U.S.

mid–Jan   *Can't Buy Me Love* is written in Paris.   BAB–201 (Feb 13,
enroute to Miami)

Jan 15–   Performances by The Beatles of *Can't Buy Me Love* and
Feb 5   *You Can't Do That* are recorded during this period in
Paris and London.

JAN 16   French newspapers report on The Beatles' tour of Paris
the previous day.

Mersey Beat runs the very first photographs of The
Beatles ever taken after the Ringo Starr/Pete Best
switch. The photos were taken by Peter Kaye at the
behest of Brian Epstein, but were never printed before.

The Beatles perform at the Olympia Theater in Paris,
France, with Trini Lopez and Sylvie Vartan. BAB–
193 (Jan 15)   PMB–197 (Jan 15)   TB–193 (Jan 15)

Backstage at the Olympia, pandemonium breaks out and
a fist fight begins when a French cameraman is barred
from taking exclusive pictures; the police must be
summoned.

JAN 17   The French press gives The Beatles mixed reviews after
their opening night at the Olympia.

I Want to Hold Your Hand/I Saw Her Standing There (45)
hits number 1 on the *Cash Box* charts in the U.S.
CON–9 (early Feb)

New Musical Express reports that 7,000,000 LPs, EPs and
singles by The Beatles were sold in the U.K. during 1963.

JAN 18   *I Want to Hold Your Hand* enters the *Billboard* singles
charts at number 45, remaining on the charts for 15
weeks during which it reaches a high point of number 1.

JAN 19   The Beatles do three shows at the Olympia; partially
recorded by French radio.

The Beatles' shows from the Olympia are broadcast on
French radio, and can be heard in England.

JAN 20   The Beatles are interviewed on French radio; the broadcast
can be received in England.

Meet The Beatles! (LP) is released in U.S. by Capitol.
JLS–115 (Jan 14)   PMS–135 (Jan 14)

JAN 21   *A World Without Love*, written by Lennon/McCartney, is
recorded at EMI's Abbey Road studios, London, by
Peter and Gordon for their single released February 28
in the U.K.

JAN 22   ORTF films Beatles' performance at the Olympia in Paris.

JAN 24   *Cash Box* magazine reports the interest of American record

companies in British records is due largely to the effect
of The Beatles.

JAN 25   *She Loves You* enters the *Billboard* singles charts at
number 69, remaining on the charts for 15 weeks during
which it reaches a high point of number 1.

JAN 27   **Introducing The Beatles** (LP) is released in U.S., with *P.S.*
I Love You and *Baby, It's You* replaced by *Ask Me Why*
and *Please Please Me.*   BF–208 (Feb)   TBD–9 (Feb)
My Bonnie/The Saints (45) by Tony Sheridan and The
Beatles, is released in U.S.

JAN 28   *I Want to Hold Your Hand* (45) becomes The Beatles' first
number 1 single on the U.S. charts, according to Mark
Shipper's humorous spoof of Beatle history, *Paperback*
Writer.

JAN 29   *You Can't Do That* instrumentals are recorded at EMI's
Abbey Road studios, London.
Komm, Gib Mir Deine Hand and *Sie Liebt Dich* are re–
corded at Pathe Marconi studios in Paris.   BD–7 (Jun)
Do You Want to Know a Secret/Bad to Me (45) written by
Lennon/McCartney and recorded by Billy J. Kramer
with The Dakotas, is released in U.S.

JAN 30   *Please Please Me/From Me to You* (45) is released in the
U.S. on Vee Jay Records.
Brian Epstein's assurance that Paul McCartney is not and
has no plans to be engaged or married – to Jane Asher
or anyone else – is printed in *Mersey Beat.*
Mersey Beat prints a photograph of a new Beatles' wall–
paper being sold to fans.
Pending publication of *John Lennon in His Own Write* is
announced in *Mersey Beat*; much of the book is taken
from Lennon's "Beatcomber" column which ran in
Mersey Beat.

JAN 31   Drummer Pete Best, former Beatle, and his group The All
Stars reportedly sign with Decca Records.
A *New Musical Express* report on U.S. Beatles' sales
appears: *She Loves You*, almost 1,000,000 records;
I Want to Hold Your Hand, 2,000,000; **Meet The**
Beatles (LP) over 750,000 copies.
I Wanna Be Your Man, written by Lennon/McCartney, is
released in the U.S. on The Rolling Stones' LP **Ready**
Steady, Go.
Sweet Georgia Brown/Nobody's Child (45), by Tony
Sheridan and The Beatles, is released in the U.K. by
Polydor Records.

LATE JANUARY

American columnist Sheilah Graham has tea in Paris with The
Beatles.

FEBRUARY

We Love You Beatles, adapted from the movie musical "Bye Bye
Birdie," becomes the unofficial anthem of Beatlemaniacs in the
U.S. during the group's visit to America.

The Beatles prepare to start their first film, "A Hard Day's Night."

The Beatles record the soundtrack for their film, "A Hard Day's
Night," in three eighteen--hour days.

Al Aronowitz first introduces The Beatles to Bob Dylan.

This Boy/It Won't Be Long, by The Beatles, is included on Capitol
Records promotional LP **Balanced for Broadcast.**

An industry in Beatles' memorabilia, most of it unauthorized and
deceptive, springs up in the U.S., the sale of novelties, souvenirs
and merchandise grossing in the tens of millions by year's end.

Tony Sheridan records but never releases *Tell Me If You Can,*
claiming to have co--authored it with Paul McCartney.

EARLY FEBRUARY

American stores begin to sell Beatle wigs, shirts, dolls, rings, lunch--
boxes, buttons, notebooks, ice cream ("Beatle Nut"), and tennis
shoes.

FEB 1   **Meet The Beatles** (LP) enters the *Billboard* album charts at
number 92, remaining on the charts for 69 weeks during
which it reaches a high point of number 1.

I Want to Hold Your Hand hits number 1 on the *Billboard*
singles charts, remaining there for seven weeks; The
Beatles' first number 1 single.

I'm in Love by The Fourmost, written by Lennon/
McCartney, reaches its highest point on the *Melody
Maker* singles charts: number 15.

I Saw Her Standing There enters the *Billboard* singles
charts at number 117.

Please Please Me enters the *Billboard* singles charts at
number 68, spending 13 weeks on the charts during
which time it reaches a high point of number 3.

FEB 3   *I Want to Hold Your Hand* (45) is certified as a Gold Record by the R.I.A.A. in the U.S.

Meet The Beatles (LP) certified as a Gold Record by R.I.A.A. in the U.S.

The Beatles with Tony Sheridan and Their Guests (LP) is released in U.S. on MGM Records. GBR–15 (**And Guests**) TBD–8 (March)

FEB 5   The Beatles return from Paris.

FEB 6   Ringo Starr's parents serve tea and pose for photographs with fans who traveled over 50 miles to see Ringo, who wasn't at the Starkey residence.

Brian Sommerville, The Beatles' publicity man, flies to U.S.

FEB 7   Four Beatle–related records reportedly released in the U.S.: The Swans' *The Boy with the Beatle Hair*; Sonny Curtis' *A Beatle I Want to Be*; The Liverpools' LP **Beatle Mania in the USA**; The Buddies' *The Beatles.*

All My Loving (EP) is released in U.K. LCP–274 (Feb 7, 1963).

Feb   Enroute to the U.S. for their first tour, The Beatles hold a press conference in Heathrow Airport's VIP lounge be-- fore boarding their flight; thousands of screaming, banner waving fans keep amazed authorities busy. TOL–104 (Aug)

The Beatles leave London Airport on Pan American flight 101 for their first tour of the U.S., along with Brian Epstein, Neil Aspinall, Mal Evans, and Cynthia Lennon.

Over WNEW radio, New York, William Williams, aping the lyrics of *I Want to Hold Your Hand*, comments that a lot of people would like to hold their noses over The Beatles' music.

The Beatles land at New York's Kennedy Airport, beginning their first American tour.

The Beatles land at Kennedy Airport aboard a TWA airliner, a plane which later became a collector's item for Beatle maniacs, according to Mark Shipper's humorous spoof of Beatle history, *Paperback Writer.*

Feb   Upon arrival at Kennedy Airport for their first U.S. tour, The Beatles are rushed directly to the Hotel Plaza in air--conditioned Cadillac limousines, avoiding both cus-- toms inspection and thousands of screaming fans.

The Beatles hold their first press conference in the U.S.

Sid Bernstein tries to convince Brian Epstein to hold a Beatles' concert in Madison Square Garden instead of the

already scheduled Carnegie Hall; Epstein decides not to
change the venue.

The conservative Hotel Plaza is surrounded by fans as The
Beatles begin a week--long stay which places the hotel
under a virtual state of siege; Hotel spokesmen state they
would never have granted the booking if they'd known
their guests were to be -- "them."

Chet Huntley ends the day's "Huntley--Brinkley Report"
by stating that he sees no need to show the national
audience the film NBC cameramen made of The Beatles
arriving at Kennedy Airport.

FEB 8   In the morning, John, Paul and Ringo, accompanied by an
estimated 400 girls, walk through Central Park in New
York City; George remains behind with a sore throat.

The Beatles tape an interview with The Ronettes asking
the questions.

Feb   Shortly after The Beatles settle in at the Plaza Hotel,
American disc jockey Murray the K interviews them live
over the phone on his radio show; he soon comes to the
hotel, leading to his "adoption" of the group for the
rest of the tour.

Murray the K shows The Beatles around New York City;
they meet Tuesday Weld, Stella Stevens and other
celebrities during their nightclubbing.

The Beatles must become members of the trade union
AFRA before commencing rehearsals at CBS studios
for the "Ed Sullivan Show."

John, Paul and Ringo rehearse for their first Ed Sullivan
appearance at the CBS 53d Street studios in the after--
noon, leaving George at the hotel with a sore throat,
nursed by his sister Louise.

I Saw Her Standing There enters the *Billboard* Hot 100
charts at number 68, remaining there for 11 weeks
during which time it reaches a high point of number 14.

Capitol Records hosts a dinner for three Beatles at the
exclusive 21 Club, followed by motor--tour of New
York night life; George remains at the hotel answering
phone calls from across the country.

The Beatles, in New York, have a radio interview aired
over the BBC's "Saturday Club" radio program.

The Beatles spend the day rehearsing for their appearance
on the "Ed Sullivan Show."

My Bonnie enters the *Billboard* singles charts at number
107.

Introducing The Beatles (LP) enters the *Billboard* album
charts at number 59, remaining on the charts for a period
of 49 weeks during which time it reaches a high point
of number 2.

All My Loving (EP) enters the *Melody Maker* singles charts
in the U.K. at number 42.

FEB 9   During the day, a dress rehearsal for the "Ed Sullivan
Show" is conducted, along with taping another "Sullivan"
show to be aired February 23.

The Observer reports that a factory in the U.S. is manu–
facturing 35,000 Beatle wigs a day; huge business in other
Beatle souvenirs and memorabilia is discussed.

The Beatles' first live TV appearance in America is broad–
cast on CBS's "Ed Sullivan Show," drawing the largest
audience in the history of television for an entertainment
program.   ATC–23 (Jan)   TOL–106 (Aug)

Wally Podrazik, co–author (a decade later) of the standard
recording history of The Beatles, *All Together Now*,
watches "Walt Disney's Wonderful World of Color"
instead of The Beatles performance on the "Ed Sullivan
Show"; he continues to ignore The Beatles for nearly
two more years.

Murray the K takes three Beatles to the Playboy Club, while
George returns to bed, and then on to the Peppermint
Lounge.

Interview with The Beatles is recorded for **The Beatles
American Tour with Ed Rudy** (LP), released June 9.

FEB 10   The Beatles give interviews to the press all day long.

The New York *Daily News* reports on the "Beatle Bounce"
performed by the frenzied teenage studio audience
which witnessed The Beatles' first appearance on the
"Ed Sullivan Show" the night before.

I'm in Love, written by Lennon/McCartney and recorded
by The Fourmost, is released on a single in the U.S.

The Beatles again make the club rounds in the evening –
the Headliner, and the Improvisation in Greenwich
Village -- calling it a day around 4 a.m.

FEB 11   Anthony Burton, in the New York *Daily News*, editorially
welcomes The Beatles as a diversion from the troubles
besetting the world.

The Beatles travel by train in a snow storm from New York

to Washington, DC in a special coach, with picture takers
and reporters at every major stop along the way.
CON–17 (Feb 10)

The Beatles are interviewed on radio station WWDC, the
first station in the U.S. to play a Beatle record.

A press conference is held at the Washington Coliseum
before The Beatles' performance.

After the press conference, The Beatles check in at the
Shoreham Hotel, occupying the whole seventh floor.

The Beatles' first outdoor concert in the U.S. is held at
the Washington Coliseum, Washington, DC; CBS–TV
films the performance.

After their performance, The Beatles meet show promoter
Harry Lynn in his office; Tommy Roe calls to congratu-
late them.

The Australian Fan Club wires congratulations to The
Beatles on their conquest of the U.S., with a promise
that a bigger welcome is awaiting them in Australia.

In Washington, The Beatles attend an evening masked ball
as the guests of Sir David Ormsby–Gore, Lord Harlech,
British Ambassador to the U.S.; Ringo Starr curses out a
woman who snips off some of his hair as a souvenir.
TOL–113 (Aug, after visiting Miami)

FEB 12   The Beatles return to New York from Washington by train
during the afternoon, snow having grounded all commercial flights.

Thousands of fans greet The Beatles on return to New York
from Washington, both at the train station and at the
Hotel Plaza.

Sir Alec Douglas–Home, British Prime Minister, arrives in
Washington, having postponed his planned arrival there
the day before because it coincided with the concert by
The Beatles.

Two Beatles' concerts held at New York's Carnegie Hall.
BIR–124 (Feb 7)

Shirley Bassey calls The Beatles between their shows at
Carnegie Hall.

EMI records the two 35–minute Carnegie Hall Beatles'
concerts in stereo; never released.

Mrs. Nelson (Happy) Rockefeller, wife of New York's
Governor, attends The Beatles' Carnegie Hall concert
with two of her children.

FEB 13   *Mersey Beat* carries a full page ad for "Sunday Night at

The Cavern," a new 30–minute radio show to be broad--
cast Sunday nights at 10:30 over Radio Luxembourg;
The Cavern is billed as "The Home of The Beatles."

George Harrison discusses the pending publication of a
book by Robert Freeman called *Beatles Limited* in a
piece printed in *Mersey Beat.*

The New York Times reports that nearly 3,000 shrieking
Beatle fans held a concert at Carnegie Hall the previous
evening, with The Beatles as inaudible accompanists.

Mersey Beat reports on the increasing availability of Beatle
wigs, boots, stockings, talcum powder, wall paper, hats,
sweaters, chewing gum and Beatle cakes.

The Beatles fly to Miami, Florida, in tourist class, someone
having called the airline and changed their first–class
reservations as a practical joke.

Thousands greet The Beatles on arrival at Miami airport;
the Beatles are whisked away when the crowd surges
through the barriers toward the plane.

The Beatles check into the Deauville Hotel in Miami Beach.

During the evening, Murray the K takes The Beatles to the
Peppermint Lounge in Miami to see Hank Ballard.

FEB 14   **The Fourmost Sound** (EP), containing *I'm in Love* and
Hello Little Girl by Lennon/McCartney, is released in
the U.K.

The Beatles take the day off, using a luxurious houseboat
offered by Bernard Castro, except for a private session
with photographers from *Life* magazine.

Miami police assign a personal bodyguard, Sgt. Buddy
Bresner, to The Beatles; The Beatles visit him and his
family in his home for dinner.

Feb   The Beatles policeman/bodyguard arranges an incognito
getaway for the group, who are picked up at the kitchen
entrance of their hotel by a meat wagon; they spend the
day at a beachfront Miami home.

The Beatles spend the evening at floor shows in the Deau--
ville Hotel – Don Rickles, Myron Cohen, dancer Carol
Lawrence.   BB9–13 (Rickells)

FEB 15   **The Beatles with Tony Sheridan and Their Guests** (LP)
enters the *Billboard* album charts at number 147, re--
maining on the charts for 14 weeks during which time it
reaches a high point of number 68.

My Bonnie enters the *Billboard* Hot 100 charts at number
67, remaining on the charts for six weeks during which
time it reaches a high point of number 26.
Meet The Beatles (LP) hits number 1 on the *Billboard*
album charts, remaining there for eleven weeks.
The "Stamp Out Beatles" movement moves from Detroit
to Miami and threatens to demonstrate outside the
Deauville Hotel.
The Beatles' dress rehearsal for their second appearance on
the "Ed Sullivan Show."
FEB 16   The Beatles appear for the second time on CBS's "Ed
Sullivan Show," broadcast from Deauville Hotel's
Mau Mau Club, Miami Beach.   BCE--42 (Beauville Hotel)
Songs from The Beatles' "Ed Sullivan Show" performance
are illegally recorded, later to be included on the follow--
ing bootleg LPs: **Renaissance Minstrels Volume I**, and
Abbey Road Revisited.   DI1--15 ("Ed Sullivan Show" at
Carnegie Hall)
After the "Ed Sullivan Show," Maurice Lansberg, owner of
the Deauville Hotel, throws a party for Ed Sullivan and
The Beatles.
FEB 17   Newspaper reports indicate that Joe Louis and Sonny
Liston attended The Beatles show.
All My Loving/This Boy (45) is released in Canada.
BU14--16 (Mar)
I Wanna Be Your Man, written by Lennon/McCartney and
recorded by The Rolling Stones, is released on a single
in the U.S.
The Beatles concentrate on learning water--skiing most of
the day.
FEB 18   The Beatles visit Muhammed Ali, then Cassius Clay, unseated
heavyweight boxing champ, at his training camp during
his preparation for the upcoming rematch with the
champion, Sonny Liston.
Newspaper reports quote "Sullivan Show" TV technicians
as calling The Beatles the most friendly and cooperative
performers they've ever worked with.
The Beatles attend a barbecue at a millionaire's home,
then watch film "Fun in Acapulco," starring Elvis
Presley, at a drive--in theatre.
late Feb The Beatles are interviewed by WQAM radio while in
Miami.

FEB 19   The Beatles relax on the beach in Miami, Florida, and shop
–21   for the latest records in local stores.

FEB 21   *My Bonnie/The Saints* (45) is reissued in the U.K.

Reports appear of Variety Club of Great Britain's selection of The Beatles as the Show Business Personalities of the Year.

The Beatles fly back to England, arriving early the next morning, the 22nd.

FEB 22   *From Me to You* re–enters the *Billboard* singles charts at number 120.

The Beatles return from the U.S. to England, greeted by thousands of fans at London Airport.

FEB 23   The Beatles film an appearance at Teddington Studios for the "Big Night Out" television show, aired on the 29th.

The Beatles' third appearance (filmed) on the "Ed Sullivan Show" is aired in the U.S.

FEB 24   *Newsweek* carries news of The Beatles as their cover story.

FEB 25   George Harrison's 21st birthday.

Can't Buy Me Love and *You Can't Do That* vocals are recorded at EMI's Abbey Road studios, London; versions of *Long Tall Sally, I Call Your Name, Slowdown* and *Matchbox* are also recorded.

FEB 26   **Jolly What! The Beatles and Frank Ifield on Stage (LP)** is released in the U.S. on the Vee Jay label. TBD–9 (Jun)

FEB 27   *Mersey Beat* carries a half–page advertisement for Sayers "Beatles Cake," party–sized and decorated with "real photographs" of one Beatle per cake.

Two previously unpublished poems by John Lennon, "The Tales of Hermit Fred" and "The Land of Lunapots," are published in *Mersey Beat*.

FEB 28   *Why/Cry for a Shadow* (45), by Tony Sheridan and The Beatles, is released in the U.K.

Interview with Brian Epstein appears in *New Musical Express*.

A World Without Love, written by Lennon/McCartney and recorded by Peter and Gordon, is released on a single in the U.K. BF–212 (Mar)

FEB 29   The Beatles appear on ABC–TV's "Big Night Out" show in the U.K., filmed February 23.

Beatles' songs, merely lip–synched from recordings for the show, are recorded from the "Big Night Out" television show, later to appear on the bootleg recording **Sunday**

Night at the London Palladium.

Introducing The Beatles (LP) reaches its highest position on the *Billboard* album charts, number 2, remaining there for nine weeks.

All My Loving (EP) reaches its highest point on the *Melody Maker* singles charts: number 12.

Brian Epstein appears on BBC's "Juke Box Jury" television show.

From Me to You (45) enters the *Billboard* singles charts, remaining there for six weeks during which time it reaches a high point of number 41.

MARCH

Madame Tussaud's wax museum places effigies of The Beatles on display.

One and One Is Two, written by John Lennon and Paul McCartney, is recorded by Mike Shannon with The Strangers.

A special edition of "Thank Your Lucky Stars," featuring The Beatles, becomes the British entry in the Montreux Festival.

On the set of "Ready Steady Go," Paul McCartney denies rumors that he is married to Jane Asher.

The Beatles learn they will take the biggest U.S. concert tour of any British entertainers in August.

British fans eagerly pursue copies of the German version of *I Want to Hold Your Hand.*

The news is released that Jack Good, television producer, is planning to produce an hour–long TV special featuring The Beatles.

Ringo Starr is elected a vice--president of Leeds University.

The Beatles hold the first six positions on the Australian top ten: *I Saw Her Standing There, Love Me Do, Roll Over Beethoven, All My Loving, She Loves You* and *I Want to Hold Your Hand.*

Cry for a Shadow/Why, by Tony Sheridan and The Beatles, is released in Germany on the Polydor label.

MAR 2   The Beatles begin filming "A Hard Day's Night" at London's Twickenham studios. PMS--137 (Liverpool)
George Harrison meets Pattie Boyd the first day of filming of "A Hard Day's Night."
Twist and Shout/There's a Place (45) is released in the

U.S. on the Tollie label.

Mar 2– Fifteen songs are recorded by The Beatles during the period
Apr 27 of the filming of "A Hard Day's Night."

*Tell Me Why, I'll Cry Instead, I'm Happy Just to Dance
with You, I Should Have Known Better, If I Fell, And I
Love Her* are recorded at EMI's Abbey Road studios,
London.

Murray the K interviews The Beatles during the period of
filming of "A Hard Day's Night."

MAR 3 The Beatles' appearance on ABC–TV's "Big Night Out,"
broadcast elsewhere in the U.K. on February 29, is
aired in the London area.

MAR 5 *Komm, Gib Mir Deine Hand/Sie Liebt Dich* (45) is released
in Germany on the Odeon label. IR–128 (Jan 29)

MAR 7 *From Me to You* enters the *Billboard* Hot 100 charts at
number 86.

The publisher of *The Beatles Book* launches another
publication focused on another Brian Epstein group,
Gerry and The Pacemakers.

MAR 12 Reminiscences of Bill Turner, a former schoolmate of
John Lennon, appear in *Mersey Beat*; memories deal
with Lennon's early writings – poems, stories, cartoons –
in a notebook called "The Daily Howl," and with
Lennon's early skiffle group, The Quarrymen.

MAR 13 *Cash Box* reports four Beatles' songs in top four singles
positions: *She Loves You, I Want to Hold Your Hand,
Please Please Me, Twist and Shout.*

Meet The Beatles (LP) is reported to have sold over
3,600,000 copies in the U.S., the most in recording
history to that date.

Can't Buy Me Love is reported to have advance sales of
1,700,000 copies in the U.S.

MAR 14 *Please Please Me* reaches highest position on *Billboard*
singles charts: number 3.

Twist and Shout enters the *Billboard* singles charts at
number 55; it reaches a high point of number 2 during
a stay on the charts of eleven weeks.

Roll Over Beethoven enters the *Billboard* singles charts at
number 102.

My Bonnie reaches highest position on *Billboard* singles
charts: number 26.

MAR 14 Film of The Beatles' Washington Coliseum concert is
–15   shown on closed circuit TV.
MAR 16 *Can't Buy Me Love/You Can't Do That* (45) is released in
            the U.S. BM–96 (Mar 30)   PMB–200 (Mar 30)
MAR 17 *Can't Buy Me Love* reported to have advance orders of
            over 1,000,000 copies.
MAR 20 *I'll Keep You Satisfied*, written by Lennon/McCartney, is
            released in U.K. on an EP of the same name by Billy J.
            Kramer with The Dakotas.
            Can't Buy Me Love/You Can't Do That (45) is released in
            the U.K. BAB–200 (Mar 24)   BFC–4 (Mar 30)
               LCP–273 (Mar 30)
            The Beatles tape an appearance on "Ready, Steady, Go"
            television program (Rediffusion Television); the show is
            aired April 27.
MAR 21 *Roll Over Beethoven* enters the *Billboard* Hot 100 charts
            at number 79, remaining on the charts for four weeks,
            during which time it reaches a high point of number 68.
            I Saw Her Standing There reaches its highest point on
            Billboard singles charts: number 14.
            She Loves You hits number 1 on the *Billboard* singles
            charts, remaining there two weeks.
            World Without Love by Peter and Gordon, written by
            Lennon/McCartney, enters the *Melody Maker* singles
            charts in the U.K. at number 30.
            The Beatles simultaneously hold twelve slots in the top
            100 songs in the U.S.
            The Beatles appear on the cover of the *Saturday Evening
            Post.*
MAR 23 The Beatles receive two Carl Allen Awards for 1963: the
            most outstanding beat group; the most outstanding
            vocal record for dancing (*She Loves You*).
            John Lennon in His Own Write is published in U.K., the
            title suggested by Paul McCartney.
            John Lennon's *In His Own Write* wins the coveted Foyle's
            Literary Prize.
            Do You Want to Know a Secret/Thank You Girl (45) is
            released in the U.S. on the Vee Jay label.
            The Beatles (EP) is released in the U.S. on Vee Jay.
MAR 25 The Beatles appear on BBC TV's "Top of the Pops."
MAR 26 Pete Best flies to the U.S. to appear on the TV show, "I've
            Got a Secret."
            The Beatles film scenes for "A Hard Day's Night" at

Scala Theatre in London.

MAR 27 *Why/Cry for a Shadow* (45), by Tony Sheridan and The Beatles, is released in U.S. by M.G.M. GBR--2 (Mar 9)

In Australia, eleven of the top thirty tunes are by The Beatles, ten of them in the top twenty, six of them in the first six positions on the charts.

MAR 28 *Can't Buy Me Love* enters the *Billboard* singles charts at number 27, remaining on the charts for ten weeks during which time it reaches a high point of number 1.

Can't Buy Me Love enters the *Billboard* British top twenty singles charts, remaining on the charts for nine weeks during which time it reaches a high point of number 1.

All My Loving enters the *Billboard* singles charts at number 71, remaining on the charts for a period of six weeks during which it reaches a high point of number 45.

Do You Want to Know a Secret enters the *Billboard* singles charts at number 78, remaining on the charts for eleven weeks during which time it reaches a high point of number 2.

You Can't Do That enters the *Billboard* singles charts at number 115.

Can't Buy Me Love enters the *Melody Maker* singles charts in the U.K. at number 1, remaining in that position for three weeks.

MAR 30 "I've Got a Secret," featuring Pete Best as one of the guests, is aired on American TV.

Bad to Me, written by Lennon/McCartney, is released in the U.S. on a single by Billy J. Kramer with The Dakotas.

The Beatles Bank Holiday radio show is broadcast on the BBC.

A profile on Brian Epstein is broadcast on the BBC's "Panorama" television program. BBS--54 (Feb 30)

Mar 30-- The Beatles perform at the Empire in Liverpool,
Apr 4 England.

MAR 31 Beatles' songs hold the top five chart positions for *Billboard* singles in the U.S., plus an additional seven registering in the *Billboard* Hot 100.

Can't Buy Me Love (45) is certified as a Gold Record by the R.I.A.A. in the U.S.

late Mar John and Cynthia Lennon, George Harrison and Pattie Boyd fly to Ireland on a private plane for Easter weekend.

SPRING

"What's Happening U.S.A.," film of The Beatles' visit to the U.S.
in February, is aired on British television.

The Beatles music finishes its rock–and–roll stage of development
with *Can't Buy Me Love.*

APRIL

George Martin announces The Beatles' next album, containing
eleven new Lennon–McCartney songs, and *Don't Bother Me* by
George Harrison.

The Beatles are presented with outstanding entertainer awards by
the Variety Club of Great Britain.

In the U.K., The Beatles emerge at the top of a pop–music paper's
Top Ten singles analysis of chart placements, more than 100
points ahead of the second place group; they also top the LP
list analysis, the sheet music listings, and score four times as
many points as Bobby Vinton in an American *Billboard* chart
analysis.

The news is announced that Princess Margaret will attend the
premiere of "A Hard Day's Night," set for July 6.

It is announced that The Beatles will play the Hollywood Bowl
during their upcoming summer tour of the U.S.

During a break in filming, The Beatles go to the Playhouse Theatre,
where they record songs for broadcast on "Easy Beat."

The Beatles receive news that they've been booked for Rediffusion
Television's "Around The Beatles," due to be aired May 6.

You're My World/Suffer Now I Must (45) by Cilla Black, managed
by Brian Epstein, is released in the U.K., later to hit number 1
on the charts.

Nobody I Know, written by John Lennon and Paul McCartney,
is recorded at EMI's Abbey Road studios by Peter and Gordon.

Filming continues at London's Scala Theatre in London on "A
Hard Day's Night," under the directorship of Richard Lester.

From "The Beatles' Second Album" (EP), a special juke box EP
featuring six songs from **The Beatles' Second Album** (LP), is
released on Capitol.

Like Dreamers Do, written by John Lennon and Paul McCartney,
is recorded by The Applejacks.

Start of filming of The Beatles' television special produced by Jack
Good.

Love Me Do/P.S. I Love You (45) is released in Canada by Capitol
of Canada.

Highlights From "The Beatles' Second Album," featuring an interview and three songs from **The Beatles' Second Album** (LP), is issued to radio stations by Capitol.

APR 4   *You Can't Do That* enters the *Billboard* top 100 singles charts at number 65, remaining on the charts for four weeks, during which time it reaches a high point of number 48.

         Twist and Shout reaches its highest position on the *Billboard* singles charts: number 2.

         Can't Buy Me Love hits number 1 on the *Billboard* singles charts, remaining there for five weeks.

         Jolly What! The Beatles and Frank Ifield on Stage (LP) enters the *Billboard* album charts at number 135, re-- maining on the charts for six weeks during which time it reaches a high point of number 103.

         Thank You Girl enters the *Billboard* singles charts at number 79, remaining on the charts for a period of seven weeks during which it reaches a high point of number 35.

         Roll Over Beethoven reaches its highest position on the *Billboard* singles charts: number 68.

         From Me to You reaches its highest 1964 position on *Billboard* singles charts: number 41.

         The Beatles appear on the BBC Light Programme, "Saturday Club."

         Beatles songs occupy the top five positions on the *Billboard* Hot 100 singles charts.

APR 6   *P.S. I Love You* reaches its highest position on the *Billboard* singles charts: number 10.

         I Wanna Be Your Man, written by Lennon/McCartney, is released on a Rolling Stones single in the U.S.

APR 10   *Love of the Loved*, written by Lennon/McCartney and recorded by Cilla Black, is released on the EP **Anyone Who Had a Heart** in the U.K.

         The Beatles' Second Album (LP) is released in U.S.

APR 11   The Beatles have five records in the American top ten, six in the top twenty, eight in the top fifty, and 14 in the top 100.

         Can't Buy Me Love enters Dutch radio's (VARA) "Time for Teenagers" Top 10 charts at number 4.

         You Can't Do That reaches its highest position on the *Billboard* singles charts: number 48.

         There's a Place enters the *Billboard* singles charts at number

74, going no higher, remaining in that position for one
week.

Love Me Do enters the *Billboard* singles charts at number
81, remaining on the charts for fourteen weeks during
which it reaches a high point of number 1.

Why enters the *Billboard* singles charts at number 131.

APR 12   The Beatles film more scenes for the film "A Hard Day's
Night" at London's Marylebone Railway Station.

APR 13   **The Beatles' Second Album** (LP) is certified as a Gold
Record by the R.I.A.A.

mid–Apr Beatles' songs occupy fourteen positions in the *Billboard*
Hot 100 singles charts.

APR 16   *A Hard Day's Night* is recorded at the Abbey Road studios.
The Beatles are interviewed at London's Twickenham
studios by Ed Sullivan while filming "A Hard Day's
Night." BEA3–13 (Mar)

APR 18   *Why* reaches its highest position on the *Billboard* top 100
singles charts: number 88.

World Without Love by Peter and Gordon, written by
Lennon/McCartney, hits number 1 on the *Melody Maker*
charts, remaining there for two weeks.

Jolly What! The Beatles and Frank Ifield on Stage (LP)
reaches its highest position on the *Billboard* album
charts: number 104.

The Beatles appear on ATV's "Morecambe and Wise Show."

The Beatles with Tony Sheridan and Their Guests (LP)
reaches its highest position on the *Billboard* album
charts: number 68.

APR 19   *A World Without Love*, written by Lennon/McCartney,
is re–recorded by Peter and Gordon at London's
Prince of Wales Theatre for their LP **Tribute to Michael
Holiday**.

early   The evening before John Lennon is to be honored at Foyle's
1964   literary society, John and Cynthia celebrate at the Adlib
Club, returning early in the morning and, after four hours
sleep, wake up with hangovers.

APR 23   John and Cynthia Lennon attend the Christina Foyle literary
luncheon organized for him.   TOL–99 (early 1964)

early   At Foyle's literary luncheon for John Lennon, the audience
1964   is amazed when, expecting a speech, they receive a brief

thanks from Lennon, who quickly resumes his seat.

APR 24   Final day of shooting for the film "A Hard Day's Night."

APR 25   **The Beatles' Second Album** (LP) enters the *Billboard*
album charts at number 16, remaining on the charts for
a period of 55 weeks during which period it reaches a
high point of number 1.

Fans wait outside the apartment shared by George Harrison
and Ringo Starr in Knightsbridge for a glimpse of the
pair.

All My Loving reaches its highest position on the *Billboard*
singles charts: number 45.

APR 26   The Beatles perform at the *New Musical Express* Poll
Winner's Concert at the Wembley Empire Pool, London.

ABC--TV films The Beatles at the Wembley Poll Winner's
Concert in London.

An interview with Walter Shenson, producer of "A Hard
Day's Night," appears in the New York *Times.*

APR 27   John Lennon's *In His Own Write* is published in the U.S. by
Simon and Schuster. BEA3–13 (Apr 25)

Love Me Do/P.S. I Love You (45) is released in the U.S.

Rediffusion Television broadcasts The Beatles' performance
on "Ready, Steady, Go," taped March 20.

The Beatles begin two days of filming for a Rediffusion
Television show.

A World Without Love, written by Lennon/McCartney
and recorded by Peter and Gordon, is released on a
single in the U.S.

APR 27   Eleven songs are recorded by The Beatles at EMI's Abbey
–28   Road studios, later to appear on the bootleg recording
Cinelogue VI.

APR 29   The Beatles perform in Edinburgh, Scotland.

APR 30   The Beatles perform at the Odeon in Glasgow, Scotland.

late Apr   George Harrison develops a heavy cold, resulting in an
avalanche of throat lozenges and cough medicines being
sent to the Fan Club's London offices.

MAY

From a Window, written by John Lennon and Paul McCartney, is
recorded at EMI's Abbey Road studios by Billy J. Kramer with
The Dakotas.

Ain't She Sweet/Take Out Some Insurance on Me Baby, by Tony

Sheridan and The Beatles, is released in Germany on Polydor.
Brian Epstein reveals that The Beatles will begin another tour of
the U.K. in October, beginning in Bradford.
It's For You, written by John Lennon and Paul McCartney, is re–
corded at EMI's Abbey Road studios, London, by Cilla Black.
It is announced that "A Hard Day's Night" will open simultaneously
in 500 American theaters, rather than having a single--theater
premiere.
It is reported that a ticker--tape reception for The Beatles is
being planned for their arrival in San Francisco in mid--August.
The Beatles spend most of the month vacationing, returning in
late May.
George Harrison, vacationing in the Caribbean, nearly water--skis
into a razor--sharp coral reef; he does manage to cut his thumb
open with the fin of a fish he caught.

EARLY MAY

George Martin informs The Beatles that he'd just completed a
recording session with Ella Fitzgerald, who had recorded her
version of *Can't Buy Me Love.*

MAY--JUNE

Brian Epstein produces a number of star--studded concerts on
Sundays at the Prince of Wales Theatre, London, The Beatles
being only one of the acts presented.

MAY 2   **The Beatles' Second Album** (LP) hits number 1 on the
Billboard album charts, remaining there for five weeks.
A Beatles' fan travels to Liverpool to meet Ringo Starr's
mother, who sends her off in a taxi to meet George
Harrison's mother, father and brother; Mrs. Harrison
drives her to see Paul's father in Allerton (not at home),
then on for a visit with John's Aunt Mimi in Woolton.
A World Without Love by Peter and Gordon, written by
Lennon/McCartney, enters the *Billboard* singles charts
at number 105.
A "secret" vacation for The Beatles and their wives and
girlfriends begins, using coded names, with destinations
like the Virgin Islands (two couples), and Tahiti (two
couples). Three hundred fans intercept George and John
enroute in Vancouver, and catch Paul and Ringo enroute
in Puerto Rico.
MAY 6   "Around The Beatles," filmed April 27–28, is shown as a

TV special in the U.K.

Songs from The Beatles' BBC–TV show "Around The Beatles" are recorded, later to be illegally included on the following bootleg LPs: **Some Other Guy, Gone Are the Days, The E.M.I. Outakes, Cinelogue Six,** and **Around The Beatles -- Live 1964.**

MAY 8   Four cuts by Tony Sheridan and The Beatles appear on an anthology LP **Let's Do the Twist, Hully Gully, Slop, Surf, Locomotion, Monkey,** released in the U.K.

One and One Is Two, written by Lennon/McCartney, appears on a single by The Strangers with Mike Shannon in the U.K.

Instrumental versions of *All My Loving* and *I Saw Her Standing There* are released in the U.K. by Beatles' pro–ducer George Martin on Parlophone.

MAY 9   *Thank You Girl* reaches its highest position on the *Billboard* singles charts: number 35.

Do You Want to Know a Secret reaches its highest position on the *Billboard* singles charts: number 2.

P.S. I Love You enters the *Billboard* singles charts at num–ber 64, remaining on the charts for eight weeks during which time it reaches a high point of number 10.

MAY 10   Radio Luxembourg airs the first part of a show on The Beatles, "This Is Their Life." BBS--54 ("That's Their Life")

MAY 11   *I Want to Hold Your Hand* and *I Saw Her Standing There* are included on **Chart Busters Vol. 4** (LP), released in the U.S.

Four by The Beatles (EP) is released in the U.S. on Capitol. GBR--13 (Aug 19) TBD--7 (Mar)

Long Tall Sally (LP) is released in Canada.

MAY 15   *Love Me Do* hits number 1 in the U.S. on the *Cash Box* charts.

I Call Your Name, written by Lennon/McCartney and recorded by Billy J. Kramer with The Dakotas, appears on the EP **I'll Keep You Satisfied No. 2** in the U.K.

MAY 17   The second portion of Radio Luxembourg's "This Is Their Life" is aired.

MAY 18   The Beatles Whit Monday Bank Holiday radio show is broadcast on BBC.

MAY 21   *Sie Liebt Dich/I'll Get You* (45) is released in the U.S. on the Swan label. TBD--4 (Apr)

MAY 23   *All My Loving* enters Dutch radio's (VARA) "Time for Teenagers" Top 10 charts at number 9.

Bad to Me by Billy J. Kramer with The Dakotas, written
by Lennon/McCartney, enters the *Billboard* singles charts
at number 120.

MAY 24   A Beatles' interview and performance of *You Can't Do That* is
aired on the "Ed Sullivan Show," filmed during making of
"A Hard Day's Night."

MAY 29   *Ain't She Sweet/If You Love Me, Baby* (45) is released in
the U.K. on the Polydor label.

Nobody I Know, written by Lennon/McCartney, is released
in the U.K. on a single by Peter and Gordon.

MAY 30   *Love Me Do* hits number 1 on the *Billboard* singles charts,
dropping to number 2 the next week.

Sie Liebt Dich enters the *Billboard* singles charts at number
108.

MAY 31   The Beatles perform two concerts at the Prince of Wales
Theatre in London, England, at Brian Epstein's "Pops
Alive!" show.

LATE MAY--EARLY JUNE

Before leaving on tour, Paul McCartney buys an Aston Martin
automobile.

JUNE

Songs broadcast over the BBC are recorded, later to be illegally
included on the bootleg recordings **Their Never Released, The
New Mary Jane, Nassau Colliseum,** and **Live from Germany**.

NEMS Enterprises signs a new contract with Stramsact, increasing
NEMS' share of income from 10% to 45%.

The True Story of The Beatles, by Billy Shepherd, is published in
the U.S. by Bantam Books.

It is reported that The Beatles were recently fearful that they had
contracted chicken pox from Roy Orbison's son, 6--year--old
Roy Dewayne, who had come with his father to visit them;
the group soon has an "all--clear" from their doctor, however.

The British Beatles fan club sends out a special 32--page magazine
of pictures and feature stories to its membership.

Harry Epstein, Brian Epstein's father, decides to sell most of the
family business in Liverpool.

JUNE--JULY

The Beatles Fan Club reaches 50,000 members in the U.K.

JUNE–NOVEMBER
   Continuous world touring by The Beatles.

JUN 1   *Sweet Georgia Brown/Take Out Some Insurance on Me,*
            Baby (45), by Tony Sheridan and The Beatles, is re–
            leased in the U.S.   GBR–3 (Jun 25) TBD–2 (Sep)

JUN 1   *Anytime at All, Things We Said Today, When I Get Home,*
–3   and *I'll Be Back* are recorded at the Abbey Road studios.

JUN 3   Ringo Starr collapses on eve of The Beatles' world tour,
            remaining behind until his arrival in Australia on June
            12.

JUN 4   Paul, George and John are driven to London Airport;
            boarding the plane before other passengers, they sign
            autographs for the flight crew.   BIR–30 (Jun 3)
               PMS–139 (Jun 3)
            John, Paul and George sign in at the Royal Hotel, Copen–
            hagen, opposite the Tivoli Gardens.
            Before show–time, The Beatles rehearse with stand–in
            drummer, Jimmy Nicol.
            The British Ambassador in Copenhagen visits The Beatles.
            The Beatles perform at the Tivoli Gardens in Copenhagen,
            Denmark, on their world tour, Jimmy Nicol subbing
            for Ringo.   BCE–43 (KB Hall)
            Nine songs recorded at The Beatles' second concert in
            Copenhagen later appear on such bootlegs as **Copen–**
            hagen 1964 and **John, George, Paul, Jimmy**.
            After the concerts, The Beatles receive a call from Brian
            Epstein: Ringo is improving but still has a temperature
            of 103°.

Jun 4–   The Beatles perform in more than 50 cities on four
Nov 10   continents.

JUN 5   *KFWBeatles/You Can't Do That* (45), featuring an inter–
            view with The Beatles by KFWB radio in Los Angeles
            and *You Can't Do That*, is issued by KFWB and Music
            City record store.
            Like Dreamers Do, written by Lennon/McCartney and re–
            corded by The Applejacks, appears on a single in the U.K.
            A World Without Love, written by Lennon/McCartney,
            appears on **Peter and Gordon** (LP), is released in the U.K.
            The Beatles fly into Schiphol Airport near Amsterdam,
            Holland.
            The Beatles rehearse at Treslong Studios in Hillegom, 26
            miles outside Amsterdam.   BB12–23 (Tres Long restau–
            rant, Hillegram)

	The Beatles are videotaped by Dutch television (VARA Broadcasting Co.), and are interviewed prior to the show at Treslong Studios, Hillegam.
JUN 5 --6	The Beatles visit Amsterdam's "red--light" district, called the Walletjes, and reportedly spend the night at a brothel; John Lennon is reportedly photographed on hands--and--knees, too drunk to walk, in the doorway of a brothel.
JUN 6	The Beatles take an hour--long glass--topped boat trip through Amsterdam's canals.
Jun	While in Amsterdam, John Lennon criticizes the Dutch police for manhandling Beatle fans too roughly.

The Beatles tour the city of Amsterdam; a crowd of 50,000 fills the streets.

Like Dreamers Do, written by Lennon/McCartney and re--corded by The Applejacks, appears on a single in the U.S.

The Beatles travel in two white Cadillacs to the Exhibition Hall in Blokker, 36 miles from Amsterdam, escorted by motorcycle police.

Four by The Beatles (EP) enters the *Billboard* singles charts at number 105.

Nobody I Know by Peter and Gordon, written by Lennon/McCartney, enters the *Melody Maker* singles charts in the U.K. at number 45.

The Beatles perform at the Exhibition Hall in Blokker, Holland, on their world tour.   BBS--26 (Denmark) LCP--269 (Denmark)   TBA--234 (Denmark)

While The Beatles rest and sleep between shows at the Exhibition Hall, they unknowingly miss a civic reception at a local restaurant and a tour of a Dutch village planned for them.

Cynthia Lennon joins The Beatles in Amsterdam, and re--turns to London with them.

Following their concert, The Beatles rush from the Blokker Exhibition Hall direct to Schiphol Airport, Amsterdam, fly BOAC to London Airport where they hold a news conference, then immediately leave for Hong Kong on another plane.

JUN 8	Dutch television (VARA) broadcasts The Beatles perfor--mance filmed June 5.

Three songs penned by Lennon/McCartney appear on **Little Children** (LP) by Billy J. Kramer with The Dakotas, re--leased in the U.S.

101

"Around The Beatles" television show is shown for the
second time in U.K. BBS–54 (Jun 18)
The Beatles fly to Hong Kong via Beirut, Lebanon, be–
ginning their Far East tour.

JUN 9   **The Beatles American Tour with Ed Rudy (LP)** is released.
GBR–26 (Oct 23)

JUN 10   The Dutch television show videotaped on June 5 is broad–
cast.
The Beatles perform two shows at the Princess Theater in
Hong Kong, on their world tour. BBS–26 (Jun 9)
BCE–45 (Jun 9)   LCP–269 (Jun 9)

JUN 11   In the U.K., Ringo Starr is discharged from University College
Hospital.

JUN 12   Ringo Starr flies to Australia via San Francisco, arriving
at Melbourne Airport to a crowd of 5,000 fans.
Over 300,000 people, the biggest crowd ever to receive
The Beatles, fill the streets of Adelaide, Australia.

**JUN 12
–13**   The Beatles perform at the Centennial Hall in Adelaide,
Australia, on their world tour, with Jimmy Nicol still
subbing for Ringo.

JUN 13   **Four by The Beatles** (EP) enters the *Billboard* Hot 100
charts at number 97, remaining on the charts for three
weeks during which time it reaches a high point of
number 92.
Like Dreamers Do by The Applejacks, written by Lennon/
McCartney, enters the *Melody Maker* singles charts in
the U.K. at number 41.
Ain't She Sweet enters the *Melody Maker* singles charts in
the U.K. at number 36.
The Beatles' American Tour (LP) by Ed Rudy enters the
Billboard album charts at number 96; during 13 weeks
on the charts, it reaches a high point of number 20.
ATN–357 (Jun 6)

JUN 15   *A World Without Love*, written by Lennon/McCartney,
appears in the U.S. on an album with same name by
Peter and Gordon. BU14–14 (Aug)
A Beatles' Melbourne, Australia, concert is held at Festival
Hall; 250,000 people line the streets in greeting.
JLS–119 (Jun 12)   PMS–139 (Jun 12)
Songs by The Beatles are recorded at their Melbourne,
Australia, concert, later to be included on the bootleg
LPs **Second to None, Melbourne 1964,** and **Back in the
Saddle.**

Nobody I Know, written by Lennon/McCartney, is released in the U.S. on a single by Peter and Gordon.

Souvenir of Their American Visit (EP) is released in the U.S. on Vee Jay.

Jimmy Nicol vacates the drummer's spot as Ringo Starr returns to the tour.

JUN 16   The Beatles perform at Festival Hall, Melbourne; Ringo Starr on drums.

JUN 17   The Beatles leave Melbourne and return to Sydney.

JUN 18   Paul McCartney's 22nd birthday.

JUN 18   The Beatles perform at Sydney Stadium in Sydney, Aus--
–20   tralia, on their world tour.

JUN 19   **The Beatles' First** (LP) is released in the U.K. on Polydor.
            BBS--52 **(Firsts) PMS--139 (Firsts)**

I'm Gonna Knock on Your Door/Why Did I Fall in Love with You (45), by Pete Best and The All Stars, is released in the U.K. on Decca.

Long Tall Sally (EP) is released in the U.K.

JUN 20   **Little Children** (LP) by Billy J. Kramer with The Dakotas, featuring three songs written by Lennon/McCartney, enters the *Billboard* album charts at number 149.

JUN 21   The Beatles fly to Auckland, New Zealand. BB36–21 (Jul)

JUN 22   The Beatles perform in concert in Wellington, New Zealand,
–23   on their world tour.

JUN 24   The Beatles perform in concert in Auckland, New Zealand,
–25   on their world tour.

JUN 26   The soundtrack LP, **A Hard Day's Night**, is released in the U.S. by United Artists. TBD--13 (Jul)

JUN 26   The Beatles perform in concert in Christchurch, New
–27   Zealand, on their world tour.

JUN 27   **A World Without Love** (LP) by Peter and Gordon, with the title song written by Lennon/McCartney, enters the *Billboard* album charts at number 114.

Ain't She Sweet reaches its highest point on the *Melody Maker* singles charts: number 24.

Long Tall Sally enters Dutch radio's (VARA) "Time for Teenagers" Top 10 charts at number 5.

Four by The Beatles (EP) reaches its highest position on *Billboard* singles charts: number 92. BU3–16 (97)

Sie Liebt Dich reaches its highest position on *Billboard* singles charts: number 97.

Nobody I Know by Peter and Gordon, written by Lennon/McCartney, reaches its highest point on the *Melody*

Maker charts: number 6.

late Jun   A gang of New Zealanders hide in a linen closet at The
           Beatles' hotel, hoping to cut off the groups' hair to im--
           press their girlfriends; they are discovered and exit
           hurriedly down a fire escape.

JUN 28   The Beatles leave New Zealand for Brisbane, Australia, after
           having performed in Auckland, Dunedin and Christ--
           church. BB12--25 (Jun 27)

JUN 29   The Beatles perform in Brisbane, Australia, on their world
           tour.

late Jun   While in Brisbane, Australia, a group of students throw
           rotten eggs, pies and slabs of wood at The Beatles; only
           police intervention saves the students from crowds of
           angry fans.

MID--1964

Soon after the increase of NEMS' Seltaeb royalty from 10% to 45%,
relations between the firms worsen; NEMS files a suit claiming
non--payment of full royalties and excessive business expenses
on the part of Seltaeb, which countersues NEMS.

This Is The Savage Young Beatles (LP), with 1961 tracks by Tony
Sheridan and The Beatles, is released, the first bootleg of The
Beatles. GBR--26 (Aug)

Release of the interview recording of The Beatles by New York disc
jockey Murray the K.

JULY

Paul McCartney purchases a house for his father outside Liverpool,
England.

From "Something New" (EP), special jukebox EP featuring six
songs from **Something New** (LP), is released on Capitol in the
U.S.

George Harrison buys a bungalow in Esher, England.

The Beatles' publicity director, Brian Sommerville, sets up a
publicity organization devoted to keeping most people *away*
from the group, so great is the demand for interviews, appear--
ances and performances.

John Lennon purchases a house in Weybridge, England, for
£20,000.

JUL 2   The Beatles arrive in London after touring Australia and
           New Zealand.

JUL 3   *I'm Gonna Knock on Your Door/Why Did I Fall in Love*

with You (45) by The Pete Best Four is released in the
U.K.

JUL 4   The Beatles are "enroute" through Kastrup Airport,
Copenhagen, Denmark.
Twist and Shout enters the Dutch radio's (VARA) "Time
for Teenagers" Top 10 charts at number 9.
Long Tall Sally (EP) enters the *Melody Maker* singles charts
at number 20 in U.K.

JUL 6   Paul McCartney reveals the purchase of Drake's Drum, a
racehorse, for his father.
World premiere in London of "A Hard Day's Night,"
attended by Princess Margaret and Lord Snowdon;
Piccadilly Circus is closed to traffic.
Jim McCartney's 62nd birthday.
Like Dreamers Do, written by Lennon/McCartney and re-
corded by The Applejacks, appears on a single in the
U.S.
Ain't She Sweet/Nobody's Child (45), early songs by The
Beatles and Tony Sheridan, is released in the U.S. on the
ATCO label.

JUL 7   Ringo Starr's 24th birthday.

JUL 8   The Beatles appear on the BBC's "Top of the Pops"
television show.
Songs by The Beatles are recorded from the BBC radio
show "Top of the Pops," later to be illegally included
on the bootleg LP **No Obvious Title.**

JUL 10   **Off The Beatle Track** (LP), by Beatles' producer George
Martin, featuring instrumental versions of Beatles'
songs, is released in the U.K.
A Hard Day's Night (LP) is released in the U.K. BB18–
24 (Aug 7)   BB19–26 (Aug 10)
The Beatles arrive back at Liverpool Airport after a flight
from London, and hold a press conference at the fan-
packed air terminal to announce their personal attendance at the Liverpool premiere of "A Hard Day's Night."
100,000 fans line the streets of Liverpool to welcome The
Beatles on their arrival for the premiere of "A Hard
Day's Night" in Northern England, at the Odeon.
A Hard Day's Night/Things We Said Today (45) is released
in the U.K.
New Musical Express reports that the film "A Hard Day's
Night," which cost a quarter–million pounds to make, is
expected to gross a minimum of a million pounds in the

U.K. alone.

It is reported that the first U.S. pressing of the LP **A Hard Day's Night** will run 2,000,000 copies.

I'll Keep You Satisfied, written by Lennon/McCartney, appears on a single by Billy J. Kramer with The Dakotas in the U.S.

JUL 11   The Beatles appear on the TV show, "Thank Your Lucky Stars."

JUL 12   **A Hard Day's Night** (LP) enters the *Billboard* album charts at number 12; it remains on the charts for 51 weeks during which time it reaches a high point of number 1.
    BF–37 (Jul 18)

George Harrison is slightly injured in a crash.

The Beatles perform at the Hippodrome in Brighton, England, with The Fourmost and Jimmy Nicol.

More film of The Beatles is aired in the U.S. on the "Ed Sullivan Show."

JUL 13   *A Hard Day's Night/I Should Have Known Better* (45) is released in the U.S.

JUL 14   Film critic for *Variety* compares The Beatles' performance in "A Hard Day's Night" to the zaniness of the Marx Brothers.

JUL 15   "The Road to Beatlemania" is televised in the U.K. on ATV.

JUL 16   *The Film Daily* review of "A Hard Day's Night" calls the film noisy, confused, weak, shoddily acted, poorly recorded, and an unquestioned commercial success.

The Beatles appear on the BBC's "Brian Matthew Intro– duces . . . " radio program.

JUL 17   *From a Window*, written by Lennon/McCartney, appears in the U.K. on a single by Billy J. Kramer with The Dakotas.

New Musical Express reports the recording of a parody of The Beatles by "The Bumblers," comprised of Frank Sinatra, Sammy Davis, Jr., Bing Crosby and Dean Martin.

New Musical Express reports that sales of **A Hard Day's Night** (LP) have reached one–and–a–half million in the U.S.

JUL 18   *Like Dreamers Do* by The Applejacks, written by Lennon/ McCartney, reaches its highest point on the *Melody Maker* singles charts: number 17.

Dutch television (VARA) rebroadcasts The Beatles' per– formance filmed June 5.

A *Hard Day's Night* enters the Dutch radio's (VARA) "Time for Teenagers" Top 10 charts at number 6.

A *Hard Day's Night* enters the *Billboard* British top twenty singles charts, remaining on the charts for 10 weeks during which time it reaches a high point of number 1.

A Hard Day's Night (LP) enters the *Melody Maker* album charts in the U.K. at number 1, remaining there for 21 weeks.

A *Hard Day's Night* enters the *Billboard* singles charts at number 21, remaining on the charts for 13 weeks during which time it reaches a high point of number 1.
    BF–36 (Jul 19)

Ain't She Sweet enters the *Billboard* singles charts at num-- ber 90, remaining on the charts for a period of nine weeks during which time it reaches a high point of number 19.

I Should Have Known Better enters the *Billboard* singles charts at number 119.

A *Hard Day's Night* enters the *Melody Maker* singles charts in the U.K. at number 1, remaining there for four weeks.

Long Tall Sally (EP) reaches its highest point on the *Melody Maker* singles charts: number 14.

JUL 19   The Beatles appear on "Big Night Out," a TV program broad-- cast live from Blackpool.

JUL 20   **Something New** (LP) is released in the U.S.
    And I Love Her/If I Fell (45) is released in the U.S.
    I'll Cry Instead/I'm Happy Just to Dance with You (45) is released in the U.S.

JUL 21   A review of "A Hard Day's Night" notes the screaming audience was sent into a frenzy with each appearance of The Beatles on screen at New York's Beacon Theatre.

JUL 23   The Beatles appear at a charity show at the London Palladium called "The Night of 100 Stars."

JUL 24   *Nobody I Know*, written by Lennon/McCartney, appears in the U.K. on an LP with the same name by Peter and Gordon.
    A World Without Love, written by Lennon/McCartney, and recorded by Peter and Gordon, appears on the LP **Tribute to Michael Holiday** in the U.K.

JUL 25   George Harrison appears on BBC's "Juke Box Jury" tele-- vision program.

Ringo's Theme by George Martin enters the *Billboard* singles charts at number 94.

A Hard Day's Night (LP) hits number 1 on the *Billboard* album charts, remaining there for 14 weeks.

The Beatles' American Tour (LP) by Ed Rudy reaches its highest position on the *Billboard* album charts: number 20.

I'll Keep You Satisfied by Billy J. Kramer with The Dakotas, written by Lennon/McCartney, enters the *Billboard* singles charts at number 85.

And I Love Her enters *Billboard* singles charts at number 80, remaining on the charts for nine weeks during which it reaches a high point of number 12.

I'm Happy Just to Dance with You enters *Billboard* singles charts at number 113.

I'll Cry Instead enters the *Billboard* singles charts at number 115.

I Should Have Known Better enters the *Billboard* Hot 100 charts at number 75, remaining on the charts for four weeks and reaching a high point of number 53.

From a Window by Billy J. Kramer with The Dakotas, written by Lennon/McCartney, enters the *Melody Maker* singles charts in the U.K. at number 27.

JUL 26   The Beatles perform at the Opera House in Blackpool, England.

JUL 28   The Beatles fly to Sweden for a concert tour.

Three thousand fans greet The Beatles on arrival at Arlanda Airport, outside Stockholm, Sweden.

JUL 28   The Beatles perform at the Ice Hockey Stadium in Stock-
–29   holm, Sweden; John and Paul receive electrical shocks during the performance.

JUL 30   Brian Epstein's and John Lennon's comments regarding the cancellation of immediate plans for a follow--up book to *In His Own Write* are published in *Mersey Beat*.

Plans to publish a book of photographs in America taken by Ringo Starr are discussed in *Mersey Beat*.

Mersey Beat prints a piece on The Beatles' rehearsals for the upcoming TV show, "Blackpool Night Out."

The Beatles return to London from Stockholm.

JUL 31   George Martin, Beatles' producer, releases a single in the U.S. with instrumental versions of *Ringo's Theme (This Boy)* and *And I Love Her*.

It's For You, written by Lennon/McCartney, appears in the

U.K. on a single.

SUMMER
George Harrison moves into a new Ł 20,000 house in Surrey.
The Beatles' Fan Club has risen to 50,000 members.
Paul McCartney and George Harrison are photographed discussing
   their vacations soon after their returns.

AUGUST
A woman is shot and killed at the Hilton Hotel in San Francisco;
   the murder is undiscovered for several hours because her
   screams, heard by a chambermaid, are ignored as routine
   accompaniment for other guests at the hotel: The Beatles.
Print runs of the monthly *Beatles Book* reach 350,000 copies.
In Chicago, John Lennon decides to join Paul McCartney in some
   fried eggs for breakfast; a "ghastly looking" chicken embryo is
   found in one of the eggs, which nearly makes Paul sick. Lennon,
   nonplussed: "It's not Easter or anything, is it?"
A Beatles' performance of *Shout* made during this period is later in--
   cluded on the bootleg LP **Live from Germany**.
The Beatles record a special interview album for Vee Jay, **Hear The
   Beatles Tell All**. BD-5 (January)
Brian Epstein concludes his book, *A Cellarful of Noise.*
Dean Martin and Frank Sinatra are unable to get tickets to The
   Beatles' concert at the Hollywood Bowl.
A World Without Love by Peter and Gordon, written by Lennon/
   McCartney, is included on Capitol Records promotional LP
   Balanced for Broadcast.

EARLY AUGUST
I Don't Want to See You Again, written by John Lennon and Paul
   McCartney, is recorded at EMI's Abbey Road studios, London,
   by Peter and Gordon.

AUGUST--SEPTEMBER
"Beatlemania" sweeps the U.S.

AUG 1   *And I Love Her* by George Martin enters the *Billboard*
             singles charts at number 105, dropping off the following

week.

Ringo Starr appears on BBC's "Juke Box Jury" television show.

I'll Cry Instead enters the *Billboard* Hot 100 charts at number 62, remaining on the charts for seven weeks during which time it reaches a high point of number 25.

If I Fell enters *Billboard* singles charts at number 92, remaining on the charts for a period of nine weeks during which time it reaches a high point of number 53.

A World Without Love (LP) by Peter and Gordon, with the title song written by Lennon/McCartney, reaches its highest position on the *Billboard* album charts: number 21.

A Hard Day's Night hits number 1 on the *Billboard* singles charts, remaining there for two weeks.

I'm Happy Just to Dance With You reaches highest position on *Billboard* singles charts: number 95. BF–36 (enters the charts at 95)

AUG 2   The film "A Hard Day's Night" goes into general release in theatres in England.

The Beatles perform at the Gaumont in Bournemouth, England.

After the Bournemouth concert, The Beatles stop at a cafe in a small town for some tea; Paul and George engage in a loud mock "brawl," waking residents who call the police. Once the police determine the "brawl" was a joke, The Beatles sign autographs for them and continue on their way.

AUG 3   BBC broadcast a Bank Holiday radio show by The Beatles.

"Follow The Beatles," a film on the making of "A Hard Day's Night," is rebroadcast on BBC television.

Off The Beatle Track (LP) by Beatles' producer George Martin, featuring instrumental versions of Beatles' songs, is released in the U.S.

AUG 6   "Beatles Blow It," *Time* magazine's review of the one and only Beatles' film, "A Hard Day's Night," urges readers to avoid the movie "at any cost," according to Mark Shipper's humorous spoof of Beatle history, *Paperback Writer.*

AUG 7   *Life* magazine's review of "A Hard Day's Night" also notes some "Marx Brothers surrealism" in the film.

George Martin, Beatles' producer, releases a single in the U.K. with instrumental versions of *Ringo's Theme (This Boy)* and *And I Love Her.*

The proposed date for the release of *No Reply*, recorded by Tommy Quickly; not released.

AUG 8   The Beatles appear on the cover of the *Saturday Evening Post.*

Something New (LP) enters the *Billboard* album charts at number 12, remaining on the charts for a period of 41 weeks during which it reaches a high point of number 2.

It's For You by Cilla Black, written by Lennon/McCartney, enters the *Melody Maker* singles charts in the U.K. at number 27.

AUG 9   The Beatles perform at the Futurist in Scarborough.

AUG 10 *Do You Want to Know a Secret/Thank You Girl* (45) released in the U.S. by Vee Jay.

Love Me Do/P.S. I Love You (45) is released in the U.S. by Vee Jay.

Please Please Me/From Me to You (45) is released in the U.S. by Vee Jay.

Twist and Shout/There's a Place (45) is released in the U.S. by Vee Jay.

AUG 11 The Beatles have a recording session for several possible selections for a new single; no choice of songs is expected until after their North American tour.

New York premiere of "A Hard Day's Night."

AUG 12 "A Hard Day's Night" opens in 500 theaters across the U.S.

From a Window and *I'll Be on My Way*, written by Lennon/McCartney, is released in the U.S. on a single by Billy J. Kramer with The Dakotas.   BU18–7 (Aug 7)

AUG 13 The Los Angeles *Herald–Examiner* film critic finds The Beatles "amusing" and "engaging" in "A Hard Day's Night."

A review of "A Hard Day's Night" in the Los Angeles *Times* compares The Beatles to Mack Sennett and the Marx Brothers.

AUG 15 *I Should Have Known Better* reaches its highest position on *Billboard* singles charts: number 53.

New Musical Express reports that 15,000 copies of the film "A Hard Day's Night" were made for distribution to theaters, more prints than any other film in history.

From a Window by Billy J. Kramer with The Dakotas, written by Lennon/McCartney, reaches its highest point on the *Melody Maker* singles charts: number 12.

AUG 16 Bosley Crowther, New York *Times* film critic, finds The Beatles in "A Hard Day's Night" reminiscent of the

Marx Brothers.

The Beatles perform in concert at the Opera House in Blackpool, England.

The Beatles perform at the Futurist in Scarborough, England. TBA--235 (Futuris)

AUG 17   *It's for You*, written by Lennon/McCartney, appears in the U.S. on a single by Cilla Black.

AUG 18   The Beatles fly out of London Airport for San Francisco.

The Beatles begin their first North American tour. BAB--203 (Aug 19)   MB--83 (Aug 15)

AUG 19   The Beatles perform at San Francisco's Cow Palace, beginning of their first American tour.

The Beatles are filmed in concert at San Francisco's Cow Palace

Aug 19--   Tracks for the interview albums **Ed Rudy with the New**
Sep 20   **U.S. Tour, Volume 3; Remember, We Don't Like Them, We Love Them; Hear The Beatles Tell All** and **The Beatles' Story** are recorded.

AUG 20   The Beatles perform at Convention Hall in Las Vegas on their first American tour.

AUG 21   The Beatles perform at Municipal Stadium in Seattle, Washington, on their first American tour.

AUG 22   **Something New** (LP) reaches its highest position on the *Billboard* album charts, number 2, remaining there for nine weeks.

From a Window by Billy J. Kramer with The Dakotas, written by Lennon/McCartney, enters the *Billboard* singles charts at number 92.

Ain't She Sweet reaches its highest position on the *Billboard* singles charts: number 19.

The Beatles' Vancouver, Canada, concert is held at Empire Stadium.

Beatles are filmed in concert at the Empire Stadium in Vancouver, B.C., Canada.

The Beatles' live performance at Empire Stadium in Vancouver is illegally taped from the public address system and from a radio broadcast for the bootleg LP **The Beatles -- Vancouver 1964**.

I'll Keep You Satisfied by Billy J. Kramer with The Dakotas, written by Lennon/McCartney, reaches its highest position on the *Billboard* singles charts: number 30.

late Aug   Elsie Starkey, Ringo Starr's mother, Louise Harrison, George Harrison's mother, and other friends and relatives gather at The Cavern for a Ł110 trans--Atlantic

phone call with American disc jockeys at Radio WROD
in Florida.

AUG 23   The Beatles in concert at the Hollywood Bowl, Los Angeles.
Songs from The Beatles' performance at the Los Angeles
Hollywood Bowl are illegally recorded, later to be in--
cluded on the following bootleg LPs: **Back in 1964 at
the Hollywood Bowl, Live at the Hollywood Bowl,
Get 'Cher Yeah Yeahs Out, Live at the Hollywood Bowl,
Los Angeles, Hollywood Bowl 1964, The Shea Stadium
Concert, For the Last Time, Live in Vancouver, Canada,
Munich at Least, Wizardo's Greatest Hits, Back Upon Us
All, Second to None, 30 Nostalgia Hits,** and **The Tour
Album (Third Amendment).**
Towels used by The Beatles to dry their faces after their
Hollywood Bowl concert are later cut up in small squares,
which are mounted on certificates as a "Beatles Souvenir."
Twist and Shout (live version) is recorded at the Hollywood
Bowl.

AUG 24   *Newsweek*'s review of "A Hard Day's Night" terms it
"daring and fresh."
The Chipmunks Sing The Beatles Hits (LP) by The Chip--
munks, now a Beatle collector's item, is released in the
U.S.
Something New (LP) is certified as a Gold Record by the
R.I.A.A.
Slow Down/Matchbox (45) is released in the U.S.

AUG 25   *A Hard Day's Night* (45) is certified as a Gold Record by the
R.I.A.A.

AUG 26   The Beatles perform at Red Rock Stadium in Denver,
Colorado, on their first American tour. PMS–142 (Red
Rocks Amphitheatre)

AUG 27   The Beatles perform at the Gardens in Cincinnati, Ohio,
on their first American tour.

AUG 28   The Beatles appear on the cover of *Life* magazine.
The Beatles perform at Forest Hills Stadium in New York,
on their first American tour.
The Beatles are recorded at Forest Hills Stadium, New
York; tracks later appear on the bootleg **Forest Hills
Tennis Stadium** (LP).

Summer   The Beatles spend several hours with Bob Dylan while
they are performing in New York, their second meeting
with Dylan.

AUG 29   *I'll Cry Instead* reaches its highest position on the *Billboard* singles charts: number 25.

It's for You by Cilla Black, written by Lennon/McCartney, enters the *Billboard* singles charts at number 128.

AUG 30   The Beatles perform at the Convention Hall in Atlantic City, N.J.

SEPTEMBER

Well over 100,000 people have already purchased tickets to The Beatles' Christmas Show at the Hammersmith Odeon, London, December 24, 1964 – January 16, 1965.

I Knew Right Away, with Paul McCartney playing tambourine, is recorded at EMI's Abbey Road studios, London, by Alma Cogan.

Brian Epstein has lunch with Colonel Tom Parker, Elvis Presley's manager, in Memphis, Tennessee.

An interview is recorded which later appears on the bootleg re-cording **KFWB Beatles.**

The Beatles Introduce New Songs (45), with John Lennon intro-ducing Cilla Black's *It's for You* and Paul McCartney introducing Peter and Gordon's *I Don't Want to See You Again*, is released to radio stations by Capitol as a promotional disc.

George Harrison and John Lennon are mobbed by fans while in Dallas.

SEP 2   The Beatles' Philadelphia concert at Convention Hall, source of the bootleg **Whiskey Flats** LP; songs also later appear on the bootleg LP **Liverpool Flash.**   BU20–23 (Aug 2)

SEP 3   *Mersey Beat* carries a piece consisting of reminiscences by Ringo Starr's mother, Elsie Starkey, dealing with Ringo's early years.

The Beatles perform at the State Fair Coliseum in Indiana-polis, Indiana, on their first American tour.

SEP 4   The Beatles perform at the Milwaukee Auditorium on their first American tour.

SEP 5   *It's for You* by Cilla Black, written by Lennon/McCartney, reaches its highest point on the *Melody Maker* singles charts: number 8.

Slow Down enters *Billboard* singles charts at number 99, remaining on the charts for a period of seven weeks during which it reaches a high point of number 25.

Matchbox enters *Billboard* singles charts at number 81, remaining on the charts for a period of eight weeks during which time it reaches a high point of number 17.

Off The Beatle Track (LP) by George Martin enters the
Billboard album charts at number 130.

Little Children (LP) by Billy J. Kramer with The Dakotas,
featuring three songs written by Lennon/McCartney,
reaches its highest position on the *Billboard* album charts,
number 48.

And I Love Her reaches its highest position on *Billboard*
singles charts: number 12.

If I Fell reaches its highest position on the *Billboard* singles
charts: number 53.

The Beatles perform at the International Amphitheater in
Chicago, Illinois, on their first American tour.

SEP 6   The Beatles perform at Olympia Stadium in Detroit,
          Michigan, on their first American tour. BB14--29
          (Olympic) LCP--269 (Olympic)

SEP 7   *Can't Buy Me Love* and *You Can't Do That* (by The
          Beatles) and *A World Without Love* and *Nobody I Know*
          (written by Lennon/McCartney and recorded by Peter
          and Gordon) are included on **The Big Hits from England
          and the USA** (LP), released in the U.S.

          The Beatles perform at Maple Leaf Gardens in Toronto,
          Canada, on their first American tour.

SEP 8   The Beatles perform at the Forum in Montreal, Canada,
          on their first American tour.

SEP 11   *I Don't Want to See You Again*, written by Lennon/
          McCartney, appears in the U.K. on a single by Peter and
          Gordon.

          The Beatles perform at the Gator Bowl in Jacksonville,
          Florida, on their first American tour.

          George Harrison forms Harrisongs, his own music pub--
          lishing company.

SEP 12   Brian Epstein reports he has purchased controlling interest
          in Liverpool's *Mersey Beat* newspaper.

          Ringo's Theme, by George Martin, reaches its highest
          position on the *Billboard* singles charts: number 53.

          The Beatles perform at the Boston Gardens in Boston,
          Massachusetts, on their first American tour.

SEP 13   The Beatles perform at the Civic Center in Baltimore,
          Maryland, on their first American tour.

SEP 14   The Beatles perform at the Civic Arena in Pittsburgh,
          Pennsylvania, on their first American tour. BCE--49
          (Civic Center)

SEP 15   *I Should Have Known Better* enters Dutch radio's (VARA)

"Time for Teenagers," Top 10 charts at number 9.

Their Biggest Hits (EP), a Beatles' bootleg with a fake Tollie label, is released in the U.S.

The Beatles perform at the Public Auditorium in Cleveland, Ohio, on their first American tour.

SEP 16   An Associated Press story reports that Police Inspector Carl Bear of Cleveland's Juvenile Bureau ordered The Beatles off the stage of the Cleveland Public Auditorium for 15 minutes to allow the young audience to calm down.

The Beatles perform at City Park Stadium in New Orleans, Louisiana, on their first American tour.

SEP 17   The Beatles perform at the Municipal Stadium in Kansas City on their first American tour, after Charles O. Finley offers them $150,000 to add Kansas City to their tour, a figure higher than any ever paid to an American artist.   BBS--27 (rest day)   LCP--270 (rest day)

SEP 18   The Beatles perform at the Memorial Coliseum in Dallas, Texas, on their first American tour.

SEP 19   The review of "A Hard Day's Night" in *Saturday Review* places The Beatles' humor between the Marx Brothers and the Three Stooges.

John Lennon grants permission for use of his drawing, "The Fat Budgie," on a Christmas card; half--a--million cards are printed.

Off The Beatle Track (LP) by George Martin reaches its highest position on the *Billboard* album charts: number 111.

Brian Epstein's 30th birthday, the day before the Beatles' final New York City concert on their American tour.

The Beatles rest at a ranch in Missouri.

SEP 20   The Beatles perform at a charity concert at the Paramount Theater in New York City, ending their first American tour.

The Beatles are seen again on the "Ed Sullivan Show."

SEP 21   The Beatles return to England from their tour of America and Canada.

George Martin, Beatles' producer, releases a single in the U.S. with instrumental versions of *I Should Have Known Better* and *A Hard Day's Night.*

The Rutles appear on the cover of *Life International,* accord--ing to the album send--up of The Beatles,' **The Rutles.**

I Don't Want to See You Again, written by Lennon/
McCartney, appears in the U.S. on a single by Peter and
Gordon.

Sep 21--   The Beatles record songs for their **Beatles For Sale** (LP) at
Oct 8   EMI's Abbey Road studios; two tracks, *You'll Know
            What to Do* and *Always and Only*, go unreleased.

SEP 25   Brian Epstein reports he was offered £3,500,000 for his
            interest in The Beatles by an American business syndi-
            cate.

SEP 28   Four Lennon/McCartney songs appear in the U.S. on **I'll
            Keep You Satisfied** (LP) by Billy J. Kramer with The
            Dakotas.

FALL

Release of interview single by U.S. disc jockey Tom Clay, *Remember, We Don't Like Them, We Love Them.*

Hear The Beatles Tell All (LP), a promotional interview record, is
released in the U.S. on Vee Jay. GBR--26 (Apr 18) TBD--10 (Sep)

The Beatles' individual styles of humor emerge clearly defined,
having been sharpened at innumerable press conferences and
public appearances over the past year.

OCTOBER

The Beatles record *Echoes of the Mersey Side.*

Geoffrey Ellis joins NEMS Enterprises in London as a senior
executive, becoming a director in 1965.

Date of the issue of the *Mersey Moptop Faverave FabGearBeat*
contained in *National Lampoon*'s October 1977 send--up issue
devoted to The Beatles.

A Cellarful of Noise by Brian Epstein and Derek Taylor is published
in the U.K.

Brian Epstein records portions of his autobiography, *A Cellarful
of Noise*, for an LP planned for release in the U.S.; never re--
leased.

EARLY OCTOBER

Ringo Starr passes his driving test and begins to look for a new car.
I Feel Fine and *She's a Woman* are recorded.

EARLY--MID--OCTOBER
The Beatles hold enough recording sessions to provide an abund--
ance of material for their next album.

OCT 1   *Mersey Beat* prints an article by Brian Epstein about The
Beatles' American tour.
The Beatles Vs. The Four Seasons (LP) is released in the
U.S. on Vee Jay. TBD--10 (Nov)

OCT 3   *I Don't Want to See You Again* by Peter and Gordon,
written by Lennon/McCartney, enters the *Billboard*
singles charts at number 84.
I Should Have Known Better by George Martin enters the
Billboard singles charts at number 114.
It's for You by Cilla Black, written by Lennon/McCartney,
reaches its highest position on the *Billboard* singles
charts: number 79.
A Hard Day's Night by George Martin enters the *Billboard*
singles charts at number 122, dropping off the following
week.
From a Window by Billy J. Kramer with The Dakotas,
written by Lennon/McCartney, reaches its highest
position on the *Billboard* singles charts: number 23.
Matchbox reaches its highest position on the *Billboard* singles
charts: number 18.

OCT 5   **Ain't She Sweet** (LP), by Tony Sheridan and The Beatles,
is released in the U.S. on the ATCO label.

OCT 9   Beatles record three songs for the U.S. TV show "Shindig"
before a live audience at London's Granville Theatre; an
additional tune, *The House of the Rising Sun*, goes un--
released.
The Beatles begin a tour of the U.K. with Mary Wells,
Tommy Quickly and others.
The Beatles perform at the Gaumont in Bradford, England,
at the start of their four--week autumn tour.

OCT 10 The Beatles perform at De Montfort Hall in Leicester,
England, on their autumn tour.
I Should Have Known Better by George Martin reaches its
highest position on the *Billboard* singles charts: number
111.

If I Fell enters Dutch radio's (VARA) "Time for Teenagers"
Top 10 charts at number 8.

Slow Down reaches highest position on *Billboard* singles
charts: number 25.

The Beatles Vs. The Four Seasons (LP) enters the *Billboard*
album charts at number 147, reaching its highest position
the following week: number 142, during a stay on the
charts of three weeks.

OCT 11   The Beatles perform at the Odeon in Birmingham, England,
on their autumn tour.

OCT 12   **Songs, Pictures and Stories of The Fabulous Beatles** (LP) is
released in the U.S. on Vee Jay.

OCT 13   The Beatles perform at the ABC in Wigan, England, on
their autumn tour.

OCT 14   The Beatles perform at the Apollo in Manchester, England,
on their autumn tour. BCE--51 (Ardwicke Apollo)
PMS--143 (Ardwick Apollo)
ABC--TV films Beatles in concert at the Apollo in Man--
chester, England.

OCT 15   The Beatles perform at the Globe in Stockton, England, on
their autumn tour.

OCT 16   *If I Fell/Tell My Why* (45) is released in Europe on Parlo--
phone.
The Beatles appear live on "Ready, Steady, Go" television
show.
The Beatles perform at the ABC in Hull, England, on their
autumn tour.

OCT 19   The Beatles perform at the ABC in Edinburgh, Scotland, on
their autumn tour.

OCT 20   The Beatles perform at Caird Hall in Dundee, Scotland, on
their autumn tour.

OCT 21   The Beatles perform at the Odeon in Glasgow, Scotland, on
their autumn tour.

OCT 22   The Beatles perform at the Odeon in Leeds, England, on
their autumn tour.

OCT 23   *It's for You*, written by Lennon/McCartney, appears in the
U.K. on an EP of the same name by Cilla Black.
The Beatles perform at the Gaumont State in Kilburn, on
their autumn tour.

OCT 24   The Beatles perform at the Odeon in Lewisham, England.
The Beatles perform at the Granada in Walthamstow,
England, on their autumn tour. PMS--143 (Oct 23)

OCT 25   The Beatles are awarded five Ivor Novello Awards by

British Music Industry for the year 1963: most outstanding contribution to music; *She Loves You*, most
broadcast song, and top selling record; *I Want to Hold
Your Hand,* second top selling record; and, *All My
Loving*, second most outstanding song.

The Beatles perform at the Hippodrome in Brighton,
England, on their autumn tour.

OCT 26
–28
Another Beatles Christmas Record is recorded at EMI's
Abbey Road studios, London.   BD--8 (Nov)

OCT 28
The Beatles perform at the ABC in Exeter, England, on
their autumn tour.

OCT 29
The Beatles perform at the ABC in Plymouth, England, on
their autumn tour.

OCT 30
A single by Alma Cogan is released in the U.K.; Paul plays
tambourine.

The Beatles perform at the Gaumont in Bournemouth,
England, on their autumn tour.

OCT 31
Songs, Pictures and Stories of The Fabulous Beatles (LP)
enters the *Billboard* album charts at number 121, remaining on the charts for a period of 12 weeks during
which time it reaches a high point of number 63.

The Beatles perform at the Gaumont in Ipswich, England,
on their autumn tour.   PMS--143 (Odeon in Southend)

NOVEMBER

Love Me Do: The Beatles' Progress by Michael Braun is published
in the U.K. by Penguin.

Broadcast of a Beatles' appearance on BBC radio's "Top of the
Pops."

NOV 1
The Beatles perform at the Astoria in Finsbury Park,
London, on their autumn tour.

NOV 2
George Martin, Beatles' producer, releases **A Hard Day's
Night** (LP) in the U.S., featuring instrumental versions
of Beatles' songs.

The Beatles perform at the Ritz in Belfast, Northern
Ireland, on their autumn tour.

NOV 4
Extracts from the Film A Hard Day's Night (EP) is released in the U.K.

The Beatles perform at the Ritz in Luton, England, on their
autumn tour.

NOV 5   The Beatles appear at the Odeon in Nottingham, England,
         on their autumn tour.
NOV 6   *From a Window*, written by Lennon/McCartney, appears
         in the U.K. on an EP of the same name by Billy J.
         Kramer with The Dakotas.
         Extracts from the Album A Hard Day's Night (EP) is re--
         leased in the U.K.
         The Beatles appear at the Gaumont in Southampton,
         England, on their autumn tour.
NOV 7   *I Don't Want to See You Again* by Peter and Gordon,
         written by Lennon/McCartney, reaches its highest
         position on the *Billboard* singles charts: number 16.
         The Beatles appear at the Capitol in Cardiff, England, on
         their autumn tour.
NOV 8   The Beatles appear at the Empire in Liverpool, England, on
         their autumn tour.
NOV 9   The Beatles perform at City Hall in Sheffield, England, on
         their autumn tour.
NOV 10   The Beatles appear at Colston Hall in Bristol, England, last
         stop on their autumn tour.
NOV 12   *Mersey Beat* reports that, while in Liverpool on their U.K.
         tour, John Lennon was allowed to select one of Stu
         Sutcliffe's paintings during a visit with Sutcliffe's parents.
NOV 13   *America/Since You Broke My Heart* (45) by Rory Storm
         and The Hurricanes, for which Ringo Starr had previously
         played drums, is released in the U.K.
NOV 15   Portions of the British TV special, "Around The Beatles,"
         are shown in the U.S.
NOV 21   The Beatles appear on the TV show "Thank Your Lucky
         Stars." BBS--54 (Nov 1)
NOV 23   **The Beatles Story** (LP) is released in the U.S.
         I Feel Fine/She's a Woman (45) is released in the U.S.
         BM--97 (Aug 24)   GBR--4 (Nov 13)
NOV 24   James McCartney, Paul's father, marries his second wife,
         Mrs. Angela Williams, after nearly ten years as a widower.
         BAB--244 (Jan 1965) BEA2--17 (Jan 1965) TB--
         244 (Jan 1965)
NOV 26   The Beatles appear on the BBC Light Programme "Top
         Gear."
NOV 27   *I Feel Fine/She's a Woman* (45) is released in the U.K. on
         the Parlophone label.
         The Beatles appear on the "Ready, Steady, Go" television
         show.

NOV 28   **A Hard Day's Night** (EP) enters the *Melody Maker* singles
     charts in the U.K. at number 48.

DECEMBER
   John Lennon has a demo studio built in his house.
   It is reported that Ringo Starr recently received a telegram from
      Burt Lancaster promising that Ringo's guns, which Lancaster
      had promised to send to England after meeting Ringo in the
      U.S., would still be sent if Ringo could arrange for an import
      license.
   Reports begin to circulate that a show devoted to The Beatles will
      start on Radio Luxembourg, hosted by DJ Chris Denning.
   Gifts given The Beatles during their summer tour of Australia and
      New Zealand finally reach England, including a stuffed five--
      foot tall kangaroo given to Paul McCartney.

EARLY--MID--DECEMBER
   George Harrison vacations in Nassau, Paul McCartney visits his
      father and stepmother in Liverpool, while Ringo is in hospital
      having his tonsils removed.

DEC 1   Ringo Starr enters University College Hospital, London,
     for a tonsillectomy; he rejects requests to have them as
     souvenirs. BF--31 (Nov)
DEC 3   The Beatles appear on the BBC's "Top of the Pops" tele--
     vision show.
DEC 4   The Beatles Fan Club newsletter announces a current
     membership of 65,000.
     Beatles For Sale (LP) is released in the U.K. on Parlophone.
     BAB--344 (Nov)   BBS--52 (Nov 27)   BIR--36 (Nov 27)
     LCP--263,275 (Nov 27)
DEC 5   **Songs, Pictures and Stories of The Fabulous Beatles** (LP)
     reaches its highest position on the *Billboard* album charts:
     number 63.
     I Feel Fine (45) enters the *Billboard* British top twenty
     singles charts, remaining on the charts for ten weeks
     during which it reaches a high point of number 1.
     I Feel Fine enters the *Billboard* singles charts at number
     22, remaining on the charts for 11 weeks during which
     time it reaches a high point of number 1.
     She's a Woman enters the *Billboard* singles charts at num--
     ber 46, remaining on the charts for nine weeks during
     which time it reaches a high point of number 4.
     I Feel Fine enters Dutch radio's (VARA) "Time for

Teenagers" Top 10 charts at number 5.

I Feel Fine enters the *Melody Maker* singles charts at
number 1 and remains there for six weeks.

A Hard Day's Night reaches its highest point on the *Melody
Maker* singles charts: number 34.

DEC 8   Paul McCartney is quoted about plans to marry Jane Asher,
though, he adds, nothing is imminent.

DEC 9   A filmed Beatles' appearance on the BBC's "Top of the
Pops" television show is broadcast.

DEC 10 Ringo Starr leaves the hospital following his tonsilectomy.

DEC 11 *I Don't Want to See You Again* and *Nobody I Know*,
written by Lennon/McCartney, appear in U.S. on the
LP **I Don't Want to See You Again** by Peter and Gordon.

DEC 12 **The Beatles Story** (LP) enters the *Billboard* album charts
at number 97, remaining on the charts for 17 weeks
during which it reaches a high point of number 7.

Beatles For Sale (LP) enters the *Melody Maker* album charts
in the U.K. at number 1, remaining there for nine weeks,
dropping to number 2 for ten weeks, and returning to
number 1 for an additional six weeks.

DEC 15 **Beatles '65** (LP) is released in the U.S. on Capitol.

DEC 18 *I Don't Want to See You Again*, written by Lennon/
McCartney, appears in the U.K. on the LP **In Touch
with Peter and Gordon.**

EMI announces two--week sales of **Beatles For Sale** (LP) at
750,000 copies.

Another Beatles Christmas Record is released by the Fan
Club. PMS--144 (Dec 24)

DEC 21 The Beatles begin rehearsals for their Christmas stage show,
and the monthly *Beatles Book* reports that The Beatles
will switch positions in the instrument department for
at least one performance of the show.

DEC 22 The Beatles and cast of the Christmas show assemble in
London for rehearsals.

Dec 24-- The Beatles Christmas show runs at the Odeon in Hammer--
Jan 16   smith, London, excluding Sundays.

Christ-- The Beatles send Norman Smith, their recording balance--
mas   and--control engineer, a pair of gold cuff--links addressed
to "Two D--Bs Smith," Paul McCartney's nickname for
Smith.

Brian Epstein gives a large rocking horse to John Lennon's
son, Julian, for Christmas.

The Beatles Fan Club membership rises to over 65,000 in

Britain.

The Beatles give Neil Aspinall a 2.4 gray Jaguar for Christ‐
mas.

Attending one of the performances at The Beatles'
Christmas Show in Hammersmith, Pattie Boyd is
attacked by teenage girls resentful of her place in
George Harrison's life. BAB‐316 (Christmas 1965)

DEC 26 The Beatles appear on the BBC's "Saturday Club" radio
program.

I Feel Fine hits number 1 on the *Billboard* singles charts,
remaining there for three weeks.

She's a Woman reaches its highest position on the *Billboard*
singles charts: number 4.

DEC 31 *I Feel Fine* (45) is certified as a Gold Record by the
R.I.A.A.

Beatles '65 (LP) is certified as a Gold Record by the
R.I.A.A.

The Beatles' Story (LP) is certified as a Gold Record by
the R.I.A.A.

LATE 1964

I'm a Loser reflects Bob Dylan's influence on John Lennon's mus‐
ical composition.

Derek Taylor ‐‐ Beatles' press agent ‐‐ leaves The Beatles' employ
due to continual disagreements with Brian Epstein.

I saw a film today oh boy

A DAY
IN THE
LIFE

The Beatles
Day-By-Day

1965

DURING THIS YEAR ...

Die Beatles: Fabelwesen Unserer Zeit by Christine Ehrhardt is
published in West Germany by Wolf Frhr. von Tucher.

The Beatles purchase a customized $100,000 Rolls Royce
Phantom.

Leurs 14 Plus Grands Succes (LP) is released in France by Odeon.

The following Beatles' singles are released in Holland: *No Reply/
Rock 'n' Roll Music, Ticket to Ride/Yet It Is, Help/I'm Down,
Dizzy Miss Lizzy/Yesterday, We Can Work It Out/Day Tripper.*

An interview record, **All About The Beatles** (LP) by Louise
Harrison Caldwell, George Harrison's sister, is released in U.S.

The Beatles Monthly Book, published in England, polls readers to
select their favorite Beatles song: *Help!* tops a list of ten.

The Beatles' Greatest (LP) is released in Germany by Odeon.

The following singles by The Beatles are released in Australia:
*Rock and Roll Music/Honey Don't, Ticket to Ride/Yet It Is,
Help!/I'm Down, Yesterday/Act Naturally, Day Tripper/We
Can Work It Out.*

Joshua Rifkin records his LP, **The Baroque Beatles Book**, a tribute
to The Beatles, with their songs rendered in the style of Baroque
composers.

Angie and The Chiclettes release *Treat Him Tender Maureen* (45)
shortly after Ringo Starr's wedding.

The following EPs by The Beatles are released in Australia: **With
The Beatles, A Hard Day's Night, Beatles For Sale (1), Beatles
For Sale (2).**

Help! The Beatles is published in the U.S. by Random House.

I Should Have Known Better, words and music by Lennon/McCartney,
is re--copyrighted in the U.K. by Northern Songs Ltd.

The following songs, words and music by George Harrison, are copy--
righted in the U.K. by Northern Songs Ltd.: *I Need You, Think
For Yourself* and *You Like Me Too Much.*

125

The Beatles record an unreleased version of *I Do Like to be Beside the Seaside* during their appearance on the TV show, "Black--pool Night Out."

Beatles No. 5 (LP) is released in Japan by Odeon.

The Beatles Nel Film "Aiuto" (LP) is released in Italy, featuring the same songs as the British **Help!** (LP).

The Beatles (EP) is released in Mexico by Capitol.

The recording *The Girl I Love*, incorrectly rumored to be by The Beatles, is released.

A rare stereo version of *I'm Down* is released in Japan on an EP called **Help!**

Ringo Starr gets a new Ludwig drum kit for use in the film "Help!"

Ticket to Ride/Yet It Is (45) is released in Japan by Odeon.

The following album by The Beatles is released in Australia:
Beatles For Sale. BF--41 (1964)

Beatles 7 (LP) is released in Italy by Parlophone.

Pete Best gives up his attempts to remain as a performer in show business.

The Beatles Greatest Hits, Volume 2 (LP) is released in Singapore by Parlophone.

Help! (LP) is released in Germany by Odeon.

The Beatles are photographed in front of the Milan Cathedral on their trip to Italy.

George Harrison's father, Harold, leaves work after 31 years as a bus driver.

Les Beatles 1965 (EP) is released in France by Odeon.

John Lennon buys a supermarket for £20,000 for a school friend, Pete Shotten.

Les Beatles (EP) is released in France by Parlophone (Odeon).

George Harrison's parents move from Liverpool to Warrington, fifteen miles from Liverpool.

The Beatles (EP) is released in France by Odeon.

The Ronettes tour with The Beatles.

A rare stereo version of *She's a Woman* is released on an Australian LP called **Beatles' Greatest Hits, Vol. 2.**

The album **The Beatles Live in Italy** is rumored to have been re--corded at the Beatles' performance at the Cinema Adriano in Rome.

Communism, Hypnotism, and The Beatles by Rev. David A. Noebel is published in the U.S. by The Christian Crusade.

The following singles by The Beatles are released in Italy: *Rock 'n' Roll Music/I'll Follow the Sun, I Feel Fine/Kansas City, Eight Days a Week/I'm a Loser, Ticket to Ride/Yes It Is, Long Tall Sally/She's a Woman, Yesterday/The Night Before, I Need You/Dizzy Miss Lizzy, We Can Work It Out/Day Tripper,* and, *Help!/I'm Down.*

Help! by Al Hine, a novel based on The Beatles' film, is published in the U.S. by Dell.

A Spaniard in the Works, by John Lennon, is published in the U.S. by Simon & Schuster.

EARLY 1965

A dentist friend of George Harrison's first introduces LSD to both George and John Lennon by secretly dosing their cups of coffee with it during a dinner in London. ATC--66 (summer 1966)

Pattie Boyd and George Harrison begin living together.

The Rutles play at Che Stadium, "named after the Cuban guerilla leader Che Stadium," according to the album send--up of The Beatles' career: **The Rutles.**

Denny Laine's *Go Now* reaches the number 1 chart position in the U.K.

By the time Sid Bernstein receives Brian Epstein's contract covering the Shea Stadium concert, over $180,000 in tickets have already been sold.

JANUARY

Brian Epstein and The Beatles decide on the schedule for the year -- tours, radio, TV, recording, etc.

You've Lost That Lovin' Feelin'/Is It Love (45) by Cilla Black, managed by Brian Epstein, is released in the U.K., later reaching a high point of number 2 on the charts.

During a phone call, New York promoter Sid Bernstein and Brian Epstein arrange The Beatles' summer Shea Stadium concert, The Beatles are to receive $100,000 or 60% of the receipts, whichever proves higher.

JAN 1   Dick James, Beatles' music publisher, releases a medley of Beatles' songs in the U.K. called *Sing a Song of Beatles* (45).

JAN 2   *I Feel Fine* enters Holland's Radio Veronica Top 40 at number 1.

        I Don't Want to See You Again (LP) by Peter and Gordon, with the title song written by Lennon/McCartney, enters the *Billboard* album charts at number 133.

Beatles '65 (LP) enters the *Billboard* album charts at number 98, remaining on the charts for 70 weeks during which it reaches a high point of number 1.

If I Fell enters Holland's Radio Veronica Top 40 at number 26.

The Beatles' Story (LP) reaches its highest position on the *Billboard* album charts, number 7.

I Should Have Known Better enters Holland's Radio Veronica Top 40 at number 40.

JAN 9   John Lennon reads his poems on the BBC's "Not Only . . . But Also" radio show.

Beatles '65 (LP) hits number 1 on the *Billboard* album charts, remaining there for nine weeks.

JAN 16   Beatles' Christmas show ends at the Odeon in Hammer-smith, England.

mid–Jan   George Harrison vacations at home, and Paul McCartney travels to Tunisia after The Beatles' Christmas show.

JAN 19   It is reported that four out of seven R.I.A.A. gold records awarded during 1964 went to Beatles' singles.

JAN 20   TV show "Shindig" is aired in the U.S., featuring The Beatles performing three songs.

JAN 22   The Beatles are reported to have been America's top song-writers during 1964.

JAN 27   George Harrison acts as best man at the wedding of his brother, Peter.

John and Cynthia Lennon begin a ten–day skiing vacation in the Alps along with George Martin and his wife Judy; Martin sprains his ankle at St. Moritz, an injury that requires a plaster cast.

JAN 28   Merger of Brian Epstein's NEMS and the Vic Lewis Organisation is reported.

JAN 29   *If I Fell/Tell Me Why* (45) is released in the U.K.

JAN 30   **I Don't Want to See You Again** (LP) by Peter and Gordon, with the title song written by Lennon/McCartney, reaches its highest position on the *Billboard* album charts: number 95.

FEBRUARY

It is reported in the monthly *Beatles Book* that Ringo Starr is responsible for the song titles *A Hard Day's Night* and *Tomor-row Never Knows.*

Cilla (LP) by Cilla Black, managed by Brian Epstein, is released in the U.K.

The Beatles begin work on their second film.

Two songs by George Harrison are recorded by The Beatles.

Sid Bernstein, U.S. promoter, signs a contract for an August 15
   Beatles' concert at Shea Stadium, unaware that the booking
   might conflict with a New York Met's home game, according to
   Mark Shipper's humorous spoof of Beatle history, *Paperback
   Writer.*

FEBRUARY--MAY

"Help!" is filmed, The Beatles' second motion picture.

EARLY FEBRUARY--EARLY MARCH

*The Night Before, You've Got to Hide Your Love Away, I Need
You, Another Girl, You're Gonna Lose That Girl* are recorded at
EMI's Abbey Road studios, London.

FEB 1   **4 by The Beatles** (EP) is released in the U.S.

FEB 11   Ringo Starr marries Maureen Cox; John and Cynthia
          Lennon and George Harrison attend the wedding, but
          Paul McCartney is in the U.S. at the time. (GUB--35
          (Maureen Taylor) WT9--23 (Feb 2)

FEB 12   Murray the K records an interview with Ringo Starr.
          RO--13 (interviews all four)
          Ticket to Ride and *Yes It Is* are recorded by The Beatles.

FEB 15   John Lennon passes his driving test.
          The Beatles begin recording songs for their new film,
             "Help!"
          Eight Days a Week/I Don't Want to Spoil the Party (45)
             is released in the U.S.

FEB 18   Northern Songs Ltd., The Beatles' music publishing com--
          pany, opens its stock to public ownership.

FEB 19   The Beatles tape tracks from the day's recording session
          onto portable tape recorders to take with them for
          listening.
          The Chipmunks Sing The Beatles Hits (LP) by The Chip--
          munks, now a Beatle collector's item, is released in the
          U.K.
          Music from "A Hard Day's Night" (EP), featuring instru--
          mental versions of Beatles' songs, is released in the U.K.
          by Beatles' producer George Martin.

FEB 20   *Eight Days a Week* enters the *Billboard* singles charts at
          number 53, remaining on the charts for ten weeks

during which it reaches a high point of number 1.

Eight Days a Week/Baby's in Black enters Holland's Radio Veronica Top 40 at number 10.

I Don't Want to Spoil the Party enters the *Billboard* singles charts at number 81, remaining on charts for six weeks, during which it reaches a high point of number 39.

FEB 22   The Beatles leave for the Bahamas to begin filming "Help!" BEA2--17 (Feb 18)

FEB 25   Members of The Beatles' party are each given copies of a book on Indian philosophy while in the Bahamas.

George Harrison's 22nd birthday.

"KRLA Beat" news sheet announces the employment of Derek Taylor – former Beatles' press agent -- as an exclusive reporter for KRLA in Los Angeles.

FEB 27   **4 by The Beatles** (EP) enters the *Billboard* singles charts at number 81, remaining on the charts for five weeks during which it reaches a high point of number 68.

MARCH

It is reported that George Harrison has acquired a white Aston Martin like Paul McCartney's, changing from his E--type Jaguar.

The Beatles film scenes for "Help!" in the Bahamas.

MAR 12   The Beatles stop off briefly in England on their way to the Austrian Alps.

MAR 12   After landing in England and before embarking for Austria,
–13   The Beatles pick out *Ticket to Ride* and *Yes It Is* as the flip--sides for their next single.

MAR 13   The Beatles fly to Austria for more filming of "Help!"

Eight Days a Week hits number 1 on the *Billboard* singles charts, remaining there for two weeks.

MAR 19   An instrumental version of *I Feel Fine* is released in the U.K. on a single by Beatles' producer George Martin.

MAR 20   *I Don't Want to Spoil the Party* reaches its highest position on the *Billboard* singles charts: number 39.

The Beatles are interviewed by phone from Austria on the BBC's "Saturday Club" radio program.

MAR 22   **The Early Beatles** (LP) is released in the U.S.

Mar 22--   Songs recorded by The Beatles during this period later
May   appear on the LP **Help!**

MAR 27   *Rock and Roll Music/No Reply* (45) enters Holland's Radio Veronica Top 40 at number 18.

4 by The Beatles (EP) reaches its highest position on the

Billboard singles charts: number 68.

SPRING

Datebook magazine carries an interview with Paul McCartney by
Alan Freeman.

The Rolling Stones' managers, Eric Easton and Andrew Oldham,
appoint Allen Klein to renegotiate the Stones' recording con--
tract with Decca Records.

Murray the K individually interviews three of The Beatles in Lon--
don, New York and Miami; the interviews are later included on
the bootleg LP **Soldier of Love.**

The Beatles' **Help!** (LP) is released, partially comprised of songs
drawn from the 15,000 submitted to The Beatles as a result of
their search for new material via a classified ad, according to
Mark Shipper's humorous spoof of Beatle history, *Paperback
Writer.*

SPRING--SUMMER

Songs by The Beatles released in this period reflect their growing
inventiveness during a period of transition.

APRIL

John Lennon and Neil Aspinall take the London subway home to
Tottenham Court Road after an evening with Keith Richard
and Mick Jaggar of The Rolling Stones; they go unrecognized
by the workmen and cleaners who inhabit the early morning
subway.

Denny Laine's *Go Now* reaches number 10 in the U.S. *Billboard*
charts.

Auntie Gin's Theme and *Scrambled Eggs*, written by John Lennon
and Paul McCartney, are recorded at EMI's Abbey Road studios,
London, by George Martin's Orchestra.

I've Been Wrong Before/I Don't Want to Know (45) by Cilla Black,
managed by Brian Epstein, is released in the U.K.

That Means a Lot, written by John Lennon and Paul McCartney, is
recorded by P.J. Proby.

APR 1   Technicians and actors in the film studios shooting "Help!"
wait for a practical joke by The Beatles to celebrate
April Fool's Day; nothing happens.

Brian Epstein buys controlling interest in London's
Saville Theatre.

APR 3   *Mersey Beat* reports the break--up of the Pete Best Combo.

	The Beatles appear on ITV's "Thank Your Lucky Stars."
APR 4	John Lennon and Paul McCartney write *Help!*
APR 6	**Beatles For Sale** (EP) is released in the U.K.
APR 9	*Ticket to Ride/Yes It Is* (45) is released in the U.K.
APR 11	Murray the K again interviews The Beatles, the interviews later appearing on the bootlegs **Murray the K Fan Club** and **Soldier of Love**.

The Beatles perform at the *New Musical Express* Poll Winner's Concert at the Empire Pool in Wembley, England.

ABC--TV films The Beatles in concert at the Wembley Poll Winner's Concert in London.

Beatles' performance of *She Loves You* at the Wembley concert is recorded, later to be illegally included on the bootleg LP **Soldier of Love**.

The Beatles appear on "The Eamonn Andrews Show" on ABC--TV.

APR 12	**George Martin Scores Instrumental Versions of the Hits** (LP), including songs *I Feel Fine, P.S. I Love You*, and *No Reply*, is released in the U.S.
APR 13	Two versions of *Help!* are recorded at EMI's Abbey Road studios, London.
APR 14	It is reported that Paul McCartney has purchased a Victorian house in St. John's Wood, London.
APR 15	The Beatles appear on BBC's "Top of the Pops."
mid--Apr --May 12	Continued shooting of "Help!" at Twickenham Studios, London.
APR 16	John Lennon and George Harrison are interviewed on the live TV show, "Ready Steady Goes Live."
APR 17	*Ticket to Ride* (45) enters the *Billboard* British top twenty singles charts, remaining on the charts for nine weeks during which it reaches a high point of number 1.

Ticket to Ride enters the *Melody Maker* singles charts in the U.K. at number 1, remaining there for five weeks.

APR 18	Film of The Beatles at the *New Musical Express* Poll Winner's Concert is aired on ABC--TV.
APR 19	*Ticket to Ride/Yes It Is* (45) is released in the U.S.
APR 24	*Ticket to Ride* enters Holland's Radio Veronica Top 40 at number 10.

The Early Beatles (LP) enters the *Billboard* album charts at number 132, remaining on the charts for 33 weeks during which it reaches a high point of number 43.

Yes It Is enters the *Billboard* singles charts at number 115.

Ticket to Ride enters the *Billboard* singles charts at
number 59, remaining on the charts for eleven weeks
during which it reaches a high point of number 1.

APR 25   The second half of the *New Musical Express* Poll Winner's
Concert is broadcast on TV.

MAY

Part I of "The Beatles and Me," by Neil Aspinall, is published in
16 Magazine.

It is generally believed that The Beatles' forthcoming film, "Help!"
will be called "Eight Arms to Hold You."

The Beatles attend Bob Dylan's London concert, and spend several
hours with him after the show.

The Beatles' February 1964 performance on British TV's "Big
Night Out" is aired in the Cleveland, Ohio, area.

MAY--JUNE

John Lennon again records *Keep Your Hands Off My Baby* – un--
released.

MAY 1   *Yes It Is* enters the *Billboard* Hot 100 charts at number
71, remaining on the charts for a period of four weeks,
during which it reaches a high point of number 46.

early May The Beatles stay at the "Antrobus Arms," Amesbury,
while shooting sequences for "Help!" in Salisbury Plain.

MAY 4   Thieves steal some clothing from John Lennon's car while
he is being filmed on Salisbury Plain.

MAY 10 *You Like Me Too Much, Bad Boy, Dizzy Miss Lizzie,* and
--11   *Tell Me What You See* are recorded at EMI's Abbey
Road studios, London.

MAY 12 "Help!" filming is concluded. BB23--2 (May 15)

MAY 15 *Yes It Is* reaches its highest position on the *Billboard* singles
charts: number 46.

MAY 22 *Ticket to Ride* hits number 1 on the *Billboard* singles charts,
dropping to 2 the next week.

LATE MAY--EARLY JUNE

Two versions of *I'm Down*, along with final and unreleased versions
of *Act Naturally, It's Only Love, I've Just Seen a Face* and
Yesterday are recorded at the Abbey Road studios; unreleased
versions of other songs are recorded under the working titles
That's a Nice Hat, Scrambled Eggs, Auntie Gin's Theme and
Eight Arms to Hold You.

JUNE

The Beatles are interviewed, the session later appearing on **The Sound of the Stars Interviews (LP)**.

The Beatles are photographed playing with their spaghetti dinners during the Italian part of their European tour.

The Beatles are interviewed, the recording later used as part of the bootleg **ABC Manchester**.

JUN 4   **Beatles For Sale (No. 2) (EP)** is released in the U.K.

JUN 7   The Beatles' two–hour BBC Whit Monday radio show is aired.

JUN 10   1,337 different versions of Beatles' songs by various artists worldwide are reported to have been made.

JUN 12   **The Early Beatles (LP)** reaches its highest position on the *Billboard* album charts: number 43.

Queen Elizabeth includes The Beatles in the birthday honors list, naming them as members of the Most Excellent Order of the British Empire and awardees of the MBE.   PMB–216 (MBC)

JUN 14   Several MBE holders return their awards in protest over The Beatles' being awarded the same honor.

Beatles VI (LP) is released in the U.S.

JUN 15   The *Daily Mirror* reports that two MBEs have been returned by recipients to protest Beatles' award of the honor.

JUN 17   Controversy continues in U.K. over award of MBEs to The Beatles.

JUN 18   John Lennon discusses his book, *A Spaniard in the Works*, on the BBC's "Tonight" television show.

The Beatles leave for a tour of France, Italy and Spain.

Paul McCartney's 23rd birthday.

Peter Carver's "Thursday's Requests" show on Radio Luxembourg plays a recording requested by a fan in Germany for Paul McCartney's birthday.

Two more MBE recipients return their awards.

JUN 20   The Beatles perform at the Palais des Sports in Paris, France, beginning their European tour; the concert is telecast in France.

Paris–TV (ORTF) videotapes The Beatles in concert at the Palais des Sports in Paris.

JUN 21   Another MBE is returned by author Richard Pape.

JUN 22   The Beatles perform at the Palais d'Hiver in Lyons, France, on their European tour.

JUN 24 The Beatles perform at the Velodromo Vigonelli in Milan,
        Italy, on their European tour.
        A Spaniard in the Works by John Lennon is published.
        John Lennon is interviewed on ITV's "Today" television
        show.
JUN 26 **Beatles VI** (LP) enters the *Billboard* album charts at num–
        ber 149, remaining on the charts for 41 weeks during
        which it reaches a high point of number 1.
        The Beatles perform at the Palazzo Degli Sport in Genoa,
        Italy on their European tour. BB23–4 (Jun 25) BCE–55
        (Palazzo Degli Sport) TBA–236 (Palais de Sports)
JUN 27 The Beatles perform at the Adriana Hotel in Rome, Italy,
        on their European tour.
        EMI records Beatles' Adriana Hotel concert in Rome in
        stereo; later, an Italian LP is recalled by EMI (after the
        sale of about 1,000 copies) because release was made
        without consent of The Beatles.
JUN 27 The Beatles tour Rome late in the evening of the 27th and
–28   early morning of the 28th to avoid crowds of fans.
JUN 28 The Beatles leave Rome for Cote d'Azur, and hold a press
        conference at the Hotel Negresco after arrival.
JUN 29 Paul McCartney and George Harrison are entertained aboard
        the yacht of producer Felix Marouani.
JUN 30 The Beatles perform at the Palais des Fetes in Nice, France,
        on their European tour.

SUMMER
   Kansas City/Boys (45) by Pete Best, The Beatles' drummer prior
      to Ringo Starr, is released in the U.S.
   The Byrds' *Mr. Tambourine Man*, blending the influence of Bob
      Dylan's lyrics and George Harrison's 12–string electric guitar
      stylistics, tops the British and American charts.
   Paul McCartney and Jane Asher tour the Tate Gallery in London.

MID–1965
   Peter Brown, manager of a Whitechapel NEMS record shop, leaves
      Liverpool to join Brian Epstein at the London NEMS office.
   Playboy magazine publishes an interview with The Beatles which
      covers controversial subjects.

JULY
   Sid Bernstein makes the second payment – $50,000 – to Brian
      Epstein for The Beatles' upcoming Shea Stadium concert in

August.
An interview with George Harrison by Robin Bean about the making
of "Help!" appears in *Films and Filming* magazine.

JUL 1   The Beatles fly to Madrid, Spain.
          Beatles VI (LP) is certified as a Gold Record by R.I.A.A.
          The Beatles perform in Jerez, Spain.
JUL 2   The Beatles perform at the Monumental Bullring in Madrid,
          Spain, on their European tour. BCE–55 (Plaza de Toros
          Monumental)
JUL 3   The Beatles perform at the Barcelona Bullring in Barcelona,
          Spain, ending their European tour.
          A John Lennon interview about his book, *A Spaniard in the
          Works*, is aired on BBC's "World of Books" radio pro–
          gram.
JUL 4   The Beatles return to London's Heathrow Airport.
JUL 5   *That Means a Lot*, written by Lennon/McCartney, appears
          in the U.S. on a single by P.J. Proby.
JUL 7   Ringo Starr's 25th birthday.
JUL 10   **Beatles VI** (LP) hits number 1 on the *Billboard* album
          charts, remaining there for six weeks.
          Begins a period of three weeks during which no Beatles–
          related material appears on *Billboard* singles charts.
JUL 17   Beatles' performances are aired on "Thank Your Lucky
          Stars" and "Blackpool Night Out."
          An excerpt from the film "Help!" is aired on ABC–TV's
          "Thank Your Lucky Stars."
JUL 19   *Help!/I'm Down* (45) is released in the U.S.
JUL 23   *Help!/I'm Down* (45) is released in the U.K.
JUL 24   Ringo Starr purchases a house in Weybridge.
JUL 28   BBC1 televises a show called "Songwriters," about the
          songs of John Lennon and Paul McCartney.
JUL 29   World premiere of film "Help!" in London, attended by
          Princess Margaret and Lord Snowdon.
JUL 30   UPI distributes a photo of Princess Margaret meeting Paul
          McCartney at the premiere of The Beatles' film "Help!"
JUL 31   *Help!* enters Holland's Radio Veronica Top 40 at number
          4.
          Help! (45) enters the *Billboard* British top twenty singles
          charts, remaining on the charts for ten weeks during
          which it reaches a high point of number 1.
          Help! enters the *Billboard* singles charts at number 110.
          Help! enters the *Melody Maker* singles charts in the U.K.

at number 1, remaining there for four weeks.

AUGUST

George Martin leaves EMI after a fifteen--year association as a salaried employee, forming his own Associated Independent Recordings.

Brian Epstein stays at the New York home of Nat Weiss during the period of the Shea Stadium concert, because Epstein was being plagued by phone calls at his Waldorf Astoria Hotel suite.

Brian Epstein meets Colonel Tom Parker and Elvis Presley in New York just after the Shea Stadium concert and just before The Beatles' departure for California.

I Need You and *You Like Me Too Much*, George Harrison's second and third songs for The Beatles, appear on the LP **Help!**

The Beatles in Help! a novel by Al Hine based on the film and screenplay by Marc Behm, is published.

The introduction of new musical instruments, after *Yesterday*, marks a new stage in development of The Beatles' music.

EARLY AUGUST

It is announced that the next Beatles' film will be based on the book, *A Talent for Loving*, to be shot on location in Mexico or Spain.

You've Got to Hide Your Love Away, written and produced by John Lennon and Paul McCartney (with Paul playing rhythm guitar and George Harrison playing tambourine), is recorded at Fontana studios, London, by The Silkie.

AUG 1   The film "Help!" opens in a theatre in Aldershot, Hamp--shire, England.

The Beatles last live TV appearance for nearly a year on "Blackpool Night Out." PMS--148 ("Big Night Out")

A special plane, hired by Brian Epstein to fly The Beatles from Blackpool to London, carries only Ringo, while John, Paul and George travel back by car.

Songs from The Beatles' performance on ABC--TV's "Blackpool Night Out" are recorded, later to be in--cluded on the bootleg album **Sunday Night at the London Palladium.**

AUG 3   A review of "Help!" in *The Hollywood Reporter* focuses on The Beatles' "grace and humor" as central to their appeal.

The Beatles announce that Subafilms, their film company,

will make a color documentary of the National Jazz Festival at Richmond, England.

AUG 4   *Variety* again notes the Marx Brothers' character of the Beatles' performance in "Help!"

AUG 6   **Help!** (LP) is released in the U.K. IR–42,126 (Aug 13)

John Lennon purchases a bungalow for his Aunt Mimi near Bournemouth, England.

AUG 7   *Help!* enters the *Billboard* Hot 100 charts at number 42, remaining on the charts for thirteen weeks during which it reaches a high point of number 1.

I'm Down enters the *Billboard* singles charts at number 118.

AUG 8   John Lennon and George Harrison attend the Richmond Jazz Festival.

AUG 11   A review of "Help!" from the London *Observer* is reprinted in the Los Angeles *Times*, calling the film "ferociously ephemeral."

AUG 13   The Beatles leave London for their third concert tour of the U.S.

The Beatles arrive at Kennedy International Airport, the plane moving to an isolated area two miles from hun–dreds of fans gathered at the terminal building.

At Beatles' behest, Brian Epstein signs Paddy, Klaus (Voorman) and Gibson (Kemp) to a management con–tract.

Stu Sutcliffe's passport issued August 13, 1960, expires.

Help! (LP) is released in the U.S.

London's *Evening News* reports that each Beatle was in–sured for £1,000,000 before their U.S. tour; London's *Evening Standard* reports a figure of £2,000,000.

The Beatles hold a press conference in the lobby of the Warwick Hotel, New York City.

The Beatles are visited in their suite at the Warwick Hotel by Bob Dylan.

AUG 14   **Help!** (LP) enters the *Melody Maker* album charts at num–ber 1, remaining there for nine weeks, dropping to num–ber 2 for one week, and returning to number 1 for an additional six weeks.

The Beatles are convoyed from the Warwick Hotel to CBS television studios by New York police, who clear busy streets to allow the cars to pass unmolested.

The Beatles record six songs before a live audience for future airing on the "Ed Sullivan Show" at CBS television studios.

An appearance by The Beatles on the British TV show
"Big Night Out" is broadcast in the New York area
during the evening.

AUG 15   The Beatles travel from the Warwick Hotel to a waterfront
heliport by limousine, from the heliport to the World's
Fair by helicopter, and from the World's Fair to Shea
Stadium via Wells Fargo armored van.

John Lennon's British passport issued August 16, 1960
expires.

Jane Asher reportedly confirms wedding plans with Paul
McCartney.

AUG 15   The Beatles perform at New York's Shea Stadium on their
–16   American tour; with 56,000 in the audience, it is the
largest outdoor concert in history to date. Ed Sullivan
introduces The Beatles, who do 12 songs in 30 minutes.
BAB–208 (Aug 23)

AUG 15   The Beatles in concert at New York's Shea Stadium; John
Lennon is robbed on stage by three Cuban gunmen,
according to Mark Shipper's humorous spoof of Beatle
history, *Paperback Writer.*

The documentary, "The Beatles at Shea Stadium," is
filmed.

Songs from The Beatles' Shea Stadium concert are recorded,
later to be included on the following bootleg LPs:
**Cavern Club, Live Performance Shea 15–08–1965, Last
Live Show,** and **Dawn of Our Innocence.**

Teenager Lou O'Neill, Jr. meets with Paul McCartney; they
are photographed together.

The Beatles leave Shea Stadium, again, in an armored Wells
Fargo van.

AUG 16   The Beatles sleep late, record some DJ interviews, and are
visited by The Supremes, The Exciters, The Ronettes,
Del Shannon and Bob Dylan.

AUG 17   The Beatles fly from New York to Toronto by charter
plane.

The Beatles perform at Maple Leaf Stadium in Toronto,
Canada, on their American tour.

AUG 18   A review of "Help!" in the *Motion Picture Herald* proclaims
it "high comedy."

The Beatles fly from Toronto to Atlanta.

The Beatles perform at Atlanta Stadium in Atlanta,
Georgia, on their American tour.

The Beatles fly from Atlanta to Houston, Texas, arriving

at 2:00 a.m. in the morning.

The film "Help!" premieres at the Uptown Theatre in Kansas City.

AUG 19 The Beatles perform two concerts at the Sam Houston Coliseum in Houston, Texas, on their American tour; 25,000 attend each concert.

The Beatles' second show at the Houston Coliseum is re--corded, the songs later appearing on the bootleg LP **Houston**.

AUG 20 The Beatles arrive in Chicago on an early morning flight from Houston.

The Beatles perform in Comiskey Park in Chicago, Illinois, on their American tour.

AUG 21 The Beatles arrive from Chicago at the airport in Minnea--polis in the afternoon, and are spirited away from 4,000 fans waiting for them.

The Beatles hold a press conference which is broadcast live on a local Minneapolis radio station.

The Beatles perform in Minneapolis, Minnesota, before an audience of 30,000, netting themselves $90,000.00 for 35 minutes of show--time. LCP--271 (Metropolitan Stadium, Minneapolis)

The Beatles leave Metropolitan Stadium in Minneapolis in a laundry truck, spending the evening in the Lemington Motor Inn in downtown Minneapolis.

AUG 22 In the early morning hours, the Minneapolis police vice squad pounds on Paul McCartney's apartment door, forcing him to open the door under fear of arrest. His female companion identifies herself as a 21--year--old president of a fan club, who, according to police Inspector Dwyer, didn't look 16.

The Beatles fly from Minneapolis to Portland, Oregon, arriving in the early afternoon. One of the chartered plane's engines catches fire and smokes just before land--ing.

The Beatles are visited in their dressing room by Carl Wilson and Mike Love of The Beach Boys.

The Beatles perform at the Portland Coliseum in Portland, Oregon, on their American tour.

AUG 23 The Beatles arrive in Los Angeles on an early morning flight from Portland; they stay at a rented house in Beverly Hills, 2850 Benedict Canyon.

Help! (LP) is certified as a Gold Record by the R.I.A.A.

New York premiere of film "Help!"

That Means a Lot, written by Lennon/McCartney, appears
in the U.S. on a single by P.J. Proby.

The Beatles begin spending six days in Los Angeles.

AUG 24   During the day, The Beatles are visited by Eleanor Bron
and The Byrds at their Beverly Hills house, surrounded
by fans and police.

Alan Livingstone of Capitol Records holds an early evening
party for The Beatles, attended by many celebrities.

The Beatles watch a private showing of "What's New
Pussycat?" in the late evening; Paul McCartney and
George Harrison miss the end of the film, leaving to
attend a recording session by The Byrds.

Northern Songs Ltd. reports profits of Ł 620,000 for the
year.

AUG 25   Four female fans hire a helicopter to overfly the Beatles'
Beverly Hills house so they can shout down their greet-
ings.

AUG 26   The Beatles continue to sunbathe and swim at their
Beverly Hills retreat; mail and gifts fill two corners of
the main living room.

AUG 27   Elvis Presley invites The Beatles to his Bel Air mansion,
where they socialize and play music together for three
hours. The meeting is not publicized, and Elvis even
denies subsequently that it took place. BB38--22 (Sep)
BU15--4 (Aug 17)

AUG 28   The *Saturday Review* finds the Beatles' performance in
"Help!" more reminiscent of Abbott and Costello than
of the Marx Brothers.

The *New Yorker's* review of "Help!" appears, calling the
screenplay a complex plundering of works by Sax
Rohmer, Edgar Wallace, Rider Haggard and S.J. Perelman.

The Beatles make the two--hour ride from Beverly Hills
to San Diego aboard a bus outfitted with a refrigerator,
wardrobes, and a bathroom with a shower.

The Beatles perform at Balboa Stadium in San Diego,
California, on their American tour.

The Beatles, en route from San Diego back to Los Angeles
on their luxurious bus, are forced to stop at a mortuary
to transfer to limousines when the bus breaks down.

Help! (LP) enters the *Billboard* album charts at number
148, remaining on the charts for 44 weeks during which
it reaches a high point of number 1.

John Lennon and Paul McCartney have reportedly been
insured by Northern Songs Ltd. for £1,000,000, costing
£9,975 in premiums.

AUG 29 Bosley Crowther's review of "Help!" in the New York
Times labels the film "surrealistic slapstick."

Alan Livingstone, President of Capitol Records, presents
The Beatles with a gold record for the **Help!** album at
an afternoon press conference.

The Beatles are driven from the Capitol Tower to the
Hollywood Bowl in an armored truck.

AUG 29 The Beatles perform at the Hollywood Bowl in Los Angeles,
–30   California, on their American tour. BBS--27 (Aug 23)

EMI records The Beatles' two Hollywood Bowl concerts
in stereo, unreleased until 1977.

AUG 30 Before their Hollywood Bowl concert, The Beatles host a
poolside party at their Beverly Hills home for reporters
and disc jockeys.

The Beatles' second Hollywood Bowl concert; it, too, is
recorded.

AUG 31 A review of "Help!" in the Hollywood *Citizen News* refers
to it as a string of TV sight--gag commercials rather than
a motion picture.

George Harrison quits The Beatles on religious grounds after
John Lennon's reference to The Beatles being bigger
than Jesus, according to Mark Shipper's humorous spoof
of Beatle history, *Paperback Writer.*

The Beatles fly from Los Angeles to San Francisco.

The Beatles perform at the Cow Palace in San Francisco,
California, final concert on their American tour.
PMB--218 (San Diego)

Scores of fans at the Cow Palace concert faint in the rush of
the crowd toward the stage.

SEPTEMBER--OCTOBER
The Beatles vacation during this period.

FALL
Brian Epstein and Nat Weiss form Nemperor Artists; Weiss had
earlier assumed management of the group The Cyrkle, of *Red
Rubber Ball* fame.

SEP 1   The *Dallas Morning News* headlines -- "George Harrison
Quits Beatles" -- makes public Harrison's departure from

the group on religious grounds, according to Mark
Shipper's humorous spoof of Beatle history, *Paperback
Writer.*

The Beatles return to London after their third American
tour.

EMI reports that **With The Beatles** (LP) has sold over
1,000,000 copies in England.

SEP 2   A review of "Help!" in the Los Angeles *Herald–Examiner*
proclaims it a box–office success.

Help! (45) is certified as a Gold Record by the R.I.A.A.

SEP 4   *Help!* hits number 1 on the *Billboard* singles charts, re–
maining there for three weeks.

SEP 6   George Martin, Beatles' producer, releases **Help!** (LP) in
the U.S., containing instrumental versions of The
Beatles' songs.

SEP 7   Brian Epstein reportedly signs The Moody Blues to a con–
tract.

SEP 10   *You've Got to Hide Your Love Away*, written by Lennon/
McCartney, appears in the U.K. on a single by The
Silkie; the single is produced by Lennon and McCartney.

SEP 11   **Help!** (LP) hits number 1 on the *Billboard* album charts,
remaining there for nine weeks.

I'm Down reaches its highest position on the *Billboard*
singles charts: number 101.

SEP 12   A filmed Beatles' performance of six songs is aired on the
"Ed Sullivan Show."   BM–120 (Sep 9)   LCP–264
(Sep 9)

Songs from The Beatles' "Ed Sullivan Show" performance
are recorded, later to be included on the bootleg LP
L.S. Bumble Bee.

SEP 13   *Yesterday/Act Naturally* (45) is released in the U.S.

A son -- Zak -- is born to Ringo Starr and wife Maureen,
their first child, at Queen Charlotte's Hospital, Hammer--
smith, London.   BF–41 (Sep 14)   WT14–21 (Dec 12)

SEP 16   *Eight Days a Week* (45) is certified as a Gold Record by
the R.I.A.A.

SEP 17   *That Means a Lot*, written by Lennon/McCartney, appears
on a single in the U.K. by P.J. Proby.

SEP 18   *Yesterday* enters the *Billboard* singles charts at number 106.

Act Naturally enters the *Billboard* singles charts at number
109.

SEP 20   *I Can't Do Without You/Keys to My Heart* (45) by Pete

Best, Beatles' drummer prior to Ringo Starr, is released in the U.S.

You've Got to Hide Your Love Away, written by Lennon/McCartney, appears in the U.S. on a single by The Silkie; the single is produced by Lennon and McCartney.

SEP 25   The *New Republic*'s review of "Help!" notes that any second film effort by The Beatles would suffer by comparison with the first.

Yesterday enters the *Billboard* Hot 100 charts at number 45, remaining on the charts for eleven weeks during which it reaches a high point of number 1.

You've Got to Hide Your Love Away by The Silkie, written by Lennon/McCartney, enters the *Melody Maker* singles charts in the U.K. at number 37.

A weekly cartoon series on The Beatles begins on American television.

Act Naturally enters the *Billboard* Hot 100 charts at number 87, remaining on the charts for seven weeks during which it reaches a high point of number 1.

That Means a Lot by P.J. Proby, written by Lennon/McCartney, enters the *Melody Maker* singles charts in the U.K. at number 46.

OCTOBER

Prince Philip, on tour in Canada with Queen Elizabeth, is quoted as saying that The Beatles were "on the wane."

The Beatles record new material after their tour of 36 U.S. cities, according to Mark Shipper's humorous spoof of Beatle history, *Paperback Writer.*

A cover version of *Yesterday* by Matt Monro, written by Lennon/McCartney, is released in the U.K., later reaching a high point on the British *Billboard* top ten position of number 8.

John's Aunt Mimi moves from Liverpool to a house in Bournemouth which he purchased for her.

EARLY OCTOBER

Paul McCartney returns briefly to Liverpool to visit family and friends.

OCT 1   **Eine Kleine Beatlemusik** (LP), an early presentation of Beatles' songs in classical form, is released in the U.K.

Yesterday hits number 1 on the *Cash Box* and *Billboard* charts.

144

OCT 8   *People Say/I'm Walking* (45), falsely rumored to be a re--
         cording by John Lennon and Paul McCartney, is released
         in the U.K.

OCT 9   John Lennon's birthday.
         Yesterday hits number 1 on the *Billboard* singles charts,
         remaining there for four weeks.
         You've Got to Hide Your Love Away by The Silkie, written by
         Lennon/McCartney, enters the *Billboard* singles charts
         at number 104.

OCT 11   *Boys/Kansas City -- Hey--Hey--Hey--Hey* (45) is released in the
         U.S.
         Do You Want to Know a Secret/Thank You Girl (45) is
         released in the U.S.
         Love Me Do/P.S. I Love You (45) is released in the U.S.
         Please Please Me/From Me to You (45) is released in the
         U.S.
         Roll Over Beethoven/Misery (45) is released in the U.S.
         Twist and Shout/There's a Place (45) is released in the U.S.

OCT 12   The Beatles begin recording tracks for **Rubber Soul** (LP)
         at EMI's St. John's Wood studios, the sessions lasting
         into early November; five songs from the sessions go
         unreleased: *Rubber Soul, Maisy Jones, Baby Jane, If
         You've Got Troubles* and *That Means a Lot.*

OCT 16   *You've Got to Hide Your Love Away* by The Silkie,
         written by Lennon/McCartney, reaches its highest point
         on the *Melody Maker* singles charts: number 24.
         That Means a Lot by P.J. Proby, written by Lennon/
         McCartney, reaches its highest point on the *Melody
         Maker* singles charts: number 25.

OCT 17   *Help!* enters the Polish radio station -- Rozglosnia
         Harcerska -- charts at number 10.

OCT 19   *The Beatles Third Christmas Record* is recorded.

OCT 20   *Yesterday* (45) is certified as a Gold Record by the R.I.A.A.

OCT 22   The Beatles are reported to have declined an invitation to
         appear at the Royal Variety Show.

OCT 23   *Act Naturally* reaches its highest position on the *Billboard*
         singles charts: number 47.

OCT 26   The Beatles are given their MBEs (awarded June 12) in the
         Great Throne Room at Buckingham Palace by the Queen
         of England.

OCT 29   **The Beatle Cracker Suite** (LP), an early presentation of
         Beatles' songs in classical form, is released in the U.K.

OCT 30   *Yesterday* enters Holland's Radio Veronica Top 40 at number 23.

Boys enters the *Billboard* singles charts at number 102, dropping off the following week.

OCT 31   Tickets go on sale for The Beatles' December tour of the U.K.

Ticket to Ride enters the Polish radio station -- Rozglosnia Harcerska -- charts at number 16.

NOV 1   The Beatles record for a Granada TV special on their music, to be aired December 17.

early Nov   *We Can Work It Out* and *Day Tripper* are recorded at the Abbey Road studios.

NOV 12   George Martin, Beatles' producer, releases a single in the U.K. with instrumental versions of *Yesterday* and *Another Girl.*

The Beatles in Italy (LP), consisting of old studio tracks but widely assumed to have been taped during The Beatles' Italian concert tour, is released in Italy. (This is not **The Beatles Live in Italy**, a supposed 1965 recording.)

NOV 13   Brian Epstein is reported to have persuaded Capitol Records to withdraw release of a U.S. single, *Boys/ Kansas City* (45), as unrepresentative of current Beatle music.

NOV 14   *Yesterday* enters the Polish radio station -- Rozglosnia Harcerska -- charts at number 12.

I Need You enters the Polish radio station -- Rozglosnia Harcerska -- charts at number 15.

You've Got to Hide Your Love Away enters the Polish radio station -- Rozglosnia Harcerska -- charts at number 17.

NOV 15   A special edition of *The Beatles Book* monthly goes on sale in the U.K.   WT23-20 (Dec; "Christmas Extra")

NOV 19   George Martin, Beatles' producer, releases **Help!** (LP) in the U.K., containing instrumental versions of Beatles' songs.

NOV 22   **You've Got to Hide Your Love Away** (LP) by The Silkie (produced by Lennon and McCartney) is released in the U.S., containing *You've Got to Hide Your Love Away,* written by Lennon/McCartney.

NOV 25   For two hours after closing to the public, The Beatles purchase Christmas gifts at Harrod's department store in London.

NOV 27   *You've Got to Hide Your Love Away* by The Silkie, written by Lennon/McCartney, reaches its highest position on the *Billboard* singles charts: number 10.

DECEMBER
It is reported that The Beatles have cancelled plans for doing a
third film, "A Kind of Loving," based on the book *A Talent
for Loving*, because they don't want to play the parts of cow--
boys.
Woman, written by Paul McCartney, is recorded at EMI's Abbey
Road studios, London, by Peter and Gordon.
Paul McCartney records an unreleased Christmas record.
Think for Yourself and *If I Needed Someone,* George Harrison's
fourth and fifth songs for The Beatles, appear on the LP
Rubber Soul.

DEC 2   Filmed broadcast of a Beatles' performance on BBC's
           "Top of the Pops," featuring *Day Tripper* and *We Can
           Work It Out.*
           Songs by The Beatles are recorded from the BBC radio
           show "Top of the Pops" later to be included on the
           bootleg LP **On Stage.**
           The Beatles and others, driven by Neil Aspinall in an
           Austin Princess, drive through the night enroute to
           Berwick--on--Tweed, 100 miles from their destination --
           Glasgow.
           George Harrison's rehearsal guitar, a Ⱡ 300 Gretsch Country--
           man, falls off the top of the group's Austin Princess
           enroute to Scotland on their concert tour, and is run
           over at least fourteen times before the pieces are re--
           covered.
DEC 3   The Beatles arrive in Glasgow, Scotland, from Berwick--on--
           Tweed, where they check in at their hotel, The Central.
           A large press conference precedes The Beatles show at the
           Odeon in Glasgow.
           The Beatles are visited in their dressing room at the Odeon
           by Mike Berry of a new pirate radio station, Radio
           Scotland; DJ Berry records an interview with the group
           for broadcast from a ship in the North Sea.
           The Beatles perform at the Odeon in Glasgow, Scotland,
           beginning their last tour of the U.K.   TBA--18 (tour
           begins Dec 17)
           During The Beatles' show at the Odeon in Glasgow, John

147

Lennon's cousin, Stanley, arrives at the stage door but is refused admittance by a security guard; Neil Aspinall finally lets him in to see John.

We Can Work It Out/Day Tripper (45) is released in the U.K.

Rubber Soul (LP) is released in the U.K. BBS–52 (Dec 3, 1963) PMS–150 (Dec 1)

DEC 4   In Glasgow, The Beatles make an early start for Newcastle to beat the morning snow, which is falling fast.

The Beatles perform at City Hall in Newcastle, England, on their last tour of the U.K.

The Beatles appear on "Thank Your Lucky Stars" television program.

DEC 5   The Beatles perform at the Empire in Liverpool, England, on their last tour of the U.K.

Backstage after their Empire concert, two girls meet with The Beatles to discuss their campaign to save The Cavern Club.

DEC 6   **Rubber Soul** (LP) is released in the U.S.

We Can Work It Out/Day Tripper (45) is released in the U.S.

The Beatles' Million Sellers (EP) is released in the U.K. IR–50 (Dec 5)

DEC 7   The Beatles perform at the Ardwick Apollo in Manchester, England, on their last tour of the U.K.

Film producer Walter Shenson meets with The Beatles in Manchester to discuss their next film, scheduled to be a cowboy farce loosely based on *A Talent for Loving*.

DEC 8   The Beatles perform at City Hall in Sheffield, England, on their last tour of the U.K. BB31–14 (Gaumont)

Dec   The Moody Blues and The Beatles eat dinner together at their hotel after their Sheffield concert.

DEC 9   The Beatles perform at the Odeon in Birmingham, England, on their last tour of the U.K.

DEC 10   *A Hard Day's Night/Help!* (45) by Peter Sellers, is released in the U.K.

The Beatles perform at the Odeon in Hammersmith, London, on their last tour of the U.K.

DEC 11   *Day Tripper* enters the *Billboard* singles charts at number 103.

We Can Work It Out enters the *Billboard* singles charts at number 101.

Rubber Soul (LP) enters the *Melody Maker* album charts at number 1, remaining there for 13 weeks.

We Can Work It Out/Day Tripper (45) enters the *Billboard* British top twenty singles charts, remaining on the charts for ten weeks during which it reaches a high point of number 1.

We Can Work It Out/Day Tripper enters the *Melody Maker* singles charts in the U.K. at number 3.

The Beatles perform at the Astoria in Finsbury Park, London, England, on their last tour of the U.K.

BBS--27 (London, Hammersmith Odeon)

DEC 12 The Beatles perform at the Capitol in Cardiff, England, the final concert on their last tour of the U.K.

DEC 15 The Beatles watch the Rediffusion TV show, "Here Come the Pops," between performances; John Lennon ex--presses a desire to perform on the show.

A World Without Love/Nobody I Know (45), recorded by Peter and Gordon, is released in the U.S.

DEC 16 "The Music of Lennon and McCartney" is shown on Granada TV in London area only.

DEC 17 "The Music of Lennon and McCartney," special 50--minute television show on the music of Lennon/McCartney, is broadcast on Granada TV nation--wide.

The Beatles Third Christmas Record is released by the Fan Club.

DEC 18 *We Can Work It Out/Day Tripper* hits number 1 on the *Melody Maker* singles charts, remaining there for four weeks.

Day Tripper enters the *Billboard* Hot 100 charts at number 56, remaining on the charts for ten weeks during which it reaches a high point of number 5.

We Can Work It Out enters the *Billboard* Hot 100 charts at number 36, remaining on the charts for twelve weeks during which it reaches a high point of number 1.

DEC 24 **Rubber Soul** (LP) is certified as a Gold Record by the R.I.A.A.

DEC 25 *We Can Work It Out/Day Tripper* enters Holland's Radio Veronica Top 40 at number 1.

Christ-- George Harrison proposes to Pattie Boyd while driving to
mas Day London.

Paul McCartney reportedly reinterates plans to eventually marry Jane Asher.

149

The Beatles appear on a special "Saturday Club" Christmas show on BBC radio.

Rubber Soul (LP) enters the *Billboard* album charts at number 106.

Christ-
mas
Meat -- The Beatles (LP), featuring the famed "butcher cover," is released, then recalled by Capitol Records after adverse public reaction, according to Mark Shipper's humorous spoof of Beatle history, *Paperback Writer.*

Four copies of **Paul's Christmas Album** are pressed, a special recording made for John, George and Ringo.

DEC 31
That's My Life/The Next Time You Feel Important (45) by Freddie Lennon, John Lennon's father, is released in the U.K.

Well I just had to laugh

A DAY
IN THE
LIFE
The Beatles
Day-By-Day
1966

DURING THIS YEAR . . .

Royalties on albums by The Beatles increase from 6 cents to
39 cents per album as of this year.

Jimmy McCulloch, later a guitarist for Wings, plays with a band
called One in a Million at age 13.

The following singles by The Beatles are released in Australia:
*Nowhere Man/Norwegian Wood, Paperback Writer/Rain, Yellow
Submarine/Eleanor Rigby.*

Linda Eastman has become a determined and practical New York
photographer, specializing in shooting rock stars.

Revolver (LP) is released in Germany by Odeon.

Brian Epstein takes George and Pattie Harrison on a week--long
vacation in the south of France.

The following Beatles' singles were released in Holland: *Michelle/
Girl, Paperback Writer/Rain,* and *Yellow Submarine/
Eleanor Rigby.*

Reappearance of the bootleg album, **This Is the Savage Young
Beatles** (LP), first released in mid--1964.

George Harrison begins to write songs, accumulating a store, some
of which later appear on **All Things Must Pass** (LP).

The Penguin John Lennon, a paperback with both *In His Own Write*
and *A Spaniard in the Works,* is published in the U.S. by Penguin.

Brian Epstein and New York attorney Nat Weiss take a yacht trip
together.

"The Music of Lennon and McCartney" TV special is chosen as
the British entry in the Montreux Festival.

"Little Malcolm and His Struggle Against the Eunuchs," a London
stage play, first appears, later to be the basis of the 1974 Apple
Films production of the same name.

Australian Robert Stigwood joins Brian Epstein's NEMS Enter--
prises.

151

Olivia Trinidad Arias, later George Harrison's second wife, graduates from Hawthorne High School, Hawthorne, California.

Rubber Soul (LP) is released in Italy with a different sleeve from the U.S./U.K. version.

The following singles by The Beatles are released in Italy: *Run for Your Life/Michelle, Paperback Writer/Rain, Eleanor Rigby/ Yellow Submarine, Girl/Nowhere Man.*

Cilla Black tours the U.K., does television shows, works live in cabarets, appears in the pantomime show "Little Red Riding Hood," and makes a film called "Work Is a Four–Letter Word."

The following EPs by The Beatles are released in Australia: **Yesterday, Nowhere Man.**

Murray the K Tells It Like It Is, Baby by Murray Kaufman, with and introduction by George Harrison, is published in the U.S. by Holt, Rinehart & Winston.

Paul McCartney hires George Kelly as his butler, a man later to relate his experiences with Paul and The Beatles in his memoirs.

The Beatles appear in concert at Los Angeles' Dodger Stadium, according to Mark Shipper's humorous spoof of Beatle history, *Paperback Writer.*

The Beatles (EP) is released in France by Odeon.

The Beatles' "break–up" actually begins as, more and more, they start to live apart, cease their touring and their previously communal way of life.

The Beatles Greatest Hits, Vol. 1 & Vol. 2 are released by Parlo– phone in Australia, Singapore, Malaysia and Hong Kong.
    BU26–8 (1967)

Ron Nasty is quoted as having asserted the The Rutles are bigger than God. In the face of fans burning Rutles' albums across America, Nasty claims that a journalist has misquoted him and that he actually said that The Rutles were bigger than "Rod," meaning Rod Stewart, according to the album send–up of The Beatles, **The Rutles.**

EARLY 1966

Brian Epstein, learning of Herb Alpert's interest in The Beatles, hosts a small party at his Belgravia home where The Beatles and wives meet not only Alpert but also The Tijuana Brass.
    BEA3–13 (Apr 1964)

The Beatles' album, **Meat -- The Beatles,** stays on top of the charts around the world, according to Mark Shipper's humorous spoof of Beatle history, *Paperback Writer.*

Photographer Robert Whitaker conducts The Beatles' photo session
which leads to the original "butcher cover" for **Yesterday and
Today** (LP), withdrawn by Capitol soon after release.

JANUARY

The monthly *Beatles Book* reports that a poll of Beatles' fans
overseas reveals *I Want to Hold Your Hand* as their favorite
song, and *Yesterday* their favorite from the **Help!** album.

A cover version of *Michelle* by The Overlanders, written by John
Lennon and Paul McCartney, is released, later reaching a high
point on the British *Billboard* top ten charts of number 1.

George Harrison gets rid of his Aston Martin, which has only 4,000
miles on it, buying a green Ferrari through Brian Epstein's garage;
the monthly *Beatles Book* reports that John Lennon's Ferrari,
with only 1,000 miles on the odometer, is also up for sale. John,
however, will keep his black Rolls Royce.

Love's Just a Broken Heart/Yesterday (45) by Cilla Black, managed
by Brian Epstein, is released in the U.K.

The monthly *Beatles Book* reveals that The Beatles had originally
preferred *We Can Work It Out* as the "A" side of their December
1965 single, but others preferred *Day Tripper*. The record was
released with promotional effort for the record as a "double–A"
sider.

JAN 1   **Rubber Soul** (LP) enters the *Billboard* Hot 100 album
charts, remaining on the charts for 49 weeks during
which it reaches a high point of number 1.
A Paul McCartney *Melody Maker* interview appears.

JAN 6   *We Can Work It Out* (45) is certified as a Gold Record by
the R.I.A.A.

JAN 8   **Rubber Soul** (LP) hits number 1 on the *Billboard* album
charts, remaining there for six weeks.
We Can Work It Out hits number 1 on the *Billboard* singles
charts, remaining there for three out of the next four
weeks.

JAN 10   *Woman*, written by Paul McCartney, appears in the U.S. on
a single by Peter and Gordon.

JAN 21   George Harrison marries Patricia Anne Boyd at the Epsom
Register Office, Surrey; Paul McCartney is the only
Beatle in attendance.

JAN 22   *Day Tripper* reaches its highest position on the *Billboard* singles charts: number 5.

JAN 23   *Day Tripper* enters the Polish radio station -- Rozglosnia Harcerska -- charts at number 17.

JAN 31   *A Hard Day's Night/Help!* (45) by Peter Sellers is released in the U.S.

FEBRUARY

The monthly *Beatles Book* indicates that John Lennon has amassed a collection of amplifiers, guitars, record players and juke boxes in a special music room in his London home.

The Beatles announce a late summer tour of the U.S. and a possible visit to Japan.

The Lennons and Starrs vacation during the month, Paul McCartney is seen frequently in London clubs, George Harrison and Pattie honeymoon in Barbados, West Indies.

Rubber Soul (LP) is on top of the charts, **Help!** (LP) is still on the charts, as is *We Can Work It Out/Day Tripper* (45).

EARLY FEBRUARY

Scheduled time for the completion of construction of a home Paul McCartney is having built in London.

FEB 4   The Beatles reportedly receive three R.I.A.A. Gold Records for singles released in the U.S.

FEB 6   *Michelle* enters the Polish radio station – Rozglosnia Harcerska -- charts at number 10.

FEB 11   *Woman*, written by Paul McCartney, appears in the U.S. on a single by Peter and Gordon.

FEB 12   *Michelle* by The Beatles enters Holland's Radio Veronica Top 40 charts at number 1.

Woman, by Peter and Gordon, written by Lennon/McCartney, enters the *Billboard* singles charts at num-- ber 83.

FEB 13   *Girl* enters the Polish radio station (Rozglosnia Harcerska) charts at number 18.

mid--Feb *That's My Life/The Next Time You Feel Important* (45) by Freddie Lennon, John Lennon's father, is released in the U.S.

FEB 21   *Nowhere Man/What Goes On* (45) is released in the U.S.
IR--126 (Feb 7)   PMB--220 (Feb 7)

FEB 25   George Harrison's 23rd birthday.

FEB 26   *Woman* by Peter and Gordon, written by Paul McCartney,

enters the *Melody Maker* singles charts at number 47.
FEB 28   Liverpool's Cavern Club closes with debts of Ł 10,000;
police must break in through barricades erected by
Beatle fans inside the club who resist the closing, The
Hideaways playing as a backdrop to all the chaos.

MARCH
Paul McCartney's London Home, unfinished when expected in late
December 1965, will reportedly be ready this month.
"The Beatles at Shea Stadium" is broadcast in the U.S. on ABC--
TV.
It is announced that The Beatles will tour the U.S., Germany and
Japan in the summer.
Alfie/Night Time Is Here (45) by Cilla Black, managed by Brian
Epstein, is released in the U.K.
A special double issue of the monthly *Beatles Book* is published.

EARLY--MID--MARCH
The Beatles are scheduled to record songs for their next film at
EMI studios, London; the songs are expected to have a country--
and--western flavor to reflect the "cowboy" slant of the film.

MAR 1   "Beatles at Shea Stadium" film is broadcast on BBC
television in color.
MAR 4   **Yesterday** (EP) is released in the U.K.
A John Lennon interview with Maureen Cleave is published
in London's *Evening Standard,* first appearance of his
contention that The Beatles are more popular than
Jesus.   ATC--27 (Summer)   BF--57 (Feb)   BU11--11
(May)
MAR 5   *Nowhere Man* enters the *Billboard* singles charts at number
25, remaining on the charts for nine weeks during which
it reaches a high point of number 3.
What Goes On enters the *Billboard* singles charts at number
118, remaining on the charts for two weeks during which
it reaches a high point of number 81.
MAR 7   Phil Spector produces Tina Turner's version of *River Deep,*
Mountain High; when later released in the U.S. as part
of an album, a sticker on the cover features an accolade
by George Harrison about the song.
Woman (LP) by Peter and Gordon appears; it includes
Woman, written by Paul McCartney, a song credited on
the album to "Bernard Webb."

MAR 12   *What Goes On* enters the *Billboard* Hot 100 charts at number 89.

MAR 19   *What Goes On* reaches its highest position on the *Billboard* singles charts: number 81.

MAR 22   Paul McCartney and Jane Asher reportedly vacation at Klosters, a skiing resort in Switzerland; he ferries his own car across the channel in order to travel inconspicuously.

MAR 25   Paul McCartney interview in London's *Evening Star* is published.

MAR 26   Paul McCartney and his father watch the latter's racehorse win the Hylton Plate at Aintree at odds of 20 to 1.

          Nowhere Man reaches its highest position on the *Billboard* singles charts: number 3.

          Woman by Peter and Gordon, written by Paul McCartney, reaches its highest point on the *Melody Maker* singles charts: number 21.

LATE MARCH

The Beatles begin recording sessions for a new single and LP later than originally planned.

LATE MARCH--EARLY APRIL

Paul McCartney confirms that he is "Bernard Webb," composer of *Woman*, recorded by Peter and Gordon; he had concealed the fact to see if the song would be successful if not identified as a Lennon/McCartney tune. It was.

SPRING

"Sound of the Stars" interview is recorded.

The Beatles make more far--reaching changes in the content and arrangement of their music.

APRIL

Paul McCartney has the corner of one of his front teeth chipped off in an accident.

The Beatles hold marathon press interviews and photographic sessions on a day set aside for this at a studio in Chelsea.

Completion of the first authorized biography of The Beatles by Hunter Davies is reported; publication is set for October.

Most of the month is spent in songwriting and recording sessions.

The Beatles are interviewed, the session later appearing on the bootleg recording **Beatles Interview**.

Month originally scheduled for The Beatles to begin filming their
third motion picture based on the book *A Talent for Loving.*

EARLY APRIL
A special repeat issue of the *Beatles Book* with all the best pictures
from preceding monthly issues is published, in response to re--
quests for copies of earlier issues now out--of--print.

EARLY APRIL--MID--JUNE
*Taxman, Eleanor Rigby, Love You To, Here, There and Every--
where, Yellow Submarine, She Said, She Said, Good Day Sun--
shine, For No One, I Want to Tell You, Got to Get You Into
My Life,* and *Tomorrow Never Knows* are recorded at the Abbey
Road studios.

APR 1   *Nowhere Man* (45) is certified as a Gold Record by the
          R.I.A.A. BEA3-13 (Mar)
APR 2   *Woman* by Peter and Gordon, written by Lennon/McCart--
          ney, reaches its highest position on the *Billboard* singles
          charts: number 14.
APR 5   Lennon and McCartney reportedly sell more shares in
          Northern Songs Ltd., bringing each of them Ł 146,000.
APR 6   The Beatles write and record a song called *The Void*, which
          later appears on **Revolver** (LP) as *Tomorrow Never
          Knows*, at EMI's Abbey Road studios.
APR 11   Rumored date of a trip by The Beatles to Memphis,
          Tennessee, for recording sessions with touted American
          engineers and sound technicians.
APR 13   *Paperback Writer* is recorded at the Abbey Road studios.
          BB35--2 (Apr 13--14) BEA3--13 (Apr 13--14)
APR 16   **Woman** (LP) by Peter and Gordon, with the title song
          written by Paul McCartney, enters the *Billboard* album
          charts at number 133.
APR 18   Liverpool's Cavern Club is sold by a court receiver after
          bankruptcy.
APR 20   The vocals for *Eleanor Rigby* are recorded. BD--12 (Apr
          20--27)
APR 27   The strings track for *Eleanor Rigby* is recorded.

LATE APRIL
Rain is recorded.

157

LATE APRIL--EARLY MAY
> *I'm Only Sleeping, Dr. Robert* and *And Your Bird Can Sing* are recorded at EMI's Abbey Road studios.

MAY
> Paul McCartney and Neil Aspinall meet with Bob Dylan at Dolly's Club in London soon after Dylan arrives from the U.S.; also present are Keith Richard and Brian Jones of The Rolling Stones. Afterward, they retire to Dylan's room at the Mayfair Hotel.
> **Cilla Sings a Rainbow** (LP) by Cilla Black, managed by Brian Epstein, is released in the U.K.
> The Beatles make the promotional film--clips for their new songs *Paperback Writer* and *Rain.*
> The monthly *Beatles Book* reports that Ringo Starr's home in Surrey has been completed by Ringo's own company, Bricky Builders. PMS--157 (indicates Brickey Building Co. began Sep 24)
> *Don't Answer Me/The Right One Is Left* (45) by Cilla Black, managed by Brian Epstein, is released in the U.K.

MAY 1   The Beatles appear for the last time in concert in the U.K. at the *New Musical Express* Poll Winner's Show, Empire Pool, Wembley.

MAY 7   Begins a month--long period during which no Beatle--related records appear on the *Billboard* singles charts.

MAY 14   *Melody Maker* reports that The Beatles have sold over 1,000,000 records in Denmark.

MAY 19   The Beatles film performances at EMI studios and Chis--
  --20   wick House, London, which are aired on "Top of the Pops" (June 9) in the U.K. and the "Ed Sullivan Show" (June 5) in the U.S.

MAY 21   **Bad Boy** (EP) enters Holland's Radio Veronica Top 40 charts at number 40.

MAY 30   *Paperback Writer/Rain* (45) is released in the U.S. (BIR--120 (May 23)   PMB--221 (May 23)

JUNE
> George Harrison meets Ravi Shankar for the first time at George's home in Esher.
> Ravi Shankar and his tabla player, Alla Rakha, return to George Harrison's home in Esher for the second time to give a private performance for The Beatles and some friends.
> John Lennon is reported to own three cars -- a black Mini--Cooper, a black Rolls Royce, and a black Ferrari; George Harrison has a

, black Mini–Cooper and a green Ferrari; Paul McCartney a green Mini–Cooper and a blue Aston Martin; and Ringo Starr a maroon Mini–Cooper, a maroon Facel Vega, and a Rolls Royce currently up for sale.

Brian Epstein organizes Nemperor Artists in the U.S., to handle NEMS interests in America.

A Tony Barrow interview discussing the "butcher cover" of the LP **Yesterday and Today** is recorded, later to be included on the bootleg LP **Some Other Guy**.

JUN 3   The "butcher cover" photo (original cover of the U.S. album **Yesterday and Today** is used in an ad in *New Musical Express* for *Paperback Writer* (45).

JUN 4   The Beatles appear on the BBC's "Saturday Club" radio program.

JUN 5   Promotional film clip of The Beatles performing *Paperback Writer* and *Rain* is shown on the "Ed Sullivan Show" in the U.S.

The Beatles are filmed in London for another "Ed Sullivan Show" broadcast; the interview later appears on the bootleg recordings **Supertracks Vol. 2** and **ABC Man–chester**.

JUN 7–   Three versions of *Yellow Submarine* are recorded at EMI's
10   Abbey Road studios, London.

JUN 9   A Beatles' appearance is aired on the BBC's "Top of the Pops" television show: filmclips of the group singing *Paperback Writer* and *Rain.*

JUN 10 *Paperback Writer/Rain* (45) is released in the U.K.

JUN 11 A color photo from The Beatles' photo session with Robert Whitaker for the original "butcher cover" for **Yesterday and Today** (LP) appears on the cover of *Disc* magazine.

Paul McCartney interview with *Disc and Music Echo.*

Woman (LP) by Peter and Gordon, with the title song written by Paul McCartney, reaches its highest position on the *Billboard* album charts: number 60.

Paperback Writer enters the *Billboard* singles charts for ten weeks during which it reaches a high point of number 1.

Rain enters the *Billboard* singles charts at number 72, re-- maining on the charts for seven weeks during which it reaches a high point of number 23.

JUN 15 **Yesterday and Today** (LP) is released in the U.S. with the "butcher cover."

Jun   Capitol Records recalls the "butcher cover" version of the

U.S. LP **Yesterday and Today.**

JUN 16   Reports of the withdrawal of the "butcher cover" of the
U.S. version of **Yesterday and Today** (LP) appear in the
U.K.

Martha, Paul McCartney's favorite sheepdog, is born in High
Wycombe; she is registered as "Loakes Park Winter--
stale."

The Beatles appear live on BBC--TV's "Top of the Pops."

Songs from The Beatles' performance on "Top of the Pops"
are recorded, later to appear on the bootleg LP **Rock
'n' Roll.**

JUN 17   Paul McCartney reportedly purchases a 183--acre farm in
Kintyre, Scotland.

Woman, written by Paul McCartney, appears in the U.K.
on the album **Peter and Gordon.**

JUN 18   The Beatles appear on ABC's "Thank Your Lucky Stars"
television show in the U.K.

Paperback Writer enters the *Billboard* British top twenty
singles charts, remaining on the charts for seven weeks
during which it reaches a high point of number 1.

Paperback Writer enters the *Melody Maker* singles charts at
number 1, remaining there for four weeks.

JUN 20   **Yesterday and Today** (LP) is re--released in the U.S., this
time without the famous "butcher cover."   ATN--54
(lists 20th as original release date)

JUN 22   The Beatles attend opening night of Sibylla's discotheque
in London; the club is partially financed by George
Harrison.

JUN 23   The Beatles leave London for Munich, Germany, beginning
what is to be their last world tour.

Following their arrival at Munich Airport, Tony Barrow
has The Beatles and Brian Epstein driven to the Bayer--
ischer Hof Hotel in a white Mercedes; they quickly
occupy their suite on the fifth floor.

On their way down from their suite to attend a press con--
ference, The Beatles are stuck for ten minutes between
floors as the elevator jams.

At the press conference, The Beatles are presented with an
award by *Bravo Magazine*, organizers of the tour.

The Beatles spend the evening in their hotel.

JUN 24   The Beatles awake around noon, and spend the afternoon
practicing for their performance at the Circus Krone.

The Beatles' last world tour begins in Munich, Germany, at

the Circus Krone. BB34--29 (Kroner) PMS--154 (Kroner)

German television, ZDR, videotapes The Beatles in concert at the Circus Krone in Munich, Germany.

JUN 25 Seven white Mercedes take The Beatles' party to the rail-- way station in the early morning for the trip to Hamburg.

Paperback Writer enters Holland's Radio Veronica Top 40 charts at number 4.

The Beatles travel to Hamburg on a special train, used by Queen Elizabeth the year before; they have their own suite of rooms – a dining area, lounge, four bedrooms and bathrooms.

Paperback Writer hits number 1 on the *Billboard* singles charts, drops to 2 the following week, and then returns to first position for a week.

En route to Hamburg, The Beatles' train stops in Essen around 4:30 p.m., for their performance at the Gruge-- halle.

Film of Beatles performing *Paperback Writer* and *Rain* is aired in the U.K. on "Thank Your Lucky Stars" TV show.

The Beatles perform at the Grugahalle in Essen, Germany, on their last world tour. BB37--9 (Grugehalle) BCE-- 62 (Grugahalle) BU5--18 (Gruga Halle)

The Beatles have a meal in their dressing room and hold a press conference between shows at the Grugahalle in Essen.

JUN 25 The Beatles arrive back at the railway station at 12:30
--26 a.m., having waited at the Grugahalle for the crowds to disperse.

JUN 26 The Beatles' train arrives in Hamburg around 6:00 a.m.; they are quickly driven off to the Schloss Hotel in Tremsbuttel, thirty miles from Hamburg.

The Beatles sleep in until one--thirty; they appear on the balcony of their suite to satisfy a crowd of several hundred fans.

John Lennon visits Astrid Kirschner, Stu Sutcliffe's former fiance, and she gives him several letters written by Sutcliffe before his death in Hamburg.

Paul McCartney takes an old girlfriend to visit the Indra and the Star Club in Hamburg's Reeperbahn; together they also see Doctor Bernstein, The Beatles' doctor during their Hamburg period.

The Beatles perform at the Ernst Merck Halle in Hamburg,
Germany, for the first time in three years, as part of
their last world tour.

Songs by The Beatles from their Hamburg concert are
illegally recorded, later to be included on the bootleg
LPs **Munich at Least** and **The Tour Album (Third
Amendment)**.

Backstage at the Merck Halle, The Beatles are reunited
with many old friends from their early days in Hamburg,
including Bert Kaempfert.

After two shows and a press conference, The Beatles re–
turn to their hotel for a quiet evening with a few old
friends.

JUN 27 The Beatles leave Hamburg, Germany, on their flight to
Tokyo.

The Beatles are forced to land in Anchorage, Alaska, en
route to Japan, because of a typhoon warning.

Jun 30– The Beatles perform at the Martial Arts Hall in Tokyo,
Jul 2 Japan, on their last world tour. TBA–238 (Jun 30–
Jul 1)

JUNE–JULY

The Beatles tour the Far East.

MID--1966

George Harrison records *Pink Litmus Paper Shirt* and John Lennon
sings lead vocal on *Colliding Circles*, both unreleased. RO--18
(Sep)

Best of The Beatles (LP) by Pete Best, Beatles' drummer prior to
Ringo Starr, is released in the U.S.

The Beatles voice a good number of outlandish and controversial
opinions by mid--year.

SUMMER

Billy J. Kramer parts company with The Dakotas.

JULY

Got to Get You into My Life, written by John Lennon and Paul
McCartney, is recorded at EMI's Abbey Road studios, London,
by Cliff Bennett and The Rebel Rousers.

JUL 1 The Beatles perform at the Martial Arts Hall in Tokyo, Japan. LCP--271 (Budo Kan Hall)

Songs from The Beatles concert in the Martial Arts Hall are illegally recorded, later to be included on the bootleg LP **The Great Take--Over.**

Japan--TV videotapes The Beatles in concert at the Martial Arts Hall, Tokyo, in color.

JUL 2 The Beatles perform at the Martial Arts Hall in Tokyo, Japan, on their last world tour.

JUL 3 The Beatles arrive in Manila, Philippines, greeted by a crowd of 50,000.

JUL 4 The Beatles perform in Araneta Coliseum in Manila, the Philippines, to a crowd of 100,000, the final concert on their last world tour. BBS--27 (Areneta) BCE--62 Aranesa) OBF--8 (National Football Stadium)

JUL 5 **The Best of Peter and Gordon** (LP) is released in the U.S.; it includes *A World Without Love, I Don't Want to See You Again*, and *Woman.* BU14--14 (May)

The Beatles' party leaves Manila for London on KLM flight 862, stopping over in New Delhi.

JUL 6 The Beatles begin three days of rest in New Delhi, India.

JUL 8 **Yesterday and Today** (LP) is certified as a Gold Record by the R.I.A.A.

The Beatles return to London, vowing never to return to the Philippines.

Nowhere Man (EP) is released in the U.K.

JUL 9 **Yesterday and Today** (LP) enters the *Billboard* album charts at number 120, remaining on the charts for 31 weeks during which it reaches a high point of number 1.

Rain reaches its highest position on the *Billboard* singles charts: number 23.

JUL 12 Lennon/McCartney win three Ivor Novello Awards: *We Can Work It Out* (top selling single of 1965); *Yesterday* (most outstanding song of the year); *Help!* (second best selling single of the year).

JUL 14 *Paperback Writer* (45) is certified as a Gold Record by the R.I.A.A.

late Jul The decision is made to release the single *Yellow Sub--marine/Eleanor Rigby* (45) in the U.K. in about two weeks; it had previously only been slated for U.S. release.

JUL 23 The Cavern Club re--opens in Liverpool; Prime Minister Harold Wilson attends, and The Beatles send a wire.

JUL 29 The Beatles reportedly reject an offer to tour South Africa.

JUL 30 **Yesterday and Today** (LP) hits number 1 on the *Billboard* album charts, remaining there for five weeks.

The Best of Peter and Gordon (LP) by Peter and Gordon, featuring three songs by Lennon/McCartney, enters the *Billboard* album charts at number 130.

JUL 31 A bonfire of Beatle records in Birmingham, Alabama, be-- gins U.S. reaction to John Lennon's statement that The Beatles are more popular than Jesus.

AUGUST

The *Datebook*, an American teenage magazine, prints John Lennon's comments on Christianity out of context.

Brian Epstein arrives in New York to help John Lennon explain his comments about The Beatles being bigger than Jesus.

Cilla's Hits (EP) by Cilla Black, managed by Brian Epstein, is re-- leased in the U.K.

Yesterday and Today (LP) occupies *Billboard*'s number 1 album slot despite the furor over John Lennon's remarks about the relative popularity of Jesus and The Beatles.

A cover version of *Got to Get You into My Live* by Cliff Bennett, written by John Lennon and Paul McCartney, is released in the U.K., later reaching a high point on the British *Billboard* top ten charts of number 6.

"Beatles Views 1966 by Ken Douglas" is recorded, released on the LP **BV 1966. RO--17 (Beatles Views)**

Taxman, I Want to Tell You, and *Love You To,* George Harrison's sixth, seventh and eighth songs for The Beatles, appear on the LP **Revolver.**

The Beatles begin serious experimentation in their music with the last track of **Revolver** (LP) and the whole of the **Sgt. Pepper** album.

Film of Beatles performing *Paperback Writer* and *Rain* is aired on the "Ed Sullivan Show."

The government of South Africa bans the playing of The Beatles' music because of John Lennon's remarks about the relative popularity of Christ and The Beatles; the ban lasts five years, until The Beatles break--up in 1970, when Paul, George and Ringo can once again be heard solo in South Africa – but not John.

The Beatles tour 34 American cities, according to Mark Shipper's humorous spoof of Beatle history, *Paperback Writer.*

AUG 4   Beatle records are banned from broadcast at radio stations
           across the U.S. due to Lennon's remarks.
AUG 5   *That Means a Lot*, written by Lennon/McCartney is released
           in the U.K. on the EP **P.J.'s Hits**, by P.J. Proby.
           Revolver (LP) is released in the U.K.
           Got to Get You into My Life, written by Lennon/McCart–
           ney, appears in the U.K. on a single by Cliff Bennett
           and The Rebel Rousers; the record is produced by Paul
           McCartney.
           Yellow Submarine/Eleanor Rigby (45) is released in the
           U.K. BIR–58 (Aug 8) LCP–274 (Aug 8)
AUG 6   A total of 30 U.S. radio stations have reportedly banned
           Beatle records.
           Paul McCartney appears on the BBC's "David Frost at the
           Phonograph" radio program.
AUG 8   **Revolver** (LP) is released in the U.S.
           Yellow Submarine/Eleanor Rigby (45) is released in the
           U.S.
AUG 11   The Beatles leave for the U.S. on what is to be their last
           American tour.
AUG 12   The Beatles arrive in Chicago and, at a news conference,
           John Lennon apologizes for his statement about the
           popularity of The Beatles versus the popularity of Jesus.
             GUB–62 (Aug 11)
           The Beatles perform at the International Amphitheater
           in Chicago, Illinois, beginning their last American tour.
             BIR–57 (Aug 13)
           The Beatles are filmed in concert at Chicago's International
           Amphitheatre.
AUG 13   *Yellow Submarine/Eleanor Rigby* enters the *Billboard*
           British top twenty singles charts, remaining on the charts
           for eight weeks during which it reaches a high point of
           number 1.
           Yellow Submarine/Eleanor Rigby enters the *Melody Maker*
           singles charts in the U.K. at number 4.
           Revolver (LP) enters the *Melody Maker* album charts at
           number 1, remaining there for nine weeks.
           The Beatles perform at Olympia Stadium in Detroit,
           Michigan, on their last American tour. BBS–27
             (Olympic) LCP–272 (Olympic)
           A public bonfire of Beatle records is sponsored by radio

station KLUE, Longview, Texas, in protest over John
Lennon's remarks about Jesus.

AUG 14 Radio station KLUE, Longview, Texas, is knocked off the
air when a bolt of lightning strikes their broadcast
tower, ruining electronic equipment and knocking the
news director unconscious.

The Beatles perform at the Municipal Stadium in Cleveland,
Ohio, on their last American tour.

I Feel Fine is illegally recorded at The Beatles' Cleveland
concert, later to appear on the LP **BV 1966**.

mid–Aug The Beatles tape an NBC Special TV show, the "Lenny
Bruce Variety Hour," never released due to Bruce's
death, according to Mark Shipper's humorous spoof of
Beatle history, *Paperback Writer*.

AUG 15 **This Is Where It Started** (LP), by Tony Sheridan and The
Beatles, is released in the U.S.

The Beatles perform at Washington Stadium in Washington,
D.C., on their last American tour.

The Beatles are filmed in concert at Washington Stadium,
Washington, D.C.

AUG 16 The Beatles perform at Philadelphia Stadium in Phila–
delphia, Pennsylvania, on their last American tour.

AUG 17 John Lennon, at a Toronto press conference, expresses his
encouragement for young Americans who wish to come
to Canada instead of being drafted to fight in Viet Nam.

The Beatles perform at the Maple Leaf Gardens in Toronto,
Canada, on their last American tour.

AUG 18 The Beatles perform at the Suffolk Downs Racetrack in
Boston, Massachusetts, on their last American tour.

AUG 19 The Beatles perform at the Memphis Coliseum in Memphis,
Tennessee, on their last American tour.

As a result of John Lennon's remarks about Jesus Christ,
six Ku Klux Klansmen picket The Beatles' concert at
the Memphis Coliseum; debris is hurled on stage from
the audience and a firecracker explodes.

AUG 20 *Yellow Submarine/Eleanor Rigby* (45) enters Holland's Radio
Veronica Top 40 charts at number 5.

Yellow Submarine enters the *Billboard* singles charts at
number 52, remaining on the charts for nine weeks
during which it reaches a high point of number 2.

Eleanor Rigby enters the *Billboard* singles charts at num–
ber 101, remaining on the charts for nine weeks during
which it reaches a high point of number 11.

Yellow Submarine/Eleanor Rigby (45) hits number 1 on the
Melody Maker singles charts, remaining there for three
weeks.

Got to Get You into My Life by Cliff Bennett and The
Rebel Rousers, written by Lennon/McCartney, enters
the *Melody Maker* singles charts at number 43.

The Beatles perform at Crosley Field in Cincinnati, Ohio,
on their last American tour.

AUG 21   The Beatles perform at Busch Stadium in St. Louis,
Missouri, on their last American tour.

AUG 22   **Revolver** (LP) is certified as a Gold Record by the R.I.A.A.

AUG 23   Before the Shea Stadium concert, The Beatles are pre--
sented with a large cake by the management. Upon
learning that the cake did *not* contain a scantily--clad
woman, John Lennon reportedly said: "We don't want
any of your fucking cake."

AUG 23   The Beatles perform at New York's Shea Stadium on their
--24   last American tour.

AUG 23   The crowd reaction at The Beatles' Shea Stadium concert
is recorded, later to be released as an LP called **Beatles
Blast at Stadium Described by Erupting Fans**, by *Audio
Journal.*

AUG 25   The Beatles perform at the Seattle Coliseum in Seattle,
Washington, on their last American tour.

Ringo Starr hides in a cleaning closet at the Edgewater
Inn, Seattle, to escape fans who have stormed the
hotel's hallways, randomly knocking on doors in search
of The Beatles.

AUG 26   Paul McCartney denies that he and Jane Asher will wed
while in Los Angeles.

AUG 27   *Eleanor Rigby* enters the *Billboard* Hot 100 charts at
number 65.

AUG 28   The Beatles perform at Dodger Stadium in Los Angeles,
California, on their last American tour. BB34--29
(Dodge Stadium) JLS--132 (Dodge Stadium)
PMS--157 (Dodge Stadium)

AUG 29   The Beatles' last live concert in held in San Francisco's
Candlestick Park, ending all touring by the group.

The Beatles' last concert is filmed and recorded by Beatles'
press officer Tony Barrow; the performance is not re--
leased.

Songs from The Beatles' Candlestick Park performance are
recorded, later to be illegally included on the bootleg

LP **Live at San Francisco Candlestick Park**.
Got to Get You into My Life, written by Lennon/McCart–
ney, appears in the U.S. on a single by Cliff Bennett
and The Rebel Rousers; the record is produced by Paul
McCartney.

late Aug   Brian Epstein's briefcase, containing pills and compromising
correspondence, is stolen from his room at a Beverly
Hills hotel; a ransom note threatening exposure leads
police to a former boyfriend of Epstein's, but Epstein
refuses to press charges.

AUG 30   The Beatles leave for London.

AUG 31   The Beatles return to London.

SEPTEMBER

Yoko Ono arrives in England to attend a symposium at London's
Institute of Contemporary Arts.

From Head to Toe, with Paul McCartney playing tambourine, is
recorded by The Escourts.

Brian Epstein takes an overdose of pills in an attempt to commit
suicide; quick hospitalization saves his life.

The monthly *Beatles Book* reports that nearly a dozen cover
versions of songs from **Revolver** (LP) have been released by
other recording artists in the U.K.

SEPTEMBER–OCTOBER

John Lennon cuts his hair off for his role in "How I Won the War."

"How I Won the War," featuring John Lennon, is filmed in Ger–
many and Spain, beginning near Celle, north Germany.

SEP 1   "Action for Crippled Children" charity reportedly receives
a Christmas card design donated by John Lennon.

SEP 3   John Lennon flies to Germany to begin filming "How I
Won the War."

Revolver (LP) enters the *Billboard* album charts at number
45, remaining on the charts for 77 weeks during which
it reaches a high point of number 1.

SEP 10   **Revolver** (LP) hits number 1 on the *Billboard* album charts,
remaining there for six weeks.

The Best of Peter and Gordon (LP) by Peter and Gordon,
featuring three songs written by Lennon/McCartney,
reaches its highest position on the *Billboard* album

charts: number 72.

SEP 12   *Yellow Submarine* (45) is certified as a Gold Record by the R.I.A.A.

SEP 17   *Yellow Submarine* reaches its highest position on the *Bill--board* singles charts: number 2.

Got to Get You into My Life by Cliff Bennett and The Rebel Rousers, written by Lennon/McCartney, reaches its highest point on the *Melody Maker* singles charts: number 6.

SEP 19   A *Sunday Times* interview with Paul McCartney appears. John Lennon flies to Spain to play Gripweed in the film "How I Won the War."

SEP 24   *Eleanor Rigby* reaches its highest position on the *Billboard* singles charts: number 11.

OCTOBER

George and Pattie Harrison vacation in Bombay, India, George studying Indian music and taking sitar lessons from Ravi Shankar. BAB--227,228 (Sep) PMS--157 (Sep 20) TB--227, 228 (Sep)

Brian Epstein takes a trip to the U.S.

A Fool Am I/For No--One (45) by Cilla Black, managed by Brian Epstein, is released in the U.K.

Another segment of Neil Aspinall's article "The Beatles and Me," appears in *16 Magazine.*

Ringo Starr vacations in Spain.

OCT 6   *Yellow Submarine* enters the Polish radio station (Roz--glosnia Harcerska) charts at number 12.

Eleanor Rigby enters the Polish radio station (Rozglosnia Harcerska) charts at number 16.

Taxman enters the Polish radio station (Rozglosnia Harcerska) charts at number 20.

OCT 9   The last Phil Spector single is released on the Philles label, *I Can Hear Music*, by The Ronettes.

OCT 13   Denny Laine leaves The Moody Blues.

OCT 14   *New Musical Express* reports on Paul McCartney's role in writing the musical score for the film later called "The Family Way."

OCT 17   **The Amazing Beatles and Other Great English Group Sounds** (LP) is released in the U.S. TBD--8 (1964)

OCT 22   Begins a three--and--one--half month period during which no Beatle–related recording appears on the *Billboard* singles charts.

OCT 24   Cardinal Cushing, Archbishop of Boston, agrees that The Beatles are better known throughout the world than Jesus.

LATE OCTOBER
George and Pattie Harrison return to England after five weeks in India.

NOVEMBER
British newspapers carry stories that Paul McCartney was involved in a car accident late one night after leaving Abbey Road studios, the germinus for the "Paul Is Dead" story.

Brian Epstein begins to deny rumors of a Beatles' break--up, stemming from the cessation of group touring and the pursuit of personal interests by group members.

Paul McCartney composes soundtrack music for "The Family Way" film.

The Beatles do not perform live from this point until February 9, 1967, adding fuel to rumors that Paul McCartney's double is being trained to take his place in The Beatles.

Pantomime: Everywhere Is Christmas and *Please Don't Bring That Banjo Back* are recorded by The Beatles.

Recording sessions begin which result in the single *Penny Lane/ Strawberry Fields Forever* and **Sgt. Pepper's Lonely Hearts Club Band** (LP).

John Lennon meets Yoko Ono at the Indica Gallery, London, preview of her art exhibition.

After completing his score for "The Family Way," Paul McCartney travels by car through France and Spain, then flies to Nairobi, Kenya.

NOVEMBER–DECEMBER
The Family Way (LP), containing songs written by Paul McCartney, is recorded by The George Martin Orchestra at EMI's Abbey Road studios, London.

NOV 9   Paul McCartney is supposedly involved in a fatal car crash, his head severed from his body; according to "Paul Is Dead" rumors circulated in 1969, Paul is replaced at this time by a double, William Campbell.

NOV 9--   "Unfinished Paintings and Objects by Yoko Ono" are
12   exhibited at the Indica Gallery in London.
NOV 10   The date Paul McCartney is allegedly "Officially Pro--
           nounced Dead," according to the "Paul Is Dead" rumors
           of 1969.
NOV 11   An interview with Ringo Starr appears in the *New Musical
           Express.*
NOV 14   Brian Epstein denies reported rumors that two of The
           Beatles have approached Allen Klein to take over
           management of their careers.
NOV 15   Brian Epstein denies rumors that The Beatles are splitting
           up.
           Annual general meeting of Northern Songs Ltd. is held.
NOV 18   *From Head to Toe/Night Time*, a single by The Escourts,
           produced by Paul McCartney, is released in the U.K.
NOV 19   Paul McCartney returns from a vacation in Kenya.
           In London, John, George and Ringo express irritation over
           the Allen Klein reports.
NOV 24   The Beatles start their first recording sessions since the end
           of their American tour.
NOV 25   **The Beatles Fourth Christmas Record** (LP) is recorded.
NOV 28   **The Beatle Girls** (LP) by Beatles' producer George Martin,
           with instrumental versions of Beatles' songs, is released
           in the U.S.
           Take Out Some Insurance on Me, Baby, recorded by Tony
           Sheridan and The Beatles, appears on **The Original
           Discotheque Hits** (LP) released in U.S.

DECEMBER

   The Beatles unsuccessfully work at EMI studios, London, in an
      attempt to devise a follow--up to **Revolver** (LP), for release
      before Christmas; the tracks are later used for the **Sgt. Pepper**
      album.
   Another special "Christmas Extra" magazine is published by
      the monthly *Beatles Book.*
   Ringo Starr vacations in Spain.
   The Beatles begin work on the **Sgt. Pepper** LP at EMI studios,
      London.
   When I'm Sixty--Four is recorded at the Abbey Road studios.

DEC 10   **A Collection of Beatle Oldies . . . But Goldies** (LP) is re--
           leased in the U.K. BIR--59 (Nov) PMS--158 (Dec 9)
           Love in the Open Air and *Theme from "The Family Way,"*

171

written by Paul McCartney, are recorded by The George Martin Orchestra.

Strawberry Fields Forever is recorded at the Abbey Road studios.

DEC 13   John Lennon appears on the cover of *Look* magazine.

DEC 16   **The Beatles Fourth Christmas Record** (LP) is released by the Fan Club. BU17–14 (Dec 17)

DEC 17   **A Collection of Beatles Oldies . . . But Goldies** (LP) enters the *Melody Maker* album charts at number 7.

DEC 18   London world premiere of the film, "The Family Way," with music by Paul McCartney.

Fan Club members receive the fourth Beatles' Christmas record.

DEC 23   *Love in the Open Air/Theme from "The Family Way"* (45), written by Paul McCartney and recorded by The George Martin Orchestra, is released in the U.K.

DEC 24   An article appears in the Los Angeles *Times* about jazz musician Herbie Mann, who is quoted as calling Lennon and McCartney "the Rodgers and Hart of this generation."

DEC 26   John Lennon appears on the BBC's "Not Only . . . But Also" radio program, with Peter Cook and Dudley Moore.

DEC 28   *Variety*'s film critic calls McCartney's score for the film, "The Family Way," "neat" and "resourceful."

DEC 29   *Billboard* reports that The Beatles hold number 1 hits in thirteen countries.

DEC 31   **A Collection of Beatles Oldies . . . But Goldies** (LP) reaches its highest position on the *Melody Maker* album charts: number 4.

A Paul McCartney interview appears in *New Musical Express*.

LATE 1966

Brian Epstein's use of drugs to escape business pressures has become severe.

Paul McCartney buys a three–story house in St. John's Wood, London, near the EMI recording studios, for Ł40,000.

Brian Epstein makes another, more halfhearted, attempt to commit suicide.

About a lucky man
who made the grade

A DAY
IN THE
LIFE
The Beatles
Day-By-Day
1967

DURING THIS YEAR . . .

The Beatles write the songs *Jessie's Dream* and *Shirley's Wild Accordian*, performed for the "Magical Mystery Tour" TV special by accordianist Shirley Evans, unreleased as recordings.

Brian Epstein hires Robert Stigwood to be co--director of NEMS Enterprises.

Robert Stigwood negotiates a complete takeover of NEMS Enter--prises with Brian Epstein.

Paul McCartney's father turns 64, and *When I'm Sixty--Four* (originally written in 1962 or 1963) is revised in his honor for the **Sgt. Pepper** album.

The World's Best -- The Beatles (LP) is released in Germany by Odeon. BF--68 (1967) BF--211 (1968)

The Beatles seriously consider acting in a movie adaptation of J.R.R. Tolkien's *Lord of the Rings*, with Paul probably por--traying Frodo, Ringo as Sam, George as Gandalf and John as Gollum.

Denny Laine writes and records his composition *Say You Don't Mind* as a member of The Electric String Band.

The first 45 rpm Beatles record – featuring *All You Need Is Love* – is issued in France, where only EPs were issued before.

The Beatles record their unreleased album **Rabbi Saul** for Queenie Epstein soon after the death of her son Brian, according to the *National Lampoon* parody of Beatles' history; the album con--tains songs like: *Hey, Juden, Helter Schmelter,* and *P.S.I.O.U.*

Jimmy McCulloch, 14--year--old guitarist later to join the line--up of Paul McCartney's Wings, joins the group Thunderclap Newman.

The Beatles consider dramatic roles in a film called "Shades of a Personality."

The following singles by The Beatles are released in Italy: *Penny Lane/Strawberry Fields Forever, All You Need Is Love/Baby*

173

You're a Rich Man, and *Hello Goodbye/I Am the Walrus.*
Ringo Starr and Paul McCartney are photographed while on a trip
   to Greece.
Hello Goodbye/I Am the Walrus (45) is released in Japan by Odeon.
Tea drinking heavily influences the creation of The Rutles' greatest
   work, **Sergeant Rutter's Only Darts Club Band**, according to the
   album send–up of The Beatles, **The Rutles.**
Strawberry Fields Forever/Penny Lane (45) is released in France
   by Odeon.
Mal Evans buys a home in Sunbury, near homes owned by John,
   Ringo and George.
Yoko Ono stages her "Wrapping Event" in London's Trafalgar
   Square.
All You Need Is Love/Baby You're a Rich Man (45) is released in
   Japan by Odeon.
Drummer Joe English joins the band Jam Factory, where he remains
   until the band's breakup in 1973–74. PMB–46 (1968)
Paul McCartney first becomes interested in The Beatles' business
   affairs.
The following singles by The Beatles are released in Australia:
   *Penny Lane/Strawberry Fields Forever, All You Need Is Love/
   Baby You're a Rich Man,* and *Hello Goodbye/I Am the Walrus.*
Scaffold, with Paul McCartney's brother -- Mike McGear – gets a
   record in the top ten: *Thank U Very Much.*
The following Beatles' singles are released in Holland: *Strawberry
   Fields Forever/Penny Lane, Hello Goodbye/I Am the Walrus,*
   and *All You Need Is Love/Baby You're a Rich Man.*
Paul McCartney first meets Linda Eastman at the Bag O'Nails
   Club, London; afterward they go to the Speakeasy Club together.
The following EP by The Beatles is released in Australia: **Help!**

EARLY 1967
George Martin's Associated Independent Recordings produces not
   only The Beatles, but Cilla Black, Adam Faith, Tom Jones,
   Gerry and The Pacemakers, Manfred Mann, Shirley Bassey, and
   others.
John Lennon announces that he considers himself a Buddhist.
The sitar, influenced by the George Harrison/Ravi Shankar associ-
   ation, begins to find its way into the recordings of many other
   Western performers.

Brian Epstein buys an historic country mansion near Heathfield,
Sussex, for ₤ 25,000.

Sgt. Pepper (LP) is recorded under top secret conditions, according
to Mark Shipper's humorous spoof of Beatle history, *Paperback
Writer.*

You Know My Name recorded.

Paul McCartney finally takes his first LSD trip after his resistance
is broken down by others around him; by the time of the release
of the **Sgt. Pepper** album in June, The Beatles conclude nearly
a year of experimenting with LSD.

JANUARY

The Beatles sign a new contract with EMI Records; previously
receiving only pennies per album sold, they are now to receive
10% of wholesale price, and 17½% for albums sold in the U.S.

The Beatles make public their decision not to do live tours any
more.

Paul McCartney displays a new moustache, heralding The Beatles'
psychedelic period.

The Beatles return to Liverpool to make a promotional TV film
to help sales of *Strawberry Fields Forever/Penny Lane*, soon to
be released.

Rescheduled date for Beatles' trip to India, according to Mark
Shipper's humorous spoof of Beatle history, *Paperback Writer.*

Brian Epstein brings in Robert Stigwood, an Australian, as co--
managing director of NEMS; many of Epstein's proteges are
upset when he turns his full attention to The Beatles, giving
up most daily responsibilies and other work to Stigwood
to handle.

EARLY JANUARY--LATE APRIL

Sgt. Pepper's Lonely Hearts Club Band (and *Reprise*), *With a Little
Help from My Friends, Lucy in the Sky with Diamonds, Getting
Better, Fixing a Hole, She's Leaving Home, Being for the Benefit
of Mr. Kite, Within You Without You, Lovely Rita, Good
Morning Good Morning,* and *A Day in the Life* are recorded.

JAN 1   George and Pattie Harrison, Brian Epstein and Eric Clapton
         are asked to leave Annabol's in London because George
         isn't wearing a tie.

JAN 1-- Three versions of *Penny Lane* are recorded at EMI's Abbey
14   Road studios. ATN--61 (Dec 1966)

JAN 6   **The Family Way** soundtrack album, with songs written by
Paul McCartney, is released in the U.K. BF--206 (Feb)

JAN 7   A rumor circulates in England that Paul McCartney has
been killed in a car accident.

The Beatles are reported to have won six R.I.A.A. Gold
Records in 1966.

JAN 8   There is a *Sunday Times* report stating that the National
Theatre's invitation to Paul McCartney to write music
for the songs in Shakespeare's "As You Like It" was
rejected by him.

JAN 15   Paul Harrison, George Harrison's nephew, is seven years old.

JAN 16   Jane Asher begins a tour of the U.S. with the Bristol Old
Vic Company.

JAN 18   Paul McCartney's body is found in the front seat of his car
in Wimbledon Common, Surrey; the coroner rules
accidental death, even though Paul has been garroted,
stabbed, shot, and run over by a car, according to *National
Lampoon's* parody of Beatles' history.

Jan 19-- *A Day in the Life* is recorded at EMI's Abbey Road studios,
Feb 10   London.

JAN 21   George and Pattie Harrison's first wedding anniversary.

Brian Epstein's NEMS Enterprises merges with the Robert
Stigwood Group.

JAN 25   Thieves, attempting to steal John Lennon's car parked out--
side Brian Epstein's home, are interrupted in the process
by an anti--theft device.

JAN 27   *Got to Get You into My Life*, written by Lennon/McCart--
ney, appears on an album of the same name by Cliff
Bennett and The Rebel Rousers.

George Harrison's brother and sister--in--law, Peter and
Pauline, celebrate their second wedding anniversary.

The LS Bumble Bee/Bee Side (45), by Peter Cook and
Dudley Moore, incorrectly attributed to John Lennon, is
released in the U.K.

JAN 30   John Lennon, Paul McCartney and Brian Epstein attend a
concert by The Who and The Jimi Hendrix Experience.

JAN 31   *Penny Lane/Strawberry Fields Forever* (45) is aired for the
first time in the U.K.

LATE JANUARY

Two performances by The Beatles of *Strawberry Fields Forever*
and *Penny Lane* are filmed by Peter Goldmann.

FEBRUARY

Promo film "Strawberry Fields Forever" is first shown in the U.S. on the "Hollywood Palace" TV show, and later on "American Bandstand."

George and Pattie Harrison first meet the Maharishi Mahesh Yogi.

Pattie Harrison becomes a member of the Spiritual Regeneration Movement.

Two film clips of The Beatles performing *Strawberry Fields Forever* and *Penny Lane* are shown on the "Ed Sullivan Show."

FEB 1	A version of *Sgt. Pepper's Lonely Hearts Club Band*, with horns and without Ringo, is recorded at the Abbey Road studios.
FEB 2	*Penny Lane/Strawberry Fields Forever* (45) is aired for the first time in the U.S.
FEB 6	The Beatles sign a new nine--year contract with EMI. HHG7--5 (Feb 7) EMI announces that The Beatles' world record sales (con--verted to singles units) have topped 180 million units.
FEB 7	National Beatle Day. BBC repeats "Not Only . . . But Also" radio show featuring John Lennon, originally broadcast December 26, 1966.
FEB 9	"Penny Lane" and "Strawberry Fields" films made in late January are shown on the BBC's "Top of the Pops" television show.
FEB 11	Ringo and Maureen Starr's second wedding anniversary.
FEB 13	*Penny Lane/Strawberry Fields Forever* (45) is released in the U.S.; special DJ copies differ in length from those commercially released.
FEB 14	The *Daily Express* reports that John Lennon has refused his wife Cynthia the services of a nanny to care for their son Julian.
FEB 16	*Good Morning Good Morning* is recorded at the Abbey Road studios. "Penny Lane" and "Strawberry Fields" films first shown February 9 are repeated on the BBC's "Top of the Pops" television show. JLS--135 (Feb 17)
FEB 17	*Being for the Benefit of Mr. Kite* is recorded at the Abbey Road studios. *Penny Lane/Strawberry Fields Forever* (45) is released in the U.K., the first quarter million with a special sleeve.
FEB 18	*Penny Lane* enters the *Billboard* singles charts at number 116.

Strawberry Fields Forever enters the *Billboard* singles charts at number 118.

FEB 20   John Lennon, Ringo Starr and their wives attend a Chuck Berry performance at Brian Epstein's Saville Theatre.

FEB 21   *Fixing a Hole* is recorded at EMI's Abbey Road studios.

FEB 22   *Lovely Rita* is recorded at the EMI studios.

Northern Songs Ltd. predicts profits for the fiscal year 1966–67 at at least Ł 810,000.

FEB 25   George Harrison's 24th birthday.

Penny Lane/Strawberry Fields Forever enters the *Melody Maker* singles charts in the U.K. at number 3.

Strawberry Fields Forever enters the *Billboard* Hot 100 charts at number 83, remaining on the charts for nine weeks during which it reaches a high point of number 8.

Penny Lane/Strawberry Fields Forever enters Holland's Radio Veronica Top 40 charts at number 4.

Penny Lane/Strawberry Fields Forever enters the *Billboard* British top twenty singles charts, remaining on the charts for eight weeks during which it reaches a high point of number 2.

A film clip promoting *Penny Lane* and *Strawberry Fields Forever* is shown on "Hollywood Palace."   BEA3–13 (Mar)

Penny Lane enters the *Billboard* Hot 100 charts at number 85, remaining on the charts for ten weeks during which it reaches a high point of number 1.

FEB 26   Brian Epstein's purchase of a house in East Sussex, England, is reported.

MARCH

Paul McCartney proposes the creation of a whole Beatles' album devoted to the theme of social injustice to John Lennon (**Sgt. Pepper**), according to Mark Shipper's humorous spoof of Beatle history, *Paperback Writer.*

Photo sessions for the covers of the **Sgt. Pepper** LP are held.

MAR 2   *Lucy in the Sky with Diamonds* is recorded at the Abbey Road studios, London.

MAR 3   **The Beatle Girls** (LP) by Beatles' producer George Martin, with instrumental versions of Beatles' songs, is released in the U.K.

MAR 4   *Penny Lane/Strawberry Fields Forever* hits number 1 on the *Melody Maker* singles charts, remaining there for three weeks.

MAR 9   *Getting Better* is recorded at the Abbey Road studios, London.

MAR 10 Louise Harrison, George's mother, celebrates a birthday.

MAR 11 The Beatles receive three Grammy Awards from American Academy of Recording Arts & Sciences for 1966: *Michelle*, song of the year (composing); *Eleanor Rigby*, best contemporary solo vocal performance; **Revolver** (LP), sleeve design.

Dick James reports that 446 versions of *Yesterday* have been recorded by various artists since its release on the **Help!** album in August 1965.

MAR 15 *Within You Without You* is recorded at EMI's studios on Abbey Road, London.

mid–Mar John Lennon and Paul McCartney finish writing *With a Little Help from My Friends* for Ringo's feature on the **Sgt. Pepper** album.

The Beatles are close to the end of recording the **Sgt. Pepper** LP.

MAR 17 *She's Leaving Home* is recorded at EMI's St. John's Wood studios on Abbey Road, London.

Pattie Harrison's 23rd birthday.

MAR 18 *Penny Lane* hits number 1 on the *Billboard* singles charts.

MAR 20 *Penny Lane* (45) is certified as a Gold Record by the R.I.A.A.

MAR 25 The Beatles receive two Ivor Novello Awards from the British Music Industry for the year 1966: *Michelle*, most performed work; *Yellow Submarine*, top selling single.

MAR 28 Derek Taylor throws a farewell party before his departure for England (the following day) to join Apple.

MAR 29 *Sgt. Pepper's Lonely Hearts Club Band* (with Ringo) is recorded at the Abbey Road studios.

Derek Taylor leaves California for England to become Apple press officer and publicist.

MAR 30 *With a Little Help from My Friends* is recorded at EMI's Abbey Road studios.

SPRING

Brian Epstein suffers extreme paranoia as a result of heavy drug use.

Nat Weiss "sobers up" Brian Epstein, bringing him around from a heavy dose of Seconal, in time to do an interview with Murray the K at WOR radio, New York.

Plans for the film "Magical Mystery Tour" are announced.

Brian Epstein, about to fly to London after a visit to New York, has a premonition of death and fears the plane will crash in the sea.

Step Inside Love is recorded by Paul McCartney, later to be included on the bootleg LP **Abbey Road Revisited.**

APRIL

Brian Epstein holds a meeting at New York's Waldorf Astoria Hotel with Nat Weiss, Robert Stigwood and Sid Bernstein to discuss plans for expanding his management organization.

George Harrison's ninth song for The Beatles, *Within You, Without You*, appears on the **Sgt. Pepper** album.

The partnership, The Beatles & Co., is formed.

APR 1   *Strawberry Fields Forever* reaches its highest position on the *Billboard* singles charts: number 8.

APR 2   The Beatles finish work on the **Sgt. Pepper** album.

APR 3   Paul McCartney flies to the U.S., arriving in San Francisco.

APR 4   Paul McCartney attends a rehearsal by The Jefferson Airplane.

APR 5   Jane Asher, touring with the Old Vic in Denver, is joined by Paul McCartney to celebrate her 21st birthday.

APR 6   Paul McCartney and Jane Asher spend the day in the Colorado Rockies.

APR 7   Paul McCartney and Jane Asher attend a Greek theatre in Denver.
Decca Records releases the Denny Laine single *Say You Don't Mind/Ask the People.*

APR 8   *Penny Lane* enters the Polish radio station (Rozglosnia Harcerska) charts at number 13.
Julian Lennon's fourth birthday.
Paul McCartney attends a performance of "Romeo & Juliet" in Denver, featuring Jane Asher.

APR 9   Paul McCartney flies from Denver to Los Angeles on Frank Sinatra's private Lear jet.

APR 10   Paul McCartney visits with John and Michelle Phillips, and attends a Beach Boys' recording session.

APR 11   Paul McCartney first conceives the idea for the film "Magical Mystery Tour" on flight back to England from the U.S.

On Top of Old Smokey, with Paul McCartney playing bass
guitar, is recorded by The Beach Boys, but not released.

Vegetables, produced by Paul McCartney and The Beach
Boys, is recorded by The Beach Boys.

APR 12   Gordon R. Caldwell, George Harrison's nephew, celebrates
his tenth birthday.

Paul McCartney arrives back in London.

APR 19   Deed of partnership forming "The Beatles & Co." is exe--
cuted, with the Apple organization to manage the
partnership.

APR 24   *Love in the Open Air,* written by Paul McCartney, appears
in the U.S. on a single by George Martin & His Orchestra.

Apr 25--   Two versions of *Magical Mystery Tour* are recorded at
May 3   EMI's Abbey Road studios.

MAY

Brian Epstein gives a huge party at his home in Sussex; John
Lennon brings along a large quantity of LSD.

The Beatles, arms around one another, pose for the well known
"thumbs up" photograph.

Brian Epstein confides to Nat Weiss that he feels Robert Stigwood
is too extravagant with NEMS' money, and that he, Epstein, is
losing control of NEMS to Stigwood.

The *Beatles Monthly* awards a free subscription to a fan who wrote
of her pride in The Beatles for not indulging in drugs, unaware
(as most people were) that the group had been using drugs,
especially LSD, for some two years.

Queen magazine in the U.K. quotes Brian Epstein as attributing
the new mood in the country as growing out of the use of
hallucinatory drugs.

Paul McCartney tells a reporter for *Life* that he has taken LSD.
ATC--68 (Apr)

You Know My Name is recorded at the Abbey Road studios.

MAY--JUNE

Not Unknown, Anything and *India,* written by George Harrison,
and *Annie,* written by Lennon and McCartney, are recorded;
unreleased.   BBS--62 (*Pink Litmus Paper Shirt* and *Colliding Circles*)

MAY 1   EMI announces that sales of Beatle records (converted to
singles units) have reached 200 million.

I Don't Want to See You Again/Woman (45), by Peter and

Gordon, is released in the U.S.

MAY 6   Begins a two--and--a--half month period during which no Beatle--related recording appears on the *Billboard* singles charts.

MAY 11   *Baby You're a Rich Man* is recorded at the Abbey Road studios.

MAY 12   *Sgt. Pepper's Lonely Hearts Club Band* is first aired in the U.K.

MAY 20   Harold and Louise Harrison, George's parents, celebrate a wedding anniversary.

BBC radio bans broadcast of *A Day in the Life*, contending that the song encourages drug use.

MAY 25   John Lennon has his Rolls Royce painted in psychedelic colors and designs.

MAY 27   John Lennon, in a *Melody Maker* interview, states that The Beatles will do no more touring.

MAY 28   Harold Harrison, George's father, celebrates a birthday.

LATE MAY

All You Need Is Love is written.

Brian Epstein throws a press party to preview the new **Sgt. Pepper** album.

JUNE

An interview with Ringo Starr is recorded, later to appear on the bootleg recording **Radio London's Last Hour.**

What Good Am I/Over My Head (45) by Cilla Black, managed by Brian Epstein, is released in the U.K.

A cover version of *With a Little Help from My Friends* by The Young Idea, written by John Lennon and Paul McCartney, is released in the U.K., later reaching a high point on the British *Billboard* top ten charts of number 10.

An issue of the monthly *Beatles Book* is published, for the first time with a color photograph (from the **Sgt. Pepper** (LP) photo sessions) used on the front and back covers.

The first outdoor rock concert is held in Monterey, California, with George Harrison listed as one of the board of advisors.

We Love You, with John Lennon and Paul McCartney doing backing vocals, is recorded at Olympia Studios, London, by The Rolling Stones.

What A Shame Mary Jane Had A Pain At the Party and *Peace of Mind* are recorded at EMI's Abbey Road studios; the first goes unreleased the second later appears on the bootleg **Peace of Mind.** ATN--258

(mid–1967; *Not Unknown*, *Anthing*, *India*, *Annie*, *What's the News Maryjane* and *Peace of Mind*)

JUN 1   **Sgt. Pepper's Lonely Hearts Club Band** (LP) is released in the U.K. ATC–69 (May) BAB–345 (Apr) BBS–52 (Jul 1)

JUN 2   **Sgt. Pepper's Lonely Hearts Club Band** (LP) is released in the U.S.

JUN 3   **Sgt. Pepper's Lonely Hearts Club Band** (LP) enters the *Melody Maker* album charts in the U.K. at number 1, remaining there for 22 weeks.

JUN 10 Gordon Caldwell, George Harrison's brother–in–law, celebrates a birthday.

JUN 12 **The Family Way** soundtrack album, with songs written by Paul McCartney, is released in the U.S.
        Irene Harrison, George Harrison's neice, celebrates a birth–day.

JUN 14 Recording sessions for *All You Need Is Love* begin at Olympic
–25   studios.

JUN 15 **Sgt. Pepper's Lonely Hearts Club Band** (LP) is certified as a Gold Record by the R.I.A.A.

mid–Jun *All Together Now* and *It's All Too Much* are recorded.

JUN 16 The Beatles appear on the cover of *Life* magazine.

JUN 18 Paul McCartney's 25th birthday.

JUN 19 Paul McCartney interview on his use of LSD appears in the *Daily Mirror.*
        Paul McCartney appears on British television, discussing LSD and other drugs.

JUN 20 **Sgt. Pepper** (LP) is completed, according to Mark Shipper's humorous spoof of Beatle history, *Paperback Writer.*

JUN 21 Billy Graham announces his prayer efforts for Paul McCartney, after revelation of McCartney's experi–mentation with LSD.

JUN 24 The Beatles hold a press photo session; the "placard" photos for *All You Need Is Love* are taken.
        Sgt. Pepper's Lonely Hearts Club Band (LP) enters the *Billboard* album charts at number 8, remaining on the charts for 121 weeks during which it reaches a high point of number 1. BF–97 (Jun 23)

JUN 25 *All You Need Is Love* is recorded at EMI studios, London, as part of the first live world–wide TV program, "Our World," seen in 24 countries by 400 million people.
        BF–86 (700 million) TB–230 (Jul)
        All You Need Is Love, recorded from The Beatles'

appearance on "Our World" TV broadcast, is later in--
cluded on the bootleg album **L.S. Bumble Bee.**
JUN 28   New York premiere of film "The Family Way" with music
by Paul McCartney.

LATE JUNE
George Harrison in fined the equivalent of $16.80 for speeding in
Roehampton Lane, Putney, England, in a Mini Cooper.

SUMMER
Brian Epstein stages a number of rock shows at the Saville Theatre.
The "Drone of Ark," a Cherry Hill, New Jersey girl – member of
an offshoot cult of Beatlemaniacs known as "the Drones"
because of their practice of listening to the drone of the piano
chord at the end of *A Day in the Life* for years at a stretch –
begins a drone listening session which lasts until the summer of
1976, according to Mark Shipper's humorous spoof of Beatle
history, *Paperback Writer.*
Cilla Black, upset by Brian Epstein's inattention to her career,
leaves NEMS Enterprises, but the business disagreement is later
resolved and their friendship improved.
The regular use of drugs, especially LSD, takes The Beatles into a
mystical/philosophical period.
Public outcry against "seasoning discrimination" in the British
military grows as a result of the release of the **Sgt. Pepper** album,
according to Mark Shipper's humorous spoof of Beatle history,
Paperback Writer.
Wally Podrazik, co–author (eight years later) of the standard re--
cording history of The Beatles *All Together Now*, participates
in a Beatle singalong in the back of a bus touring the British
countryside.
Ringo Starr builds a large extension on his mock--Tudor house in
Weybridge, Surrey.
The *Financial Times* estimates Brian Epstein's wealth at seven
million pounds.
Ravi Shankar, his reputation bolstered by his association with
George Harrison, holds his first large outdoor festival in
Monterey, California.

MID--1967
The construction firm of which Ringo Starr is co--owner closes

down due to an inability to sell the houses they have been
building.
Exhausted from the creation of **Sgt. Pepper**, Paul McCartney vaca--
tions in Scotland, George Harrison returns to India to study the
sitar with Ravi Shankar, Ringo Starr goes to Switzerland for
postgraduate study in billiards, and John Lennon moves in with
Yoko Ono, according to Mark Shipper's humorous spoof of
Beatle history, *Paperback Writer*.

JULY

The Beatles sign a petition to have marijuana legalized.
The Beatles search for an island to buy off the coast of Greece;
all but George and Pattie Harrison stay for three weeks.
Brian Epstein's father dies.
Paul McCartney comments that *All You Need Is Love* was written
in two weeks as a "message" song to the world audience soon
to view The Beatles recording it.
Nat Weiss calls Brian Epstein and informs him that Robert Stigwood
has chartered a yacht for The Bee Gees, then also under NEMS'
management, to tour the U.S.; Epstein determines that Stig--
wood will have to be eased out of the company.
Ringo Starr is interviewed on Radio London's "Last Hour" show.
Thank You Very Much is recorded at EMI's Abbey Road studios,
London, by Scaffold, co--produced by Paul McCartney.

JUL 1   **Sgt. Pepper** (LP) is released, the title referring to the
         "seasoning discrimination" prevalent in the British
         military (sergeants getting better pepper than enlisted
         men), according to Mark Shipper's humorous spoof of
         Beatle history, *Paperback Writer*.
         Sgt. Pepper's Lonely Hearts Club Band (LP) hits number 1
         on the *Billboard* album charts, remaining there for 15
         weeks.
JUL 3   Gordon and Louise Caldwell, George Harrison's brother--
         in--law and sister, celebrate their 13th wedding anni--
         versary.
JUL 5   George and Pattie Harrison visit George's parents in
         Cheshire.
JUL 6   *All You Need Is Love* enters the Polish radio station
         (Rozglosnia Harcerska) charts at number 1.
         All You Need Is Love/Baby You're a Rich Man (45) is
         aired on radio for the first time.

JUL 7   *All You Need Is Love/Baby You're a Rich Man* (45) is released in the U.K.

George and Pattie Harrison return home from visiting George's parents in Cheshire.

Ringo Starr's 27th birthday.

JUL 15   *All You Need Is Love* enters Holland's Radio Veronica Top 40 charts at number 2.

All You Need Is Love enters *Billboard*'s British top twenty singles charts, remaining on the charts for ten weeks during which it reaches a high point of number 1.

All You Need Is Love enters the *Melody Maker* singles charts in the U.K. at number 3.

JUL 17   *All You Need Is Love/Baby You're a Rich Man* (45) is re-- leased in the U.S.   IR--127 (Jul 24)   PMB--228 (Jul 24)

JUL 20   Harold J. and Peter Harrison, George's brothers, celebrate their respective birthdays, ages 33 and 27.

JUL 22   Paul McCartney interview in *New Musical Express* reveals that *All You Need Is Love* was written especially to bring the worldwide audience The Beatles' message: love.

All You Need Is Love enters the *Billboard* singles charts at number 71, remaining on the charts for eleven weeks during which it reaches a high point of number 1.

Baby You're a Rich Man enters the *Billboard* singles charts at number 115.

All You Need Is Love hits number 1 on the *Melody Maker* singles charts, remaining there for three weeks.

JUL 24   Full--page ad in the London *Times* protesting Britain's marijuana laws, signed by The Beatles and others, appears.

JUL 28   Allen Klein purchases 48% of Cameo--Parkway Record Company, 297,000 shares at $1.75 per share.

JUL 29   *Baby You're a Rich Man* enters the *Billboard* Hot 100 charts at number 64, remaining on the charts for five weeks during which it reaches a high point of number 34.

JUL 31   Beatles' fan Pattie Emerson meets George Harrison at his home in Esher, later writing about it in the American magazine *Datebook*.

LATE JULY

George Harrison has his house in Esher painted in psychedelic colors.

Catcall, written by Paul McCartney, is recorded by The Chris
Barber Band.

AUGUST
The Beatles give up their experimentation with drugs as they
delve deeper into spiritual matters.
World premiere of Yoko Ono's film, "Film No. 4."
Cilla Black is deeply affected by the death of Brian Epstein.

AUG 1   George and Pattie Harrison fly to Los Angeles to attend a
         Ravi Shankar concert at the Hollywood Bowl.
         George Harrison composes *Blue Jay Way.*
AUG 2   George and Pattie Harrison visit Ravi Shankar's music
         school.
AUG 3   George Harrison and Ravi Shankar hold a press conference
         at Shankar's music school.
AUG 4   **The Beatles' First** (LP) is reissued in the U.K.
         Maureen Starkey's 21st birthday.
         George and Pattie Harrison attend Ravi Shankar's Holly–
         wood Bowl concert.
AUG 5   George and Pattie Harrison go shopping and sightseeing in
         Los Angeles.
AUG 6   Pattie Harrison, sister Jenny Boyd, and Neil Aspinall go to
         Disneyland.
AUG 7   *Black Is Black/Have You Seen Your Mother Baby Standing
         in the Shadows* (45) by Lord Sitar, incorrectly attributed
         to George Harrison, is released in the U.S.
         George and Pattie Harrison fly to San Francisco.
AUG 8   George Harrison visits San Francisco's Haight–Asbury
         district, and wanders through the hippie neighborhood
         followed by "flower children" as he sings *Baby You're
         a Rich Man.*
         George and Pattie Harrison fly from San Francisco to New
         York.
         John Lennon and son Julian pose for fans' photographs
         outside their house in St. George's Hill Estate off
         Cavendish Road, Weybridge, Surrey.
AUG 9   George and Pattie Harrison fly from New York to London.
AUG 12   *Baby You're a Rich Man* reaches its highest position on
         the *Billboard* singles charts: number 34.
AUG 13   *With a Little Help from My Friends* enters the Polish radio
         station (Rozglasnia Harcerska) charts at number 11.
         Lucy in the Sky with Diamonds enters the Polish radio

station (Rozglasnia Harcerska) charts at number 15.

AUG 14 –24 Mrs. Queenie Epstein, Brian Epstein's mother, visits him for ten days.

mid–Aug Newspaper advertisements announce that the Maharishi will soon give a public lecture in London.

AUG 16 Louise Caldwell, George Harrison's sister, has her 36th birthday.

AUG 17 A review of "The Family Way" in the Los Angeles *Herald–Examiner* calls Paul McCartney's score "unobtrusively right."

AUG 18 Peter Brown visits with Brian Epstein and his mother, Queenie.

The Rolling Stones' *We Love You/Dandelion* (45), featuring Lennon and McCartney as backing vocalists on *We Love You*, is released in the U.K.

AUG 19 Ringo Starr and wife Maureen welcome a new son, Jason Starkey, their second child, born at Queen Charlotte's Hospital, Hammersmith, London.

All You Need Is Love hits number 1 on the *Billboard* singles charts, dropping to second position the following week.

AUG 20 *A Day in the Life* enters the Polish radio station (Rozglasnia Harcerska) charts at number 19.

AUG 21 Nat Weiss writes to Brian Epstein.

Aug 22– Sep 25 *Your Mother Should Know* is recorded at the Abbey Road studios.

AUG 22 –23 Nat Weiss and Brian Epstein talk by phone between New York and London.

AUG 23 Brian Epstein writes a letter to Nat Weiss, four days before his death, indicating his plans to come to the U.S. for a visit, beginning September 2.

John and Cynthia Lennon's fifth wedding anniversary.

AUG 24 Mrs. Queenie Epstein, Brian Epstein's mother, returns to Liverpool after a ten–day visit with her son in London.

Plans are worked out by The Beatles with Brian Epstein for filming of the TV special, "Magical Mystery Tour."

John Lennon, Paul McCartney and George Harrison attend a lecture at the London Hilton Hotel by Maharishi Mahesh Yogi; in a private meeting afterwards, the Maharishi invites them to attend lectures at his University College, Bangor, North Wales. BM–139 (all four attend) TB–230 (all four attend)

Brian Epstein has dinner with Simon Napier–Bell at Carrier's Restaurant in Islington, London.

AUG 25   The Beatles travel by train to Bangor, Wales, with the
Maharishi, to study transcendental meditation.
Brian Epstein leaves London to spend a bank–holiday
weekend at his country home in Sussex, with Peter
Brown and Geoffrey Ellis to follow him.
Brian Epstein, Peter Brown and Geoffrey Ellis have dinner
at Epstein's country home in Sussex.
Around ten o'clock in the evening, Brian Epstein returns
to London from his country home in Sussex.
AUG 26   The Beatles and members of their party are initiated into
the International Meditation Society.
Brian Epstein calls Peter Brown in Sussex, apologizes for
not returning Friday evening, sounding drowsy from
having taken sleeping pills the night before.
AUG 27   The Beatles study transcendental meditation with the
Maharishi in Bangor, North Wales.
Sunday Express reports that Beatles' former drummer,
Pete Best, currently works in a Liverpool bakery for
Ł18 a week.
Brian Epstein's butler and housekeeper call Epstein's
secretary, Joanne, when he does not leave his bedroom
Saturday and Sunday. Epstein is later found dead in
his bed from a drug overdose. BU2--8 (Aug 12)
After talking with Peter Brown on the phone, Paul McCart–
ney breaks the news of Brian Epstein's death to the
other Beatles in Bangor.
AUG 28   The Rolling Stones' *We Love You/Dandelion* (45),
featuring Lennon and McCartney as backing vocalists
on *We Love You*, is released in the U.S.
An autopsy is held to determine the cause of Brian
Epstein's death.
The Beatles announce plans to study meditation in India.
AUG 29   Brian Epstein is buried in a cemetary in Long Lane,
Liverpool.
AUG 30   Clive Epstein, Brian's brother, becomes Chairman of NEMS
Enterprises. HHG7--7 (Aug 28)
AUG 31   The Beatles reportedly announce that they will assume
management of their own affairs, following the death of
Brian Epstein.

SEPTEMBER
The Beatles originally plan to visit the Maharishi in India this
month, but the trip is postponed in order to begin shooting

"Magical Mystery Tour."

Apple Electronics Ltd. is formed to handle patents of electronic inventions of Alexis Mardas.

Harold and Louise Harrison, George Harrison's parents, visit George's sister Louise Caldwell in the U.S.

Apple Publishing is founded to handle song publishing.

Public reaction to **Sgt. Pepper** (LP) leads to total ban on "seasoning discrimination" in the British military, according to Mark Shipper's humorous spoof of Beatle history, *Paperback Writer*.

Yoko Ono's "Yoko Plus Me" exhibit, sponsored by John Lennon, opens at the Lisson Gallery in London.

Versions of *The Fool on the Hill* and *I Am the Walrus* are recorded, later surfacing on the bootleg recording **Studiooutakes**.

SEPTEMBER--OCTOBER

How I Won the War, with vocals by John Lennon, is recorded by Musketeer Gripweed and The Third Troop. RO--58 (1966)

Magical Mystery Tour, The Fool on the Hill, Flying, Blue Jay Way, Your Mother Should Know, I Am the Walrus are recorded.

SEPTEMBER--NOVEMBER

Filming of "Magical Mystery Tour," produced and directed by The Beatles, the first "Apple" product.

Following the death of Brian Epstein, The Beatles (owners of 10% of NEMS Enterprises) make it clear to Clive Epstein, Brian's brother, that they wish to have the option offered by Brian Epstein to Robert Stigwood (to purchase 51% of NEMS) withdrawn, as they wish to operate without Stigwood.

SEP 1   A general conference on future recording and film plans is held by The Beatles and staff at Paul McCartney's home in St. John's Wood.

SEP 2   *Melody Maker* runs a piece on Brian Epstein.

The date Brian Epstein had intended to begin a vacation in the U.S.

NEMS' press officer, in a *Melody Maker* interview, tells of The Beatles' continued state of shock after death of Brian Epstein.

Paul McCartney interview by *New Musical Express* confirms that he feels no one could replace Brian Epstein as his manager.

SEP 6   Two versions of *Blue Jay Way* are recorded by George Harrison at the Abbey Road studios.

SEP 7   Two versions of *I Am the Walrus* are recorded by John

	Lennon at the Abbey Road studios, London.
SEP 8	*Flying* is recorded by The Beatles at the Abbey Road studios.
	A Coroner's Court terms Brian Epstein's death accidental, due to a cumulative overdose of bromide in a drug he had been taking called Carbitral.
SEP 10	Cynthia Lennon's 28th birthday.
SEP 11	The Magical Mystery Tour bus sets off for filming of the TV special in Cornwall.
	All You Need Is Love (45) is certified as a Gold Record by the R.I.A.A.
SEP 12	**England's Greatest Hits** (LP), including The Silkie perform-- ing *You've Got to Hide Your Love Away* (written and produced by Lennon/McCartney) is released in the U.S.
SEP 13	Zak Starkey's second birthday.
mid--Sep	The Beatles switch over from bus--touring to filming at a military air base in West Malling for the "Magical Mystery Tour" special.
SEP 15	The filming of "Magical Mystery Tour" is completed.
SEP 18	**Smiley Smile** (LP) by The Beach Boys, including *Vegetables* (produced by Paul McCartney and The Beach Boys) is released in the U.S.
SEP 19	George Harrison's mother, Louise, flies to the U.S. to visit George's sister, Louise Caldwell.
SEP 22	The Beatles appear on the cover of *Time* magazine.
	Time magazine reports on the reaction in the U.S. to the **Yesterday and Today** (LP) original "butcher cover," terming it a "serious lapse of taste."
SEP 25	*The Fool on the Hill* is recorded at EMI's Abbey Road studios in St. John's Wood, London.
SEP 29	George Harrison's niece, Leslie Caldwell, celebrates her 8th birthday.
SEP 30	Frank Zappa, in a *Disc and Music Echo* interview, says that John Lennon was correct in his assessment that The Beatles were more popular than Jesus.
	John Lennon, George Harrison and the Maharishi appear on David Frost's television show.

LATE SEPTEMBER--EARLY NOVEMBER
The Beatles spend six weeks editing the film for the TV special, "Magical Mystery Tour."

OCTOBER
The management of Cameo–Parkway Record Company announces an agreement in principle to combine Allen Klein and Co. with Cameo–Parkway Record Company.

OCT 4   John Lennon and George Harrison again appear on David Frost's TV show in the U.K.

OCT 5   George Harrison's mother, Louise, flies to Canada to visit one of her three brothers.

OCT 7   First reports appear that Ringo Starr will act in the film "Candy."
The Beatles reject a $1 million offer for a concert appear-- ance at Shea Stadium.
Begins a month--and--a--half period during which no Beatle--related recordings appear on the *Billboard* singles charts.

OCT 9   John Lennon's 27th birthday.

OCT 10   George Harrison's mother, Louise, flies home to England.

OCT 13   *How I Won the War*, with vocalist John Lennon, appears in the U.K. on a single by Musketeer Gripweed (Lennon) and The Third Troop.

OCT 17   A memorial service for Brian Epstein is held at the New London Synagogue, Abbey Road, London.
Mick Jagger of The Rolling Stones indicates that The Stones and The Beatles have discussed opening a jointly owned recording studio, but denies that a business partnership between the groups is in the offering.

OCT 18   World premiere in London of film "How I Won the War," with John Lennon.

OCT 20   *Catcall*, written by Paul McCartney, appears in the U.K. on a single by The Chris Barber Band.

OCT 22   "How I Won the War," reviewed in the London *Observer,* is termed the "dourest and sourest" picture since "Dr. Strangelove."

OCT 23   **Pandemonium Shadow Show** (LP) by Harry Nilsson, is released, containing a medley of Beatles' songs called *You Can't Do That*, directly sparking Nilsson's subse-- quent career involvement with The Beatles.

OCT 24   "A Hard Day's Night" is shown in the U.S. on NBC--TV.
The Hollywood Reporter's review of "How I Won the War" calls John Lennon's presence in the film as one intended to provide "insurance and curiosity."

OCT 25   *Variety*'s review of "How I Won the War" notes that John

Lennon's billing far exceeds his role in the film.

OCT 26 Second anniversary of The Beatles' receipt of the MBE.

OCT 29 George Harrison's sister--in--law, Pauline, celebrates her 24th birthday.

FALL

John Lennon invites Pete Shotten (a childhood friend) to leave the management of a supermarket, which John had purchased for him, and come to London to work for Apple -- managing the Apple Botique.

Ringo Starr finds Jesus, and the other Beatles help him record their unreleased album **Good Night Vicar**, according to *National Lampoon*'s parody of Beatles' history. The album contains songs like: *He's Looking Through You, I'll Follow the Son,* and *Revelations No. 9.*

NOVEMBER

I Only Live to Love You/From Now On (45), by Cilla Black, is released in the U.K.

EARLY NOVEMBER

An additional "Fool on the Hill" sequence is filmed in the south of Spain for The Beatles' TV special, "Magical Mystery Tour."

NOV 1 A five million dollar lawsuit against Allen Klein and Cameo--Parkway, filed by Lucarelli Enterprises (which charged that the defendants had conspired to interest Lucarelli Enterprises in the acquisition of capital Cameo stock merely to stimulate an artificial rise in the price of public stock) is dismissed.

NOV 4 *Hello Goodbye* is recorded. BD--14 (Oct 2) RO--20
--5 (Oct 2)

NOV 5 George Harrison's mother, Louise, flies to New York City to do TV and radio appearances; his father, Harold, flies on to Illinois to see their daughter, Louise.

A review of "How I Won the War" in *Our Sunday Visitor* calls John Lennon's appeal "enormous," though his part is minor.

NOV 7 Three photographic portraits of The Beatles by John Bratby go on sale at the Zwemmer Gallery.

NOV 8 New York premiere of film "How I Won the War," with John Lennon.

NOV 10 At the Saville Theatre, London, The Beatles make film clips to promote *Hello Goodbye.*

NOV 16   Ian Harrison is born, son of George Harrison's brother Peter and sister--in--law Pauline.

NOV 17   Louise and Harold Harrison, George's parents, fly back to England.

NOV 20   **Smiley Smile** (LP) by The Beach Boys, including *Vegetables* (produced by Paul McCartney and The Beach Boys) is released in the U.K.

NOV 23   *Rolling Stone* magazine reports on the first bootleg LP to contain songs by The Beatles -- Best of 1967 -- and other artists, the album surfacing in the New York City area.
"Sgt. Pepper" film clips are banned from broadcast by BBC's "Top of the Pops" and "Late Night Line Up" pro-- grams because of a musician's union controversy.

NOV 24   *Hello Goodbye/I Am the Walrus* (45) is released in the U.K. BIR--69 (Nov 14) BU22--16 (Dec) HHG7--9 (Nov 13)

NOV 26   Film of Beatles performing *Hello Goodbye* is broadcast in the U.S. on the "Ed Sullivan Show."

NOV 27   *Hello Goodbye/I Am the Walrus* (45) is released in the U.S.
Magical Mystery Tour (LP) is released in the U.S.

NOV 28   *Christmas Time Is Here Again!* is recorded.

NOV 29   First airplay of **Magical Mystery Tour** (LP).

LATE NOVEMBER--MID--DECEMBER

Filming of "Candy," featuring Ringo Starr as Emmanuel the Gardener.

DECEMBER

Blue Jay Way, George Harrison's tenth song for The Beatles, appears on **Magical Mystery Tour** (LP).

George Harrison records English--title tracks in London for his **Wonderwall Music** (LP).

EARLY DECEMBER

Scheduled time for broadcast of an ABC--TV interview with Louise Harrison, George's mother, in the U.S.

DECEMBER 1967--JANUARY 14, 1968

Tracks for George Harrison's **Wonderwall Music** (LP) are recorded at EMI studios in Bombay and at EMI's Abbey Road studios, London.

DEC 2   *Hello Goodbye* enters the *Billboard* singles charts at
           number 45, remaining on the charts for eleven weeks
           during which it reaches a high point of number 1.
           I Am the Walrus enters the *Billboard* singles charts at
           number 102.
           Hello Goodbye enters *Billboard*'s British top twenty singles
           charts, remaining on the charts for ten weeks during
           which it reaches a high point of number 1.
           Hello Goodbye enters the *Melody Maker* singles charts in
           the U.K. at number 3.
           Hello Goodbye enters Holland's Radio Veronica Top 40
           charts at number 4.
           It is reported that one of The Beatles' companies is dis-
           cussing the possibility of opening a chain of "Sgt.
           Pepper Lonely Hearts Clubs" in the U.S.
           John Lennon is interviewed by Kenny Everett on BBC
           radio's "Where It's At" program.
DEC 4   Ringo Starr flies to Rome to begin filming of "Candy."
           HH13–1 (Dec 1–11)
DEC 6   **Their Satanic Majesties Request** (LP) by The Rolling Stones,
           incorrectly rumored to include background vocals by Paul
           McCartney on the cut *Sing This All Together*, is released
           in the U.S.
DEC 7   The Apple Botique opens in 94 Baker Street, London;
           Jenny Boyd, Pattie's sister, works as one of the shop
           employees. BF–94 (Dec 5)   TBA–22 (Dec 4)
           Universal Beatle Day.
DEC 8   **Their Satanic Majesties Request** (LP) by The Rolling Stones,
           incorrectly rumored to include a background vocal by Paul
           McCartney on the cut *Sing This All Together,* is released
           in the U.K.
           Magical Mystery Tour (EP) is released in the U.K.
DEC 9   *I Am the Walrus* enters the *Billboard* Hot 100 charts at
           number 64, remaining on the charts for four weeks during
           which it reaches a high point of number 56.
           Hello Goodbye hits number 1 on the *Melody Maker* singles
           charts, remaining there for four weeks.
DEC 10   George Harrison and Ravi Shankar appear in an educational
           TV show broadcast from the U.N. Building, New York;
           Harrison's 20 minutes were taped in London some days
           before.
DEC 11   Paul McCartney and Jane Asher, vacationing on Paul's
           farm in Scotland, reiterate their plans to marry.

DEC 12   George Harrison's brother and sister--in--law, Harry and
          Irene, celebrate their ninth wedding anniversary.

DEC 15   The Beatles' Christmas record, *Christmas Time Is Here
          Again!* is released by the Fan Club; the sleeve is de--
          signed by Julian Lennon.   JLS--139 (Dec 21)   PMS--
          163 (Dec 11)

          Magical Mystery Tour (LP) is certified as a Gold Record
          by the R.I.A.A.

DEC 16   **Magical Mystery Tour** (EP) enters the *Billboard* British
          top twenty singles charts, remaining on the charts for
          nine weeks during which it reaches a high point of
          number 2.

          Magical Mystery Tour (EP) enters Holland's Radio
          Veronica Top 40 charts at number 15.

          Magical Mystery Tour (EP) enters the *Melody Maker* singles
          charts in the U.K. at number 17.

DEC 17   The Beatles throw a Christmas party for their Fan Club
          area secretaries.

DEC 21   The Beatles throw a gala Christmas party for their friends
          and the production staff of "Magical Mystery Tour."

DEC 21   George Harrison's parents spend eight days at George and
--28   Pattie's home.

DEC 23   *I Am the Walrus* reaches its highest position on the *Bill--
          board* singles charts: number 56.

          Magical Mystery Tour (LP) enters the *Billboard* album
          charts at number 157, remaining on the charts for 82
          weeks during which it reaches a high point of number 1.

late Dec Just before Christmas, John Lennon writes to his father,
          Freddie Lennon, who is sick in bed, and a few days
          later sends a car to bring his father for a visit with him
          and his family in Weybridge.

DEC 25   Paul McCartney and Jane Asher announce their engagement.
          The Beatles spend the day at home with their respective
          families.

Christmas George Harrison buys his parents a new car.

          George Harrison's parents spend eight days at George and
          Pattie Harrison's home.

DEC 26   World premiere of film "Magical Mystery Tour" on BBC--1
          TV, seen by 13 million viewers; broadcast in black--and--
          white.

DEC 27   Critics begin to attack the "Magical Mystery Tour" tele--
          vision show of the evening before.

          Evening Standard interview with Paul McCartney over the

"Magical Mystery Tour" film, which he directed, is published.

Paul McCartney appears on "The Frost Programme" television show.

DEC 28   George Harrison's parents return home after spending eight days with George and Pattie.

The Los Angeles *Times* coverage of "Magical Mystery Tour" is headlined: "Critics and Viewers Boo: Beatles Produce First Flop with Yule Film."

DEC 29   John Lennon leaves for a brief vacation in Morocco.

DEC 30   George Harrison's parents have a dinner for their other two sons, Harold and Peter, and their families.

Hello Goodbye hits number 1 on the *Billboard* singles charts, remaining there for three weeks.

DEC 31   *Hello Goodbye* enters the Polish radio station (Rozglasnia Harcerska) charts at number 2.

George Harrison's eldest maternal uncle dies at age 59.

LATE 1967

John Lennon has his Rolls Royce painted with psychedelic designs.

John Lennon and Yoko Ono begin a period of years during which they are inseparable, according to Mark Shipper's humorous spoof of Beatle history, *Paperback Writer*.

After a year of allowing the house and ground to fall into disrepair, Paul McCartney decides to fix up the house he had purchased in St. John's Wood, London, in late 1966.

The Beatles are invited to dine with Members of Parliament; Ringo Starr inhales some of the famous "Sergeant's Pepper," leading him to a sneezing bout which keeps him in bed for three days and establishes the Guinness world record for sneezing, according to Mark Shipper's humorous spoof of Beatle history, *Paperback Writer*.

Grapefruit becomes the first group signed to Apple Publishing.

LATE 1967--EARLY 1968

Soundtrack of the film "Yellow Submarine" is recorded.

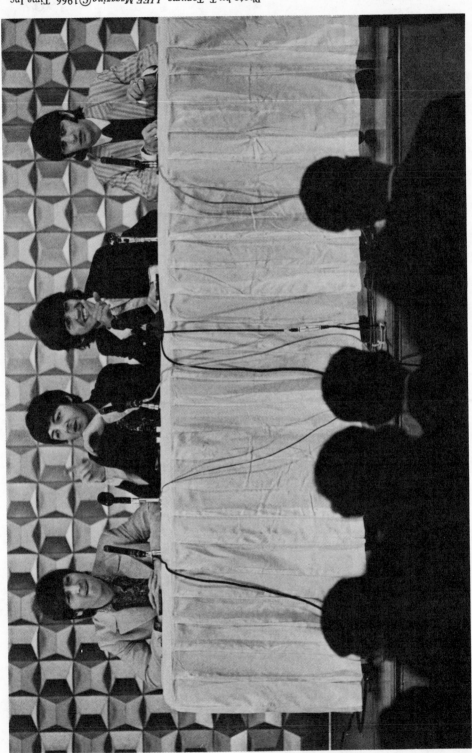

A crowd of people
turned away

A DAY
IN THE
LIFE

The Beatles
Day-By-Day

1968

DURING THIS YEAR . . .

Ringo Starr remarks that he was once called by someone from the *Jewish Chronicle* who assumed he was Jewish because of his large nose.

Beatles and Co. by Juan Carlos Kreimer is published in Argentina by Editorial Galerma.

Richard Hamilton, who designed a cover of an album for the Rolling Stones, declines Paul McCartney's request that he do a similarly "trendy" collage for the next Beatles album; Hamilton suggests that the cover be blank, with a photographic collage as an insert, and the albums numbered.

The songs recorded for the "white album" are all individual efforts, with no co-writing between Lennon and McCartney.

John Lennon's two books, *In His Own Write* and *A Spaniard in the Works*, are adapted for the London stage by Victor Spinetti and Adrienne Kennedy.

Flying, credited to Lennon/McCartney/Harrison/Starkey, is copyrighted in the U.K. by Northern Songs Ltd.

The Beatles: A Study in Sex, Drugs, and Revolution by Rev. David A. Noebel is published in the U.S. by the Christian Crusade.

The following singles by The Beatles are released in Australia: *Lady Madonna/The Inner Light, Hey Jude/Revolution.*

The following EPs by The Beatles are released in Australia: **Norwegian Wood, Magical Mystery Tour, Penny Lane.**

It's All Too Much and *Only a Northern Song* are copyrighted, and *I Want To Tell You* and *The Inner Light* recopyrighted in the U.K. by Northern Songs Ltd., words and music by George Harrison.

The Beatles: The Real Story, by Julius Fast, is published in the U.S. by Putnam.

The Beatles, Paul McCartney on lead, record unreleased versions

of *Step Inside Love* and *Goodbye; Step Inside Love* is later
recorded and released by Cilla Black.

EMI--Italiana begins to issue Beatles albums and singles in Italy,
taking over from Carish S.P.A.

The following singles by The Beatles are released in Italy: *Lady
Madonna/The Inner Light, Hey Jude/Revolution, Ob--la--di,
Ob--la--da/Back in the U.S.S.R.*

The Beatles by Anthony Scaduto is published in the U.S. by Signet.

The Lennon Play: In His Own Write, by John Lennon, Adrienne
Kennedy and Victor Spinetti, is published in the U.S. by Simon
& Schuster.

John Lennon's artistic work deliberately changes dramatically,
revealing more honestly and candidly -- too candidly, for some --
the "real" John behind the celebrity facade.

The Magical Mystery Tour (LP) is released in Germany by Apple.

Thank God for the Beatles, by Dr. Timothy Leary, is published by
the League for Spiritual Discovery.

Ringo Starr develops a new drum technique copied by drummers
the world over.

The Beatles Book, edited by Edward E. Davis, is published in the
U.S. by Cowles.

The Beatles: Words Without Music, edited by Rick Friedman, is
published in the U.S. by Grosset & Dunlap.

The following Beatles' singles are released in Holland: *Lady
Madonna/The Inner Light, Hey Jude/Revolution, Ob--la--di,
Ob--la--da/While My Guitar Gently Weeps.*

Dirk McQuickly and Ron Nasty fly to New York to announce the
Rutles' formation of Rutle Corps, according to the album
send-up of The Beatles, **The Rutles.**

The Yellow Submarine Gift Book is published in the U.S. by
World.

Yellow Submarine by Max Wilk is published in the U.S. by Signet
Books.

EARLY 1968

The Beatles watch a preview of the King Features film, "Yellow
Submarine."

Paul McCartney begins to write *Back in the U.S.S.R.* in India,
with a chorus added by Mike Love of The Beach Boys.

Clive Epstein discusses the possible sale of NEMS with Leonard

Richenberg, managing director of Triumph Investment Trust.
Chris O'Dell begins to work at Apple.
Paul McCartney, George Harrison and Ringo Starr pick the name
"Apple" for their new record company in the billiards room at
Paul's home, according to Mark Shipper's humorous spoof of
Beatle history, *Paperback Writer.*

JANUARY

George Harrison agrees to write the music for the film "Wonderwall."
John and Cynthia Lennon and actor Victor Spinetti vacation for
six days in Casablanca, Morocco.
It is reported that John Lennon's father, Alfred, recently married
a 19--year--old girl.
Total versions of Lennon--McCartney songs recorded by other
artists and groups reaches over 1,000.
Every Beatles single released to this date has sold over one
million units worldwide; 26 records -- singles and LPs -- have
sold over a million each in the U.S. alone; total sales -- counting
singles, EPs (as two singles), and LPs (as five singles) come to
225 million records.
McGough and McGear (LP) is recorded; produced by Paul McCartney.
Kenny Everett interview with John Lennon.
Proposed month for the visit to U.S. by Geoffrey Ellis, managing
director of NEMS, to arrange an American telecast of "Magical
Mystery Tour"; bad press in the U.K. keeps the film off U.S.
television.
Esquire's assessment of John Lennon's performance in "How I
Won the War": "adequate."
The Apple organization instructs the clothing design group, The
Fool, to make no further expenditures without written per--
mission.
Songs by The Beatles from the Kenny Everett interview are
recorded, later to be included on the bootleg LP **No Obvious
Title.**
John Lennon gives his wife, Cynthia, a puppy named Bernard.
Ringo Starr returns from Rome after a fortnight's filming of
"Candy."
George Harrison partially records tracks for the film "Wonderwall"
at EMI studios in London.

EARLY JANUARY

The price of shares in the Cameo--Parkway Record Company,

48% owned by Allen Klein, rises to an all–time high of 76 5/8.

JAN 1   Jane Asher visits with Paul McCartney's family.
JAN 5   *Time* magazine notes that the "flop," "Magical Mystery
          Tour," will net The Beatles $2 million.
          "Magical Mystery Tour" film is rebroadcast in color over
          BBC television.
JAN 6   *Daily Mirror* reports that John Lennon and his father,
          Alfred, have been reunited; Alfred Lennon had left
          home when John was a child.
          Magical Mystery Tour (LP) hits number one on the *Bill–
          board* album charts, remaining there for 8 weeks.
          Brian Epstein's estate reportedly set at Ł 486, 032 before
          taxes, the administration of which he willed to his mother.
JAN 9   John Lennon appears on the cover of *Look* magazine.
          George Harrison begins ten days in Bombay, India, com–
          posing, arranging and recording music for the film
          "Wonderwall" (and album, **Wonderwall Music**) at De
          Lane Lea studios; he is visited by Peter Tork of The
          Monkeys, and Eric Clapton of Cream.   ATN–68 (Indian
          title tracks only, recorded Jan. 9–15)
JAN 11   Instrumentals for *The Inner Light* are recorded in Bombay
          by George Harrison.
JAN 13   **Magical Mystery Tour** (LP) hits number one on the *Melody
          Maker* singles charts, dropping to number two the
          following week.
JAN 15   Paul Harrison, George Harrison's nephew, is 8 years old.
JAN 19   *Dear Delilah/The Dead Boot* (45) by Grapefruit, the
          first group signed by Apple, is released in the U.K. on
          the RCA/Victor label.
JAN 21   George and Pattie Harrison's second wedding anniversary.
          George and Pattie Harrison receive flowers sent to them by
          members of U.S. based Official George Harrison Fan
          Club for their anniversary.
JAN 27   George Harrison's brother and sister–in–law, Peter and
          Pauline, have their third wedding anniversary.
JAN 30   Start of Cilla Black's BBC television show.

FEBRUARY
The Beatles Fan Club moves from Liverpool to London.
John Lyndon, head of Apple Retail, claims in his correspondence
    with The Fool that the design group has taken a large amount
    of clothing without paying for it.

John Lennon ships his Rolls Royce to the U.S. for his use there.

Paul McCartney vacations on his farm in Scotland; Ringo Starr spends time in Rome.

The British press speculates on who controls the Apple Botique, since only John Lennon and George Harrison attended the opening in December 1967.

Neil Aspinall is appointed Director of Apple Corps; Alistair Taylor becomes General Manager.

Beatles Monthly begins to appear as a special supplement inside the U.S. magazine, *Teen Datebook.*

Neil Aspinall and Gene Mahon first discuss the apple label design to appear on all Apple Records.

And the Sun Will Shine and *The Dog Presides*, Paul McCartney on drums, are recorded by Paul Jones at EMI's Abbey Road studios.

Mal Evans discovers the Welsh group, The Iveys (later, Badfinger), who eventually sign with Apple.

The Beatles, Ltd. changes its name to Apple Corps, Ltd., parent company to Apple Electronics, Ltd., Apple Music Publishing, Apple Records, Apple Films Ltd., Apple Television, Apple Wholesale and Apple Retail.

It's All Too Much is recorded.

A version of *Think for Yourself* and the soundtrack for the film "Yellow Submarine" are recorded, later to appear on the bootleg recordings **Cinelogue Yellow Submarine** and **Cinelogue 2.**

Jenny Boyd, Pattie (Boyd) Harrison's sister, acts as a sales assistant in the Apple Botique.

Paul McCartney writes and records *Step Inside Love*; his version of the song is unreleased, but later appears on the bootleg recording **Those Were the Days.**

Apple Films Ltd. is founded as successor to Beatles Film Productions to handle financing and distribution of motion pictures and television productions.

Two film clips of The Beatles are made for the promotion of *Lady Madonna.*

Paul McCartney gives his song *Step Inside Love* to Cilla Black, to use as the theme song for her television show.

FEB 3   George and Pattie Harrison meet their new nephew, Ian, for the first time.

Lady Madonna is recorded by Paul McCartney and session musicians at Abbey Road studios. ATN--67 (Feb 3--4)

FEB 4   *Across the Universe* is partially recorded at the Abbey Road studios. ATN--83 (version one, recorded 4th *through* 8th)   RO–20 (4th *and* the 8th)

FEB 5   Paul McCartney appears at London press conference held to publicize the Leicester Arts Festival.

FEB 6   Ringo Starr sings *Act Naturally* with Cilla Black on her TV show.
Vocals for *The Inner Light* are recorded in London at Abbey Road studios.

FEB 7   National Beatle Day.

FEB 8   Recording of *Across the Universe* is completed.

FEB 10   "Magical Mystery Tour" film is broadcast over Dutch television.
Paul McCartney and Jane Asher attend a performance by Paul's brother, Mike McGear (with Scaffold).

FEB 11   Ringo and Maureen Starr have their third wedding anniver--sary.
Only a Northern Song and *Hey Bulldog* are recorded at EMI's Abbey Road studios.

FEB 13   Ringo Starr appears with Cilla Black on BBC–TV, singing *Do You Like Me Just a Little Bit.*

mid–Feb   Just prior to their trip to India, George Harrison and Ringo Starr shave off their moustaches.

FEB 16   George and Pattie Harrison, Jenny Boyd, and John and Cynthia Lennon fly to India to begin their meditation with the Maharishi.   BU3–7 (February 4th; also with Donovan and Mal Evans)

FEB 17   Begins a month--long period during which no Beatle--related recording appears on the *Billboard* singles charts.
It is reported that Hunter Davies is writing the Beatles' official biography.

FEB 19   Paul McCartney, Jane Asher, and Ringo and Maureen Starr join John and George in Rishikesh, India.

FEB 23   The Securities and Exchange Commission suspends trading in shares of the Cameo--Parkway Record Com--pany, 48% of the shares owned by Allen Klein, with the price of shares at 55 1/8.

FEB 24   Paul McCartney interview with *Evening Standard* appears, describing the formation of Apple.

FEB 25   George Harrison's 25th birthday is celebrated with songs, balloons and flowers by everyone at the Maharishi's retreat.

FEB 29   *AOS* is recorded at the Royal Albert Hall, London, by Yoko Ono (later appears on **Yoko Ono/Plastic Ono Band (LP)**; John Lennon plays guitar.

MARCH

Klaus Voorman creates the artwork for the cover of George
   Harrison's **Wonderwall Music** (LP).

Victor Spinetti produces and directs a stage adaptation of some of
   the contents of John Lennon's two books.

George Harrison sells his shares in Northern Songs when his
   song--writing contract expires.

John Lyndon, head of Apple Retail, warns the design group, The
   Fool, that they will be excluded from all clothing work rooms
   if they do not stop taking garments without payment.

Mal Evans becomes general manager of Apple Records, and Derek
   Taylor arrives from California to become Apple's publicity
   manager.

The Bonzo Dog Dah Doo Band records *I'm the Urban Spaceman*,
   produced by Paul McCartney.

MAR 1   The world is introduced to *Lady Madonna/The Inner
             Light*.
             Ringo Starr leaves the Maharishi's retreat after only two
             weeks, describing it as being like Butlin's, a British
             vacation camp, but with food too spicy for his tastes.

MAR 8   *Step Inside Love*, written by Paul McCartney and recorded
             by Cilla Black, is released in U.K. on a single.
             A single, *And the Sun Will Shine/The Dog Presides*, is re--
             leased in U.K., with Paul McCartney playing drums on
             And the Sun Will Shine.

MAR 9   The Beatles receive four Grammy Awards from the
             National Academy of Recording Arts & Sciences for
             1967: **Sgt. Pepper's Lonely Hearts Club Band** (LP) takes
             best album, best contemporary album, best album cover,
             best engineered recording.

MAR 10   George Harrison's mother, Louise, has a birthday.

MAR 14   A film clip made for the promotion of *Lady Madonna* is
             broadcast on British TV's "Top of the Pops."

MAR 15   A medley -- *Indian Ropetrick* and *Happy Birthday Mike
             Love* -- are recorded in Rishikesh, India, later to be in--
             cluded on the bootleg LP **Indian Rope Trick**.
             Lady Madonna/The Inner Light (45) is released in the U.K.

MAR 17   Pattie Harrison's 24th birthday, celebrated at the Mahar--
             ishi's retreat.

MAR 18   *Lady Madonna/The Inner Light* (45) released in U.S.
             TBD--6 (April)

MAR 23   *Step Inside Love* by Cilla Black, written by Paul
             McCartney, enters the *Melody Maker* singles charts in the

          U.K. at number 14.

MAR 23   *Lady Madonna* enters Holland's Radio Veronica Top 40 charts at number 7.

          Lady Madonna enters the *Billboard* British top twenty singles charts, remaining on the charts for six weeks, during which it reaches a high point of number 1.

          Lady Madonna enters the *Billboard* singles charts in the U.S. at number 23, remaining on the charts for eleven weeks during which it reaches a high point of number 4.

          The Inner Light enters the *Billboard* singles charts in the U.S. at number 117.

          Lady Madonna enters the *Melody Maker* singles charts in U.K. at number 3.

MAR 26   Paul McCartney and Jane Asher fly back to England.

MAR 30   *The Inner Light* reaches the highest position on the *Billboard* singles charts: number 96.

          Lady Madonna reaches its highest point on the *Melody Maker* singles charts: number 2.

          A promotional film--clip of *Lady Madonna* is shown on "Hollywood Palace."

MAR 31   Net profits for The Beatles' partnership combined with those of Apple Corps Ltd. reach one--and--a--half million pounds for the preceding 16 months.

          From this date until the end of 1970, no financial accounts of The Beatles' partnership are prepared or made to the partners.

APRIL

Apple Corps Ltd. sets up operations at 95 Wigmore Street in London.

Apple Publicity company is founded to handle advertising and publicity for all Apple enterprises.

Paul McCartney spends time at his farm in Scotland.

Sher--oo (LP) by Cilla Black is released in the U.K.

John Lennon and Yoko Ono marry, recording their wedding night for later release as an album (**Wedding Album**), according to Mark Shipper's humorous spoof of Beatle history, *Paperback Writer*.

Apple Publishing signs The Iveys (later Badfinger) to a publishing contract.

APRIL–JULY
> Most tracks for the album **Raga** are recorded by Ravi Shankar in
> India and Los Angeles, produced by George Harrison.

APR 1   The president of the Official George Harrison Fan Club in
          the U.S. receives a letter written by George Harrison
          expressing his thanks for the anniversary flowers received
          January 21st; the letter is written on stationary bearing
          the letterhead: Spiritual Regeneration Movement
          Foundation of India Under the Divine Guidance of His
          Holiness Maharishi Mahesh Yogi of Uttar Kaski.

APR 5   Jane Asher's 22nd birthday.

APR 6   *Step Inside Love* by Cilla Black, written by Paul McCartney,
          reaches its highest position on the *Melody Maker* singles
          charts: number 7.
          Apple is reported to have declared its openness to nomina-
          tions for new, worthwhile artists to record.
          The Inner Light occupies the 107th position on the *Bill-
          board* singles charts.

APR 7   The Beatles reportedly have sold the "Magical Mystery Tour"
          television show for broadcast in Japan.

APR 8   *Lady Madonna* (45) certified a Gold Record by the R.I.A.A.
          Julian Lennon's fifth birthday.

APR 12   George Harrison's nephew, Gordon Caldwell, has his 11th
          birthday.

APR 20   Apple announces its intention to promote unknown com-
          posers and musicians.
          Lady Madonna reaches its highest position on the *Billboard*
          singles charts: number 4.
          John and Cynthia Lennon arrive back in England from
          India.

APR 22   George and Pattie Harrison arrive back in England from
          India.

APR 25   It is reported that Brian Epstein's town house in Belgravia
          and his country home near Heathfield have been sold.

APR 27   Final day of the meditation course at the Maharishi's retreat
          in Rishikesh; all of The Beatles "dropped–out" before
          completion, Ringo and Maureen claiming they missed
          their children and didn't appreciate the spicy camp diet,
          Paul and Jane simply because they were rested and had
          "had enough," George, Pattie, John and Cynthia claim-
          ing they didn't wish to be part of a film about the
          Maharishi which an American company had begun at
          the camp.

MAY

While in Paris, France, George Harrison trips a photographer; Harrison pays a fine of $200.00 the following January.

Apple Management company is founded to act as theatrical agent for Apple artists.

John Lennon and Yoko Ono spend their first evening together at John's home in Weybridge.

Apple Overseas company is founded to handle foreign artists, who will record in their own countries for Apple.

John Lennon and Yoko Ono open their first art exhibit together at the Arts Lab in London.

Month announced for the first release of the film "Yellow Submarine," not released until July.

Paul McCartney attends a reception for the Leister College Arts Festival.

John Lennon orders an engraved silver--plated plaque to commemorate the Acorn Event.

MAY 4   Mary Hopkin, soon to be Apple's first female "discovery," wins a competition on the television show "Opportunity Knocks."

MAY 5   Fashion model Twiggy tells Paul McCartney about performer Mary Hopkin.

MAY 6   *Step Inside Love*, written by Lennon/McCartney and re--corded by Cilla Black, is released in the U.S. on a single.

MAY 8   George and Pattie Harrison originally scheduled to return to England from India on this date.

MAY 11 John Lennon, Paul McCartney, Neil Aspinall, Derek Taylor, Mal Evans and Ron Kass fly from London to New York to introduce Apple to the U.S. HH15--2 (also: Dennis O'Dell & Brian Lewis)

A three--and--a--half month period begins with no Beatles records on the *Melody Maker* charts in U.K., running through Aug. 31, 1968.

MAY 12 A special screening of "Magical Mystery Tour" takes place
--13   at the Straight Theatre in San Francisco as part of a benefit drive by radio station KMPX--FM.

MAY 13 Date of a London Palladium show organized to raise funds for British Olympic teams competing in the Mexico games; The Beatles earlier declined the request by Queen Elizabeth that they appear in the show.

mid--May "Magical Mystery Tour" has four showings at the Los Feliz Theatre, Los Angeles, and two at the Esquire

Theatre in Pasadena.

MAY 15   George and Pattie Harrison, with Ringo and Maureen
Starr, fly to France to attend a special screening of
"Wonderwall." HH15–2 (May 17)

John and Paul talk about Apple on the "Tonight" show,
hosted by Joe Garagiola; they also renounce their
association with the Maharishi. HH15–2 (May 14)

In U.S., John Lennon and Paul McCartney hold a press
conference to promote Apple, where Paul meets Linda
Eastman for the second time.

May   Linda Eastman slips Paul McCartney her phone number at
the New York press party held for the launching of Apple,
he calls her that very night.

May   Following the New York press party held for the launching
of Apple, Linda Eastman stays the night with John
Lennon and Paul McCartney at Nat Weiss's apartment,
and goes to the airport with them the next day.

Spring   By the time of the New York announcement of the forma--
tion of Apple by John Lennon and Paul McCartney, the
organization is riddled with hangers--on draining off
the company's revenue.

MAY 16   John Lennon and Paul McCartney return to London.

MAY 17   World premiere of the film "Wonderwall," with music by
George Harrison, at the Cannes Film Festival.

McGough and McGear (LP), co–produced by Paul
McCartney, is released in the U.K.

MAY 18   George and Pattie, with Ringo and Maureen, attend a
special screening of "Wonderwall" at the Cannes Film
Festival.

MAY 19   George, Pattie, Ringo and Maureen fly back to England
from France.

After returning from France, George and Pattie Harrison
drive to George's mother's in Appleton, Cheshire, then
on to Penketh, Warrington, Lancashire, to attend the
christening of their new nephew, Ian, at St. Mary's
Church.

George and Pattie Harrison leave Penketh around 7:00 p.m.
for London; George indicates he has a recording session
later in the evening.

The Beatles begin recording songs for their next album,
most of them selected from 34 songs written by the
four -- including Ringo's first song -- while in India.

Lady Madonna enters the Polish radio station (Rozglasnia Harcerska) charts at number 5.

MAY 20   George Harrison's parents have a wedding anniversary.

MAY 21   Prior to their attendance at his performance at the Royal Albert Hall, Andy Williams lunches with Paul McCartney and Jane Asher.

MAY 22   John Lennon declares the war in Viet Nam to be insanity in an interview aired on an American television show.

In London, John Lennon, Yoko Ono, and George and Pattie Harrison hold a press conference to promote Apple Tailoring.

MAY 23   George Harrison and John Lennon open a shop called Apple Tailoring in King's Road, Chelsea, managed by clothing designer John Crittle.

MAY 28   George Harrison's father has a birthday.

MAY 30   An unreleased 10--minute version of *Revolution* and of *Revolution No. 9* are recorded at Abbey Road studios.

LATE MAY

John Lennon and Yoko Ono record tracks for **Unfinished Music No. 1 -- Two Virgins** (LP) at Ascot Sound studios.

LATE MAY -- MID--OCTOBER

The Beatles spend nearly every weekday at the Apple offices on Wigmore Street; tracks for **The Beatles** (LP) are recorded.

JUNE

Total songs written by Lennon/McCartney and recorded by The Beatles reaches 105, with an additional 17 songs written for and recorded by other artists.

George Harrison and Ravi Shankar hold a press conference in Los Angeles to announce production of a film about Indian art and culture, "Raga."

Mary Hopkin begins recording *Those Were the Days/Turn Turn Turn* at Trident Studios, London; she also begins to record Italian, French, German and Spanish versions of *Those Were the Days*. Paul McCartney plays instruments and produces all the recordings, the sessions ending in September.

Where Is Tomorrow/Work Is a Four--Letter Word (45), by Cilla Black is released in the U.K.

John Lennon and Yoko Ono fly to County Mayo, Ireland, for a

few days' vacation.

Total songs written by George Harrison and recorded by The Beatles reaches 11.

Paul McCartney's accountant is told by Apple accountants that the combined net profits for Beatles' partnership, and for Apple Corps Ltd., were about one--and--a--half--million pounds for the periods ending March 31, 1968, the same amount netted by The Beatles over all the years prior to December 31, 1967.

The Fool, a design group, moves from an association with the Apple organization to a new arrangement with Mercury Records.

JUNE--AUGUST
Apple begins to move into new offices in Savile Row, London.

EARLY JUNE
The first version of *Revolution* is recorded by the Beatles.

JUN 7   George and Pattie Harrison, along with Ringo and Maureen Starr and Mal Evans, come to California so George can film a guest appearance in the Ravi Shankar film, "Messenger of the East." HH15--3 (mid--June)

JUN 8   In North Wales, Paul McCartney and Jane Asher attend the wedding of Paul's brother, Mike McGear, to Angela Fishwick; Paul is best man.

Begins a three month period during which no Beatle--related recording appears on the *Billboard* singles charts.

Paul McCartney interview in *Melody Maker* reveals that twenty new songs were written by The Beatles while visiting the Maharishi in India.

JUN 10   George Harrison's brother--in--law, Gordon Caldwell, Sr., has a birthday.

Lord Sitar (LP) by Lord Sitar, wrongly attributed to George Harrison, is released in U.S.

JUN 11   *Blackbird* is recorded by Paul McCartney at Abbey Road studios, London.

JUN 12   George Harrison's sister--in--law, Irene, has a birthday.

JUN 15   John Lennon and Yoko Ono's "Acorn Event" at the National Sculpture Exhibition, Coventry Cathedral.

JUN 16   George, Pattie, Ringo, Maureen and Mal fly to New York City.

JUN 18   Paul McCartney invites fans inside 93--94 Waldor Street for his 26th birthday party of champagne and a cake they had presented him with earlier.

John Lennon, Yoko Ono and Neil Aspinall attend the opening of the National Theatre production of John's one--act play, *In His Own Write*, at London's Old Vic.

Paul McCartney attends the opening of a play featuring Jane Asher, instead of attending the opening of John Lennon's play.

JUN 19   George, Pattie, Ringo, Maureen and Mal fly back to England from New York.

JUN 20   Paul McCartney flies to Los Angeles on Apple business.

Apple Records reportedly reaches a distribution agreement with EMI in the U.K. and Capitol in the U.S.

JUN 20 --24   Paul McCartney shares a bungalow at the Beverly Hills Hotel with Linda Eastman.

JUN 21   Paul McCartney, in Hollywood for a Capitol Records Convention, announces that all future records by The Beatles will be released on the Apple label.

JUN 22   Paul McCartney, according to *New Musical Express*, has filmed an hour--long interview with David Frost for American television.

Apple Records is reported to have purchased 3 Savile Row as a recording studio for a half--million pounds.

John Lennon discusses stage adaptations of his books, *In His Own Write* and *A Spaniard In the Works*, on BBC's "Release."

JUN 24 --26   George Harrison plays lead guitar and produces recordings of *Sour Milk Sea* (written by George) and *The Eagle Laughs at You*, recorded at Trident studios, London, by Jackie Lomax.

JUN 25   Paul McCartney and Mike McGear leave Paul's home in St. John's Wood after fixing a leak in their green Mini.

JUN 30   *Thingumybob* and *Yellow Submarine*, are recorded by John Foster and Sons Ltd. Black Dyke Mills Band for Apple Records at Victoria Hall, Bradford, England, conducted and produced by Paul McCartney. PMS--165 (April 30)

JUNE--JULY

Originally scheduled time frame for the release of the "Wonder--wall" film, not released generally until January 1969.

MID--1968

Paul McCartney writes *Maxwell's Silver Hammer*.

SUMMER

Paul McCartney records *Jubilee*, later called *Junk*.

John Lennon, watching student riots in Paris under the influence
of LSD, is inspired to lead The Beatles in the creation of their
unreleased album, **The Little Red Album**, according to *National
Lampoon*'s parody of Beatles' history. The album contains
songs like: *Love Mao Do, Rice Paddies Forever*, and *Paperback
Tiger*.

George Harrison writes and records *Not Guilty* for the "white album,"
but it goes unreleased until his 1979 album **George Harrison**.
BU25–13 (1967)

At a press interview, after being asked what new material Apple was
about to release, John Lennon launches into versions of *Those
Were The Days* and *Don't Let Me Down*.

JULY

Employees of the Apple Botique are given two weeks' notice.

Paul McCartney holds a photo session in the yard of his home.

Apple Records signs The Iveys (later Badfinger) to a recording
contract.

Paul McCartney receives a citation for speeding in Coventry.

EARLY JULY

Concert promoter Vic Lewis goes to Moscow to try and arrange a
Beatles concert in the Soviet Union.

JULY–OCTOBER

James Taylor (LP) is recorded for Apple at Trident studios,
London, by James Taylor; Paul McCartney plays bass guitar
on *Carolina In My Mind*.

JUL 1   John Lennon's first art exhibit at the Robert Frazer
Gallery in London, "You Are Here," dedicated to Yoko
Ono. JLS–141 (Frazer) PMS–166 (Fraser)
Goodnight is recorded at EMI's Abbey Road studios.

JUL 2   Recording of *Ob–la–di, Ob–la–da* begins at EMI studios in
Abbey Road, London.

JUL 3   Fourteenth wedding anniversary of Louise and Gordon
Caldwell, George Harrison's sister and brother–in–law.

JUL 6   An excerpt from the cartoon film "Yellow Submarine" is broadcast on the BBC's "Release" show.

"A Hard Day's Night" is re--run on NBC--TV in the U.S.

JUL 7   Ringo Starr's 28th birthday; he receives a go--kart from his wife Maureen.

Pattie Harrison is reported to be opening an art shop in Chelsea, England.

JUL 8   At the behest of actor David Peel, Apple underwrites the cost of a children's show on a Brighton beach.

JUL 9   *Somewhere in the Crowd*, with Ringo Starr on backing vocals, is recorded at EMI's Abbey Road studios, London, by Solomon King.

Revolution is recorded at EMI's Abbey Road studios, St. John's Wood, London. ATN--67 (mid--July)

JUL 12   John Lennon puts his home up for sale, asking $96,000.00.

Don't Pass Me By is recorded by Ringo Starr at the Abbey Road studios.

JUL 13   An advertisement appears in *Record Mirror* offering for sale a 1961 Citroen 2CV for no less than Ł300, the car having been hand--painted by George Harrison and Klaus Voorman.

mid--Jul John and Julian Lennon and Yoko Ono go to visit John's Aunt Mimi for a weekend.

Apple Records in launched.

Mary Hopkin records *Those Were the Days/Turn! Turn! Turn!* (45) for Apple Records, produced by Paul McCartney.

An as yet undecorated Apple studios on Savile Row begins to be occupied.

JUL 15   *Cry Baby Cry* is recorded by John Lennon at EMI's Abbey Road studios.

JUL 17   World premiere at the Pavilion in London of the film "Yellow Submarine"; all The Beatles attend except Ringo.

A celebration party is held in the "Yellow Submarine Discoteque Room" at the Royal Lancaster Hotel, London, following the premiere of the film "Yellow Submarine."

JUL 18   At the Abbey Road studios, The Beatles begin recording versions of *Helter Skelter*, which continue throughout August.

JUL 19   Recording of *Sexy Sadie* begins at EMI studios in Abbey Road, London.

An excerpt from the cartoon film "Yellow Submarine" is

shown on BBC TV's "How It Is."
JUL 20   Jane Asher appears on the "Simon Dee Show" on BBC--
          TV, announcing that her seven--month engagement to
          Paul McCartney has been ended -- by Paul. BIR--74
          (August)   IR--74 (August)
          George Harrison's brothers, Harry and Peter, celebrate,
          respectively, their 34th and 28th birthdays.
JUL 21   Further comments by Jane Asher and Paul's father on the
          broken engagement appear in the British press.
          Daily Telegraph reports that Northern Songs Ltd. is under--
          valued on the stock exchange.
JUL 23   *The Hollywood Reporter* finds the ending of "Yellow
          Submarine" to be "painfully long and pretentiously
          cute."
          Variety predicts "Yellow Submarine" will succeed with
          Beatles fans and pop audiences in general.
          Recording of *Everybody's Got Something to Hide (Except
          Me and My Monkey)* begins at EMI studios in Abbey
          Road, London.
JUL 25   Recording of *While My Guitar Gently Weeps* begins at
          EMI studios in Abbey Road, London, and is finished
          much later.
JUL 26   John Lennon spends the day finishing *Hey Jude* at Paul
          McCartney's home.
JUL 27   The decision is made to close down the Apple Boutique.
late Jul Pattie Harrison and Jenny Boyd open a stall in Chelsea's
          Antique Market, selling art nouveau.
JUL 29   The Beatles are filmed for "Experiment in Television"
          during the recording sessions of *Hey Jude*; the film is
          first shown on August 30.
JUL 30   Variant recording *Hey Jude* is made, later to appear on the
          bootleg LP **L.S. Bumble Bee.**
          Paul McCartney announces the closing of the Apple
          Boutique.
          Apple Boutique cashiers begin to inform customers that
          there will be no charge for the merchandise they select.
JUL 31   Apple Boutique closes in London, the merchandise given
          away to the public.   PMW--9 (July 1969)
          Daily Telegraph reports that Paul McCartney's St. John's
          Wood home is included in a preservation order covering
          buildings of architectural or historic note.
          Another version of *Revolution* is recorded by John Lennon
          and Paul McCartney at the Abbey Road studios.

JUL 31   *Hey Jude* is recorded at the Abbey Road studios.
–AUG 1

LATE JULY
Four versions of *Revolution* have been recorded since early June.

AUGUST
Francie Schwartz moves in with Paul McCartney at his home in
   St. John's Wood, London; she stays only about three weeks.
George Harrison buys a guitar as a gift for Mary Hopkin; he is too
   shy to give it directly to her, and asks Mal Evans to make the
   presentation.
Kenny Everett interviews with The Beatles are recorded.
Eric Clapton gives George Harrison a new guitar, a cherry Gibson
   "Les Paul Custom," which is promptly named "Lucy." George
   uses it for recording songs for the "white album," **Let It Be** (LP),
   and **Abbey Road** (LP).
A rendition of *Fool on the Hill* by Sergio Mendes and Brazil '66,
   is released in the U.S., later to reach a high point on the
   Billboard top ten charts of number 6.

EARLY AUGUST
Stanley Gorticov, Capitol Records president, arrives in London for
   a visit at Apple Records, which Capitol distributes in the U.S.

AUG 1   The Beatles bring in a 40–piece orchestra to help record
            the climax of *Hey Jude*.
            Daily Mail publishes an interview with Paul McCartney on
            the Apple Boutique.
AUG 2   George Harrison leaves Paul McCartney's home in a cab.
            Television comedy series "Thingumybob" begins in London,
            theme song written by Paul McCartney and played by
            Apple's Black Dyke Mills Band.
AUG 3   Paul McCartney's current dating is the subject of a piece in
            Disc and Music Echo.
AUG 4   Carole Chapman joins Apple as assistant to Ron Kass, head
            of Apple's music division.
            Maureen Starkey turns 22.
AUG 5   In mid–afternoon, George Harrison encounters some fans

on Claremont Drive near his home in Esher; he invites
them to his house the next day.

AUG 6   George Harrison meets with fans in his home in Esher
around 1:00 p.m., chats, poses for photographs, signs
autographs, then excuses himself in order to eat breakfast.

AUG 7   The Beatles spend the day recording at EMI studios,
London, leaving around 5:30 a.m.
The Beatles record the long unreleased *Not Guilty*, to
which Eric Clapton adds a guitar track. ATN--260
(George and Eric Clapton only)
Paul McCartney and friends visit the now empty Apple
Boutique, painting the windows with Beatles' song
titles using whitewash.

AUG 8   George Harrison's mother, Louise, takes her grandchildren
Leslie and Gordon Caldwell for a weekend visit at
George's house in Esher.

AUG 9   Paul McCartney begins to record *Mother Nature's Son*,
a song on which no other Beatle is present, at EMI
studios in Abbey Road, London.
Louise Harrison, George's mother, brings her grandchildren
to visit with fans at the Patten Arms Hotel, Warrington.

AUG 10 Peter and Pauline Harrison, George's brother and sister--in--
law, entertain fans at their home in Weybridge.

AUG 11 National Apple Week, August 11–18, begins with the release
on the Apple label of the Black Dyke Mills Band's
Thingumybob single (conducted by Paul McCartney),
and George Harrison's **Wonderwall Music** (LP).

AUG 13 John Lennon, Yoko Ono and daughter Kyoko arrive at
EMI studios, followed by Ringo Starr in his limousine,
with George Harrison and Paul McCartney coming
together in George's white Mercedes.
John Lennon records *Yer Blues* at EMI studios in Abbey
Road, London.

AUG 14 *What a Shame Mary Jane Had a Pain at the Party* is re--
corded by John Lennon; not officially released, but
contained on the bootleg LP **Mary Jane**.

AUG 15 *Rocky Raccoon* is recorded alone by Paul McCartney at
the Abbey Road studios; only George Martin accom--
panies on piano.

AUG 16 **Lord Sitar** (LP) by Lord Sitar, wrongly attributed to
George Harrison, is released in the U.S.
George Harrison's sister, Louise Caldwell, is 37.
Apple releases Mary Hopkin's *Those Were the Days* single,

produced by Paul McCartney.

AUG 27 George and the entire Harrison family, and Mal Evans and family, leave for a vacation in Greece.

AUG 19 Jason Starkey is one year old.

AUG 20 Paul McCartney records *Wild Honey Pie* alone in EMI studios in Abbey Road, London; John, George and Ringo are absent.

AUG 21 George Harrison and Mal Evans return to England from Greece, leaving the rest of the Harrison family cruising around the Greek coastline in a boat belonging to Alex Mardas.

Hey Jude/Revolution (45) is first aired on radio.

AUG 22 Cynthia Lennon sues John Lennon for divorce on grounds of adultery.

Recording of *Back in the U.S.S.R.* begins at EMI studios in Abbey Road; Ringo Starr is absent.

AUG 23 *Halton Mill Morning*, first single by Apple Music's new song--writing group, The Web, is released.

Sixth wedding anniversary of John and Cynthia Lennon.

Reports of Cynthia Lennon's divorce plans appear.

AUG 23 Scheduled days for a convention of Beatle fans to be held
--24 in Minneapolis, Minnesota.

AUG 24 Paul McCartney interviewed by Alan Smith of *New Musical Express.*

At behest of John Lennon, Ronan O'Rahilly joins Apple as a business adviser.

AUG 26 *Hey Jude/Revolution* (45) is released in the U.S.

Thingumybob/Yellow Submarine (45), produced by Paul McCartney and recorded for Apple by John Foster and Sons Ltd. Black Dyke Mills Band, is released in the U.S.

Sour Milk Sea/The Eagle Laughs at You (45) by Jackie Lomax, produced by George Harrison, is released in the U.S.; *Sour Milk Sea* is written by George Harrison.

Mary Hopkin's *Those Were the Days/Turn! Turn! Turn!* (45) is released in the U.S., produced by Paul McCartney.

AUG 27 One year since the death of Brian Epstein.

George Harrison's niece, Janet, turns six years old.

AUG 28 Recording of *Dear Prudence* begins at Trident Studios, London.

AUG 30 Mary Hopkin's *Those Were the Days/Turn! Turn! Turn!* (45) is released in the U.K., produced by Paul McCartney.

Hey Jude/Revolution (45) by The Beatles is released in the U.K The Beatles first recording on the Apple label.

Film clip made during recording sessions for *Hey Jude* is
aired as part of a show called "Experiment in Television."
Neil Aspinall, managing director of Apple, marries Suzy
Ornstein in Chelsea; the wedding is attended by Paul
McCartney.

LATE AUGUST
George Harrison writes the liner notes for an album by Ashish
Khan, Ravi Shankar's nephew, **Young Master of the Sarod.**

SEPTEMBER
A rendition of *With a Little Help from My Friends* by Joe Cocker,
written by John Lennon and Paul McCartney, is released in the
U.K., later to reach a high point on the British *Billboard* top ten
singles charts of number 1.
Cameo--Parkway Record Company, 48% of the shares owned by
Allen Klein, takes over Allen Klein and Company; the new
company is renamed ABKCO Industries Incorporated.
Mary Hopkin concludes recording sessions for Italian, French,
German and Spanish versions of *Those Were the Days* begun in
June, all produced by Paul McCartney at Trident studios,
London.

SEP 1   The final version of *Helter Skelter* is recorded.
          The rest of the Harrison family returns to England from
             their vacation in Greece, going directly to Esher to visit
             George and Pattie.
SEP 3   During the evening, Mal Evans distributes invitations to
             fans outside EMI studios to take part in a TV perfor--
             mance by the Beatles.
SEP 4   Fans congregate outside Paul McCartney's home in St.
             John's Wood, awaiting his departure for Twickenham
             studios to film The Beatles promotional clip for *Hey
             Jude*; he leaves in a limousine with American lawyer/
             associate Nat Weiss, a friend of the late Brian Epstein.
          At London's Victoria Station, around 30 fans board a bus
             which will take them to Twickenham studios to partici--
             pate in the filming of the *Hey Jude* promotional film.
          Before beginning the recording of the *Hey Jude* promo--
             tional film at Twickenham studios, The Beatles "warm
             up" with their versions of *Hang Down Your Head, Tom
             Dooley* and other songs.
          The Beatles film versions of the *Hey Jude* promotional

film for five hours at Twickenham studios, about 50–60
invited fans participating in singing the long ending.

Near midnight, with most fans departed, David Frost
re–records his introduction to The Beatles' *Hey Jude*
promotional film; the film is to be shown on his TV
show, "Frost On Sunday."

SEP 6   *Thingumybob/Yellow Submarine* (45), produced by Paul
McCartney and recorded for Apple by John Foster and
Sons Ltd. Black Dyke Mills Band, is released in the U.K.

Sour Milk Sea/The Eagle Laughs at You (45) by Jackie
Lomax, produced by George Harrison, is released in the
U.K. on Apple; *Sour Milk Sea* is written by George
Harrison.

SEP 7   *Hey Jude* enters the *Melody Maker* singles chart in U.K.
at number 1, remaining there for four weeks.

George Harrison's cousin, Angela French, marries, coin–
cidentally, Brian French.

Hey Jude enters the *Billboard* British top twenty singles
charts, remaining on the charts for eleven weeks during
which it reaches a high point of number 1.

Those Were the Days by Mary Hopkin, produced by Paul
McCartney, enters the *Melody Maker* singles charts in
the U.K. at number 23.

SEP 8   Beatles performance of *Hey Jude*, previously filmed, is
broadcast on the David Frost Show, "Frost On Sunday."

SEP 10   Cynthia Lennon is 29.

SEP 11   Recording of *Glass Onion* begins at EMI studios in Abbey
Road, London, by John Lennon and Paul McCartney.

SEP 13   Zak Starkey turns age 3.

The Beatles appear on the cover of *Life* magazine.

Hey Jude (45) is certified as a Gold Record by the R.I.A.A.

SEP 14   *Hey Jude* enters the *Billboard* singles charts at number 10,
remaining on the charts for 19 weeks during which it
reaches a high point of number 1.

Hey Jude enters Holland's Radio Veronica Top 40 charts
at number 1.

The Beatles -- The Authorized Biography, by Hunter–Davies,
is published by Heinemann in U.K.

Revolution enters the *Billboard* singles charts at number
38, remaining on the charts for eleven weeks during
which it reaches a high point of number 12.

New Musical Express reports that 2,000,000 copies of *Hey
Jude* have been sold.

Broadcast on BBC–1 of the television special "All My
Loving," featuring interviews of The Beatles about
developments in pop music; produced by Tony Palmer.
Paul McCartney *Melody Maker* interview appears.

SEP 16   *I Will* is recorded by John Lennon, Paul McCartney and
George Harrison at EMI's Abbey Road studios.

SEP 18   *Birthday* is recorded at EMI studios in Abbey Road, London,
with John Lennon, Paul McCartney, Linda Eastman,
Yoko Ono, and Pattie Harrison on vocals.

SEP 19   *Piggies* is recorded at Abbey Road studios.
Filmed Beatles performance of *Revolution* is broadcast on
BBC's "Top of the Pops."

SEP 21   *Revolution* reaches its highest position on the *Billboard*
singles charts: number 12.
Those Were the Days by Mary Hopkin, produced by Paul
McCartney, enters the *Billboard* singles charts at number
132.

SEP 23   Recording of *Happiness Is a Warm Gun* begins at EMI
studios in Abbey Road, London.

SEP 28   *Sour Milk Sea* by Jackie Lomax, produced by George
Harrison, enters the *Billboard* singles charts at number
117, remains there the following week, dropping off
the week after.
Hey Jude hits number 1 on the *Billboard* singles charts,
remaining there for nine weeks.

SEP 29   *Hey Jude* enters the Polish radio station (Rozglasnia
Harcersha) charts at number 12.
Leslie Caldwell, George Harrison's niece, is 9 years old.
Revolution enters the Polish radio station (Rozglasnia
Harcerska) charts at number 17.

OCTOBER

While in California, George Harrison composes three new songs,
visits Eric Clapton, Donovan, Jack Cassidy, Frank Sinatra,
attends a concert by Cream, and makes a brief appearance on
the "Smothers Brothers Show."

Linda Eastman invents a photographic assignment in London in
order to see Paul McCartney again.

Paul McCartney calls Linda Eastman long distance from London to
New York and invites her to move in with him; she initially
arrives without daughter Heather.

John Lennon and Yoko Ono announce that Yoko is pregnant.

While in California, George Harrison receives the gold record for
Hey Jude, presented by Capitol Records at the Los Angeles

Playboy Club.

John Lennon records *Oh My Love*, later to appear on the bootleg recording **John Lennon**.

Badge, co--composed by Eric Clapton and George Harrison, is recorded by Cream, with George playing rhythm guitar.

EARLY OCTOBER

Freda Kelly, secretary of the Beatles fan club in the U.K., gives birth to a son, Timothy, at Sefton General Hospital, Liverpool.

Jackie Lomax goes on a promotional tour of the U.S. accompanied by Mal Evans.

OCT 1   *Honey Pie* is recorded at Trident studios, London, without Ringo Starr.

OCT 3   *Savoy Truffle* is recorded at Trident studios, London, without Ringo Starr.

OCT 4   *Martha My Dear* is recorded by John Lennon at Trident studios, London.

OCT 5   *Those Were the Days* by Mary Hopkin, produced by Paul McCartney, hits number 1 on the *Melody Maker* singles charts, remaining there for five weeks.

OCT 6   *Hey Jude* promotional film--clip is shown on the "Smothers Brothers Show" in the U.S.

OCT 8   Recording sessions for *Long Long Long* are held at Abbey Road studios, without Ringo Starr.

OCT 9   John Lennon turns 28.

I'm So Tired is recorded by John Lennon at Abbey Road studios, London.

Paul McCartney presents Mary Hopkin singing *House of the Rising Sun* on the "David Frost Presents" show aired on U.S. television.

Recording of *The Continuing Story of Bungalow Bill* begins at EMI studios in Abbey Road, London.

OCT 10   *Why Don't We Do It in the Road* is recorded at Abbey Road studios, London.

OCT 11   *I'm the Urban Spaceman*, produced by Paul McCartney, is released in the U.K. on a single by The Bonzo Dog Band.

OCT 12   "Help!" is shown on NBC--TV in the U.S.

An *Evening Standard* interview with Jane Asher appears.

OCT 13   *Revolution* promotional film is shown on the "Smothers Brothers Show" in the U.S.

Julia is recorded by John Lennon at EMI's Abbey Road studios.

OCT 14   Ringo Starr vacations in Sardinia.
OCT 16   George and Pattie Harrison arrive in California on Apple
         business, along with Jock McLean, Beatles U.S. road
         manager.
OCT 17   George Harrison records four tracks with Jackie Lomax in
         Los Angeles for Jackie's new album.
OCT 18   John Lennon and Yoko Ono are arrested on drug charges
         after a raid on Ringo Starr's London apartment, where
         they are staying.
OCT 19   John Lennon and Yoko Ono appear in Marylebone
         Magistrates Court after their arrest the previous day.
late Oct After recording sessions with Jackie Lomax are completed,
         George and Pattie Harrison go to the Joshua Tree, a
         California desert resort; after a relaxation period, they
         go to Woodstock, New York, and spend two weeks at
         Bob Dylan's home.
OCT 25   *En Aquellos Dias/Turn! Turn! Turn!* (45) by Mary Hopkin,
         produced by Paul McCartney, is released in Spain.
         It is announced that John Lennon and Yoko Ono are ex--
         pecting a child in February 1969.
         Mary Hopkin's *Quelli Erand Giorni/Turn! Turn! Turn!*
         is released in Italy, produced by Paul McCartney.
         Le Temps des Fleurs/Turn! Turn! Turn! (45) by Mary
         Hopkin, produced by Paul McCartney, is released in
         France.
         An Jenem Tag/Turn! Turn! Turn! (45) by Mary Hopkin,
         produced by Paul McCartney, is released in Germany.
         Mary Hopkin attends a New York concert by Donovan
         Leitch.
OCT 26   *The Eagle Laughs at You* by Jackie Lomax, produced by
         George Harrison, enters the *Billboard* singles charts at
         number 125, remains there an additional two weeks,
         and then drops from the charts.
         Date on which, three years before, The Beatles received
         their MBEs.
OCT 27   Mary Hopkin appears on the "Ed Sullivan Show."
OCT 28   Cynthia Lennon officially files petition for divorce.
OCT 29   George Harrison's sister--in--law, Pauline, turns 25.
OCT 30   *Motion Picture Herald* on "Yellow Submarine": "indes--
         cribable."
OCT 31   Linda Eastman leaves for England to live with Paul
         McCartney; they are married 4½ months later.

LATE OCTOBER -- EARLY NOVEMBER

John Lennon and Yoko Ono's two films, "Smile" and "Two Virgins," are first shown at the Chicago Film Festival; "Smile" wins an award.

FALL

John Lennon records *Those Were the Days* and a version of *Don't Let Me Down*, later to appear on the bootleg recordings **Abbey Road Revisited** and **Spicy Beatles Songs**.

The Beatles separately record tracks for *The Beatles 1968 Christmas Record.*

"Paul Is Dead" rumors are at their height.

NOVEMBER

A rendition of *Ob--la--di, Ob--la--da* by The Marmalade is released in the U.K., later to reach a high point on the British *Billboard* top ten charts of number 1.

Side two of **Electronic Sound** (LP) is recorded by George Harrison.

George Harrison records *No Time or Space* (later released on **Electronic Sound**) in California, with the assistance of Bernie Crause.

Linda Eastman moves in with Paul McCartney at his home in St. John's Wood, London.

Paul McCartney returns to the U.S. with Linda Eastman; he meets her father, Lee, and her brother, John, partners in the New York law firm, Eastman and Eastman.

Paul McCartney sings backing vocal and plays tambourine during Donovan Leitch's recording of *Atlantis* at American Recording Company studios, Los Angeles.

Ringo Starr records *This Is Some Friendly*, never released.

NOV 1   **Wonderwall Music** (LP) by George Harrison, the first Beatle "solo" album, is released in the U.K.

NOV 2   *Those Were the Days* by Mary Hopkin, produced by Paul McCartney, reaches its highest position on the *Billboard* singles charts: number 2.

NOV 3   The Beatles appear on BBC--TV, along with Lulu, Donovan, and Louise Harrison, George's mother.

A film clip from "Yellow Submarine" is shown on the "Ed Sullivan Show" in the U.S.

NOV 4   John Lennon and Yoko Ono record four tracks which
  –25   later appear on side two of **Unfinished Music No. 2:
             Life with the Lions** (LP) at Queen Charlotte's Hospital,
             London.

NOV 5   Paul McCartney vacations in Scotland.

NOV 8   Advertisements by John Lennon and Yoko Ono call for a
             neutral radio station, "The Peace Ship," to broadcast to
             Arab and Israeli sides in the Middle East.
             John and Cynthia Lennon granted a divorce; John Lennon
             does not appear in court because he is attending Yoko
             in hospital, who is in danger of miscarriage.
             Love of the Loved, Step Inside Love and *It's for You* are
             included on U.K. release by Cilla Black, **The Best of
             Cilla** (LP).

NOV 9   George Harrison is reported not to have renewed his con-
             tract with Northern Songs Ltd.

NOV 11   **Unfinished Music No. 1 -- Two Virgins** (LP) released in U.S.

NOV 13   New York premiere of film "Yellow Submarine" at the
             Forum and Tower East theaters. HH16-6 (Nov. 26 at
             Radio City Music Hall, New York) GUB–99 (late
             winter)

NOV 15   The review of "Yellow Submarine" in the Los Angeles
             Times calls the film "the most stupendous animation
             feat in decades."
             Maybe Tomorrow/And Her Daddy's a Millionaire (45) by
             The Iveys is released in the U.K.
             A review of "Yellow Submarine" in the Los Angeles *Times*
             calls The Beatles' appearance at the end of the film a
             "plain old let–down" compared with the magic of the
             rest of the film.

mid–Nov   The London *Observer*'s music reviewer, Tony Palmer,
             heralds the coming of **The Beatles** (LP) to appear in
             about a week.
             At least twenty U.S. companies licensed by King Features
             begin to market Beatle novelties to coincide with the
             premiere of "Yellow Submarine," beginning the second
             American wave of Beatles memorabilia.

NOV 16   Ian Harrison, George's nephew, is one year old.
             Lennon and McCartney reported to have held discussions
             with Lord Beeching about his assuming the management
             of Apple.
             "Yellow Submarine," reviewed in New York's *Cue* maga-
             zine, is assessed as offering a "gloriously conceived mod

1968

look of the 1960s."

NOV 17　The New York *Times* rates "Yellow Submarine" as "friendly" and "unpretentious," but also "of no great importance"; it is also "informed by marijuana."

NOV 20　Date originally scheduled for the release of John Lennon's **Two Virgins** (LP).

Those Were the Days by Mary Hopkin, produced by Paul McCartney, is certified as a Gold Record by the R.I.A.A.

NOV 21　Yoko Ono suffers a miscarriage.

NOV 22　*Time* magazine on "Yellow Submarine": "Bad Trip."

Atlantis by Donovan, with Paul McCartney on tambourine and backing vocal, is released on a single in the U.K.

The Beatles (LP) -- the "white album," the first Apple LP -- is released in the U.K.　JLS--143 (Nov 30)　LCP--275 (21st)　OBF--10 (21st)　PMS--170 (Nov 30)

NOV 23　*I'm the Urban Spaceman* by the Bonzo Dog Band, produced by Paul McCartney, enters the *Melody Maker* singles charts in U.K. at number 29.

NOV 24　Grapefruit leaves Apple Records without releasing any material.

NOV 25　**The Beatles** (LP) -- the "white album," first Apple LP is released in the U.S.

NOV 28　Date of trial stemming from John Lennon's October 18th arrest; Lennon is found guilty and fined ₤ 150 plus court costs on drug charges.　ODT--40 (Nov 29)

NOV 29　**Unfinished Music No. 1 -- Two Virgins** (LP) is released in the U.K.

NOV 30　**The Beatles** (LP) enters the *Melody Maker* album charts in U.K. at number 3.

New Musical Express reports that *Hey Jude* has sold nearly six million copies worldwide.

NOVEMBER--JANUARY

Paul McCartney, Mary Hopkin and Donovan Leitch record *Heather,* later included on the bootleg recording **20x4** (LP).

Paul McCartney, Mary Hopkin and Donovan Leitch record a version of *Blackbird,* later included on the bootleg recording **20x4** (LP).

DECEMBER

Andy Williams, lunching with Apple executives, discusses with them the possibility of an appearance in "The Magic Christian."

George Harrison and Ringo Starr visit Bob Dylan in Nashville, Tennessee, during the latter's recording sessions for **Nashville**

Skyline (LP).

Carlos Mendes records *Penina*, written by Paul McCartney, in Lisbon, Portugal.

It is reported that The Beatles will return to the stage, giving three live performances to be videotaped, with segments to be broad--cast as a one--hour TV special.

Total securities held in U.K. by The Beatles, Apple Corps and their other companies stands at Ł 1,091,207.00.

Ringo Starr interviewed by David Wigg at Apple offices, London.

DEC 2   **Wonderwall Music** (LP) by George Harrison is released in the U.S.   TBD--16 (Nov)

DEC 4   George Harrison advises Apple staff that his friends, some of California's Hells Angels, will probably visit Apple the following week.

early Dec   George and Pattie Harrison arrive in New York City, where they remain a couple of days.

DEC 6   Derek Taylor advises top Apple officers that he is giving Hells Angels their home phone numbers in case they need help while in London.

George and Pattie Harrison fly back to England.

The Beatles (LP) -- the "white album" -- is certified as a Gold Record by the R.I.A.A.

James Taylor (LP) is released in the U.K. by Apple, featuring Paul McCartney playing bass guitar on *Carolina in My Mind.*

Under the Jasmine Tree (LP) by The Modern Jazz Quartet is released in the U.K. by Apple.

DEC 7   Universal Beatle Day.

Reports begin to appear about Paul McCartney's new girl--friend, Linda Eastman.

The Beatles (LP) hits number 1 on the *Melody Maker* album charts in U.K., remaining there for 10 weeks.

DEC 11   The Rolling Stones' "Rock and Roll Circus," featuring John Lennon, Yoko Ono and others singing *Yer Blues* is filmed; never commercially released.   BCE--78 (1969)

Songs from The Rolling Stones' "Rock and Roll Circus," featuring John Lennon and Yoko Ono, are recorded, later to be included on the following bootleg LPs: **British Blue Jam, The Rock and Roll Circus, Gulp, Yer Blues.**

John Lennon's house at St. George's Hill, Weybridge, is reported for sale.

DEC 12   Tenth wedding anniversary of George Harrison's brother and sister--in--law, Harry and Irene.

DEC 14   **The Beatles** (LP) enters the *Billboard* album charts at number 11, remaining on the charts for 101 weeks during which it reaches a high point of number 1.

DEC 16   Mavis Smith, wife of Alan Smith of *New Musical Express,* begins work in Apple press office.

DEC 17   New York premiere of film "Candy," with Ringo Starr as Emmanuel the Gardener.
Daily Variety cites Ringo Starr's performance in "Candy" as being "very good."

DEC 17 –24   "Magical Mystery Tour" premieres in the U.S. at Boston's Savoy Theatre.

DEC 18   A review of "Magical Mystery Tour" in *Boston After Dark* terms the film "complex," "lyrical," and "sobering, but always fun."
Ringo Starr's presence in "Candy," according to the *Film and Television Daily,* is "mostly wasted."
I'm the Urban Spaceman, produced by Paul McCartney, is released in the U.S. on a single by The Bonzo Dog Band.
John Lennon and Yoko Ono appear inside a large white bag at London's Royal Albert Hall at the Underground Christmas party, "Alchemical Wedding."

DEC 20   *The Beatles 1968 Christmas Record* is released.

late Dec   Paul McCartney becomes an uncle: his brother Mike's wife, Angie, gives birth to a baby girl named Benna just before Christmas.

DEC 23   A Christmas party for the children of Apple staff and friends is held at the Apple building in Savile Row, London; John Lennon and Yoko Ono, in Santa suits, pass out gifts.

Christ- mas   The BBC broadcasts its annual review of number one hits of the year, combining *Hello Goodbye* with "Go Slow on the Brighton Line," a 4--minute time--lapse film taken from the front of a train traveling from London to Brighton.
Una Sensazionale Intervista Dei Beatles Piu Tre Dischi Apple (A Sensational Interview with The Beatles and Three Apple Records) is released as a four--record package in Italy, consisting of The Beatles interview with Kenny Everett and singles by Mary Hopkin, Jackie Lomax and The Iveys (Badfinger).

DEC 28   **The Beatles** (LP) hits number 1 on the *Billboard* album

charts, remaining there for nine of the next ten weeks.
DEC 29   *Back in the U.S.S.R.* enters the Polish radio station
  •   (Rozglasnia Harcerska) charts at number 16.
      Ob–la–di, Ob–la–da enters the Polish radio station
      (Rozglasnia Harcerska) charts at number 17.
      The *Continuing Story of Bungalow Bill* enters the Polish
      radio station (Rozglasnia Harcerska) charts at number 19.
      While My Guitar Gently Weeps enters the Polish radio
      Station (Rozglasnia Harcerska) charts at number 10.

LATE DECEMBER
Time scheduled for recording of a new single by The Beatles,
according to the monthly *Beatles Book*, which indicated a
session just before or just after Christmas was anticipated.
Louise Harrison, George's mother, is afflicted with the Hong Kong
flu, a cold, and an ear infection.

LATE DECEMBER – EARLY JANUARY
John Lennon and Yoko Ono produce "Rape," a film for Austrian
television.

LATE 1968
Ringo Starr announces, in a fit of depression, that he is leaving
The Beatles; he returns after a week's vacation.
Paul McCartney encourages plans for an elaborate series of live
concerts – the first in three years – centered around songs from
the "white album" and a commitment to such a plan is made
by Derek Taylor.
Bob Dylan, reported to have turned off The Beatles' **Sgt. Pepper**
(LP) on first hearing, counters with a disarmingly simple
album, **John Wesley Harding**.

He didn't notice that
the lights had changed

A DAY IN THE LIFE
The Beatles
Day-By-Day
1969

DURING THIS YEAR . . .

The following albums by The Beatles are released in Australia: **Sgt. Pepper's Lonely Hearts Club Band**, and **Magical Mystery Tour and Other Splendid Songs.**

Paul McCartney writes *That Would Be Something* in Scotland, later released on **McCartney (LP)**.

The following Beatles' singles are released in Holland on the Apple label:*Get Back/Don't Let Me Down, The Ballad of John and Yoko/Old Brown Shoe* and *Come Together/Something.*

Stu Sutcliffe's paintings from the 1961–62 Hamburg period are displayed at the Neptune Theatre Gallery in Liverpool.

Yellow Submarine by Lee Minoff, Al Brodax, Jack Mendelsohn and Erich Segal is published.

The minimum terms of The Beatles' exclusive recording contract with EMI, which expires in 1976, have already been fulfilled by this time.

Get Back/Don't Let Me Down (45) is released in France by Apple.

Very Together (LP) is released in Canada by Polydor, a reissue of the early Tony Sheridan–Beatles sessions.

The Beatles' Illustrated Lyrics, edited by Alan Aldridge, is published in the U.S. by Delacorte Press.

The following singles by The Beatles are released in Italy: *Get Back/Don't Let Me Down, The Ballad of John and Yoko/Old Brown Shoe,* and *Come Together/Something.*

Cilla Black marries Bobby Willis, her personal manager.

Get Back/Don't Let Me Down (45) is released in Germany by Apple.

The Ballad of John and Yoko/Old Brown Shoe (45) is released in Denmark by Apple.

The Beatles record the unreleased songs *When I Came to Town* and *Four Nights in Moscow* during the "Abbey Road" sessions.

The Young Beatles (LP) is released in Japan by Polydor.

231

Phil Spector begins to produce recordings for A&M Records.

George Harrison secretly records his unreleased album **Lifting Material from the World**, according to *National Lampoon*'s parody of Beatles' history. The album contains songs like: *My Sweet He's So Fine, My Sweet Fair Lady, My Sweet Beethoven's Ninth Symphony*, and others.

No One's Gonna Change Our World (LP) is released in England by Star Line.

Ringo Starr gets a new drum kit for use on the **Abbey Road** album.

Come Together/Something (45) is released in Japan by Apple.

Rumors circulate that Stig O'Hara of the Rutles was killed "in a flash fire at a water bed shop" and replaced in the group's performances "by a plastic and wax replica from Madame Tussauds," according to the album send–up of The Beatles, **The Rutles**.

Jimmy McCulloch is a member of the Thunderclap Newman band when its recording of *Something in the Air* reaches number 1 in the U.K., and reaches number 37 in the U.S.

The following singles by The Beatles are released in Australia: *Ob La Di, Ob La Da/While My Guitar Gently Weeps, Get Back/Don't Let Me Down, The Ballad of John and Yoko/ Old Brown Shoe*, and *Something/Come Together*.

Oh Darling/Here Comes the Sun (45) is released in Japan by Apple.

Abbey Road (LP) receives a Grammy Award from the American National Academy of Recording Arts and Sciences as best engineered recording.

JANUARY

The Beatles rehearse at Twickenham film studios and Apple recording studios in preparation for a rare live concert tentatively set for September 18, the concert to be filmed for TV broadcast.

The monthly *Beatles Book* reports that the Kremlin has pro–claimed The Beatles to be the epitome of Western decadence.

Paul McCartney arrives back in London from Portugal.

Apart from the final versions of songs later to appear on **Let It Be** (LP), tracks recorded at Twickenham studios during the month end up on bootlegs like **Abbey Road Revisited, Twickenham Jam, Watching Rainbows, Get Back Sessions 1, Let It Be Live, Let It Be 1970**, and **Liverpool Flash**; fifty–seven tracks are never released, even on bootlegs, including

All Shook Up, Blowing in the Wind, Don't Be Cruel, Hitch Hike, Little Queenie, Lucille, Michael Row the Boat Ashore, Midnight Special, Short Fat Fanny, Third Man Theme, When Irish Eyes Are Smiling, and *Whole Lotta Shakin' Goin' On.*

Rosetta, produced by Paul McCartney, is recorded by The Four--most.

Allen Klein flies from New York to London to propose becoming The Beatles' manager soon after hearing John Lennon's com--ments on the financial state of Apple.

John Lennon and Yoko Ono make plans to screen their films, "Two Virgins" and "Smile," in art--theaters and college theaters in the U.S.

Mary Hopkin's first Apple album is complete, save for a sleeve design.

George Harrison spends many nights with Apple Publicity Director Derek Taylor, writing a stage musical based on daily events at the Apple offices.

John Lennon introduces Allen Klein to the other Beatles, proposing that Klein take over management of their financial affairs.

Austrian television commissions a special hour--long film to be directed by John Lennon and Yoko Ono.

Clive Epstein tells Leonard Richenberg that the deal for the sale of NEMS to Triumph Investment Trust is cancelled; Epstein feels that The Beatles deserve the first option to buy.

Ringo Starr films portions of "The Magic Christian."

Rumors of Andy Williams' possible appearance in "The Magic Christian," along with rumors of filming in Liverpool instead of London, surface during the month.

George Harrison knocks down an office partition at Apple head--quarters with a sledge hammer.

Paul McCartney is chosen "Today's Most Admired Man" in a poll of British teenagers; Harold Wilson comes out ahead of John Lennon in the same poll.

Month set for the release of The Beatles' Christmas record to mem--bers of the U.S. fan club, Beatles (U.S.A.) Limited; the recording includes a version of *Nowhere Man* sung by Tiny Tim, and a poem to Yoko Ono by John Lennon.

Paul McCartney continues to wear his beard, despite a New Year's resolution to shave it off.

George Harrison, as a result of visiting Bob Dylan in Nashville the month before, records the unreleased *Mama You've Been on My Mind* and *I Threw It All Away*, available only on the **Sweet Apple Tracks** bootleg LP.

Friction between Allen Klein and John and Lee Eastman begins to build from the outset.

EARLY JANUARY

Paul McCartney, in Portugal over the New Year's holiday, writes a song for the bandleader of the hotel where he stays.

Paul McCartney proposes that The Beatles film their concert in Africa or some alternate but sunny place.

JAN 2   The Beatles arrive at Twickenham Film Studios to begin rehearsals for their planned concert tour, and begin to argue over the whole future of the project.

Recording sessions for what eventually becomes **Let It Be (LP)** – called variously the "Get Back sessions" and the "Let It Be sessions" – and the filming of 28 hours of footage for the "Let It Be" documentary begins.

JAN 2 –9   During the "Let It Be" recording sessions at Twickenham studios, The Beatles record 17 tracks which eventually end up only on the bootleg recording **Cinelogue 1**.

The Beatles write and rehearse three new songs.

JAN 2– 16   During the "Let It Be" recording sessions at Twickenham studios, The Beatles record 44 tracks which eventually end up only on the bootleg recordings **Hot As Sun** and **Sweet Apple Tracks**.

JAN 3   New Jersey authorities confiscate around 30,000 copies of **Unfinished Music No. 1: Two Virgins (LP)**, the nude sleeve photos having rendered the album "pornographic."

JAN 4   **The Best of Cilla (LP)** by Cilla Black, featuring three songs by Lennon/McCartney or Paul McCartney, enters the *Melody Maker* album charts at number 18.

JAN 6   Tracks are recorded during the filming of the "Let It Be" documentary which later appear on the bootleg album **Sweet Apple Trax Vol. 1 & 2**.

JAN 10   George Harrison walks out on The Beatles' planned concert tour, although all four resume rehearsals at Twickenham studios for a television special on how The Beatles make an album.

JAN 11   *I'm the Urban Spaceman* by The Bonzo Dog Band, produced by Paul McCartney, reaches its highest position on the *Melody Maker* singles charts: number 4.

Wonderwall Music (LP) by George Harrison enters the
Billboard album charts at number 197, remaining on
the charts for 16 weeks during which it reaches a high
point of number 49.

The Best of Cilla (LP) by Cilla Black, featuring three songs
by Lennon/McCartney or Paul McCartney, reaches its
highest position on the *Melody Maker* album charts:
number 17.

JAN 13   George Harrison visits his parents.
Early recordings of *Maxwell's Silver Hammer* are made.
Yellow Submarine (LP) is released in the U.S. by Apple.
GBR–21 (Jan 12)   HH17–3 (Dec 15)   LCP–281 (1968)
TBD–12 (Feb)

JAN 15   Paul Harrison, George's nephew, is nine years old.
George and Pattie Harrison's third wedding anniversary.
George Harrison again visits his parents.

JAN 17   **Yellow Submarine** (LP) is released in the U.K. by Apple.
BBS–53 (Dec 7, 1968)   BIR–76 (Dec 1968)   JLS–143
(Nov 28, 1968)

JAN 18   Tentative date set for another rare live Beatles' performance,
following their successful appearance before an audience
for the filming of the "Hey Jude" promotional short.
John Lennon is reported as predicting the financial collapse
of Apple if the firm continues losing money.

JAN 20   *Atlantis* by Donovan, with Paul McCartney on tambourine
and backing vocal, is released on a single in the U.S.
London premiere of film "Wonderwall," with music by
George Harrison.

JAN 20   During the "Let It Be" recording sessions at EMI's Abbey
–22   Road studios, The Beatles record seven tracks which
eventually end up only on the bootleg recordings
Cinelogue 1 and **Cinelogue Let It Be.**

JAN 21   George Harrison is fined $200 for tripping a photographer
the previous May in Paris.

JAN 24   *Road to Nowhere/Illusions* (45) by White Trash (later Trash)
is released in the U.K. by Apple.
Variety's review of "Wonderwall" calls George Harrison's
score untuneful, but stylistically "atmospheric."

JAN 25   *Ob–la–di, Ob–la–da* enters Holland's Radio Veronica Top
40 charts at number 24.
Begins a two–week period during which no Beatle–related
recordings appear on the *Billboard* singles charts.

JAN 26   During the "Let It Be" recording sessions at Apple studios in Savile Row, London, The Beatles record nine tracks, seven of which eventually end up only on the bootleg recordings **Cinelogue 1** and **Cinelogue Let It Be,** two of which – *Blue Suede Shoes* and *Love Me Do* – are un–released.

JAN 27   *Maybe Tomorrow/And Her Daddy's a Millionaire* (45) by The Iveys (later Badfinger) is released in the U.S. by Apple.

George Harrison's brother and sister–in–law, Peter and Pauline, celebrate their fourth wedding anniversary.

JAN 27 –30   During the "Let It Be" recording sessions at Apple studios in London's Savile Row, The Beatles record three tracks which eventually end up only on the bootleg recordings **Cinelogue 1** and **Cinelogue Let It Be.**

JAN 30   The final version of *Get Back* and *Don't Let Me Down* are recorded at Apple studios in Saville Row, London.

The Beatles' studio roof–top concert, performing (with Billy Preston) *I've Got a Feeling, One After 909, I Dig a Pony,* and *Get Back*; their last public appearance as a group, the compromise "live" concert toward which the month's work had begun. Neighbors complain about the noise and police stop the concert.

During the "Let It Be" recording sessions at Apple studios in Savile Row, London, The Beatles record seven tracks which eventually end up only on the bootleg recordings **Cinelogue 1** and **Cinelogue Let It Be.**

JAN 31   Filming of 28 hours of footage for "Let It Be" is con–cluded.

LATE JANUARY

Let It Be is recorded.

The Beatles abandon plans for a "Get Back" album, leaving over 100 songs officially unreleased from this recording period.

LATE JANUARY–EARLY FEBRUARY

The Beatles, Allen Klein and John Eastman meet, agreeing to postpone their own bid to buy NEMS from Clive Epstein until Klein has an opportunity to check out The Beatles' financial status.

Allen Klein meets with Clive Epstein, obtaining Epstein's assur–ance that a decision on the sale of NEMS to Triumph Invest–ment will be postponed for three weeks.

FEBRUARY

Allen Klein pursues his proposals to become Beatles' manager; Lee
   Eastman, backed by Paul McCartney, attempts to renegotiate
   The Beatles' association with NEMS Enterprises.

John Lennon etches a poem onto a zinc plate at the Curwen Stu--
   dion in London; the poem was created to introduce "Bag One,"
   a set of his erotic lithographs.

Brute Force records *King of Fuh* and *Nobody I Know*, produced
   by George Harrison.

The Beatles (U.S.A.) Limited fan club reports to area secretaries
   that the possibility of a quick marriage between Paul Mc--
   Cartney and Linda Eastman is just a rumor; also, rumors of
   difficulties between The Beatles or of Apple being in financial
   difficulty should be treated as "hogwash."

George Harrison receives a guitar as a gift from Robbie Robertson,
   lead singer of The Band.

"Yellow Submarine," at this point, becomes the second largest
   box office draw in U.S. theaters.

Peter Asher, head of Apple's A&R Department, visits Apple offices
   in Los Angeles and scouts for new talent in the U.S.

Late February is predicted as the release time for new Apple
   albums by Mary Hopkin, Jackie Lomax and James Taylor.

Pattie Harrison and Jenny Boyd close down their Chelsea antique
   stall, "Juniper."

Managing Director of Apple, Neil Aspinall, recuperates in a London
   hospital from a brief illness.

Ringo Starr and family purchase and move into a house in Wey--
   bridge previously owned by Peter Sellers.

It is reported that Linda Eastman was responsible for the pictures
   and photographic collage included in copies of **The Beatles** (LP).

George Harrison records versions of *Under the Mersey Wall* for his
   Electronic Sound album.   BD--20 (Feb 1970)

FEBRUARY--MARCH

A version of *Let It Be* recorded during this period later ends up
   on the bootleg **Supertracks Vol. 2.**

Theater owners Howard and Wyndham buy up around 5% of
   Northern Songs shares.

A version of *Don't Let Me Down*, recorded by The Beatles during
   the "Let It Be" rehearsal sessions, later ends up on the bootleg
   Kum Back.

Save the Last Dance for Me and *Don't Let Me Down*, recorded by
   The Beatles during the "Let It Be" sessions, later ends up on the

bootleg LP **L.S. Bumble Bee.**

Versions of *The Walk, Across the Universe* and *Let It Be*, recorded by The Beatles during the "Let It Be" sessions, later ends up on the bootleg LP **Let It Be Live.**

Thirteen songs recorded by The Beatles during this period, some versions of songs slated for **Let It Be** (LP), are later included on a **Get Back** promotional LP.

FEB 1   **Yellow Submarine** (LP) enters the *Melody Maker* album charts in the U.K. at number 14.

FEB 2   *Hey Bulldog* enters the Polish radio station (Rozglasnia Harcerska) charts at number 3.

Yoko Ono's divorce from her first husband, Anthony Cox, becomes final; Yoko reportedly receives custody of their child, Kyoko.

FEB 3   Paul McCartney plays drums, bass guitar and sings backing vocal for *My Dark Hour*, recorded by The Steve Miller Band at Air studios, London.

Allen Klein becomes The Beatles' business manager.

FEB 4   The Beatles appoint the New York law firm Eastman & Eastman as general counsel to Apple.

FEB 5   **Yellow Submarine** (LP) is certified as a Gold Record by the R.I.A.A.

Goodbye (LP) by Cream is released in the U.S., featuring *Badge*, written by George Harrison and Eric Clapton.

FEB 7   Paul McCartney is fined $36.00 in Coventry for a speeding ticket he received in July 1968, and for failing to pay the license fee on his car.

National Beatle Day.

George Harrison is admitted to a London hospital with an infected back molar which has infected his tonsils.

FEB 8   George Harrison's tonsils are removed, and he remains in hospital for a week.

Yellow Submarine (LP) enters the *Billboard* album charts at number 86, remaining on the charts for 24 weeks during which it reaches a high point of number 2.

Unfinished Music, No. 1: Two Virgins (LP), by John Lennon and Yoko Ono, enters the *Billboard* album charts at number 158, remaining on the charts for eight weeks during which it reaches a high point of number 124.

FEB 11   Ringo and Maureen Starr's fourth wedding anniversary; Ringo gives Maureen a puppy named Sophie.

FEB 14   Original date for proposed release of *King of Fuh* by Brute
         Force on Apple Records; never released on Apple.
         John Eastman, acting as Apple's legal counsel after Allen
         Klein has assumed business management functions,
         writes a letter to Clive Epstein wherein he proposes a
         meeting to discuss the "propriety" of the negotiations
         involving EMI, The Beatles, and NEMS.
FEB 15   **Goodbye** (LP) by Cream, featuring *Badge* (co--authored by
         George Harrison), enters the *Billboard* album charts at
         number 107.
         George Harrison is released from a hospital after his
         tonsillectomy.
         Maybe Tomorrow by The Iveys (later Badfinger), enters
         the *Billboard* singles charts at number 89.
         Yellow Submarine (LP) reaches its highest position on the
         Melody Maker album charts: number 4.
mid–Feb Clive Epstein writes back to John Eastman, demanding an
         explanation of Eastman's letter referring to the
         "propriety" of the negotiations between EMI, NEMS,
         and The Beatles.
FEB 16   Media in the U.S. earlier reported this as the proposed date of
         marriage of Paul McCartney and Linda Eastman.
FEB 17   **Under the Jasmine Tree** (LP) by The Modern Jazz Quartet
         is released in the U.S. on the Apple label.
         Triumph Investment Trust becomes the owner of 70% of
         Nemperor Holdings, sold to them by Clive Epstein.
         James Taylor (LP) is released in the U.S. on the Apple
         label, featuring Paul McCartney playing bass guitar on
         Carolina in My Mind.
FEB 18   Yoko Ono's birthday; John and Yoko are presently living
         in Surrey.
FEB 20   London premiere of the film "Candy," with Ringo Starr as
         Emmanuel the Gardener, at the Odeon in Kensington.
FEB 21   *Rosetta/Just Like Before* (45) by The Fourmost, is released
         in the U.K.; *Rosetta* is produced by Paul McCartney.
         Mary Hopkin's **Post Card** (LP), produced by Paul McCart-
         ney, is released in the U.K. on the Apple label.
FEB 22   **Sgt. Pepper's Lonely Hearts Club Band** (LP) drops from
         the *Billboard* album charts after 88 weeks.
FEB 24   Triumph Investment obtains control of NEMS.
FEB 25   George Harrison's 26th birthday.
FEB 26   It is reported that George Harrison has purchased an ES5
         Custom Electric Gibson guitar for over $1,000.00.

FEB 28   Goodbye (LP) by Cream is released in the U.K., featuring
         Badge, written by George Harrison and Eric Clapton.

LATE FEBRUARY

Allen Klein visits Leonard Richenberg's office in a bid to win back
royalties for The Beatles, claiming that NEMS owes the group
back unpaid sums for road shows.

Ringo Starr begins work on filming of "The Magic Christian."

LATE FEBRUARY–EARLY MARCH

The Beatles write a letter to Leonard Richenberg informing him
that NEMS, now controlled by Triumph Investment, will no
longer act as The Beatles' agent.

The Beatles send a letter to EMI instructing that royalties on
recordings be paid to them only through Beatles & Co. or
Apple Corps, not through NEMS (now controlled by Triumph
Investment.)

MARCH

Scheduled time for ground–breaking in Beverly Hills, California,
of a headquarters building for Apple in the U.S.; the twelve–
story structure is to be shared by CSC Corp. (Campbell, Silver,
Cosby Corp.), and is to include a huge recording studio complex.

George Harrison's song writing contract with Northern Songs
expires.

Scheduled month for the filming of "Captain Blood," a movie
featuring Tommy Smothers and Ringo Starr, to be made in
Jamaica.

Both Ringo Starr and George Harrison express their opposition to
any more live performances or tours by the group.

Mary Hopkin makes her first concert tour for Apple.

Month scheduled for the U.S. release of the movie "Wonderwall,"
soundtrack by George Harrison.

Paul and Linda McCartney are photographed on a New York street
for the Official Beatles Fan Club.

John Lennon and Yoko Ono record versions of *Let's Go On Flying,
Snow Is Falling All the Time* and *Don't Worry Kyoko* (released
on an Aspen Art recording), and the unreleased *Song for John.*

George Harrison records *Old Brown Shoe* at EMI's Abbey Road
studios.

Ringo Starr plays drums on *New Day,* recorded by Jackie Lomax.

George Harrison's music for "Wonderwall," according to a review
in *Films and Filming*, carries the vocal burden of dialogue for
the film.

George Harrison and Jackie Lomax co--produce the recording of
Goin' Back to Liverpool, never released.

EARLY MARCH

Leonard Richenberg has a private business report prepared on Allen
Klein, revealing that Klein is involved in a number of law suits.

The Beatles record or re--record a number of unreleased tracks,
including *What's the News Maryjane, Jubilee, Not Guilty* and *I
Should Like to Live Up a Tree.*

EARLY--MID--MARCH

Dick James, managing director of Northern Songs, visits Sir Lew
Grade of Associated Television Corporation, offering to sell his
shares in Northern to ATV; he hopes to avoid becoming em--
broiled in the impending battle over Northern's control.

MARCH--MAY

"The Magic Christian" is filmed, with Ringo Starr as Youngman
Grand.

MAR 1   **Yellow Submarine** (LP) reaches its highest position on the
          Billboard album charts: number 2.
          Wonderwall Music (LP) by George Harrison reaches its
          highest position on the *Billboard* album charts: number
          49.

MAR 1   Mary Hopkin records *Goodbye* (written by Lennon/
--2   McCartney) and *Sparrow* for an Apple single produced
          by Paul McCartney.

MAR 2   John Lennon and Yoko Ono record tracks for side one
          of **Unfinished Music No. 2: Life with the Lions** (LP)
          while at an avant--garde jazz concert at Lady Mitchell
          Hall in Cambridge, England. BD--20 (Mar 2, 1970)

MAR 3   Mary Hopkin's **Post Card** (LP) is released in the U.S. by
          Apple, produced by Paul McCartney.
          Road to Nowhere/Illusions (45) by Trash (formerly
          White Trash) is released in the U.S. on the Apple label.

MAR 4   Princess Margaret visits the set of "The Magic Christian" at
          Twickenham studios, where she watches Ringo Starr
          and Peter Sellers rehearse scenes; Paul McCartney, Linda
          Eastman and Mary Hopkin also visit.

MAR 7   *Blackbird/I Will*, by The Vic Lewis Orchestra, is released in the U.K. on the NEMS label.

        Lontano Dagli Occhi/The Game (45) by Mary Hopkin, produced by Paul McCartney, is released in Italy on the Apple label. TBA--xx (Mar 3), 157 (Mar 7)

        Prince En Avignon/The Game (45) by Mary Hopkin is re-- leased in France on the Apple label.

MAR 8–   Harold and Louise Harrison, George's parents, are taken ill
21   with Hong Kong flu and bronchitis.

MAR 10   George Harrison's mother, Louise, celebrates a birthday.

MAR 11   Paul McCartney and Linda Eastman announce their plans to marry.

        Linda Eastman visits the Register Office in Marylebone to give notice of Paul McCartney's and her own intention to marry on the next day.

        Thumbin' a Ride is recorded by Jackie Lomax for Apple Records, produced by Paul McCartney.

        Paul McCartney convinces a jeweller, who had already closed, to open his shop so that he can buy a wedding ring for his marriage ceremony the next day; the ring costs Ł12.

MAR 12   Paul McCartney marries Linda Eastman at the Marylebone Register Office, witnessed by Mike McGear (best man), Peter Brown, Mal Evans, and Linda's daughter Heather as bridesmaid.

        Following the wedding of Paul McCartney and Linda Eastman at the Marylebone Register's Office, the couple's marriage is blessed in an Anglican church in St. John's Wood, followed by a wedding reception at the Ritz Hotel.

        Scotland Yard police raid George Harrison's home while the Harrison's are out; upon their return George and Pattie are arrested for possession of marijuana dis-- covered in a binocular case by a Labrador retriever named "Yogi," and are later released from Esher jail on bond of $480.00 each. BEA3--17 (Mar 13) BIR-- 80 (Mar 13)

MAR 14   **Yellow Submarine** (LP) becomes The Beatles' 14th Gold Disc in the U.K.

MAR 15   *Maybe Tomorrow* by The Iveys, released in the U.S. by Apple, reaches its highest position on the *Billboard* singles charts: number 67.

        Goodbye (LP) by Cream, featuring *Badge* (co--authored

by George Harrison), reaches its highest position on the *Billboard* album charts: number 2.

Post Card (LP) by Mary Hopkin, produced on Apple by Paul McCartney, enters the *Melody Maker* album charts in the U.K. at number 15.

Goodbye (LP) by Cream, featuring *Badge* (co--authored by George Harrison), enters the *Melody Maker* album charts at number 2.

mid--Mar Jack Gill, finance director of ATV, begins purchase nego-- tiations for Northern Songs with Dick James and Charles Silver, controllers of 37½% of Northern Songs stock; he first advises Sir Lew Grade that the deal appears too complicated to close. In the afternoon, Grade himself meets with James and Silver, closing the deal in five minutes.

MAR 16 Paul and Linda McCartney and Linda's daughter Heather fly to New York for three weeks with Linda's family.

John Lennon and Yoko Ono fly to Paris.

MAR 17 *Carolina in My Mind*, by James Taylor with Paul McCartney on bass guitar, is released in the U.S. by Apple.

Paul and Linda McCartney, and daughter Heather, arrive in New York to visit Linda's relatives.

Pattie Harrison's 25th birthday.

Badge, written by George Harrison and Eric Clapton, is released in the U.S. on a single by Cream.

MAR 18 John Lennon appears on the cover of *Look* magazine.

George and Pattie Harrison return to court for a hearing on their March 12 drug arrest; the hearing lasts six minutes, and they are told to return on March 31.

MAR 20 John Lennon and Yoko Ono leave Paris for a half--day in Gibralter, where they are quietly married; Peter Brown attends the wedding.

The headquarters of The Beatles (U.S.A.) Limited fan club issues an announcement to area secretaries about John Lennon's wedding to Yoko Ono; it comments: "Please try and understand that we should at least give Yoko the same chance we are going to be giving Linda and that Maureen and Pattie got! I know this news is shocking, but I suppose if it will make John happy, we should all be very enthused too."

MAR 21 John Lennon and Yoko Ono fly to Amsterdam.

Allen Klein is reported to have been appointed business manager for The Beatles for a three--year term.

"Magical Mystery Tour" is scheduled to be shown at the
Carnegie Mellon Institute, Pittsburgh, PA.

Is This What You Want? (LP) by Jackie Lomax, produced
by George Harrison, is released in the U.K. by Apple.

MAR 22 **Unfinished Music, No. 1: Two Virgins** (LP), by John
Lennon and Yoko Ono, reaches its highest position on
the *Billboard* album charts: number 124.

MAR 26 John Lennon and Yoko Ono "Bed--In" at the Amsterdam
Hilton Hotel. BIR--82 (Mar 21)

John Lennon and Yoko Ono record the songs *John and
Yoko* and *Amsterdam* during their "Bed--In" at the
Amsterdam Hilton.

MAR 27 Ringo Starr announces that The Beatles will never again
give a live performance as a group.

The Apple group White Trash leaves London and arrives
in Amsterdam to perform.

MAR 28 The sale of Northern Songs to ATV is reported in British
newspapers, where The Beatles learn of it for the first
time.

White Trash visit John Lennon and Yoko Ono at the
Amsterdam Hilton.

Goodbye/Sparrow (45) by Mary Hopkin, produced by
Paul McCartney, is released in the U.K.; it is released by
Apple in 28 countries, along with a promotional film
showing Paul and Mary making the recording.
BF--212 (Apr)

MAR 29 Begins a week--long period during which no Beatle--related
recordings appear on the *Billboard* singles charts.

Post Card (LP) by Mary Hopkin, produced by Paul
McCartney, enters the *Billboard* album charts at num--
ber 104.

Goodbye (LP) by Cream, featuring *Badge* (co--authored by
George Harrison), hits number 1 on the *Melody Maker*
album charts, remaining there for five of the next six
weeks.

MAR 31 John Lennon and Yoko Ono hold a press conference in a
bag at the Sacher Hotel, Vienna, Austria, to discuss their
film "Rape (Film No. 6)."

The film "Rape," by John Lennon and Yoko Ono, premieres
on Austrian National Network Television, Vienna.

George and Pattie Harrison are fined £250 as a result of
the police drug raid on their home.

Report in the *Evening Standard* indicates that EMI (Electric

and Musical Instruments) would not attempt to counter--
bid against Sir Lew Grade's ATV (Associated Television
Corporation) offer to buy Northern Songs.

MARCH 31--DECEMBER 31
In nine months, The Beatles' partnership income grows to
Ł1,708,000, as opposed to only Ł 805,000 for the entire year
preceding March 31, 1969.

LATE MARCH
John Lennon and Paul McCartney call Allen Klein long distance
in Puerto Rico about the sale of Northern Songs; each returns
immediately to London.

LATE MARCH--EARLY APRIL
Allen Klein and The Beatles meet with Bruce Ormrod of the
London banking firm Henry Ansbacher and Company, seeking
advice on how to retain control of Northern Songs.
Tracks for **Wedding Album** (LP) are recorded.

EARLY SPRING
George Harrison goes to Eric Clapton's house instead of the Apple
offices; wandering in Clapton's garden carrying an acoustic
guitar, he writes *Here Comes the Sun.*

SPRING
Expected arrival time for the birth of Alfred Lennon's first child
by his 19--year--old wife, Pauline.
The Beatles' frustrated attempt to gain control of Northern Songs
completely alienates them from an already mistrusted business
establishment.

APRIL
It is reported that John Lennon has begun a "Nuts for Peace"
campaign; he and Yoko propose that world leaders hold peace
talks around a table inside a giant bag, and that the world
resolve that soldiers, through international agreement, be
forced to remove their trousers before going into battle.
Ringo Starr continues with filming of "The Magic Christian."
HH19--2 (finished late Mar)
Recording of *Octopus's Garden* is begun.
Scheduled date for the release of an album called **The Beatles
Get Back**, based on songs rehearsed in January; some of the

efforts recorded eventually appeared on **Let It Be** (LP).

Goodbye, written by John Lennon and Paul McCartney, is re-- corded in a session produced by George Martin; the song is not released.

Billy Preston records *That's the Way God Planned It* and *What About You?* for Apple records, produced by George Harrison, with George on guitar. RO--62 (Mar)

APRIL--MAY

George Harrison plays rhythm guitar on *Never Tell Your Mother She's Out of Tune*, recorded by Jack Bruce for his **Songs for a Tailor** (LP).

APRIL--JULY

Billy Preston records tracks for **That's the Way God Planned It** (LP), for Apple records, produced by George Harrison.

APR 1   An interview with John Lennon reveals that his finances have diminished to about Ł50,000.

John Lennon and Yoko Ono fly back to London.

John Lennon is reported to have plans to send two acorns to world leaders for ceremonial planting of seeds of peace.

APR 3   *New Musical Express* reports that Apple, at the behest of George Harrison, has signed Billy Preston to a contract.

Badge, written by George Harrison and Eric Clapton, is released in the U.K. on a single by Cream.

APR 5   *Badge* by Cream, co--authored by George Harrison, enters the *Bilboard* singles charts at number 87.

Jane Asher's 23rd birthday.

Post Card (LP) by Mary Hopkin, produced on Apple by Paul McCartney, reaches its highest point on the *Melody Maker* album charts: number 6.

It is reported that Dick James, managing director of Northern Songs Ltd., failed to get John Lennon and Paul McCartney to take the Ł9 million offer for Northern Songs made by ATV.

APR 6   A version of *Get Back* played by two disc jockeys con-- vinces The Beatles that more work is needed on the song.

APR 7   *Goodbye/Sparrow* (45), by Mary Hopkin, is released in the U.S. by Apple, produced by Paul McCartney.

George Harrison tells reporters he will never again keep marijuana in his home.

The Beatles remix *Get Back*, creating the final version.

APR 8   Julian Lennon's 6th birthday.

APR 10   The Beatles formally reject the ATV offer to purchase
            the rest of Northern Songs, 35% of which ATV
            already owns.

            The Beatles, controlling 29.7% of Northern stock, issue a
            statement that they oppose ATV's bid for minority
            shares in Northern Songs, and will make a counter–offer.

APR 11   The merchant banking firm, S.G. Warburg, acting for ATV,
            sends out a new offer to minority shareholders in
            Northern Songs, raising their offer by 10–pence per
            share.

            It is reported that The Beatles -- Lennon, McCartney and
            Harrison -- are considering a counter–offer to the ATV
            bid to purchase the balance of uncommitted shares in
            Northern Songs.

            It is reported that Tom Whyte, head of Triumph Invest–
            ment Trust (holder of about 5% of Northern Songs
            and 90% of Nemporer Holdings) has termed The
            Beatles' counter–proposal for Northern Songs illogical.

            Get Back/Don't Let Me Down (45) is released in the U.K.
            by Apple. BIR–78 (Apr 15)   PMS–173 (Apr 18)

APR 12   George Harrison's nephew, Gordon Caldwell, is twelve
            years old.

            John Lennon and Yoko Ono visit Ansbacher's, the banking
            firm, in order to discuss financing arrangements for their
            counter–bids for minority Northern shares.

            Goodbye by Mary Hopkin, enters the *Melody Maker*
            singles charts at number 16.

APR 14   *Get Back* is released for airplay in the U.S.

mid–Apr   Beginning of general release of the film "Candy," featuring
            Ringo Starr.

APR 15   Allen Klein, John Lennon and Yoko Ono again visit
            Ansbacher's to arrange financing for their counter–bid
            for minority shares in Northern Songs.

mid–Apr   John Lennon and Yoko Ono invite Anthony Fawcett to
            work for them full–time, instead of handling only art
            projects, and establish their own separate office at
            Apple headquarters.

APR 16   Share prices in Northern Songs rise due to rumors that a
            third party is interested in buying minority shares in
            Northern Songs.

APR 17   Beatles (U.S.A.) Limited fan club headquarters informs area secretaries that the monthly *Beatles Book* will cease publication with the June issue "owing to reorganization of their offices."

APR 18   The Beatles announce that they will bid only for enough shares to control Northern Songs; the price of shares drops.

APR 19   The news of The Beatles' bid for control of Northern Songs appears in newspapers.

New Musical Express reports that Apple world sales reached Ł 1,400,000 in the first four months of 1969.

Goodbye by Mary Hopkin, produced by Paul McCartney, enters the *Billboard* singles charts at number 86.

The Beatles reportedly have made a higher counter-proposal to Sir Lew Grade/ATV's offer to purchase shares in Northern Songs.

Post Card (LP) by Mary Hopkin, produced by Paul Mc-Cartney, reaches its highest position on the *Billboard* album charts: number 28.

Carolina in My Mind by James Taylor, with Paul McCartney on bass guitar, enters the *Billboard* singles charts at number 118, dropping off the following week.

APR 20   "Magical Mystery Tour" is scheduled to be shown in Toledo, Ohio.

At Ansbacher's offices, Paul McCartney refuses to commit his shares in Northern Songs as collateral to finance The Beatles' counter-bid.

APR 21   *Get Back/Don't Let Me Down* (45) is originally scheduled for U.S. record store release as of this date.

A film-clip of The Beatles doing *Get Back* will reportedly be aired on the "Glen Campbell Show" within the next two weeks.

APR 22   *The Ballad of John and Yoko* is recorded at EMI's Abbey Road studios, London.

John Lennon changes his middle name from Winston to Ono on the roof of Apple in Savile Row. HH20-4 (Apr 23) JLS-146 (Apr 26)

APR 24   The Beatles offer to purchase one million minority shares of Northern Songs public stock to prevent takeover of the music publisher by ATV; such a purchase would cost just over Ł 2 million, but would give them control of Northern.

APR 25   "Rape," a film by John Lennon and Yoko Ono, is shown at the Montreux Film Festival.

APR 26   *Octopus's Garden* is introduced for inclusion on **Abbey Road (LP)**.
          Get Back enters the *Melody Maker* singles charts in the U.K. at number 2.
          At his farm in Scotland, Paul McCartney assures reporters present that he is not dead.
          Get Back enters Holland's Radio Veronica Top 40 charts at number 9.
          Get Back enters the *Billboard* British top twenty singles charts, remaining on the charts for nine weeks during which it reaches a high point of number 1.
          Jane Asher's father is found dead in his home as a result of the effects of barbiturates and alcohol.

late Apr   A syndicate of minority shareholders in Northern Songs begins to form, with a view to the increasing value of their shares based on bids by ATV on one hand, and The Beatles on the other.

APR 28   Allen Klein calls a press conference at Apple, announcing that David Platz of the Essex Music Group is The Beatles' choice for a new managing director of Northern Songs.

APR 29   The syndicate of minority shareholders in Northern Songs announces it will attempt to block both ATV and The Beatles from gaining control of Northern Songs.

APR 30   The Beatles run advertisements in national newspapers promising shareholders that they will remain with Northern Songs and not seek to control its management in return for support of their position.
          For the fiscal year ending April 30, Northern Songs Ltd. reports profits of over £1,000,000 before taxes.

LATE APRIL

An interview with John Lennon discussing business affairs at Apple appears in *New Musical Express.*

MAY

Nowhere Man appears on a mail–order anthology album in the U.S. issued by the Do It Now Foundation.

The American group Mortimer records *On Our Way Home* for Apple Records (unreleased), later issued as *Two of Us* by The Beatles.

The end of an uninterrupted stream of Beatles' chart–toppers – except for *Penny Lane* – which began five years before with

Please Please Me.

The Beatles decide to delay the release of the LP, **The Beatles Get Back** (originally scheduled for April release), until August.

George Harrison plays guitar on tracks recorded by Billy Preston for his album **That's the Way God Planned It**, produced by George Harrison.

The film "The Magic Christian" featuring Ringo Starr, is completed in the U.S.

It is reported that Ringo Starr gave his wife Maureen a six–month–old collie named Sophie as an anniversary gift in February.

EARLY MAY

The Beatles, except for Paul McCartney, sign an agreement making Allen Klein their business manager.

Peter Brown visits The Beatles (U.S.A.) Limited offices in New York, revealing the impending release of *The Ballad of John and Yoko/Old Brown Shoe* (45).

It is reported that plans to issue a **Yellow Submarine** EP have been abandoned.

About ten tracks have been completed for the new Beatles' album (**Abbey Road**), currently due to be released in July or August.

MAY 1	Inauguration date of Apple's new "spoken word specialty music label," Zapple.
MAY 2	An early recording of *Something* is made by The Beatles; final vocals done by George Harrison on July 12, 1969.
	With their bid to purchase minority shares expiring this date, ATV reiterates its offer of Ł9 million, citing support for the purchase by 45% of Northern Songs' stockholders, and extending their purchase deadline until May 15.
early May	Some members of the syndicate of minority stockholders in Northern Songs, pressured by ATV's threat to withdraw its offer by May 15 and sell its own shares to The Beatles (thereby losing outright to The Beatles and submitting to their management), attempt to sell their shares to ATV as individuals. They are refused.
MAY 3	*Badge* by Cream, co--authored by George Harrison, reaches its highest position on the *Billboard* singles charts: number 60.
	Goodbye by Mary Hopkin, written by Lennon/McCartney, reaches highest position on *Melody Maker* singles charts: number 2.

Badge by Cream, co--authored by George Harrison, enters the *Melody Maker* singles charts in the U.K. at number 29.

Get Back hits number 1 on the *Melody Maker* singles charts, remaining there for four weeks.

MAY 4   Ringo Starr and Peter Sellers throw a party to celebrate the finish of their film, "The Magic Christian." John Lennon and Yoko Ono attend, as do Paul and Linda McCartney.

MAY 5   *Get Back/Don't Let Me Down* (45) is released in the U.S. by Apple.

MAY 6   It is reported that Paul McCartney and Ringo Starr would like to see the *Beatles Monthly* continue publication.

It is reported that John Lennon and Yoko Ono are re-cording an album about their lives from Yoko's mis-carriage to their honeymoon in Amsterdam.

MAY 7   The Beatles and Allen Klein meet with Sir Joseph Lock-wood of EMI to negotiate higher royalties for The Beatles; Lockwood refuses to settle the matter until the dispute between The Beatles and Triumph Investment over NEMS has been decided.

MAY 8   Allen Klein's ABKCO Industries Inc. is appointed to manage Apple for no less than 20% of the gross income, Paul McCartney strongly objects.

Report of the firing by The Beatles of Apple general manager, Alistair Taylor.

MAY 9   **Electronic Sound** (LP) is released in the U.K. by Apple in the Zapple series.   **BM--143 (Electronic Sounds) IR--79 (May 2; Electronic Sounds)   PMS--175 (May 3; Electronic Sounds)**

New Day/I Fall Inside Your Eyes (45) by Jackie Lomax is released in the U.K. by Apple; *I Fall Inside Your Eyes* is produced by George Harrison.

Unfinished Music No. 2: Life with the Lions (LP) is re-leased in the U.K. by Apple.

Sculptor Alan Aldridge is reportedly working on a foot-high nude sculpture of John Lennon and Yoko Ono.

MAY 10   *Get Back* enters the *Billboard* singles charts at number 10, remaining on the charts for twelve weeks during which it reaches a high point of number 1.

Don't Let Me Down enters the *Billboard* singles charts at
number 40, remaining on the charts for four weeks
during which it reaches a high point of number 35.

MAY 11 George Harrison plays guitar on *Never Tell Your Mother
She's Out of Tune*, recorded by Jack Bruce.

mid–May The syndicate of minority shareholders in Northern Songs
begins working actively on a coalition with The Beatles
to wrest control of Northern Songs from ATV, the
largest stockholder.

MAY 14 **Is This What You Want?** (LP), by Jackie Lomax, is re–
leased in the U.K. on the Apple label.

Morning scheduled for a press release announcing the
coalition of The Beatles and the syndicate of minority
stockholders, aimed at regaining control of Northern
Songs from ATV; the announcement is cancelled.

MAY 14 James Taylor plays at the Bitter End Club, New York;
–21   he is accompanied to the U.S. by Peter Asher.

MAY 15 Second expiration date for offer to purchase minority
shares in Northern Songs set by ATV.

Paul and Linda McCartney announce that they are expecting
a child in December.

mid–May Shortly after their announcement of Linda's pregnancy,
Paul and Linda McCartney leave for a vacation in France.

MAY 15 Following the failure of the syndicate/Beatles coalition,
members of the syndicate again work to ensure that
ATV does not acquire additional minority shares;
ATV's deadline expires, having attracted acceptances
totalling only 47% of the shares.

mid–May Paul McCartney begins work on a new Mary Hopkin
album.

MAY 15 In the evening, Edgar Astaire, representing the syndicate
members, again approaches ATV with another offer in
an attempt to form a coalition to prevent The Beatles
from gaining control of Northern; he is turned away.

MAY 16 The day passes with little contact between The Beatles,
ATV and the syndicate of minority shareholders.

John Lennon and Yoko Ono fail to make a planned trans–
Atlantic voyage on the Queen Elizabeth II with Ringo
and Maureen Starr, George and Pattie Harrison and
Peter Sellers, after John's application for a visa to enter
the U.S. is denied. HH20–2 (May 10; says both John and

George were denied entry)   JLS--147 (indicates John
and Yoko went on the trip)

King of Fuh/Nobody Knows (45) by Brute Force, slated for
release on the Apple label, is issued in the U.K. to DJ's
only.

MAY 16   Various brokers for the syndicate of minority shareholders
--17   in Northern Songs contact ATV as part of further
         attempts to negotiate the stock sale.

MAY 17   Neil and Sue Aspinall become parents with the arrival of
         their daughter, Gayla.

A meeting is arranged for Sunday between the minority
shareholders' syndicate and ATV at ATV House,
London.

MAY 18   The brokers acting for minority shareholders in Northern
         Songs meet with representatives of ATV at the
         "l'Epee d'Or" restaurant, Cumberland Hotel, in the
         evening; the syndicate, controlling 14% of Northern
         stock, agrees not to sell its shares in exchange for
         representation on the board of directors of Northern.

MAY 19   *Get Back* (45) is certified as a Gold Record by the R.I.A.A.

The Beatles receive the Ivor Novello Award from British
Music Industry for 1968: *Hey Jude*, top selling song
in the U.K.

Is This What You Want? (LP) by Jackie Lomax is released
in the U.S. by Apple, produced largely by George
Harrison; Ringo plays drums on *New Day*.

The Beatles' offer to purchase minority shares from stock--
holders in Northern Songs is due to expire at 3:00.

Meeting of the shareholders of Northern Songs in
Warburg's, a London bank, where the minority syndi--
cate formally signs the agreement reached the previous
evening with ATV, giving to ATV effective control
of Northern Songs and placing The Beatles and their
supporters in the minority.

MAY 20   John Lennon and George Harrison visit Bruce Ormrod at
         Ansbacher's to discuss the coalition of ATV and the
         syndicate members.

George Harrison's parents celebrate their 39th wedding
anniversary.

MAY 22   Ringo, Maureen, Zak and Jason Starkey arrive in New
         York City aboard Queen Elizabeth II, along with Peter
         Sellers; scenes for "The Magic Christian" are filmed
         during the next week.

First Vibration (LP) is released in the U.S.; it includes *Nowhere Man* by The Beatles.

MAY 23 **The Original Delaney & Bonnie (Accept No Substitutes)** (LP) is withdrawn from scheduled May 23 release in the U.K. on Apple.

It is announced that Jack Gill of ATV will become director of Northern Songs, with Dick James continuing as managing director; The Beatles are asked to nominate an official for the firm, but they ignore the offer.

Listening to Richard Brautigan (LP) is withdrawn by Apple from scheduled May 23 release in the Zapple series.

MAY 24 *Don't Let Me Down* reaches its highest position on the *Billboard* singles charts: number 35.

Get Back hits number 1 on the *Billboard* singles charts, remaining there for five weeks.

Badge, by Cream, co--authored by George Harrison, reaches its highest position on the *Melody Maker* singles charts: number 21.

John Lennon and Yoko Ono reportedly form their own record, film and book publishing firm, Bag Productions.

John Lennon, Yoko Ono and Yoko's daughter Kyoko fly to the Bahamas to stage a peace "Lie--In."

MAY 25 John Lennon, Yoko Ono and Kyoko decide to fly to Canada for their peace campaign, in order to be closer to the U.S. border.   ODT--184 (May 24)

MAY 26 John Lennon, Yoko Ono and Kyoko arrive at Toronto International Airport, where they are detained for two-- and--a--half hours by Immigration officials before being allowed to enter Canada.   ODT--185 (May 24)

John Lennon, Yoko Ono and Kyoko check into the Queen Elizabeth Hotel in Montreal, Canada, to stage their second "Bed--In," which lasts ten days.

Electronic Sound (LP) is released in the U.S. by Apple.

Unfinished Music No. 2: Life with the Lions (LP) is re-- leased in the U.S.

MAY 28 Harold Harrison, George's father, is 60 years old.

MAY 29 The Starkey family returns to England after a week in the U.S.

MAY 30 **Accept No Substitute** (LP) by Delaney & Bonnie, is re-- leased in the U.K. on the Apple label.

The Ballad of John and Yoko/Old Brown Shoe (45) is released in the U.K. by Apple.

MAY 31 *Goodbye* by Mary Hopkin, produced by Paul McCartney,
reaches its highest position on the *Billboard* singles
charts: number 13.

George and Pattie Harrison leave Esher for two weeks'
vacation in Sardinia.

LATE MAY
Mary Hopkin begins a North American tour.

JUNE
Ringo Starr records *Hunting Scene* for the **Magic Christian Music**
album.

Beatle fans in Britain participate in "June Song Poll Competition"
held by the monthly *Beatles Book*; far and away the most
popular song is *Hey Jude*, followed by *Yesterday, Help, All
You Need Is Love,* and *She Loves You.*

Paul McCartney vacations in the south of France.

George Harrison vacations in Sardinia.

John Lennon and Yoko Ono are interviewed by David Wigg.

EARLY JUNE--MID--AUGUST
Tracks for **Abbey Road** (LP) are recorded.

JUN 1 *Give Peace a Chance* is recorded at the Lennons' "Bed--In"
in the Hotel la Reine Elisabeth, Montreal, Canada.

Get Back enters the Polish radio station (Rozglasnia
Harcerska) charts at number 20.

Don't Let Me Down enters the Polish radio station (Roz--
glasnia Harcerska) charts at number 13.

JUN 2--
16 Mary Hopkin performs at the Royal Box, Americana
Hotel, New York City.

JUN 2 *New Day/Thumbin' a Ride* (45) by Jackie Lomax is released in the U.S. by Apple; Ringo Starr plays drums
on *New Day*, Paul McCartney produces *Thumbin' a
Ride.*

JUN 3 John, Yoko and Kyoko leave Montreal for Toronto,
where they seek a special hearing to have their entry
visas extended.

JUN 4 *The Ballad of John and Yoko* enters the *Billboard* British
top twenty singles charts, remaining on the charts for
eight weeks during which it reaches number 1.

The Ballad of John and Yoko/Old Brown Shoe (45) is released in the U.S. by Apple. IR–127 (Jun 26)

JUN 6   Reports appear that Paul and Linda McCartney are con–sidering the purchase of a 4,600 acre estate.

JUN 7   John Lennon, Yoko Ono, and Kyoko return to England from Canada.

John Lennon and Yoko Ono appear on "The David Frost Show."

The Ballad of John and Yoko enters the *Melody Maker* singles charts in the U.K. at number 15.

JUN 9   **Urban Spaceman** (LP) by The Bonzo Dog Band is released in the U.S.; it includes *I'm the Urban Spaceman*, pro–duced by Paul McCartney.

JUN 10   George Harrison's brother–in–law, Gordon Caldwell Sr., has a birthday.

JUN 11   Beatles (U.S.A.) Limited fan club changes its name to Beatles Fan Club Division of Apple Music Publishing Co., Inc.

JUN 12   George Harrison's sister–in–law, Irene Harrison, has a birthday.

JUN 14   Peter Asher resigns as Apple's A&R Manager.

The Ballad of John and Yoko enters Holland's Radio Veronica Top 40 charts at number 4.

The Ballad of John and Yoko enters the *Billboard* singles charts at number 71, remaining on the charts for nine weeks during which it reaches a high point of number 8.

John Lennon and Yoko Ono appear on "The David Frost Show."

JUN 16   *My Dark Hour/Song for Our Ancestors* (45), by The Steve Miller Band, is released in the U.S., with Paul McCartney playing drums, bass guitar and singing vocals on *My Dark Hour.*

Brave New World (LP) by The Steve Miller Band is released in the U.S. containing *My Dark Hour*, with Paul McCart–ney on drums, bass guitar and backing vocals.

JUN 18   Paul McCartney's 27th birthday.

JUN 20   **White Trash** (LP) by Trash is released in the U.K. by Apple.

JUN 21   **Is This What You Want?** (LP) by Jackie Lomax, largely produced by George Harrison, enters the *Billboard* album charts at number 178.

The Ballad of John and Yoko hits number 1 on the *Melody Maker* singles charts, remaining there for three weeks.

JUN 27   Ringo and Maureen Starr fly to the south of France for a vacation.

The Delaney & Bonnie album, **The Original Delaney & Bonnie (Accept No Substitutes)**, previously slated for release by Apple Records is released by Elektra.

It is reported that *Give Peace a Chance/Remember Love* (45), recorded in room 1742, Hotel La Reine, Mon-treal, Canada, will be released the week of July 4th.

That's the Way God Planned It/What About You? (45) by Billy Preston is released in the U.K. by Apple, produced by George Harrison.

JUN 28   **Unfinished Music, No. 2: Life with the Lions** (LP) by John Lennon and Yoko Ono enters the *Billboard* album charts at number 197, remaining on the charts for eight weeks during which it reaches a high point of number 174.

JUN 29   John Lennon and son Julian, and Yoko Ono and daughter Kyoko, begin a vacation tour of Scotland.

MID--1969

Lee Eastman meets with Leonard Richenberg at Claridge's, offering to buy NEMS from Triumph for one million pounds.

Radio stations are mailed copies of an album featuring songs from the "Get Back" recording sessions, but the copies are soon recalled by Apple, later to be reissued (with varying content) as the **Let It Be** album.

SUMMER

Charles Manson and followers begin a series of murders in an attempt to start a race war, the impetus for the crimes partially linked to songs on The Beatles' "White Album," which Manson considered prophetic.

The Beatles record *Bad Penny Blues, Four Nights in Moscow, Just Dancing Around, Little Eddie, My Kind of Girl, Portraits of My Love, Proud as You Are, Suicide, Swinging Days, When Every-body Comes to Town* and *Zero Is Just Another Number*; none are released.   ATN--263 (*When I Come To Town*)

Fans, bitter over Paul McCartney's marriage to Linda Eastman, scrawl graffiti on the wall surrounding their St. John's Wood home; the home is even broken into, and Linda's slides, cameras and clothing are stolen.

JULY

John Lennon and Yoko Ono purchase a Georgian mansion on 80
acres of land – Tittenhurst Park, Ascot – for Ł 150,000. JLS–
147 (May 5; 72 acres for Ł 145,000) ODT--185 (Aug)

Louise Harrison spends a week with George and Pattie at their
home in Esher.

Allen Klein concludes an agreement with Triumph Investment
Trust, ending The Beatles' relationship with NEMS.

Paul McCartney records versions of *Golden Slumbers* and *Carry
That Weight* at the Abbey Road studios that eventually end
up only on the bootleg recording **Watchin Rainbows.**

George Harrison is photographed by fans at EMI studios, London.

George Harrison produces recordings of *Hare Krishna Mantra* and
Prayer to the Spiritual Masters at the Radha Krsna Temple,
London.

EARLY JULY

Earlier recordings of *Get Back* are scrapped as unsatisfactory.

JUL 1   John Lennon, Yoko Ono, Julian and Kyoko are briefly
hospitalized after an auto accident in Golspie, Scotland,
after John loses control of the car in which they are
driving; the car is completely demolished.

Paul McCartney, George Harrison and Ringo Starr begin
recording sessions at EMI studios without John Lennon,
who is recuperating from his auto accident.

JUL 2   In Scotland, Cynthia Lennon picks up Julian at the
hospital, soon taking him off to Greece.

The Official Beatles Fan Club announces the formation of
the following chapters: The Official Heather Chapter,
The Official George Harrison Chapter, Members of the
Beatles Empire Chapter, The Official Paul McCartney
Chapter, The Walrus Waves Chapter, The Official John
Lennon Chapter, The United Beatle Fan Club Chapter;
pending chapters include the Fabulous Ringo Chapter;
The Pottie Bird Beatle Chapter, and The Flying Cow
Chapter.

Variety reports that Allen Klein plans to terminate his
month--old relationship as The Beatles' business
manager.

JUL 2
–4   Paul McCartney begins the first of three recording sessions
for the tune *Her Majesty* at Abbey Road studios, London.

JUL 3   The press reception for the *Give Peace a Chance* single is held at Chelsea Town Hall, unattended by John Lennon and Yoko Ono due to their auto accident; Ringo and Maureen Starr stand in for them.

                George Harrison's sister and brother--in--law, Louise and Gordon Caldwell, celebrate their 15th wedding anni--versary.

JUL 4   **Maybe Tomorrow** (LP) by The Iveys (later Badfinger) is released in Europe by Apple.

                Give Peace a Chance/Remember Love (45) by The Plastic Ono Band is released in the U.K. by Apple.   IR--78 (Apr 7)

JUL 5   **Electronic Sound** (LP) by George Harrison enters the *Billboard* album charts at number 192, reaches number 191 the following week, then drops from the charts.

JUL 6   Ringo and Maureen Starr return from vacationing in the south of France.

                John Lennon and Yoko Ono fly from Scotland back to England on a chartered plane.

JUL 7   *That's the Way God Planned It/What About You?* (45) by Billy Preston is released in the U.S. by Apple, pro--duced by George Harrison.

                Badge, written by George Harrison and Eric Clapton, is released in the U.S. on **Best of Cream** (LP).

                Give Peace a Chance/Remember Love (45) by The Plastic Ono Band is released in the U.S. by Apple.

                The Plastic Ono Band performs at the Chelsea Town Hall to promote their single *Give Peace a Chance*.

                Ringo Starr spends his birthday at home.

JUL 8   John Eastman writes to each of The Beatles criticizing the financial settlement reached between Allen Klein and EMI Records.

JUL 9   Paul McCartney begins recording new versions of *Max--well's Silver Hammer* at Abbey Road studios, the original version having been made some months before.

JUL 11   Paul, George and Ringo add background vocals to *Max--well's Silver Hammer* at EMI's Abbey Road studios.

JUL 12   George Harrison records final versions of his vocals for *Something*.

                Give Peace a Chance enters the *Billboard* British top twenty singles charts, remaining on the charts for nine weeks during which it reaches a high point of number 2.

                The Ballad of John and Yoko reaches its highest position

on the *Billboard* singles charts: number 8.

That's the Way God Planned It by Billy Preston, produced on Apple by George Harrison, enters the *Melody Maker* singles charts in the U.K. at 23.

Give Peace a Chance enters the *Melody Maker* singles charts in the U.K. at number 30.

JUL 14   Apple Records withdraws release of **Maybe Tomorrow** (LP) by The Iveys in the U.S.

JUL 15   The Beatles start work on *You Never Give Me Your Money* at EMI's Abbey Road studios; John Lennon is present.

JUL 16   *The Ballad of John and Yoko* (45) is certified as a Gold Record by the R.I.A.A.

mid--Jul   The Beatles record *I Want You (She's So Heavy)* and *Because* at Abbey Road studios; John Lennon is present.

JUL 17   The Beatles begin recording *Octopus's Garden* at EMI's Abbey Road studios; John Lennon is present.

JUL 18   Recording of *Oh Darling* is completed at EMI's Abbey Road studios; John Lennon is absent.

Storm in a Teacup (The Iveys), *Something's Wrong* (James Taylor), *Little Yellow Pills* (Jackie Lomax) and *Happiness Runs* (Mary Hopkin) are released on an Apple promotional record for a business firm.

My Dark Hour/Song for Our Ancestors (45) by The Steve Miller Band is released in the U.K.; Paul McCartney plays drums, bass guitar and sings backing vocal on *My Dark Hour*.

Penina, written by Paul McCartney, appears on a single by Carlos Mendes released in Portugal.

No Escaping Your Love/Dear Angie (45) by The Iveys is released in Europe by Apple. BU2--22 (*No Escape*)

Wall's Ice Cream (EP) is released in the U.K. by Apple.

JUL 19   **Best of Cream** (LP) featuring *Badge*, co--authored by George Harrison, enters the *Billboard* album charts at number 60.

Unfinished Music, No. 2: Life with the Lions (LP) by John Lennon and Yoko Ono reaches its highest position on the *Billboard* album charts: number 179.

JUL 20   George Harrison and his father, Harold, stay up all night and watch Neil Armstrong and Edwin Aldrin walk on the moon.

George Harrison's brothers, Harry and Peter, celebrate their birthdays, aged 35 and 29 respectively.

JUL 21   John Lennon resumes a regular recording schedule following a recuperation period from his automobile accident some weeks before.

Recording sessions for *Come Together* are begun at the Abbey Road studios.

JUL 22   Fans photograph John Lennon, Paul McCartney, Yoko Ono and others at EMI studios, London.

JUL 24   At EMI studios, The Beatles begin recording sessions for *Mean Mr. Mustard* and *Here Comes the Sun/Sun King*, a two–part composition later turned into separate songs for **Abbey Road** (LP).

Give Peace a Chance enters the *Billboard* singles charts, remaining on the charts for nine weeks during which it reaches a high point of number 14.

JUL 25   Paul McCartney poses for photographs and signs auto–graphs after arriving at EMI studios, London.

Linda McCartney is intercepted by fans while returning on foot to the McCartney's home in St. John's Wood.

Recording sessions for *Bathroom Window* (later *She Came in Through the Bathroom Window*) are begun.

JUL 26   George Harrison speaks in a radio broadcast in behalf of an Indian holy day peace march to commence the following day in Hyde Park.

Give Peace a Chance enters the *Billboard* singles charts at number 62.

That's the Way God Planned It by Billy Preston, produced by George Harrison, enters the *Billboard* singles charts at number 103.

Is This What You Want? (LP) by Jackie Lomax, largely produced by George Harrison, reaches its highest position on the *Billboard* album charts: number 142.

That's the Way God Planned It by Billy Preston, produced on Apple by George Harrison, reaches its highest position on the *Melody Maker* singles charts: number 7.

JUL 27   Terry Doran drives George and Pattie Harrison, and Pattie's step–sister Paula, to Apple, dropping George off and taking Pattie and Paula on to Hyde Park.

Pattie Harrison, Terry Doran and Pattie's step–sister Paula march in the peace march from Hyde Park to the Thames River, stopping for a rally in Trafalger Square; they leave the march early because Paula becomes ill.

JUL 28   Final version of *Polythene Pam* is recorded at EMI's Abbey Road studios.

JUL 29   At Apple offices, Linda McCartney is hostile to the con–tinuous attention of fans, yelling at one of them to go away.

1969

JUL 31   Paul McCartney is photographed by a fan.
Final versions of *Golden Slumbers, Carry that Weight* and *The End* are recorded at EMI's Abbey Road studios.

LATE JULY–EARLY AUGUST
The "Abbey Road" recording sessions, booked by The Beatles at EMI's Abbey Road studios.
Final versions of *You Never Give Me Your Money, Golden Slumbers, Here Comes the Sun, Sun King, Come Together* and *Mean Mr. Mustard* are recorded; *Maxwell's Silver Hammer, Bathroom Window, Oh Darling, Polythene Pam, Something,* and *Octopus's Garden* are re–recorded.
Yoko Ono, injured in the Lennon's car accident on July 1, attends the "Abbey Road" recording sessions by moving a bed into the Apple studios.

SUMMER
Allen Klein begins negotiations with Capitol Records in a bid to increase The Beatles' royalties.
ATV's share price in Northern Songs stock is greatly depressed owing to a sluggish stock market.

AUGUST
Month scheduled for John and Yoko Lennon to occupy their new $360,000.00 mansion in Ascot, a London suburb.
John Chambers, Apple's accountant, leaves the company.
Early date predicted for the release of a new album, **The Beatles Get Back.**
Pattie Harrison appears on the cover of the Italian edition of *Vogue.*
The Plastic Ono Band records *Rock Peace*; not released.
Two films by John Lennon and Yoko Ono – "The Ballad of John and Yoko" and "Number 5" – are shown in Frankfurt, Germany.
A.J. Butler, an American broker acting for The Beatles, makes cash offers to syndicate members in another bid to buy minority shares in Northern Songs.
Apple Records' artists now include: The Beatles, Mary Hopkin, Jackie Lomax, The Iveys, James Taylor, Billy Preston, Doris Troy, White Trash, The Radha Krsna Temple, The Plastic Ono Band, and The Modern Jazz Quartet.

AUG 1   *I'm the Urban Spaceman*, produced by Paul McCartney, is included on **Tadpoles** (LP) by The Bonzo Dog Band.
AUG 2   *Give Peace a Chance* reaches highest point on the *Melody Maker* singles charts: number 2.

AUG 3   Ringo and Maureen Starr, and Mal and Lil Evans attend
          the Hank Snow country & western concert at the
          London Palladium. TM4–8 (Aug 4)
AUG 4   Fans visit George Harrison outside his home in Esher just
          as he is preparing to go to the studio with Terry Doran;
          he spends 15 minutes with them posing for photos and
          signing autographs.
          Maureen Starr's 23rd birthday.
          Fans visit Ringo Starr's mansion in Elstead, Surrey,
          ostensibly to wish his wife, Maureen, a happy birthday.
AUG 8   Photograph for the cover of **Abbey Road** (LP) is taken at
          10 a.m.
          George Harrison and Mal Evans go to the Regent's Park
          zoo following the photo sessions for the cover of
          Abbey Road (LP).
AUG 9–- Mary Hopkin records *Que Sera Sera* and *Fields of St.*
    10   *Etienne*, produced by Paul McCartney, with Paul playing
          guitar and Ringo Starr on drums.
AUG 10   George Harrison picks up wife, Pattie, at the airport and,
          on his return to his home in Esher, angrily greets fans
          he finds walking down his driveway.
AUG 11   Ringo and Maureen Starr arrive at the Apple building in
          their chauffered white Mercedes; Ringo poses for
          pictures and signs autographs for fans.
          Atlantis, with Paul McCartney on tambourine and backing
          vocal, appears in the U.S. on **Barabajagal** (LP) by
          Donovan.
AUG 16   George Harrison's sister, Louise Caldwell, is 38.
AUG 19   Jason Starkey's second birthday.
AUG 20   *Variety* reports that teenage fans at the Frankfurt showing
          of "The Ballad of John and Yoko" and "Number 5"
          meet the screening with "jeers and screams."
AUG 21   The Beatles attend the annual General Meeting of Apple.
AUG 22   **That's the Way God Planned It** (LP) by Billy Preston,
          produced by George Harrison, is released in the U.K.
          by Apple.
          Hare Krishna Mantra/Prayer to the Spiritual Masters (45)
          by Radha Krsna Temple is released in the U.S. by
          Apple, produced by George Harrison. BM–143 (**Hare
          Krishna Mantra** (LP)) LCP–282 (Aug 21)
AUG 23   *That's the Way God Planned It* by Billy Preston, produced
          by George Harrison, reaches its highest position on the
          Billboard singles charts: number 62.

AUG 26   Billy Preston appears on Joey Bishop's TV show in the U.S.
AUG 27   George Harrison's niece, Janet, is seven years old.
         Brian Epstein has been dead two years.
AUG 28   George Harrison attends a press reception to promote *Hare Krishna Mantra*.
         In London, Paul and Linda McCartney welcome the birth of their new daughter Mary, named for Paul's late mother.
AUG 29   **Songs for a Tailor** (LP) by Jack Bruce is released in the U.K.; George Harrison plays rhythm guitar on the cut *Never Tell Your Mother She's Out of Tune*.
         Hare Krishna Mantra/Prayer to the Spiritual Masters (45) by Radha Krsna Temple is released in the U.K. by Apple, produced by George Harrison.
AUG 30   First birthday of Apple Electronics.
AUG 31   George and Pattie Harrison, Ringo and Maureen Starr, and John Lennon, Yoko Ono, Neil Aspinall, Mal Evans, and Chris O'Dell attend a Bob Dylan concert on the Isle of Wight.
Aug   John Lennon, George Harrison and Ringo Starr meet again with Bob Dylan during his performance at the Isle of Wight music festival.
         Bob Dylan helicopters to Tittenhurst Park, the Lennons' home, with John, Yoko and George Harrison, after his concert on the Isle of Wight.

SEPTEMBER
   John Lennon records *The Short Rap* and *The Long Rap*, released in the U.S. on the Cotillion label.
   Allen Klein reveals details of The Beatles' new contract with Capitol Records, one which nets the group from 58 cents to 72 cents per album until 1976, compared to 6 cents per album before 1966 and 30 cents per album from 1966 to 1969.
   George Harrison's mother, Louise French Harrison, is taken seriously ill in Liverpool, and is hospitalized with a cancerous brain tumor.
   John Lennon and Yoko Ono are arrested and charged with possession of cannabis.
   John Lennon and Yoko Ono are interviewed, the session later appearing on the bootleg recording **EMI Outakes**.
   Ringo Starr records *Night and Day, Star Dust*, and *Blue, Turning Grey Over You*, which later appear on his **Sentimental Journey**

(LP).   RO--29 (Oct)

George Harrison is interviewed by David Wigg.

John Lennon announces he is leaving The Beatles as a group.

Come and Get It, written by Paul McCartney, and three other
tracks are recorded by Badfinger, all produced by Paul.

The relationship between Allen Klein and John and Lee Eastman
has deteriorated to a mud--slinging, name--calling level.

London's New Cinema Club begins "Two Evenings with John and
Yoko," featuring showings of their films "Two Virgins," "Smile,"
"Honeymoon" and the world premiere of "Self--Portrait."
BM--143 ("An Evening with John & Yoko")

SEPTEMBER 1969--JANUARY 1970

Eight tracks are recorded by the Radha Krsna Temple, produced
by George Harrison.

EARLY SEPTEMBER

The syndicate of minority shareholders in Northern Songs begins
to disintegrate; ATV begins to add additional shares to its
holdings.

SEP 5   Allen Klein is reported to have re--negotiated The Beatles'
recording contract with EMI.

SEP 6   *Give Peace a Chance* reaches its highest position on the
Billboard singles charts: number 14.

SEP 8   Jack Gill reveals that ATV has increased its holdings of
shares in Northern Songs by 3%; the other syndicate
members begin to seek to sell their shares to ATV.

SEP 9   Ringo Starr enters a Middlesex hospital for examination
of a possible intestinal obstruction. OBF--14 (Sep 8--11)

SEP 10   Institute of Contemporary Arts begins showing two films
by John Lennon and Yoko Ono, "Rape" (British
premiere) and "Self--Portrait."
OBF--14 (world premiere of "Self--Portrait")

That's the Way God Planned It (LP) by Billy Preston, pro--
duced by George Harrison, is released in the U.S. by
Apple.

SEP 12   John Lennon agrees to attend the Toronto Peace Festival
during a long--distance call from Toronto to London.

The Rolling Stones LP **Through the Past Darkly** is released
in the U.K., featuring Lennon and McCartney singing
backing vocals on the cut *We Love You.*

SEP 13   John Lennon, Yoko Ono and The Plastic Ono Band fly to
Toronto to perform at the "Toronto Rock 'n' Roll

Revival" in Varsity Stadium.

Zak Starkey's 4th birthday.

Tracks of **The Plastic Ono Band -- Live Peace in Toronto 1969** (LP) are recorded by John Lennon in Varsity Stadium at the Toronto Peace Festival.

Best of Cream (LP) featuring *Badge*, co--authored by George Harrison, reaches its highest position on the *Billboard* album charts: number 3.

SEP 19   ATV purchases enough syndicate shares in Northern Songs to bring its total to just under 50%, preventing The Beatles from ever gaining control of the company.

Que Sera Sera/Fields of St. Etienne (45) by Mary Hopkin is released in France by Apple, produced by Paul McCartney.

SEP 20   *Hare Krishna Mantra* by Radha Krsna Temple, produced by George Harrison, enters the *Melody Maker* singles charts in the U.K. at number 30.

SEP 21   *Badge*, written by George Harrison and Eric Clapton, is reissued on a single by Cream.

SEP 22   A taped appearance of The Beatles performing *The Ballad of John and Yoko* is aired on the first show in a new TV series, "Music Scene."

SEP 25   Release of a White Trash version of *Golden Slumbers* is marked by a press reception at Apple studios, hosted by John Lennon and Yoko Ono.

ATV announces at its annual general meeting that ATV now controls 54% of Northern Songs.

SEP 26   **Abbey Road** (LP) is released in the U.K. by Apple.

SEP 27   Begins a three--week period during which no Beatle--related recordings appear on the *Billboard* singles charts.

SEP 29   George Harrison's niece, Leslie Caldwell, is 10 years old.

SEP 30   *Cold Turkey* and *Don't Worry Kyoko* are recorded by John Lennon and Yoko Ono.

LATE SEPTEMBER

Paul McCartney's father is hospitalized in Cheshire; Paul visits him frequently.

John Lennon and Yoko Ono's films, "Smile" and "Two Virgins," due to be shown at a benefit in Trafalgar Square for a Biafra Fund, are barred from the screen.

LATE SEPTEMBER--EARLY OCTOBER

Proposed time for another "Bed--In" by John Lennon and Yoko

Ono, this time in Japan.

FALL
Allen Klein negotiates a contract with ATV whereby The Beatles'
shares in Northern Songs would be exchanged for shares in
ATV, and whereby The Beatles' songwriting contracts would be
extended; John Eastman writes to ATV informing them that
Klein does not act for Paul McCartnev.
The rumor of Paul McCartney's death, owing to his seclusion at
his farm in Scotland, is widely believed in the U.S.

OCTOBER
Paul McCartney leaves for a vacation at his farm in Scotland
following recording sessions.
Rumored month for George Harrison to begin filming a cowboy
movie in which he plays a character named "Candy."
Four hundred people attend a four-hour screening of several
short films by John Lennon and Yoko Ono at London's
Institute of Contemporary Arts, including "Rape -- Pt. II,"
"Two Virgins," "Honeymoon," and "Self--Portrait."
Apple Records reports that the single by Trash, *Road to
Nowhere/Illusions* (45) sold 20,000 copies worldwide and failed
to make the charts anywhere, even as it announces their new
single *Golden Slumbers/Carry that Weight* backed with *Trash
Can*, and an impending album.
Paul and Linda McCartney pose for fans' photographs outside their
home in St. Johns Wood.
All That I've Got, with George Harrison playing lead guitar, is re--
corded by Billy Preston at Trident studios, London, produced
by George Harrison.
Institute of Contemporary Arts, The Mall, London, premieres the
film "Apotheosis," by John Lennon and Yoko Ono.

EARLY OCTOBER
Brief interviews with George Harrison, along with preview of
tracks from **Abbey Road** (LP), are aired on radio stations
around the U.S. through October 12.
John Lennon and Paul McCartney openly feud.

OCTOBER 1969--JANUARY 1970
Sixteen songs are recorded by Doris Troy, produced by George

Harrison and with Harrison on guitar, at Trident studios, London.

OCT 1   **Abbey Road** (LP) is released in the U.S. by Apple.
LCP--281 (Nov 1)   PMW--11 (Sep)

OCT 2   A John Lennon interview reveals that the majority of his earnings goes back into supporting Apple Records.

OCT 3   *Golden Slumbers--Carry that Weight/Trash Can* (45) by Trash (formerly White Trash) is released in the U.S. by Apple.

OCT 4   **Abbey Road** (LP) enters the *Melody Maker* album charts, remaining there for 19 weeks.

OCT 6   **Songs for a Tailor** (LP) by Jack Bruce is released in the U.S.; George Harrison plays rhythm guitar on the cut *Never Tell Your Mother She's Out of Tune.*
Something/Come Together (45) is released in the U.S. by Apple. BM--99 (Oct 13)   PMB--236 (Oct 13)

OCT 8   Paul McCartney is photographed by a fan.

OCT 9   John Lennon's 29th birthday.

OCT 9--   Yoko Ono is admitted to Kings College Hospital, Denmark
    12   Hill, London.

OCT 10   *Give Peace a Chance/Living Without Tomorrow* (45) by Hot Chocolate Band is released in the U.K. by Apple.
Brave New World (LP) by The Steve Miller Band is released in the U.K.; it contains *My Dark Hour*, with Paul McCartney on drums, bass guitar and backing vocal.

OCT 11   *Hare Krishna Mantra* by Radha Krsna Temple, produced by George Harrison, reaches its highest position on the *Melody Maker* singles charts: number 11.

OCT 12   Detroit disc jockey Russ Gibb (WKNR--FM) receives a "mysterious" phone call advising him of the various "clues" to Paul McCartney's death in certain Beatle tunes. IR--83 (Gibbs)

OCT 13   Paul and Linda McCartney and Ringo and Maureen Starr attend Mary Hopkin's opening night at the Savoy Hotel, London.

OCT 14   The Official Beatles Fan Club reports the availability of a Beatles' interview album which includes John Lennon's "apology" for remarks comparing The Beatles with Jesus; the album is being sold by the *Braille Quarterly* of Louisville, Kentucky, proceeds going to the blind.
A review of **Abbey Road** (LP) by Fred LaBour in *The Michigan Daily* furthers the mythology of Paul McCartney's death.

OCT 15   *Golden Slumbers--Carry that Weight/Trash Can* (45) by Trash
          (formerly White Trash) is released in the U.K. by Apple.
          Pattie Harrison appears on the cover of the British edition
          of *Vogue* magazine.
          Ringo and Maureen Starr fly to Los Angeles for business
          talks, along with Neil and Sue Aspinall; Ringo discusses
          recording commitments and the possibility of a TV
          special, "Startime."

OCT 16   It is announced that The Beatles will sell their shares in
          Northern Songs to ATV.

OCT 17   *Give Peace a Chance/Living without Tomorrow* (45) by
          Hot Chocolate Band is released in the U.S. by Apple.
          Everything's All Right/I Want to Thank You (45) by
          Billy Preston is released in the U.K. by Apple; *Every--
          thing's All Right* is produced by George Harrison.

OCT 18   **Abbey Road** (LP) enters the *Billboard* album charts at
          number 178, remaining on the charts for 87 weeks
          during which it reaches a high point of number 1.
          Come Together enters the *Billboard* singles charts at
          number 23, remaining on the charts for 16 weeks during
          which it reaches a high point of number 1.
          Something enters the *Billboard* singles charts at number 20,
          remaining on the charts for 16 weeks during which it
          reaches a high point of number 1.

OCT 20   **Wedding Album** (LP) is released in the U.S. by Apple.
          Cold Turkey/Don't Worry Kyoko (45) by The Plastic Ono
          Band is released in the U.S. by Apple.
          George and Pattie Harrison visit with Ravi Shankar in London.

OCT 21   Ringo and Maureen Starr, and Neil and Sue Aspinall,
          return to England from Los Angeles.   OBF--14 (Oct 22)
          The Official Beatles Fan Club reports their offices have
          been "flooded" with telephone inquiries from across the
          U.S. inquiring about Paul McCartney's alleged "death."

OCT 22   "Paul Is Dead" rumors are widespread in U.S.; Paul again
          denies the rumors.
          Paul and Linda McCartney, Heather and Mary vacation in
          Scotland.

OCT 24   *Time* magazine, released some days prior to its publication
          date, carries an article describing how Russ Gibb, of
          Detroit radio station WKNR, has uncovered Paul
          McCartney's "death" revealed in recent Beatles' albums.
          Everything's All Right/I Want to Thank You (45) by Billy
          Preston is released in the U.S. by Apple; *Everything's*

All Right is produced by George Harrison.

Space (LP) by The Modern Jazz Quartet is released in the U.K. by Apple.

Cold Turkey/Don't Worry Kyoko (45) is released in the U.K. by Apple.

Badge, written by George Harrison and Eric Clapton, is released in the U.S. on **Best of Cream** (LP).

OCT 25   *Come Together* enters Holland's Radio Veronica Top 40 charts at number 14.

OCT 26   Lee Merrick writes an article on Paul McCartney's double, Billy Shears, for the *Rat Subterranean News*.

Abbey Road (LP) enters the Polish radio station (Rozglasnia Harcerska) charts at number 1, remaining there for eleven of twelve weeks.

OCT 27   **Abbey Road** (LP) is certified as a Gold Record by the R.I.A.A.

Oct 27–   Ringo Starr records tracks for his **Sentimental Journey**
Dec   album at the Abbey Road studios, London, including *Buy Me a Beer, Mr. Shane*, not released.

OCT 27   *Something/Come Together* (45) is certified as a Gold Record by the R.I.A.A.

OCT 29   An article on Paul McCartney's replacement, Billy Shears, appears in the *Rat Subterranean News*.

OCT 30   It is reported that an album by The Plastic Ono Band called **Gossip**, originally scheduled for release in late October–early November, won't be available until late November.

OCT 31   *Something/Come Together* (45) is released in the U.K. by Apple.

LATE OCTOBER

George Harrison sits in on a recording session for an album by Rick Grech; the songs did not appear on the LP when released.

NOVEMBER

John Lennon and Yoko Ono vacation in Athens, Greece.

The Beatles separately record their 1969 Christmas record, *The Beatles Seventh Christmas Record*.

Reporter Ken Zeilig interviews John Lennon and Yoko Ono at the Apple building in Savile Row after their return from Canada.

Month predicted for the birth of Peter and Pauline Harrison's second child, making George Harrison an uncle for the sixth time.

Second scheduled month for the release of **Get Back** (LP), post--
poned to coincide with a planned Beatles' TV special.

NOVEMBER 1969--MARCH 1970
Paul McCartney records the tracks for his **McCartney** (LP) at his
home in St. John's Wood, at Morgan studios, London, and at
Abbey Road studios, London.

EARLY NOVEMBER--MID--DECEMBER
Ringo Starr records *Sentimental Journey, I'm a Fool to Care,
Dream, You Always Hurt the One You Love, Have I Told You
Lately/That I Love You,* and *Let the Rest of the World Go By,*
which later appear on his **Sentimental Journey** LP.

NOV 1   *Cold Turkey* enters the *Billboard* British top twenty singles
          charts, remaining on the charts for six weeks during
          which it reaches a high point of number 1.
          Abbey Road (LP) hits number 1 on the *Billboard* album
          charts, remaining there for eleven of the next thirteen
          weeks.
NOV 4   The New York *Daily News* runs an article debunking the
          rumors of Paul McCartney's death.
NOV 6--   "Rape -- Part II," a film by John Lennon and Yoko Ono,
   11   is shown at the Mannheim Film Festival in Germany.
NOV 7   Paul McCartney appears on the cover of *Life* magazine.
          Wedding Album (LP) is released in the U.K. by Apple.
          IR--84 (Nov 14)
NOV 8   It is reported that the "Paul Is Dead" rumors have gener--
          ated the following recordings: a documentary album
          containing excerpts from radio programs on the alleged
          death; a single, *Brother Paul*, by Billie Shears and The
          All Americans (Silver Fox Records); *The Ballad of Paul*
          by The Mystery Tour (MGM Records); *Dear Paul* by
          Jose Feliciano (RCA); *Paulbearer* on Viking Records;
          Saint Paul by Terry Knight (Capitol Records).
          The Best of Cream (LP) featuring *Badge*, co--authored by
          George Harrison, enters the *Melody Maker* album charts
          in the U.K. at number 17.
          It is reported that Capitol Records of Canada has been de--
          luged with calls about the rumored death of Paul
          McCartney, and that sales of Beatles' albums have shown
          "considerable increase."
          Cold Turkey enters the *Melody Maker* singles charts in the

U.K. at number 27.

Something/Come Together (45) enters the *Billboard* British top twenty singles charts, remaining on the charts for seven weeks during which it reaches a high point of number 4.

Something enters the *Melody Maker* singles charts in the U.K. at number 26.

NOV 9   Reports begin to appear about John Lennon and Yoko Ono's film of themselves, "Apotheosis."

NOV 10 **Space** (LP) by The Modern Jazz Quartet is released in the U.S. by Apple.

The Ballad of Paul/The Ballad of Paul (Follow the Bouncing Ball) (45) by The Mystery Tour is released in the U.S.

NOV 13 John Lennon has reportedly donated the use of his island – Dorinish – off the coast of Ireland to a group of hippies to do with as they please.

NOV 15 *Come Together* reaches its highest position on the *Bill-board* singles charts: number 2.

Sgt. Pepper's Lonely Hearts Club Band (LP) re–enters the *Billboard* album charts at number 124, sales rekindled by the "Paul Is Dead" rumors.

One of the last group shots for which The Beatles posed appears on the cover of *Rolling Stone* magazine.

Magical Mystery Tour (LP) re--enters the *Billboard* album charts at number 146, sales rekindled by the "Paul Is Dead" rumors.

Cold Turkey enters the *Billboard* singles charts at number 86, remaining on the charts for twelve weeks during which it reaches a high point of number 30.

Golden Slumbers/Carry that Weight by Trash, released in the U.S. by Apple, enters the *Billboard* singles charts at number 112, dropping off the following week.

Something reaches its highest position on the *Billboard* singles charts: number 3.

A John Lennon interview appears in *Disc and Music Echo*.

mid–Nov *All That I've Got* is recorded by Billy Preston, produced by George Harrison.

Jackie Lomax records *How the Web Was Woven* for Apple Records, produced by George Harrison.

NOV 16 Ian Harrison, George's nephew, is two years old.

Thanks   Scheduled time for Paul and Linda McCartney, and
–giving   daughters Heather and Mary, to visit Linda's family in

New York.

NOV 26   John Lennon returns his MBE.   IR–85 (Nov 25)   JLS–
         149 (Nov 23)   OBF–14 (Nov 25)

NOV 28   Expected date of birth of George Harrison's sixth niece or
         nephew, the second child of Peter and Pauline Harrison.
         Ringo Starr records at EMI studios, London.

NOV 29   *Badge*, written by George Harrison and Eric Clapton,
         appears on **Hit '69** (LP) released in the U.K.
         Something/Come Together (45) hits number 1 on the *Billboard*
         singles charts.
         Something reaches its highest point on the *Melody Maker*
         singles charts: number 4.
         Cold Turkey reaches its highest point on the *Melody Maker*
         singles charts: number 12.

LATE NOVEMBER

I Can't Get No Nookie/Cow Pie (45) by The Masked Marauders,
incorrectly rumored to feature performances by three of The
Beatles, is released in the U.S.

The Masked Marauders (LP) by The Masked Marauders, incorrectly rumored to feature performances by three of The Beatles,
is released in the U.S.

DECEMBER

John Lennon receives *Rolling Stone* magazine's first Man of the
Year award.

Apple Corps' net income for 1969 found to be about Ł 2 million.

What's the News Maryjane is almost released on a single by John
Lennon.

George Harrison records with Jackie Lomax during December, as
well as with Doris Troy.

Ringo Starr visits Los Angeles for business talks.

Sunday Express reports that Apple employees are now required to
sign statements to the effect that they will never write about
their employers.

The Beatles reject two offers of a million pounds each for concert
tours.

Doris Troy records *Ain't that Cute* and *Vaya Con Dios* for Apple
Records, the former produced by George Harrison, with George
on guitar and Ringo on drums.

Financial accounting reveals Beatles' royalties to December 1968
as three–and–a–half million pounds in the U.K.

Capitol Records is found to owe The Beatles two–and–a–half

million dollars for 3½ months of record sales in the U.S.

Expected month of birth originally announced for Paul and Linda McCartney's first natural child; the pregnancy was announced in May, and Mary McCartney was born August 28.

John Lennon and Yoko Ono discuss plans for their Toronto peace festival with John Brower and Ritchie York of Karma Productions while in Canada.

Last issue of the monthly fan newsmagazine, the *Beatles Book*, after sixandahalf years of publication.

John Lennon plasters billboards and newspapers in cities all over the free world with his new peace slogan: "War Is Over! If You Want It."

John Lennon, in a *New Musical Express* interview, declares the end of The Beatles as a group.

DECEMBER 1969JUNE 1970

Doris Troy records *Jacob's Ladder* and *Get Back* for Apple Records, George Harrison playing guitar.

DEC 1   George and Pattie Harrison and Ringo and Maureen Starr attend the opening of the "Delaney, Bonnie and Friends" tour at Albert Hall, London.

George Harrison becomes an uncle for the sixth time; Linda Harrison is born to Peter and Pauline, George's brother and sisterinlaw.

DEC 2   George Harrison joins the Delaney and Bonnie Bramlett tour.

DEC 3   George Harrison stops in to see his new niece, Linda Harrison, three days old.

George Harrison plays guitar as part of the Delaney and Bonnie Bramlett tour in Bristol.

DEC 4   George Harrison plays guitar as part of the Delaney and Bonnie Bramlett tour in Birmingham.

DEC 5   *You Know My Name/What's the News Maryjane* (45) by The Plastic Ono Band, slated for released this date in the U.K. by Apple, is not issued.

George Harrison performs as part of the Delaney and Bonnie Bramlett tour at City Hall in New Castle, England.   HH232 (Sheffield)

Come and Get It, by Badfinger, written and produced by Paul McCartney, is released in the U.K. by Apple.

Ringo and Maureen Starr and children move into a new home in North West London.

DEC 6   Ringo Starr appears on the "David Frost Show" in
           London.
           The Best of Cream (LP), featuring *Badge* (co–authored by
           George Harrison), reaches its highest position on the
           Melody Maker album charts: number 5.
           George Harrison performs as part of the Delaney and
           Bonnie Bramlett tour at the Empire in Liverpool,
           England. HH23--2 (Newcastle)
DEC 7   Universal Beatle Day.
           George Harrison (on guitar) records tracks for **Delaney
           and Bonnie on Tour** (LP) with Delaney and Bonnie
           Bramlett at Fairfield Hall in Croydon, Surrey, England.
           HH23-2 (Dec 7: Liverpool; Dec 8: Croydon)
DEC 8   "The Magic Christian" is shown to the press at 10:30 a.m.
           in London's Odeon Theatre.
           Apple company accounts reportedly showing Ł574,000
           profit for an 18–month period ending December 1966.
DEC 10   Ringo Starr appears on BBC 2's "Late Night Line Up"
           show.
           John Lennon and Yoko Ono announce plans to do a film
           about the "A6" murder case, and reveal their intention
           to bring about a public inquiry into the hanging of James
           Hanratty.
           George Harrison performs as part of the Delaney and
           Bonnie tour at the Falconer Theatre, Copenhagen,
           Denmark.
DEC 10   George Harrison tours Scandinavia with the Delaney and
  –14   Bonnie Bramlett tour.
DEC 11   An American promoter offers The Beatles a minimum of
           $2,400,000 and a possible maximum of $8,800,000 to
           do a 12--city U.S. concert tour; The Beatles reject the
           offer.
DEC 12   World premiere at London's Kensington Odeon of the film
           "The Magic Christian" with Ringo Starr as Youngman
           Grand, attended by Ringo and Maureen Starr, John
           Lennon and Yoko Ono, and Princess Margaret.
           Across the Universe (version one) appears on **No One's
           Gonna Change Our World** (LP), released in the U.K.
           by EMI.
           George Harrison plays guitar at the concert by Delaney

and Bonnie Bramlett at Falkoner Center, Copenhagen, Denmark.

The Plastic Ono Band -- Live Peace in Toronto 1969 (LP) is released in the U.K. by Apple. JLS--89 (1970) ODT--185 (Nov)

George Harrison's oldest brother and sister--in--law, Harry and Irene, mark their 11th wedding anniversary.

The Plastic Ono Band -- Live Peace in Toronto 1969 (LP) is released in the U.S. by Apple. ODT--185 (Nov)

DEC 13   **Wedding Album** (LP) by John Lennon and Yoko Ono enters the *Billboard* album charts at number 182, re-- maining on the charts for three weeks during which it reaches a high point of number 178.

DEC 14   Ringo Starr participates in taping of "A Little Help from My Friends," a documentary featuring George Martin.

DEC 15   BBC films an hour--long documentary about John Lennon for the television show "24 Hours."

John Lennon and Yoko Ono launch their "War Is Over" billboard campaign in twelve U.S. cities.

John Lennon's UNICEF benefit concert, "War Is Over If You Want It," at London's Lyceum Gallery, source of tracks for side three of **Sometime in New York City** (LP); he is joined by George Harrison and members of the Delaney and Bonnie tour.

John Lennon's UNICEF benefit concert and "War Is Over" interview are recorded, later to be included on the boot-- leg recordings **Christmas Message, Get Back to Toronto, From John and Yoko, Get Back to Toronto--High Stereo Recording**, and **Get Back to Toronto--Stereo**.

mid--Dec   Pauline Harrison, George's sister--in--law, reports that George's mother, Louise, had been in the hospital but is presently back home recuperating.

DEC 16   John Lennon and Yoko Ono fly to Toronto, Canada, to announce the Mosport Park Peace Festival.

John Lennon, Yoko Ono and Anthony Fawcett arrive at Ronnie Hawkins' farmhouse outside Toronto, Canada, for a five day stay.

DEC 17   *Variety*'s assessment of Ringo Starr's appearance in "The Magic Christian": "a distinct non--event."

John Lennon announces plans for a peace festival in Toronto, July 3--5, 1970, at a press conference at the

Ontario Science Centre.

DEC 18   John Lennon signs 3,000 lithographs for his collection,
–20   *Bag One*, at Ronnie Hawkins' farmhouse outside
             Toronto.

DEC 19   *The Beatles Seventh Christmas Record* is released by the
             Fan Club.

John Lennon and Yoko Ono meet Marshall McLuhan at
             the University of Toronto in a 45–minute interview
             filmed for television by the CBC.

DEC 21   John Lennon and Yoko Ono take a private train to Mon--
             treal and Ottawa, attending a press conference at the
             Chateau Champlain Hotel in Montreal.

DEC 22   John Lennon and Yoko Ono meet with John Munro,
             Canada's Health Minister.

John Lennon and Yoko Ono meet with Canada's Prime
             Minister, Pierre Trudeau, for nearly an hour.

DEC 23   John Lennon and Yoko Ono fly back to London.

DEC 24   Ringo Starr appears on BBC--TV's "Live" show singing
             Octopus's Garden, accompanied by The George Martin
             Orchestra.

"A Little Help from My Friends," featuring Ringo Starr,
             is broadcast on British television.

Christ–   Louise Harrison, George's mother, has dinner with her son
mas   and daughter--in--law, Peter and Pauline.

DEC 27   **Wedding Album** (LP) by John Lennon and Yoko Ono
             reaches its highest position on the *Billboard* album
             charts: number 178.

DEC 29   John Lennon and Yoko Ono fly to Aalborg, Denmark, to
             visit Kyoko, Yoko's daughter, on a farm where Kyoko
             is staying with her father Anthony Cox, and his wife
             Belinda.   ODT--68 (early Jan 1970)

John and Yoko are visited in Aalborg, Denmark by
             Hammrick and Leonard, Canadian hypnotists who
             attempt to help them give up smoking; by Ritchie York
             and John Brower, with whom they discuss plans for the
             Peace Festival; and by Allen Klein.

Linda McCartney's daughter, Heather, is seven years old.

DEC 30   It is reported that The Beatles themselves plan to resume
             publication of a new Beatles magazine, to begin publi--
             cation in Feburary 1970.

The Official Beatles Fan Club tells U.S. area secretaries to

disregard continued rumors of a Beatles' breakup; "The
four, as a group, have a whole new decade in front of
them!!!"

DEC 31   In the nine months since March 31, The Beatles' partner--
ship has grossed £1,708,000.

British television airs the three--part "Man of the Decade,"
a 20--minute portion of which is devoted to John
Lennon.

LATE DECEMBER
Paul McCartney records *The Lovely Linda* for **McCartney (LP)**.

LATE DECEMBER--EARLY JANUARY
Paul McCartney almost releases his **McCartney (LP)**, but the timing
causes bitter disagreement among The Beatles; the others feel
its release would hurt sales of the pending **Let It Be** album.

LATE 1969
Paul McCartney, attending a premiere, leaps from his car, charges
through a crowd of fans lining the street outside a theater, and
proceeds to rip a leather jacket off the back of a young girl
which resembles a custom--made jacket stolen from his St.
John's Wood home earlier in the year; the jacket proves to be
too small, and McCartney sheepishly returns it over the girl's
protestations that he keep it. It had been modeled (from a photo)
after McCartney's jacket by the girl's mother, a tailor.

Allen Klein asks Phil Spector to work with the tapes from the
"Let It Be" sessions in an attempt to salvage an album from
them.

Paul McCartney, in isolation on his sheep farm in Scotland with
his family, begins recording songs on newly installed equipment
which are eventually released as **McCartney (LP)**.

Hey Jude/Revolution (45) has sold over five million copies.

The Beatles turn over their share in Northern Songs to ATV in
exchange for loan stock in ATV itself.

And though the news was rather sad

A DAY IN THE LIFE
The Beatles
Day-By-Day

1970

DURING THIS YEAR . . .

Vice President Spiro Agnew advocates a radio ban on *With a Little Help from My Friends*, because of its references to getting "high," and on *Lucy in the Sky with Diamonds* because of its ostensible reference to LSD.

George Harrison purchases Friar Park, a 100–room mansion, for $360,000.00.

The Essential Beatles (LP) is released in Australia by Apple.

Capitol Records issues a promotional LP to celebrate "Earth Day," with *Here Comes the Sun* as one of the cuts.

Instant Karma, words and music by John Lennon, is copyrighted in the U.K. by Northern Songs Ltd.

The Beatles' earnings reach over Ł 4,350,000 ($10,440,000.00) for the entire year.

Paul McCartney records an unreleased version of his song *Penina*, written for Jotta Herre.

Oo You, words and music by Paul McCartney, is copyrighted in the U.K. by Northern Songs Ltd.

John Lennon acquires sole ownership of The Beatles' $100,000.00 customized Rolls Royce Phantom, which The Beatles had built in 1965.

The following singles by The Beatles are released in Italy: *Let It Be/You Know My Name* and *The Long and Winding Road/ For You Blue.*

Ringo Starr plays drums on a Jim Price album prior to the Bangladesh concert.

Why/Mother (45) is released in France by Apple.

John Lennon records an unreleased solo album after The Beatles' break--up, **Fuck Me! Fuck You!** consisting entirely of him screaming at people, according to *National Lampoon*'s parody of Beatles' history. The album contains songs like: *Fuck You, Fuck Your Mother, Get Fucked* and *Ah, Fuck.*

279

The following singles by The Beatles are released in Australia: *Let It Be/You Know My Name, The Long and Winding Road/ For You Blue.*

A 22–page collection of photographs and information on important dates, 1962–1969, is published in the U.K. by The Official Beatles' Fan Club, a division of Apple Records, Inc., called *The Official Beatles' Fan Club.*

Dig It, words and music by Lennon/McCartney/Harrison/Starkey, is jointly copyrighted in the U.K. by Northern Songs Ltd., Harrisongs Ltd., and Startling Music Ltd.

Cilla Black and Bobby Willis' first child is born.

George Harrison and Bob Dylan record *When Everybody Comes to Town – I'd Have You Anytime* at Dylan's house in Woodstock, later to appear on the bootleg recording **20x4 (LP).**

Beaucoups of Blues/Coochy Coochy (45) is released in France by Apple.

"The Girl Who Sang with The Beatles" and Other Stories, by Robert Hemenway, is published in the U.S. by Knopf.

Ringo Starr buys into a London furniture design business, renames it "Ringo or Robert Limited," and begins to do original furniture designs of his own.

The Beatles Get Back, by Jonathan Cott and David Dalton, is published in the U.K. by Apple Publishing.

Let It Be (LP) receives a Grammy Award from the American National Academy of Recording Arts and Sciences: best original score for film or TV.

Have You Heard the Word/Futting (45) by The Futz, incorrectly attributed to The Beatles, is released in the U.K.

The following Beatles' singles are released in Holland: *Let It Be/ You Know My Name* and *The Long and Winding Road/For You Blue.*

Apple Source – What The Beatles Are Really Like by Maurice Less (Apple gardener) is published by the Bench Press, according to Mark Shipper's humorous spoof of Beatle history, *Paperback Writer.*

EARLY 1970

Bob Dylan shows Greenwich Village, New York City, to John Lennon and Yoko Ono, who have decided to settle in the city.

John Lennon On Ronnie Hawkins (45), with Lennon introducing Hawkins' *Down in the Alley* from the latter's newly released **Ronnie Hawkins** (LP), is released to radio stations by Cotillion.

Third scheduled release time for The Beatles' **Get Back** album;

rescheduled this time to be issued as a soundtrack album at the same time as a 90--minute motion picture about the group.

JANUARY

Phil Spector comes to London at the behest of Allen Klein, to apply his expertise in recording techniques to the **Let It Be** album.

Hummingbird and *Shoot Out on the Plantation*, with George Harrison playing guitar and Ringo Starr on drums, are recorded by Leon Russell.

George Harrison is featured in the full--color photo layout in the German magazine, *Bravo*.

Ringo Starr comes to the U.S. to promote the film, "The Magic Christian."

Rumored month of a miscarriage by Linda McCartney, according to U.S. newspapers.

Radha Krsna Temple records *Govinda/Govinda Jai Jai* for Apple Records, produced by George Harrison.

Final versions of all songs for the **Let It Be** album are at last complete.

JANUARY--APRIL

Peace of Mind is recorded, appearing only on the bootleg LP **Peace of Mind.**

Versions of some sixty songs are rehearsed and recorded by The Beatles during this period, none of them ever released.

JAN 3   **Sgt. Pepper's Lonely Hearts Club Band** (LP) reaches its highest re--entry position on the *Billboard* album charts: number 101.

Magical Mystery Tour (LP) reaches its highest re--entry position on the *Billboard* album charts: number 109.

I Me Mine is recorded.

JAN 9   **Magic Christian Music** (LP) by Badfinger is released in the U.K. by Apple, produced by Paul McCartney; the cut *Come and Get It* is also written by Paul McCartney.

JAN 10   **Live Peace in Toronto** (LP) by John Lennon and Yoko Ono enters the *Billboard* album charts at number 136, remaining on the charts for 32 weeks during which it reaches a high point of number 10.

JAN 12   The Beatles' Christmas record is scheduled to be shipped to U.S. fan club members.

Come and Get It, by Badfinger, written and produced by

Paul McCartney, is released in the U.S. by Apple.

JAN 14 Paul McCartney reportedly buys the 400--acre Low
Ranadran Farm adjoining his own farm in West Scotland.

JAN 15 The London Arts Gallery opens an exhibit of John Len--
non's erotic lithographs, "Bag One," soon seized by
police as being obscene. HH23--2 (Jan 13) IR--86
(Jan 14)

George Harrison's nephew, Paul, marks his 10th birthday.

JAN 16 John Lennon's exhibit of erotic lithographs is closed down
by Scotland Yard and eight prints seized for possible
prosecution as obscene; the exhibit reopens in the
afternoon. JLS--150 (Mar)

Lontano Dagli Occhi by Mary Hopkin, produced by Paul
McCartney, is released in the U.K. by Apple.

JAN 17 Badfinger's *Come and Get It*, written by Paul McCartney,
enters the *New Musical Express* charts.

Cold Turkey reaches its highest position on the *Billboard*
singles charts: number 30.

Come and Get It by Badfinger, written and produced by
Paul McCartney, enters the *Melody Maker* singles charts
in the U.K. at number 20.

JAN 19 *Come and Get It*, written by Paul McCartney, is released in
the U.S. by The Magic Christians one week after the
Apple--released Badfinger single.

JAN 20 John Lennon and Yoko Ono have their hair cut short by a
woman barber in the barn of Anthony Cox's farm in
Denmark. IR--86 (Jan 25) ODT--186 (Dec 29, 1969)

JAN 21 George and Pattie Harrison's fourth wedding anniversary.
It is reported by the *Daily Express* that John Lennon has
cut off most of his hair in order to travel unrecognized.

JAN 23 The Beatles' Christmas Record is finally shipped to U.S.
Fan Club members.

Time magazine notes that Ringo Starr's "smirking indif--
ference" to his role in "The Magic Christian" provides
the film's only comic relief.

JAN 24 John Lennon and Yoko Ono's hair--trimming and declara--
tion of "Year One" enters the news in the U.S.

JAN 26 John Lennon writes and records *Instant Karma!* BF--137
(Jan 27)

Ringo Starr, wife Maureen and Peter Brown arrive in Los
Angeles and hold a press conference at the airport; their
arrival is timed for attendance at the premiere of "The
Magic Christian."

JAN 27   George Harrison's brother and sister--in--law, Peter and
          Pauline Harrison, have their fifth wedding anniversary.
          John Lennon offers Phil Spector a chance to produce
          Instant Karma!
          The Beatles are discussed in an editorial in *Saturday Review.*
          Ringo Starr appears on "Rowan and Martin's Laugh--In"
          TV show in the U.S.
JAN 28   U.S. premiere of "The Magic Christian" at the Four Star
          Theater, Los Angeles, attended by Ringo Starr.
          A cocktail party/press conference is held at the Beverly
          Hills Hotel after the premiere of "The Magic Christian,"
          featuring Ringo Starr.
JAN 29   *Time* magazine awards "honorable mention" to **Abbey
          Road** (LP) in its selection of best album of 1969.
          Lontano Dagli Occhi by Mary Hopkin, produced by Paul
          McCartney, is released in the U.S. by Apple.
JAN 30   Ringo Starr makes a guest appearance on "Philiben's
          People," then tapes spots for the TV show "Laugh In"
          in Burbank.
          Life magazine classes the new "bubble gum" music as
          being similar to early Beatles.
          All That I've Got/As I Get Older (45) by Billy Preston is
          released in the U.K. by Apple; *All That I've Got* is pro--
          duced by George Harrison.
JAN 31   *Come and Get It* by Badfinger, written and produced by
          Paul McCartney, reaches its highest position on the
          Melody Maker singles charts: number 4.

JANUARY--FEBRUARY

Apple hires a new company accountant, the last having resigned
in August 1969.

FEBRUARY

At EMI's Abbey Road studios, Ringo Starr records *Whispering
Grass, Bye Bye Blackbird* and *Love Is a Many Splendoured
Thing*, which later appear on his album **Sentimental Journey**;
two other recorded tracks, *Autumn Leaves* and *I'll Be Looking
at the Moon*, go unreleased.
John Lennon and Yoko Ono donate their hair, cut off in Denmark,
to Michael X's "Blackhouse" in North London.
Scheduled time for commencement of work on a film called

"Zachariah," a "rock–western" starring Ginger Baker, for
which George Harrison was asked to write a musical score.

John Lennon's erotic lithographs, "Bag One," are exhibited in Paris
at the Denise Rene Gallery.

Yoko Ono records *Who Has Seen the Wind*, with John Lennon and
George Harrison playing guitars.

"Bag One," John Lennon's show of erotic lithographs, opens in the
Lee Nordness Gallery in New York.

Yoko Ono's book, *Grapefruit,* is published in the U.S.

Ringo and Maureen Starkey are reported to have attended a per–
formance by Elvis Presley at the International Hotel, Las Vegas,
Nevada, when they came to the U.S. recently; Presley stopped
his show to introduce them to the audience, and they talked
for a couple of hours after the show.

EARLY FEBRUARY

Ringo Starr begins recording tracks for a solo album to be called
Stardust.

FEB 1   "The Magic Christian," is reviewed in the Los Angeles
Herald–Examiner; the review notes that Ringo Starr
had "precious little to do" in the film.

FEB 2   *Look* magazine captions a look back at the 1960s with the
first line from The Beatles' song *A Day in the Life*: "I
read the news today, oh boy . . . ."

FEB 6   *Instant Karma!/Who Has Seen the Wind* (45) is released in
the U.K. by Apple. LCP–208 (Mar)

How the Web Was Woven/Thumbin' a Ride (45) by Jackie
Lomax is released in the U.K. by Apple; the two sides
are produced by George Harrison and Paul McCartney,
respectively. LCP–208 (Mar)

FEB 7   *Come and Get It* by Badfinger, written and produced by
Paul McCartney, enters the *Billboard* singles charts at
number 92.

National Beatle Day.

Live Peace in Toronto (LP) by John Lennon and Yoko Ono
reaches its highest position on the *Billboard* album charts:
number 10.

Temma Harbour by Mary Hopkin, flip–side of *Lontano
Dagli Occhi* (produced by Paul McCartney), enters the
Melody Maker singles charts in the U.K. at number 16.

FEB 9   **Abbey Road** (LP) is a Grammy nominee.

FEB 10   *Look* magazine discusses Ringo Starr's role in "The Magic

Christian."

FEB 11   **The Magic Christian** (soundtrack LP) is released in the U.S.;
          it includes *Come and Get It* by Badfinger, written and
          produced by Paul McCartney; and *Hunting Scene*, pro-
          duced and with voice by Ringo Starr.
          Ringo and Maureen Starr's fifth wedding anniversary.
          New York premiere of film "The Magic Christian," with
          Ringo Starr as Youngman Grand.

FEB 12   John Lennon sings *Instant Karma!* on BBC's "Top of the
          Pops."
          John Lennon's performance of *Instant Karma!* on "Top
          of the Pops" is illegally recorded, later to appear on the
          bootleg recording **Some Other Guy**.

FEB 13   *Ain't That Cute/Vaya Con Dios* (45) by Doris Troy is
          released in the U.K. by Apple; *Ain't That Cute* is pro-
          duced by George Harrison.

FEB 14   *Temma Harbour* by Mary Hopkin, flip-side of *Lontano
          Dagli Occhi* (produced by Paul McCartney), enters the
          Billboard singles charts at number 112.

FEB 16   Plans for Apple to continue the monthly *Beatles Book*
          magazine are now finally abandoned.
          Paul McCartney is selected as best bass guitar player, and
          John Lennon and Paul McCartney as the best song-
          writers in the annual *Playboy* magazine poll; The
          Beatles enter the Playboy Hall of Fame.
          Magic Christian Music (LP) by Badfinger is released in the
          U.S. by Apple, produced by Paul McCartney; it includes
          Come and Get It, written by Paul McCartney.   LCP-
              208 (Mar)   LCP-283 (Feb 16)
          All That I've Got/As I Get Older (45) by Billy Preston is
          released in the U.S. by Apple; *All That I've Got* is pro-
          duced by George Harrison.   LCP--208 (Mar)   LCP-283
              (Feb 16)

FEB 18   Yoko Ono's 37th birthday; John Lennon throws a party for
          the occasion, and a large cake is distributed among the
          staff at Apple.

FEB 20   *Ram You Hard*, incorrectly rumored to be by John Lennon,
          is released in the U.K.
          Instant Karma!/Who Has Seen the Wind (45) is released in
          the U.S. by Apple.

FEB 21   *Instant Karma!* enters the *Billboard* British top twenty
          singles charts, remaining on the charts for six weeks
          during which it reaches a high point of number 5.

Temma Harbour by Mary Hopkin, flip--side of *Lontano Dagli Occhi* (produced by Paul McCartney), reaches its highest position on the *Melody Maker* singles charts: number 4.

Instant Karma! enters the *Melody Maker* singles charts in the U.K. at number 17.

FEB 23   Ringo Starr appears on "Laugh--In."

FEB 25   George Harrison spends his 27th birthday working.

FEB 26   A New York newspaper reports that John Lennon has dis-- avowed any connection with the Toronto Peace Festival he announced in December 1969, after it became clear to him that monies collected were being used for profit instead of for peace.

Hey Jude (LP) is released in the U.S. by Apple.   BM--90 (Feb 23)   GUB--123 (Feb 24)

FEB 28   *Instant Karma!* enters the *Billboard* singles charts at num-- ber 85, remaining on the charts for 13 weeks during which it reaches a high point of number 3.   BF--133 (Feb 29)

MARCH

The Primal Scream, a book by Arthur Janov, arrives at the Lennon's home, Tittenhurst Park.

Paul McCartney is interviewed by David Wigg at Apple offices in London.

Arthur Janov, author of *The Primal Scream*, arrives in London to begin therapy with John Lennon and Yoko Ono.

MAR 1   Film of The Beatles singing *Two of Us* and *Let It Be* is broad-- cast on the "Ed Sullivan Show."

MAR 2   *Let It Be* is aired for the first time in the Kansas City area.

MAR 4   An editorial in the *Kansas City Star* dealing with mysticism quotes John Lennon as an authority.

MAR 6   *Govinda/Govinda Jai Jai* (45) by Radha Krsna Temple is released in the U.K. by Apple, produced by George Harrison.   BM--143 (**Govinda**, their second *album*)

Let It Be/You Know My Name (45) is released in the U.K. by Apple.   BBS--51 (Feb 14)   BFC--4 (Mar 2)   BM--99 (Feb)   LCP--273 (Feb)

Hey Jude (LP) is certified as a Gold Record by the R.I.A.A.

MAR 7   *Here Comes the Sun* is played at the close of NBC's broadcast of the total eclipse.

Instant Karma! by John Lennon reaches its highest posi-- tion on the *Melody Maker* singles charts: number 4.

MAR 8   Ringo Starr records *It Don't Come Easy* in London, with Klaus Voorman, Stephen Stills and George Harrison as backup. ATN--100 (also *Early 1970*) BF--140 (late Feb) HH24--3 (ca. Mar 14)

MAR 9   *How the Web Was Woven/I Fall Inside Your Eyes* (45) by Jackie Lomax is released in the U.S. by Apple, produced by George Harrison.

MAR 10 Louise Harrison, George's mother, has her 59th birthday.

MAR 11 A New York newspaper carries an article headlined: "Lennon Pulls Out of Toronto."

Let It Be/You Know My Name (45) is released in the U.S. by Apple. BM--99 (Mar 16) IR--127 (Mar 2)

MAR 12 Paul and Linda McCartney's first wedding anniversary.

MAR 13 **Battersea Rain Dance** (LP) by The Chris Barber Band, featuring *Catcall* written by Paul McCartney, is released in the U.K.

Instant Karma! hits number 1 on the charts as *Let It Be* enters the top ten.

MAR 14 *Let It Be* enters Holland's Radio Veronica Top 40 charts at number 5.

The Magic Christian (soundtrack LP), with *Come and Get It* (produced by Paul McCartney) and *Hunting Scene* (produced by Ringo Starr), enters the *Billboard* album charts at number 185.

Let It Be enters the *Billboard* British top twenty singles charts, remaining on the charts for six weeks during which it reaches a high point of number 2.

Let It Be enters the *Melody Maker* singles charts in the U.K. at number 15.

MAR 15 A promotional film of Ringo Starr singing *Sentimental Journey* is made.

Ringo Starr is recorded singing *Sentimental* (Green-- Brown--Homer) at The Talk of the Town in London; the song later appears on the bootleg recording **Soldier of Love.**

MAR 16 *Ain't that Cute/Vaya Con Dios* (45) by Doris Troy is re-- leased in the U.S. by Apple; *Ain't that Cute* is pro-- duced by George Harrison.

MAR 17 **Live Peace in Toronto** (LP) is certified as a Gold Record by the R.I.A.A.

Pattie Harrison's 26th birthday.

Hilary French, George Harrison's cousin, reveals that family members -- and apparently the doctors -- are not really sure of the nature of Louise Harrison's illness, for which she was recently hospitalized.

Let It Be (45) is certified as a Gold Record by the R.I.A.A.

MAR 20 John Lennon and Yoko Ono's first wedding anniversary.

Que Sera Sera by Karen Young, using Paul McCartney's arrangement but with no direct involvement by McCartney, appears on a single in the U.K.

Knock Knock Who's There/I'm Going to Fall in Love Again (45) by Mary Hopkin is released in the U.K. by Apple.

MAR 21 **Hey Jude** (LP) enters the *Billboard* album charts at number 3, remaining on the charts for 33 weeks during which it reaches a high point of number 2.

All That I've Got by Billy Preston, produced by George Harrison, enters the *Billboard* singles charts at number 108, dropping to 110 the following week, then off the charts.

Let It Be enters the *Billboard* singles charts at number 6, remaining on the charts for 11 weeks during which it reaches a high point of number 1.

Let It Be reaches its highest position on the *Melody Maker* singles charts: number 3.

MAR 23 **Leon Russell** (LP) is released in the U.S., featuring George on guitar and Ringo on drums.

MAR 24 *Govinda/Govinda Jai Jai* (45) by Radha Krishna Temple is released in the U.S. by Apple, produced by George Harrison.

MAR 27 Ringo Starr's **Sentimental Journey** (LP) is released in the U.K. by Apple. BB6--ii (Apr) BM--144 (May) IR--87 (Apr 3) JLS--150 (Apr) PMS--178 (Apr 2)

MAR 28 **Hey Jude** (LP) reaches its highest position on the *Billboard* album charts, number 2, remaining there for four weeks.

Magic Christian Music (LP) by Badfinger, produced by Paul McCartney, enters the *Billboard* album charts at number 89.

Temma Harbour by Mary Hopkin, flip--side of *Lontano Dagli Occhi* (produced by Paul McCartney) reaches its highest position on the *Billboard* singles charts: number 39.

Instant Karma! by John Lennon reaches its highest position on the *Billboard* singles charts: number 3.

>   *Knock Knock Who's There* by Mary Hopkin, released on
>   Apple Records, enters the *Melody Maker* singles charts
>   in the U.K. at number 22.

MAR 29 Ringo Starr sings *Sentimental Journey* on the "David
>   Frost Show," accompanied by the George Martin
>   Orchestra; the performance later surfaces on the bootleg
>   **Soldier of Love.**

>   John Lennon and Yoko Ono announce that they are ex--
>   pecting a baby in October.

>   *Let It Be* enters the Polish radio station (Rozglasnia
>   Harcerska) charts at number 3.

SPRING

Scheduled time for the opening of a pop musical, "Jesus Christ,"
at St. Paul's Cathedral, London; John Lennon, asked to play the
part of Christ, indicated he would if Yoko Ono could play
Mary Magdalene. Neither of them appear in the play.

The Beatles record *All Together on the Wireless Machine, Mean
Mr. Mustard* and *Bye Bye Bye*, these versions ending up on the
bootleg LP **Abbey Road Revisited.**

Apple's first financial accounts are presented, revealing that three
automobiles purchased by someone using the Apple name could
not be found.

The first British bootleg comprised entirely of Beatles' perfor--
mances -- **Get Back to Toronto** -- is released.

The first U.S. bootleg LP comprised entirely of Beatles' perfor--
mances -- **Renaissance Minstrels** -- is released.

Attention again returns to the tracks recorded during the winter
(1969) for the **Let It Be** album.

APRIL

Ringo Starr plays drums at a Howlin Wolf recording session on *I
Ain't Superstitious* held at Olympic studios, London. ATN--103
(mid--1970)

Paul McCartney describes The Beatles as no longer existing as a
group.

Here Comes the Sun is included on Capitol Records promotional
LP **Balanced for Broadcast.**

APRIL--JUNE

Billy Preston records *My Sweet Lord* and *Long As I Got My Baby*,
produced by George Harrison and Billy Preston.

Billy Preston records tracks for his **Encouraging Words** album at

Trident studios, London; George Harrison plays guitar and co--
produces the LP.

APRIL--AUGUST
John Lennon and Yoko Ono attend the Primal Institute in Los
Angeles to undergo therapy, living in a rented house in Bel--Air.
John Lennon composes the songs for his **John Lennon/Plastic Ono
Band** (LP) while undergoing primal therapy in California.

APR 1   The London Arts Gallery defends in court its exhibit of
John Lennon's prints seized by police.

APR 2   A Paul McCartney interview with *Evening Standard* reveals
conflict and personal contention at Apple.

APR 7   **Delaney and Bonnie on Tour** (LP), with George Harrison
on guitar, is released in the U.S.

APR 9   Paul McCartney sings *Maybe I'm Amazed* on a five--minute
London television spot.
The U.S. headquarters of the Official Beatles Fan Club in--
forms area secretaries and chapter presidents that rumors
about Paul McCartney leaving The Beatles just because
of his work on a solo album are "not true."

APR 10   A printed publicity "interview" with Paul McCartney,
reflecting his independence and estrangement from The
Beatles as a group and due to be released April 17 with
McCartney (LP), is released prematurely and received
as an announcement of his departure from the group.
The London *Daily Mirror* reports that Paul McCartney has
left The Beatles.
News of The Beatles' break--up is headlined in the British
press.
In the *Times*, Apple denies rumors that Paul McCartney has
left The Beatles.
The Magic Christian (soundtrack LP) is released in the U.K.;
it includes *Come and Get It* by Badfinger, written and
produced by Paul McCartney; and *Hunting Scene*, pro--
duced and with voice by Ringo Starr.

APR 11   *Let It Be* hits number 1 on the *Billboard* singles charts,
remaining there for two weeks.
Knock Knock Who's There by Mary Hopkin, released by
Apple, reaches its highest position on the *Melody Maker*
singles charts: number 3.
A front page story in the *Daily Mirror* reports Paul
McCartney's departure from The Beatles.

APR 12   Paul McCartney reportedly has formed his own company,
         McCartney Productions Ltd., and is already planning
         production of a "Rupert the Bear" cartoon film.
mid–Apr Originally scheduled release time for Ringo Starr's album
         Sentimental Journey, released March 27.
APR 17   A John Lennon interview with *Rolling Stone* discusses
         Paul McCartney's departure.
         The Official Beatles Fan Club in the U.S. again reports
         that there is "nothing to worry about" in terms of
         Paul McCartney's rumored departure from The Beatles.
         Paul's **McCartney** (LP) is released in the U.K. by Apple.
         BB2--v,vii (Jul)   PMI--110,112 (May)   PMW--15,19 (Feb)
         The Paul McCartney "interview" is released by Apple to
         the press along with the release of **McCartney** (LP).
APR 18   *Come and Get It* by Badfinger, written and produced by
         Paul McCartney, reaches its highest position on the
         Billboard singles charts: number 7.
         Govinda by Radha Krsna Temple, produced by George
         Harrison, enters the *Melody Maker* singles charts in the
         U.K. at number 26, but goes no higher.
APR 20   Paul's **McCartney** (LP) is released in the U.S. by Apple.
         PMB--25,237 (Apr 17)   PMI--110,112 (May)
APR 24   Ringo Starr's **Sentimental Journey** (LP) is released in the
         U.S. by Apple. BFC--15 (Apr 23) BM--144,249 (May)
             TB--379 (**Sentimental Journal**) TBD--16 (Jun)
         Leon Russell (LP) is released in the U.K., featuring George
         Harrison on guitar and Ringo Starr on drums.
APR 25   **Magic Christian Music** (LP) by Badfinger, produced by Paul
         McCartney, reaches its highest position on the *Billboard*
         album charts: number 55.
APR 27   John Lennon's prints are declared "not obscene" and re--
         turned.
         George Harrison arrives in New York City, along with Derek
         Taylor.
Apr 27– George Harrison visits New York City; he states that he's
May 4   sure that The Beatles' break--up is only temporary.
APR 28   The U.S. based Official Beatles Fan Club advises area
         secretaries to ignore rumors of a Beatles' break--up be--
         cause "all four Beatles have the insight to realize that the
         ultimate in creative ability is the Beatles as a group."
APR 30   **McCartney** (LP), by Paul McCartney, is certified as a Gold
         Record by the R.I.A.A.

LATE APRIL

George Harrison is interviewed by Mrs. Hall, a reporter for a local Yonkers newspaper, in a meeting arranged by Pete Bennett, George's director of activities.

George Harrison does a radio interview for WABC–TV while in New York.

George Harrison goes shopping in New York, buying shirts and a white denim outfit at Kauffman's and shoes at Hudson's, and renting an electric guitar at Manny's Music Store.

MAY

George Harrison plays guitar at the King Curtis recording sessions for *Teasin* at Sunset Sound studios, London.

John Lennon and Yoko Ono have primal therapy in California.

Ringo Starr and wife Maureen attend a concert by Frank Sinatra in London.

John Lennon and Yoko Ono pose for fans' photographs in Los Angeles.

Louise Harrison, George Harrison's mother, enters a Liverpool hospital; she is unaware she is terminally ill with a brain tumor.

The contract between ATV and minority shareholders governing the control of Northern Songs expires this month.

Dialogue from the Film "Let It Be" (45) is released by United Artists to promote The Beatles' new film.

MAY 1 The U.S. based Official Beatles Fan Club reports that Paul's uncertainty about whether The Beatles split is permanent or temporary probably means the riff is only a "temporary psychological break, which will be made up simply by a phone call."

George Harrison visits the New York headquarters of the Official Beatles Fan Club.

George Harrison, back in his room at the Pickwick Hotel with officers of the U.S. fan club, poses for photographs and is interviewed for the "Datebook."

Later in the day, George Harrison and Bob Dylan record enough tracks for an album, including *I'd Have You Anytime* and *When Everybody's Come to Town*, later to appear only on the bootleg **Get Together**; *I'd Have You Anytime* is co–composed by Dylan and Harrison.

ATN–264 (mid–May) BF–142 (Jun) RO–31 (Jun)

MAY 2 **The Magic Christian** (soundtrack LP), with *Come and Get It*

(produced by Paul McCartney) and *Hunting Scene* (pro–
duced by Ringo Starr), reaches its highest position on the
Billboard album charts: number 108.
Sentimental Journey (LP) enters the *Melody Maker* album
charts in the U.K. at number 29.
McCartney (LP) enters the *Melody Maker* album charts in
the U.K. at number 10.

MAY 4   George Harrison returns to England from New York.
The Beatles -- Circa 1960 -- In the Beginning (LP), by Tony
Sheridan and The Beatles, is released in the U.S. by
Polydor.

MAY 8   **Let It Be** (LP) is released in the U.K. by Apple. IR–127
(May 15)

MAY 9   **McCartney** (LP) enters the *Billboard* album charts at
number 14, remaining on the charts for 47 weeks during
which it reaches a high point of number 1.
Sentimental Journey (LP) reaches its highest position on
the *Melody Maker* album charts: number 20.
McCartney (LP) reaches its highest position on the *Melody
Maker* album charts, number 2, remaining there for four
weeks.

MAY 11 *The Long and Winding Road/For You Blue* (45) is released
in the U.S. by Apple, last record issued by the group.
BFC–4 (May 7)   BM–99 (May 25)   IR–127 (May 7)

MAY 13 New York premiere of the film "Let It Be."
The Hollywood Reporter notes that the value of "Let It
Be" lies in its preservation of "a moment in time" for
the most important group of the '60s.
Daily Variety's review of "Let It Be" terms it "innocuous"
and "unimaginative," but fascinating as a documentary
of The Beatles' break--up.

mid–May The film "Let It Be" begins to play in theaters across the
U.S.; in a number of theaters it is double--billed with a
film called "Mercenary."

MAY 16 **The Beatles -- Circa 1960 -- In the Beginning** (LP) by Tony
Sheridan and The Beatles enters the *Billboard* album
charts at number 145, remaining on the charts for seven
weeks during which it reaches a high point of number
117.
Sentimental Journey (LP) enters the *Billboard* album charts
at number 51, remaining on the charts for fourteen
weeks during which it reaches a high point of number
22.

MAY 17 *All Together Now* enters the Polish radio station (Roz--glasnia Harcerska) charts at number 14.

A Ringo Starr promotional film clip for *Sentimental Journey* is shown on the "Ed Sullivan Show."

MAY 18 **Let It Be** (LP) is released in the U.S. by Apple. BIR--121 (May 15)   LCP--282 (May 15)   MB--91 (May 15)

The U.S. based Official Beatles Fan Club reports that there are 19 "official chapters" in the club nationwide.

MAY 20 A review of "Let It Be" in the Los Angeles *Times* calls it a warm and engaging hour--and--a--half, "immensely interesting" for its picture of The Beatles.

U.K. premiere of the film "Let It Be" in both London and Liverpool; none of The Beatles attend.

George Harrison begins to record songs for **All Things Must Pass** (LP) during the evening.

MAY 22 "Let It Be" adds up to a lively, engaging "funeral march," says a review in the Los Angeles *Herald--Examiner.*

MAY 23 Ringo Starr's **Sentimental Journey** (LP) reportedly sells half--a--million copies in two weeks in the U.S.

McCartney (LP) hits number 1 on the *Billboard* album charts, remaining there for three weeks, reportedly selling over 1,000,000 copies in four weeks.

The Long and Winding Road/For You Blue enters the *Billboard* singles charts at number 35, remaining on the charts for ten weeks during which it reaches a high point of number 1.

Let It Be (LP) enters the *Melody Maker* album charts in the U.K. at number 3.

The Long and Winding Road is reported to have sold 1,200,000 copies in the U.S. in two days by *New Musical Express.*

Let It Be (LP) is reported by *New Musical Express* to have had advance U.S. orders of 3,700,000 copies.

MAY 26 **Let It Be** (LP) is certified as a Gold Record by the R.I.A.A.

May 26--
late Aug George Harrison records tracks for his **All Things Must Pass** album at the Abbey Road studios, London.

MAY 30 Sheilah Graham, reviewer for the Hollywood *Citizen--News*, calls "Let It Be" a prime candidate for a cutting room abortion.

Record World reports that Allen Klein and ABKCO Films has announced the William K. Cash production "Come Together," with filming to begin June 1 in New York,

followed by shooting in Italy, France, England and
Yugoslavia.

Let It Be (LP) enters the *Billboard* album charts at number
104, remaining on the charts for 55 weeks during which
it reaches a high point of number 1.

JUNE
John Eastman, at the behest of Paul McCartney, writes to Allen
Klein proposing a dissolution of The Beatles' partnership,
entered into in April 1967.

Beatles' royalties for U.S. record sales from September 1969 to
June 1970 reaches $7,815,628.

John Lennon and Yoko Ono are interviewed by David Wigg at
the Apple offices in London.

George Harrison works on tracks for himself, Billy Preston and
Doris Troy.

George Harrison plays guitar and sings at recording sessions by
Derek and The Dominoes for two tracks, *Tell the Truth* and
Roll It Over.

JUNE--JULY
Stephen Stills records *To a Flame* and *We Are Not Helpless* at Island
studios, London, with Ringo Starr playing drums.

JUN 1-- Neil Aspinall begins working on a documentary film of
10   The Beatles' rise from The Cavern Club to Apple Records.

JUN 6   Let It Be (LP) hits number 1 on the *Melody Maker* album
charts, remaining there for eight weeks.

JUN 10   The U.S. based Official Beatles Fan Club assures area
secretaries that the red label on the Let It Be album does
not mean that it is The Beatles' last album, only that the
record is distributed by United Artists and not Capitol.

JUN 11   It is reported that Ringo Starr and wife Maureen were re--
cently guests of honor at the showing of "Woodstock"
at the annual Cannes Film Festival.

It is reported that John Lennon and Yoko Ono will con--
tinue vacationing in California for an extended period.

JUN 12   The *Cleveland Plain Dealer* reports that a letter written by
Paul McCartney to Jane Asher has been framed in a
$1,200 23--carat gold frame for public display in a
Cleveland department store.

JUN 13   *The Long and Winding Road/For You Blue* hits number 1
on the *Billboard* singles charts, remaining there for two

weeks.

The Beatles -- Circa 1960 -- In the Beginning (LP) by Tony Sheridan and The Beatles reaches its highest position on the *Billboard* album charts: number 117.

Let It Be (LP) hits number 1 on the *Billboard* album charts, remaining there for four weeks.

JUN 14 *The Long and Winding Road* enters the Polish radio station (Rozglasnia Harcerska) charts at number 16.

JUN 15 *I'm the Urban Spaceman* by The Bonzo Dog Band, produced by Paul McCartney, appears in the U.S. on **Progressive Heavies (LP)**.

Que Sera Sera/Fields of St. Etienne (45) by Mary Hopkin is released in the U.S. by Apple, produced by Paul McCartney.

JUN 17 A review of "Let It Be" in the *Motion Picture Herald* notes that as The Beatles have grown and progressed, they have lost their spontaneity and zaniness.

JUN 19 **Delaney and Bonnie on Tour (LP)**, with George Harrison on guitar, is released in the U.K.

JUN 20 *Record Retailer* reports the departure of Mavis Smith from the Apple press office.

Sentimental Journey (LP) reaches its highest position on the *Billboard* album charts: number 22.

JUN 27 **Get Back to Toronto (LP)**, a high quality bootleg Beatles' album, is reported on sale in London.

Jun 30-- In Nashville, Tennessee, Ringo Starr records tracks for his
Jul 1 **Beaucoups of Blues (LP)**, as well as other unreleased tracks like a 28--minute version of *Coochy Coochy* and *It Don't Come Easy*.

JULY

Ashton, Gardner and Dyke record *I'm Your Spiritual Breadman,* George Harrison on guitars, at De Lane Lea studios, London.

Ringo Starr is interviewed by David Wigg.

JUL 3 George Harrison's sister and brother--in--law, Louise and Gordon Caldwell, have their 16th wedding anniversary.

JUL 3--5 Proposed time for the peace festival to be held in Mosport Park near Toronto announced by John Lennon on December 15, 1969 but cancelled soon thereafter.

JUL 4 *The Long and Winding Road* enters Holland's Radio Veronica Top 40 charts at number 19.

Last week begins for **Let It Be** (LP) as a number 1 album
on the *Billboard* charts, the last original Beatles group
effort to hold the position.

Que Sera Sera by Mary Hopkin, produced by Paul McCartney, enters the *Billboard* singles charts at number 118.

JUL 7 Louise French Harrison, George Harrison's mother, dies
of cancer in a Liverpool hospital; her body is cremated
and she is buried July 10; George is at her bedside when
she dies.

Ringo Starr's 30th birthday.

JUL 10 Anne Nightingale of the *Daily Sketch* visits Apple's Savile
Row studios.

A funeral is held for George Harrison's mother, who passed
away July 7.

JUL 13 A *Daily Sketch* report discusses the inactivity at Apple's
Savile Row studios.

mid–Jul Canadian newspapers report that John Lennon and Yoko
Ono have set up a music publishing company called
Ono Music Ltd., primarily to publish Yoko's songs.

JUL 17 *All You Need Is Love* re–enters the Polish radio station
(Rozglasnia Harcerska) charts at number 19.

I'm the Urban Spaceman, produced by Paul McCartney,
appears in the U.K. on **The Beast of the Bonzos** (LP) by
The Bonzo Dog Band.

JUL 20 George Harrison's brothers, Harry and Peter, have their
36th and 30th birthdays respectively.

The New York–based Official Beatles Fan Club reports that
"official chapters" now number 22 nationwide.

JUL 22 **The Whale** (LP) is recorded for Apple Records by John
–24 Tavener.

JUL 25 **Sgt. Pepper's Lonely Hearts Club Band** (LP) re–enters the
Billboard album charts (for a third time) at number 159,
dropping off again four weeks later.

Record World reports that rumors about the formation of
Ono Music Ltd. are unfounded, and that Apple, managed by ABKCO, will continue to publish Yoko Ono's
songs.

Magical Mystery Tour (LP) re–enters the *Billboard* album
charts (for the third time) at number 194, rising to 192
the next week, and dropping off again thereafter.

JUL 27   The New York *Post* carries an article about Ringo Starr in which he discusses the fact that being 30 years old isn't as bad as he thought it would be.

JUL 31   Cynthia Lennon marries Roberto Bassanini at the Kensington Registry Office, London. HH26--2 (Bassinini)

AUGUST

"A sad and fascinating Apple home movie" is *Esquire*'s assessment of "Let It Be."

Yoko Ono suffers a miscarriage.

Paul McCartney writes to John Lennon suggesting dissolution of The Beatles' partnership, formed in April 1967; in an exchange of correspondence, Lennon encourages McCartney to get the other necessary signatures while he, Lennon, thinks it over.

AUG 1   *Que Sera Sera* by Mary Hopkin, produced by Paul McCartney, reaches its highest position on the *Billboard* singles charts: number 77.

AUG 2   *I'm the Urban Spaceman*, produced by Paul McCartney, appears in the U.S. on **The Beast of the Bonzos** (LP) by The Bonzo Dog Band.

AUG 4   Maureen Starkey's 23rd birthday.

The closing of the Apple press office and dismissal of two remaining press office employees is reported.

AUG 8   Begins a two--and-a--half--month period during which no Beatle--related record appears on the *Billboard* singles charts.

AUG 16   Louise Caldwell, George Harrison's sister, is 39 years old.

AUG 19   Jason Starkey is three years old.

AUG 27   Janet Harrison, George's niece, is eight years old.

AUG 28   Doris Troy's *Jacob's Ladder/Get Back* (45) is released in the U.K. by Apple, George Harrison on guitar.

Mary McCartney is one year old.

SEPTEMBER

McCartney (LP) royalty earnings for Paul McCartney reach a total of Ł 487,000.

The "Official George Harrison Chapter" of the U.S. Beatles Fan Club begins a donation drive to establish a Louise F. Harrison Memorial Cancer Fund as a result of Mrs. Harrison's death on

July 7; Louise Harrison, George's mother, had her own column in the Chapter's newsletter, and always made a special effort to answer as much of George's fan mail as possible.

SEP 4   *My Sweet Lord/Long As I Got My Baby* (45) by Billy
          Preston is released in the U.K. by Apple, produced by
          George Harrison and Billy Preston.
SEP 11   **Doris Troy** (LP) is released in the U.K. by Apple; it includes
          Ain't That Cute, produced by George Harrison, with
          George on guitar, Ringo Starr on drums.
          Encouraging Words (LP) by Billy Preston is released in the
          U.K. by Apple, produced by George Harrison and Billy
          Preston.
SEP 14   *Tell the Truth/Roll It Over* (45), by Derek and The Dom--
          inoes, is released in the U.S.; George Harrison plays
          guitar on *Tell the Truth*.
SEP 21   **Listening to Richard Brautigan** (LP), originally slated for
          release in Apple's Zapple series, is instead released in the
          U.S. on Capitol's Harvest label.
          Doris Troy's *Jacob's Ladder/Get Back* (45) is released in
          the U.S. by Apple, George Harrison on guitar.
SEP 25   Ringo Starr's **Beaucoups of Blues** (LP) is released in the
          U.K. by Apple.
          The Apple group Badfinger is slated to tour the U.S. for
          two months beginning this date, ending November 28.
          The Whale (LP) by John Tavener is released in the U.K.
          by Apple.
SEP 28   **Ashton, Gardner and Dyke** (LP) is released in the U.S.; the cut
          I'm Your Spiritual Breadman features George Harrison
          on guitar.
          Via the courts, John Lennon and Paul McCartney reported--
          ly request an accounting of all monies received by
          Northern Songs, and claim half of all such monies should
          be paid to them under the terms of a 1963 agreement.
          Ringo Starr's **Beaucoups of Blues** (LP) is released in the
          U.S. by Apple. BFC--15 (Sep 21) LCP--285 (Sep 21)
SEP 28   *Celtic Requiem* is recorded by John Tavener for his Apple
-30   album **Celtic Requiem**.

OCTOBER
Paul McCartney begins two months of soul--searching; he wishes

to sue Allen Klein, but cannot do so without suing Apple, and, thereby, suing John, George and Ringo.

Expected month of birth for a baby, announced March 29, to John Lennon and Yoko Ono.

EARLY OCTOBER

John Lennon records tracks for his album **John Lennon/Plastic Ono Band** at Ascot sound studios. ODT--186 (Apr--Aug) RO--32 (Sep)

Yoko Ono records six tracks, not including *AOS*, for **Yoko Ono/Plastic Ono Band** (LP), with John Lennon playing guitar and Ringo Starr on drums; the sessions are co--produced by John and Yoko.

OCT 3   **James Taylor** (LP) by James Taylor, featuring Paul McCart--ney playing bass guitar on *Carolina in My Mind*, enters the *Billboard* album charts at number 127.

OCT 5   Ringo Starr's *Beaucoups of Blues/Coochy--Coochy* (45) is released in the U.S. by Apple. BFC--4 (Sep) LCP--275 (Sep)

OCT 9   John Lennon turns 30.

OCT 12   *No Matter What/Carry On Till Tomorrow* (45) by Bad--finger is released in the U.S. by Apple.

OCT 16   *Think About Your Children/Heritage* (45) by Mary Hopkin is released in the U.K. by Apple.

OCT 17   **Beaucoups of Blues** (LP) enters the *Billboard* album charts at number 141, remaining on the charts for fifteen weeks during which it reaches a high point of number 65.

OCT 18   *Think About Your Children/Heritage* (45) by Mary Hopkin is released in the U.S. by Apple. LCP--283 (Oct 12)

OCT 23   Paul McCartney works on another solo album in New York; rumors continue to circulate about a solo tour of the U.S. by McCartney in the spring. Meanwhile, John Lennon works with Yoko Ono on his new solo album, while George Harrison's solo album is due to be pressed in late October.

OCT 24   *No Matter What* by Badfinger, released by Apple, enters the *Billboard* singles charts at number 101.

          Beaucoups of Blues enters the *Billboard* singles charts at number 126, remaining on the charts for five weeks during which it reaches a high point of number 87.

OCT 26   *Carolina In My Mind/Something's Wrong* (45) by James
Taylor, is released in the U.S. by Apple; Paul McCartney
plays bass guitar on *Carolina In My Mind*.

OCT 28   George Harrison and wife Pattie arrive in New York; he is
non--committal when questioned by the press at the
airport.

LATE OCTOBER

Paul and Linda McCartney have dinner with Burt Bacharach at the
exclusive New York restaurant, Daly's Dandelion.

George Harrison meets with Paul McCartney while both are in New
York.

NOVEMBER

The Official Beatles Fan Club reports that The Beatles have not
worked together in "more than a year," as each pursues "solo
ventures."

Paul McCartney and John Eastman begin proceedings to dissolve
the Beatles' partnership, triggered by a British tax authority
writ filed against the partnership for failure to file tax returns.

EARLY NOVEMBER

George Harrison leaves New York for the Bahamas and Jamaica.

NOV 6   *Carolina In My Mind/Something's Wrong* (45) by James
Taylor is released in the U.K. by Apple; Paul McCartney
plays bass guitar on *Carolina In My Mind*.

No Matter What/Better Days (45) by Badfinger is released
in the U.K. by Apple.

Let It Be (LP) is reissued in the U.K. as Apple PCS7096.

NOV 9   **Encouraging Words** (LP) by Billy Preston is released in the
U.S. by Apple, produced by George Harrison and Billy
Preston. LCP--283 (Oct 15)

The Whale (LP) by John Tavener is released in the U.S. by
Apple. BFC--21 (Oct 15)

Doris Troy (LP) is released in the U.S. by Apple; it includes
Ain't That Cute, produced by George Harrison, with
George on guitar, Ringo Starr on drums. BFC--21 &
LCP--283 (identifies this as **Ain't That Cute** (LP),
released in Oct)

No Dice (LP) by Badfinger is released in the U.S. by Apple.
BFC--21 (Oct 15)

NOV 11   Ringo and Maureen Starr's third child, Lee, is born; she is

7 pounds, 2 ounces.

NOV 13   The originally intended release date for *My Sweet Lord/ Isn't It a Pity* (45), by George Harrison -- Friday the 13th.

NOV 14   *Think About Your Children* by Mary Hopkin, released by Apple, enters the *Melody Maker* singles charts in the U.K. at number 26.

Carolina In My Mind by James Taylor, with Paul McCartney on bass guitar, enters the *Billboard* singles charts at number 99.

NOV 20   *Never Tell Your Mother She's Out of Tune*, with George Harrison on rhythm guitar, reappears in the U.K. on **Supergroups Vol. 2 (LP)**.

NOV 21   **Beaucoups of Blues (LP)** reaches its highest position on the *Billboard* album charts: number 65.

Think About Your Children by Mary Hopkin, released in the U.S. by Apple, enters the *Billboard* singles charts at number 99.

Think About Your Children by Mary Hopkin, released by Apple, reaches its highest position on the *Melody Maker* singles charts: number 20.

NOV 23   *My Sweet Lord/Isn't It a Pity* (45) by George Harrison is released in the U.S. by Apple.

Stephen Stills (LP) is released in the U.S., with Ringo Starr playing drums on the cuts *To a Flame* and *We Are Not Helpless.*

NOV 25   George Harrison and wife Pattie have returned to New York to introduce, with Allen Klein, the group Bad--finger to the New York press.

Release of **I Can Hear It Now -- The Sixties** (LP) including *I Want to Hold Your Hand* by The Beatles.

The New York--based Official Beatles Fan Club reports that the "divorce rumors" about George and Pattie Harrison appear to be groundless based on the couples' recent togetherness.

NOV 26   John Lennon and Yoko Ono go to New York. ODT--126 (Dec)

NOV 27   George and Pattie Harrison are due to return to England from New York on this date, but delay their return.

All Things Must Pass (LP) by George Harrison is released in the U.S. by Apple. GBR--22 (Nov 20) TBD--16 (Dec)

No Dice (LP) by Badfinger is released in the U.K. by Apple.

Stephen Stills (LP) is released in the U.K., with Ringo
Starr playing drums on the cuts *To a Flame* and *We Are
Not Helpless.*

NOV 28   **James Taylor** (LP) by James Taylor, featuring Paul
McCartney on bass guitar on *Carolina In My Mind*,
reaches its highest position on the *Billboard* album
charts: number 62.

No Dice (LP) by Badfinger, released in the U.S. by Apple,
enters the *Billboard* album charts at number 74.

Beaucoups of Blues by Ringo Starr reaches its highest
position on the *Billboard* singles charts: number 87.

My Sweet Lord/Isn't It a Pity by George Harrison enters
the *Billboard* singles charts at number 72, remaining
on the charts for fourteen weeks during which it reaches
a high point of number 1.

NOV 30   **All Things Must Pass** (LP) by George Harrison is released
in the U.K. by Apple. BM–144 (Dec) PMS–180 (Sep)

Rock Magazine carries an article describing the Official
Beatles Fan Club and several of its chapters.

To a Flame, with Ringo Starr on drums, appears on a
single by Stephen Stills, released in the U.S.

DECEMBER

Penina, written by Paul McCartney, is included on a single by
Jotta Herre released in Holland.

John Lennon and Yoko Ono spend time with Jonas Mekas.

Marking the break–up of the Rutles, Dirk McQuickly sues Stig
O'Hara and Ron Nasty, Barry Wom sues Dirk, Ron Nasty sues
Stig and Barry, and Stig O'Hara accidentally sues himself,
according to the album sendup of The Beatles, **The Rutles**.

DEC 3   *My Sweet Lord/Little Girl* (45), by Billy Preston, is re–
leased in the U.S. by Apple, produced by George Harri–
son and Billy Preston.

DEC 5   *No Matter What* by Badfinger, released by Apple, reaches
its highest position on the *Billboard* singles charts:
number 8.

DEC 11   **By George!** (LP) by Beatles' producer George Martin,
featuring instrumental versions of *Sgt. Pepper's Lonely
Hearts Club Band* and *I Am the Walrus*, is released in
the U.K.

Yoko Ono/Plastic Ono Band (LP), produced by John
Lennon and Yoko Ono, is released in the U.K. by Apple.
Yoko Ono/Plastic Ono Band (LP), produced by John
Lennon and Yoko Ono, is released in the U.S. by Apple.
John Lennon/Plastic Ono Band (LP), by John Lennon, is
released in the U.S. by Apple. ODT--113,188 (Oct)
John Lennon/Plastic Ono Band (LP), by John Lennon, is
released in the U.K. by Apple. ODT--113,188 (Oct)

DEC 12   *Think About Your Children* by Mary Hopkin, released in
the U.S. by Apple, reaches its highest position on the
Billboard singles charts: number 87.
John Lennon/Plastic Ono Band (LP) enters the *Melody
Maker* album charts at number 23.

DEC 14   *My Sweet Lord* (45), by George Harrison, is certified as a
Gold Record by the R.I.A.A.
Instant Karma! (45), by John Lennon is certified as a Gold
Record by the R.I.A.A.

mid--Dec First public showings of the films "Fly" and "Up Your
Leg Forever" by John Lennon and Yoko Ono are held
in New York.

DEC 17   **All Things Must Pass** (LP), by George Harrison, is certified
as a Gold Record by the R.I.A.A.

DEC 18   **From Them to You** (LP) (**The Beatles' Christmas Album**)
is released in the U.K. by the Fan Club on the Apple
label. ATN--96,294 (**From Then to Us**) BU17--23
(**From Then to You**)
The Beatles' Christmas Album (LP) is released in the U.S.
by the Fan Club on the Apple label.

DEC 19   **No Dice** (LP) by Badfinger, released in the U.S. by Apple,
reaches its highest position on the *Billboard* album
charts: number 28.
All Things Must Pass (LP) by George Harrison enters the
Billboard album charts at number 5, remaining on the
charts for 38 weeks during which it reaches a high point
of number 1.

DEC 24   Part one of John Lennon's *Rolling Stone* interview is pub--
lished.

DEC 26   *My Sweet Lord/Isn't It a Pity* by George Harrison hits num--
ber 1 on the *Billboard* singles charts, remaining there for
four weeks.
John Lennon/Plastic Ono Band (LP) by John Lennon enters
the *Billboard* album charts at number 14, remaining on
the charts for 22 weeks during which it reaches a high

point of number 6.

Carolina In My Mind by James Taylor, with Paul McCartney
on bass guitar, reaches its highest position on the *Bill–
board* singles charts: number 67.

Richard Di Lello starts to write his book on The Beatles,
The Longest Cocktail Party, which is completed in
April 1971.

All Things Must Pass (LP) by George Harrison enters the
Melody Maker album charts in the U.K. at number 20.

DEC 28   *Mother/Why* (45) by John Lennon and Yoko Ono is re--
leased in the U.S. by Apple.

DEC 31   Final date used in a court affidavit by Allen Klein to pre--
sent the total earnings raised for The Beatles from the
beginning of their management by ABKCO.

John Lennon reveals he has used drugs in one form or
another since he was 17 years old.

Balance sheet reveals total credit for the four Beatles as
only Ł738,000.

John Lennon's *Rolling Stone* interview attributes the
break--up of The Beatles to Paul McCartney's attempts
to dominate the group.

Paul McCartney files suit against The Beatles & Co. – and
thereby against John, George and Ringo -- seeking legal
dissolution of The Beatles' partnership.   IR--87 (Dec 30)
PMA--12 (Dec 30), 40 (Dec 30)   TBA--28 (Dec 30),
31 (Dec 31)

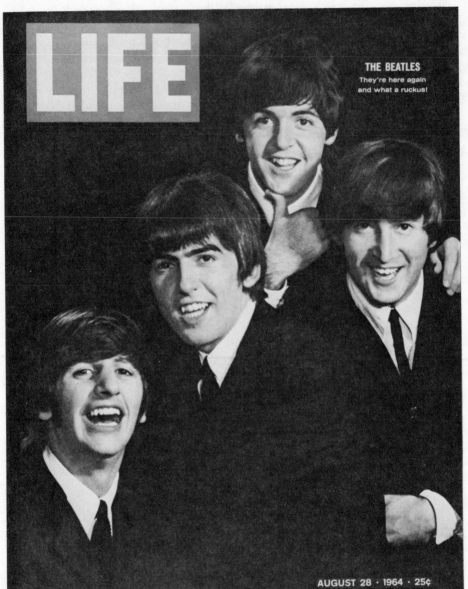

THE BEATLES
They're here again
and what a ruckus!

AUGUST 28 · 1964 · 25¢

key to the index

Indexes are rare in books about The Beatles, although a few of the more current volumes (notably *All Together Now*, *The Beatles Again* and *The Beatles Forever*) do seek to accomodate the unaccountable and perhaps unreasonable predilection of some to actually refer to the contents of a book more than once. The significance of this recent spate of workable indexes in books about The Beatles must be a barometer of something; exactly what such momentous changes in approach portend, however, is doubtless the stuff of which doctoral dissertations deserve to be made, and won't be considered here.

WHAT THE INDEX INCLUDES

Over 6,000 page references to over 2,000 different topics mentioned in the pages of *A Day In The Life* are included in the index which follows. While only a few of the countless references to The Beatles as a group and as individuals have been indexed, there is representation of virtually every other personal name, group, organization, business, magazine article, book, film, song, recording, radio program and television show, as well as a few selected places, concert venues and geographic locations (e.g., the Cavern Club; Carnegie Hall; Hamburg, Germany). A few topical entries are also included: "Jesus incident," Beatlemania, "butcher cover," "Paul Is Dead," etc.

Users of the index should be alert to the fact that, frequently, *more than one mention of a topic appears on the page cited*. More detailed indexing (citing specific dates under which a topic is discussed, for example), while helping to enumerate such multiple references, would have resulted in an index three to five times larger than the present one, a prospect better left to a later, more extravagant edition.

WHAT THE INDEX *DOES NOT* INCLUDE

As indicated, only a few salient aspects of the lives and careers of The Beatles have been cited within specific entries devoted to them as a group or as individuals. Similarly, the possibility that multiple references exist on a given page, identified by only a single page reference, has been pointed out.

Certain other types and categories of information have also been excluded from the index:

- References to songs, records and artists mentioned in connection with chart movements, and the names of periodicals which publish chart movements, are not indexed; charting usually follows close upon record release and such references, for those interested, are not difficult to find.

● Specific references to the titles of Beatles' singles and EPs released in countries other than the U.S. and the U.K. are not indexed, but are noted generally under the entry "Foreign Releases," grouped by country of origin. The titles of foreign albums, however, are specifically referred to in the index, in addition to being indexed under the general entry for foreign releases.

● The names of *most* individual and touring venues – clubs, halls, theaters, auditoriums, stadiums, etc. – have not been indexed. Concert tour venues are accessible by consulting the analytical entry for The Beatles, where the start of all tours are referenced. Specific entries for the Casbah Club, Cavern Club, and Star Club are among the few individual concert venues indexed.

● The names of *most* newspapers and magazines have not been indexed; among the few which appear (*Life, Look, Time,* etc.), cover appearances predominate.

ARRANGEMENT OF ENTRIES

Entries in the index are arranged alphabetically *word–by–word*; this arrangement will be somewhat unfamiliar to those who are used to the *letter–by–letter* order of, say, a telephone directory, but is a formalized alternative from reference and research settings which can be mastered without too much difficulty.

In *letter–by–letter* ordering, the spaces between words are ignored: "Honeymoon" (honey*m*) would precede *Honey Pie* (honey *p*); in the *word–by–word* system, however, spaces between words dictate the ordering of entries, thus placing *Honey Pie* before "Honeymoon". (Hyphenated (**Free–Wheelin'**, Ormsby–Gore) and prefixed (Di Lello) words and names are treated as one word.) The rule is generally summarized as always placing *nothing* (a blank space between words) ahead of *something* (the next letter of a longer word).

A few other unfamiliar peculiarities of the *word–by–word* alphabetizing system should also be mentioned:

● *Initial* articles (A, An, The) are ignored in alphabetizing; articles *within* an entry are regarded in ordering, however.

● Acronyms and initialisms (ABKCO, NEMS, etc.) are arranged *as if* each letter were a complete one–letter word; they are filed at the very beginning of their respective letter group (A, E, etc). Initialisms (H.M.S., P.S., etc.) are treated here in the same manner as acronyms, although they are usually subject to still other arrangement variations.

- Abbreviations (Dr., Sgt.) and arabic or roman numerals (4, VI) are filed *as if* spelled out as words.
- Surnames beginning with "Mc" and "Mac" (e.g., McCartney) are interfiled and alphabetized *as if* spelled "Mac".
- When *exactly* the same word or combination of words is used to refer to different things (e.g., The Beatles), references to persons and groups precede references to places and things. (See the next section, "Special Features of This Index," for an elaboration of this point.)
- Names of musical groups, radio and television shows, and businesses which begin with a given name (Billy J. Kramer with The Dakotas, Allen Klein & Co., "The David Frost Show," The George Martin Orchestra) are filed as an entity under the given name (Billy, Allen, etc.), *not* under the surname, although additional citations about the person may *also* be found under a surname entry.

SPECIAL FEATURES OF THIS INDEX

Changes in Type
The representational use of different type faces in the chro-nology has been continued in the index:
- regular type face refers to such things as people, places, things, groups, businesses and organizations, etc.
- regular type face within quotation marks refers to such things as concerts, art gallery shows, radio programs, television shows, magazine articles, and other topical entries
- regular type within quotation marks followed by a designation within parentheses − (film) − clarifies other references
- *italic type* refers to individual songs, including songs which are carried on singles
- *italic type* followed by other designations within parentheses − (book), (magazine) − clarify some references
- **bold type** followed by the designation (EP) refers to ex-tended play recordings
- **bold type** followed by the designation (LP) refers to long-playing recordings

Same name/Different things
As noted above, when *exactly the same* word or combination of words is used to refer to different things, a special order has been followed. The examples below will serve to illustrate both order of entry and the various type face usages already discussed:

Order of Entry	Example 1	Example 2	Example 3
individuals			
groups/organizations	The Beatles		
venues/places		Cavern Club	
song titles	*The Beatles*		*A Hard Day's Night*
EP titles	**The Beatles** (EP)		
LP titles	**The Beatles** (LP)	Cavern Club (LP)	**A Hard Day's Night** (LP)
instrumental LPs			**A Hard Day's Night** (LP; instrumental)
soundtrack LPs			**A Hard Day's Night** (LP; soundtrack)
foreign LPs	**The Beatles** (LP; Italy)		
films			"A Hard Day's Night" (film)
books	*The Beatles* (book)		*A Hard Day's Night* (book)

Year/Page cross-reference key

As an alternative to a more fully developed analytical index, one which parenthetically explains many more page references in a way similar to the entry for The Beatles, index pages instead carry headings which display the full range of yearly "chapters," together with the inclusive page numbers which correspond to those years/chapters. Hopefully, this feature will limit unnecessary searching, especially when a long list of page citations is approached with a particular year or span of years in mind.

index

1966
151–172

1967
173–197

1968
199–229

1969
231–278

1970
279–305

1966
151–172

1967
173–197

1968
199–229

1969
231–278

1970
279–305

Hines, Brian 14
Hines, Ian 16
Hit '69 (LP) 273
Hitch Hike 233
Hoffman, Dezo 36, 74
Hold Me Tight 47
Holly, Buddy   see also   Buddy Holly and
  The Crickets
Holly, Buddy 12, 13, 74
Hollywood Bowl 1964 (LP) 113
"Hollywood Palace" 177, 178, 206
Home 74
Honey Pie 222
"Honeymoon" (film) 265, 267
Hopkin, Mary 75, 208, 210, 214, 216, 217,
  218, 219, 222, 223, 226, 228, 233, 237,
  239, 240, 241, 242, 244, 252, 255, 260,
  262, 263, 266, 268, 282, 283, 288, 296,
  300
Hot As Sun 12
Hot As Sun (LP) 234
Hot Chocolate Band 268, 269
House, Jack 75
The House of the Rising Sun 118, 222
Houston (LP) 140
How Do You Do It 33, 40, 43
How I Won the War 190, 192
"How I Won the War" (film) 168, 169, 192,
  193, 201
"How It Is" 215
How the Web Was Woven 272, 284, 287
Howard and Wyndham 237
Howes, Arthur 44
Howlin Wolf 289
Hummingbird 281
Hunting Scene 255, 285, 290
Huntley, Chet 83
"Huntley–Brinkley Report" 83
The Hurricanes   see   Rory Storm and The
  Hurricanes
Hurst, Mike 60

I Ain't Not Beleebin 1
I Ain't Superstitious 289
I Am the Walrus 190, 194, 303
I Call Your Name 53, 57, 60, 65, 88, 98
I Can Hear It Now – The Sixties (LP) 302
I Can Hear Music 169
I Can't Do Without You 143
I Can't Get No Nookie 273
I Dig a Pony 236
I Do Like to be Beside the Seaside 126
I Don't Want to Know 131
I Don't Want to See You Again 75, 109, 114,
  115, 117, 123, 163, 181

I Don't Want to See You Again (LP) 123
I Don't Want to Spoil the Party 129
I Fall Inside Your Eyes 251, 287
I Feel Fine 117, 121, 124, 130, 132, 166
I Forgot to Remember to Forget 41
I Got a Woman 55
I Knew Right Away 114
I Like It 54
I Lost My Little Girl 28
I Love Ringo 76
I Me Mine 281
I Need You 125, 129, 137
I Only Live to Love You 193
"I Remember Arnold" 23
I Remember You 34
I Saw Her Standing There 47, 51, 59, 63,
  70, 78, 98
I Should Have Known Better 90, 106, 116,
  125
I Should Like to Live Up a Tree 241
I Threw It All Away 234
I Wanna Be Your Man 61, 64, 80, 87, 94
I Want to Hold Your Hand 58, 62, 64, 68,
  70, 78, 79, 80, 81, 82, 89, 98, 120, 153,
  302
I Want to Tell You 157, 164, 199
I Want to Thank You 269
I Want You (She's So Heavy) 260
I Will 221, 242
Ian and The Zodiacs 23, 24, 29
I'd Have You Anytime 280, 292
If I Fell 90, 107, 119, 128
If I Needed Someone 147
If You Love Me 21
If You Love Me Baby 99
If You've Got Troubles 145
Ifield, Frank 34, 40, 88
I'll Be Back 100
I'll Be Looking at the Moon 283
I'll Be On My Way 35, 48, 51, 54, 111
I'll Cry Instead 90, 107
I'll Follow the Son 193
I'll Get You 56, 57, 58, 60, 98
I'll Keep You Satisfied 47, 56, 64, 66, 91,
  106
I'll Keep You Satisfied (EP) 98
I'll Keep You Satisfied (LP) 117
Illusions 235, 241, 267
I'm a Fool to Care 271
I'm a Loser 124
I'm Down 126, 133, 136
I'm Going to Fall in Love Again 288
I'm Gonna Knock on Your Door 103, 104
I'm Happy Just to Dance With You 90,
  107

1966
151–172

1967
173–197

1968
199–229

1969
231–278

1970
279–305

1966
151–172

1967
173–197

1968
199–229

1969
231–278

1970
279–305

330

1966
151–172

1967
173–197

1968
199–229

1969
231–278

1970
279–305